Proceedings

20th Workshop on
Principles of Advanced and Distributed Simulation
Singapore, May 24-26, 2006

Proceedings

20th Workshop on
Principles of Advanced and Distributed Simulation
Singapore, May 24-26, 2006

Edited by

Stephen J. Turner, General Chair
Johannes Lüthi, Program Chair

Sponsored by

IEEE Computer Society Technical Committee on Simulation (IEEE-TCSIM)
ACM Special Interest Group on Simulation (SIGSIM)
Society for Modeling and Simulation International (SCS)

Los Alamitos, California
Washington • Tokyo

Copyright © 2006 by The Institute of Electrical and Electronics Engineers, Inc.
All rights reserved.

Copyright and Reprint Permissions: Abstracting is permitted with credit to the source. Libraries may photocopy beyond the limits of US copyright law, for private use of patrons, those articles in this volume that carry a code at the bottom of the first page, provided that the per-copy fee indicated in the code is paid through the Copyright Clearance Center, 222 Rosewood Drive, Danvers, MA 01923.

Other copying, reprint, or republication requests should be addressed to: IEEE Copyrights Manager, IEEE Service Center, 445 Hoes Lane, P.O. Box 133, Piscataway, NJ 08855-1331.

The papers in this book comprise the proceedings of the meeting mentioned on the cover and title page. They reflect the authors' opinions and, in the interests of timely dissemination, are published as presented and without change. Their inclusion in this publication does not necessarily constitute endorsement by the editors, the IEEE Computer Society, or the Institute of Electrical and Electronics Engineers, Inc.

IEEE Computer Society Order Number P2587
ACM Order Number **577060**
ISBN-13: 978-0-7695-2587-7
ISBN-10: 0-7695-2587-3
ISSN 1087-4097

Additional copies may be ordered from:

| ACM Order Department
P.O. Box 11414
New York, NY 10286-1414
Tel: + 1-800-342-6626
(U.S. and Canada)
Tel: +1-212-626-0500
(all other countries)
Fax: + 1-212-944-1318
E-mail: orders@acm.org | IEEE Computer Society
Customer Service Center
10662 Los Vaqueros Circle
P.O. Box 3014
Los Alamitos, CA 90720-1314
Tel: + 1 800 272 6657
Fax: + 1 714 821 4641
http://computer.org/cspress
csbooks@computer.org | IEEE Service Center
445 Hoes Lane
P.O. Box 1331
Piscataway, NJ 08855-1331
Tel: + 1 732 981 0060
Fax: + 1 732 981 9667
http://shop.ieee.org/store/
customer-service@ieee.org | IEEE Computer Society
Asia/Pacific Office
Watanabe Bldg., 1-4-2
Minami-Aoyama
Minato-ku, Tokyo 107-0062
JAPAN
Tel: + 81 3 3408 3118
Fax: + 81 3 3408 3553
tokyo.ofc@computer.org |

Individual paper REPRINTS may be ordered at: reprints@computer.org

Editorial production by Silvia Ceballos

Cover art production by Joe Daigle/Studio Productions

Printed in the United States of America by Documation LLC

IEEE Computer Society
Conference Publishing Services
http://www.computer.org/proceedings/

Proceedings

20th Workshop on
Principles of Advanced and Distributed Simulation
Singapore, May 24-26, 2006

Table of Contents

Message from the General Chair viii
Message from the Program Chair ix
Workshop Committees xi
Reviewers xiii
20th Workshop: A Brief History of PADS xiv

Session 1: Parallel Simulation

Aurora: An Approach to High Throughput Parallel Simulation 3
Alfred Park and Richard M. Fujimoto

Improving Lookahead in Parallel Multiprocessor Simulation
Using Dynamic Execution Path Prediction 11
Moo-Kyoung Chung and Chong-Min Kyung

The Distributed Open Network Emulator: Using Relativistic Time
for Distributed Scalable Simulation 19
Craig Bergstrom, Srinidhi Varadarajan, and Godmar Back

Session 2: Performance Analysis

Performance Analysis of Shared Data Access Algorithms
for Distributed Simulation of Multi-agent Systems 29
Roland Ewald, Dan Chen, Georgios K. Theodoropoulos, Michael Lees,
Brian Logan, Tom Oguara, and Adelinde M. Uhrmacher

Analysing the Performance of Optimistic Synchronization Algorithms
in Simulations of Multi-agent Systems 37
Michael Lees, Brian Logan, Chen Dan, Ton Oguara,
and Georgios Theodoropoulos

Predicting Performance of Resolution Changes in Parallel
Simulations 45
Dhananjai M. Rao and Philip A. Wilsey

Session 3: Keynote Presentation

What comes after the Semantic Web? PADS Implications
for the Dynamic Web 55
  Andreas Tolk

Session 4: Advanced Techniques and Applications

SOAr-DSGrid: Service-Oriented Architecture for Distributed
Simulation on the Grid 65
  Xinjun Chen, Wentong Cai, Stephen John Turner, and Yong Wang

Discrete-Event Execution Alternatives on General Purpose Graphical
Processing Units 74
  Kalyan S. Perumalla

Progressive Time-Parallel Simulation 82
  Tobias Kiesling

Developing an Hierarchical Simulator for Beta-binders 92
  Jan Himmelspach, Paola Lecca, Davide Prandi, Corado Priami,
  Paola Quaglia, and Adelinde Uhrmacher

Session 5: Distributed Virtual Environments

Greedy Algorithms for Client Assignment in Large-Scale Distributed
Virtual Environments 103
  Duong Nguyen Binh Ta, Suiping Zhou, and Haifeng Shen

Interest Operators: Facilitating Attribute Interest Criteria for
Formula-Based Interest Management in Distributed Virtual Environments 111
  Robert Bartlett

Using Abstraction in the Verification of Simulation Coercion 119
  Xinyu Liu, Paul F. Reynolds, and David C. Brogan

Session 6: Abstracts

Model-Based Services for Computing Grid Performance Analyses & Tuning 129
  Rob Simmonds and Brian Unger

The Reconfiguration Problem in Sensor Networks: An Optimization Approach 130
  El Moustapha Ould-Ahmed-Vall, George F. Riley, and Bonnie S. Heck

A Generic Symbiotic Simulation Framework 131
  Shell Ying Huang, Wentong Cai, Stephen JohnTurner, Wen Jing Hsu, Suiping Zhou,
  Malcolm Yoke Hean Low, Richard Fujimoto, and Rassul Ayani

Intelligent Management of Data Driven Simulations to support Model Building 132
  Catriona Kennedy and Georgios Theodoropoulos

Towards an Efficient Branching Mechanism for Simultaneous Events in Distributed Simulation 133
Patrick Peschlow and Peter Martini

Parallel Execution of Region-Scale Evacuation Traffic Models 134
Kalyan S. Perumalla

NBS Supply Chain Simulation Using Simul8 and HLA 135
Navonil Mustafee, Simon Taylor, Korina Katsaliaki, and Sally Brailsford

Session 7: Keynote Presentation

Distributed Simulation in Manufacturing and Logistics 139
Peter Lendermann

Session 8: Network Simulation

Modeling Autonomous System Relationships 143
Xenofontas Dimitropoulos and George Riley

An Efficient Routing Mechanism in Network Simulation 150
Zhiyu Hao, Xiaochun Yun, and Hongli Zhang

A Case Study in Understanding OSPF and BGP Interactions Using Efficient Experiment Design 158
David W. Bauer, Christopher D. Carothers, Murat Yuksel, and Shickumar Kalyanaram

Empirical Models of TCP and UDP End-User Network Traffic from NETI@home Data Analysis 166
Charles R. Simpson, Dheeraj Reddy, and George Riley

Session 9: High Level Architecture

Evaluation of a Fault-Tolerance Mechanism for HLA-Based Distributed Simulation 175
Martin Eklöf, Rassul Ayani, and Farshad Moradi

A Framework for Robust HLA-based Distributed Simulations 183
Dan Chen, Stephen John Turner, and Wentong Cai

Transparent Optimistic Synchronization in HLA via a Time-Management Converter 193
Andrea Santoro and Francesco Quaglia

COTS Simulation Package (CSP) Interoperability - A Solution to Synchronous Entity Passing 201
Xiaoguang Wang, Stephen John Turner, and Simon J. E. Taylor

Author Index 211

Message from the General Chair

Welcome to the 20th ACM/IEEE/SCS Workshop on Principles of Advanced and Distributed Simulation (PADS 2006). This year, for the first time, PADS takes place outside North America and Europe in the heart of South-East Asia – Singapore. Singapore was founded as a British trading colony in 1819 and became an independent nation in 1965. Since then, it has become one of the world's most prosperous countries with strong international trading links. Singapore has everything to make your stay a most memorable experience. It is a vibrant and cosmopolitan city where tradition and modernity, East and West, meet and mingle in harmony.

PADS 2006 takes place at Raffles Hotel in the centre of Singapore. Opened in 1887, the hotel was named after Sir Stamford Raffles, founder of modern Singapore. Over the years, the hotel has evolved into one of the world's most loved Grand Hotels and has welcomed innumerable celebrities, writers, and royalty. Our sessions take place in the Casuarina Suite, named after "The Casuarina Tree", a volume of short stories by Somerset Maugham, who was a regular visitor to the Hotel.

We hope that we have arranged an exciting program for you this year. Our first keynote speaker is Dr Andreas Tolk, who will discuss the question "What comes after the Semantic Web: PADS implications for the Dynamic Web!" Our second keynote speaker is Dr Peter Lendermann, who will describe the research accomplishments that have been made in Singapore in the area of "Distributed Simulation in Manufacturing and Logistics".

The workshop sessions comprise papers concerning: Parallel Simulation, Performance Analysis, Advanced Techniques and Applications, Distributed Virtual Environments, Network Simulation, and High Level Architecture. On the first morning of the workshop, Andreas Tolk will also give a tutorial on "Applying the Principles of Advanced and Distributed Simulation to the Military Domain – Training, Experimentation, and Support of Operations".

The success of a conference such as PADS depends on the efforts of many people and I would like to thank all members of the workshop committees, particularly Johannes Lüthi, our Program Chair, for his work in organizing the technical program, Wentong Cai, our Finance Chair, for his help with the planning of the conference and local arrangements, and Joo Sing Tan and Lijun Lau for their help with registration and the PADS web pages. I would also like to thank the program committee and outside reviewers, who provided high quality reviews of the many submissions. Finally, special thanks go to Silvia Ceballos and the editorial staff at IEEE Computer Society Press for their work in producing these proceedings to a very tight schedule.

Enjoy the conference and enjoy Singapore!

Stephen John Turner

Nanyang Technological University, Singapore

Message from the Program Chair

Welcome to the 2nd *Workshop on Principles of Advanced and Distributed Simulation* which is at the same time the 20th PADS workshop. You will remember that in 2005 the PADS acronym changed its meaning from "Parallel and Distributed Simulation" to "Principles of Advanced and Distributed Simulation" in order to better represent a broader scope of the workshop. This year's program shows that extending the scope (and adapting the title) of the workshop made sense as categories such as "parallel" or "distributed" only address part of the innovative character of many interesting contributions to this conference's program.

This year 43 papers were submitted (all submissions were made electronically using the WIMPE paper management system). Keeping the PADS traditions, every paper received four reviews: three from program committee (PC) members and one from an additional referee. The reviewing process was performed within a relatively tight schedule as there was just one month between the paper submission deadline and the program committee meeting. The return rate of the reviews turned out to be 96.5% which is a very good result. At the program committee meeting (held in conjunction with the 2005 Winter Simulation Conference on December 3, 2005, in Orlando, FL) 21 papers were accepted for presentation and publication. Three of these papers were conditionally accepted. A shepherd was assigned to each of the conditionally accepted papers, supervising their revision. Finally, we were happy to accept also all three conditionally accepted papers.

For several years now, the PADS workshop has included a so-called work-in-progress session. In this session, researchers can present ongoing work, new ideas, or research plans in a short talk which enables an open discussion and may help getting additional input. For PADS 2006, the program committee decided to include a list of abstracts of work-in-progress presentations which can be found in these proceedings.

Another important PADS tradition is the Best Paper Award for the most outstanding contribution. At the PC meeting the program committee nominated 7 papers that had only "accepts" and "weak accepts" as recommendations from their reviewers and at least one clear "accept" from a PC member. Extended versions of these papers will be considered for publication in a special issue of the journal *SCS Simulation*. A Best Paper subcommittee selected the best paper based on the camera ready versions of the candidates. The winner will be announced at the conference. The nominees are (in alphabetical order by paper title):

- "A Framework for Robust HLA-based Distributed Simulations" by Dan Chen, Stephen John Turner, and Wentong Cai
- "An Efficient Routing Mechanism in Network Simulation" by Zhiyu Hao, Xiaochun Yun, and Hongli Zhang
- "Analysing the Performance of Optimistic Synchronisation Algorithms in Simulations of Multi-agent Systems" by Michael Lees, Brian Logan, Dan Chen, Ton Oguara, and Georgios Theodoropoulos
- "Empirical Models of TCP and UDP End-User Network Traffic from NETI@home Data Analysis" by Charles R. Simpson, Dheeraj Reddy, and George Riley
- "Greedy Algorithms for Client Assignment in Large-Scale Distributed Virtual Environments" by Duong Nguyen Binh Ta, Suiping Zhou, and Haifeng Shen
- "Modeling Autonomous-Systems Relationships" by Xenofontas Dimitropoulos and George Riley
- "Predicting Performance of Resolution Changes in Parallel Simulations" by Dhananjai Rao and Philip A. Wilsey.

In 2005, the best paper subcommittee was equally and overwhelmingly impressed by two papers. Consequently, there were two PADS 2005 Best Papers. On behalf of the PADS 2005 Program Co-Chairs, Christopher D. Carothers and Stephen J. Turner, it is my pleasure to confirm the winners of the PADS 2005 Best Paper Award and congratulate them on their excellent papers:

- "Optimistic Parallel Discrete Event Simulations of Physical Systems Using Reverse Computation" by Yarong Tang, Kalyan S. Perumalla, Richard M. Fujimoto, Homa Karimabadi, Jonathan Driscoll, and Yuri Omelchenko and

- "Simulation of Network Traffic at Coarse Timescales" by David M. Nicol and Guanhua Yan.

I would like to thank a number of people who amply provided valuable help in organizing the PADS 2006 program. It was a pleasure to work with the General Chair Stephen J. Turner, who also occasionally helped as an unofficial Program Co-Chair (for example hosting WIMPE at Nanyang Technological University). Thank you, Steve! The work of the program committee and referees, who delivered high quality reviews within a tight schedule, is gratefully appreciated. Special thanks go to those who attended the PC meeting at Orlando, an event with lively and constructive discussions. Thank you to Brad Armstrong, General Chair of the 2005 Winter Simulation Conference, for his help in supporting the PADS 2006 PC meeting. I would like to give special thanks to Dave Goldsman for spontaneously serving as PADS referee "on-demand" during the Winter Simulation Conference. Thank you also to the three shepherds, who assisted in getting all selected papers into the final program. Last but not least, the efforts of all authors who have submitted their work to the PADS workshop are gratefully appreciated. There would be no PADS without you!

I hope you will enjoy the PADS 2006 workshop!

Johannes Lüthi

University of Applied Sciences FHS KufsteinTirol

Workshop Committees

General Chair

S. J. Turner, *Nanyang Technological University, Singapore*

Program Chair

J. Lüthi, *FHS KufsteinTirol, Austria*

Finance Chair

W. Cai, *Nanyang Technological University, Singapore*

Registration Chair

Joo Sing Tan, *Nanyang Technological University, Singapore*

Web Chair

Lijun Lau, *Nanyang Technological University, Singapore*

Steering Committee

S. J. Turner (Chair), *Nanyang Technological University, Singapore*
S. J. E. Taylor (ACM), *Brunel University, UK*
A. S. Elmaghraby (IEEE), *University of Louisville, USA*
B. W. Unger (SCS), *University of Calgary, Canada*
G. F. Riley (Elected), *Georgia Institute of Technology, USA*
D. M. Nicol (Elected), *University of Illinois Urbanna-Champaign, USA*
R. M. Fujimoto (Honorary), *Georgia Institute of Technology, USA*

Program Committee

A. Boukerche, *University of Ottawa, Canada*
W. Cai, *Nanyang Technological University, Singapore*
C. Carothers, *Rensselaer Polytechnic, USA*
D. Degroot, *Techsus, USA*
L. Donatiello, *University of Bologna, Italy*
A. S. Elmaghraby, *University of Louisville, USA*
R. M. Fujimoto, *Georgia Institute of Technology, USA*
A. Lehmann, *University Bundeswehr München, Germany*
M. Liljenstam, *Omicron, Sweden*
J. Liu, *Colorado School of Mines, USA*
A. L. M. Thom McLean, *Georgia Institute of Technology, USA*
D. M. Nicol, *University of Illinois Urbanna-Champaign, USA*
E. H. Page, *The MITRE Corp, USA*
K. Perumalla, *Oak Ridge National Laboratory, USA*
F. Quaglia, *University of Rome, Italy*
G. F. Riley, *Georgia Institute of Technology, USA*
R. Simmonds, *University of Calgary, Canada*
B. K. Szymanski, *Rensselaer Polytechnic, USA*

G. Tackett, *U.S. Army, USA*
M. Takai, *University of California Los Angeles, USA*
S. J. E. Taylor, *Brunel University, UK*
Y. M. Teo, *National University of Singapore, Singapore*
C. Tropper, *McGill University, Canada*
A. Uhrmacher, *University of Rostock, Germany*
B. Unger, *University of Calgary, Canada*
F. P. Wieland, *Sensis Corp, USA*
P. A. Wilsey, *University of Cincinnati, USA*

Reviewers

Mohamed Abdelhafez, *Georgia Institute of Technology, USA*
Emmet Beeker, *The MITRE Corp, USA*
Luciano Bononi, *University of Bologna, Italy*
Dan Chen, *University of Birmingham, UK*
Gilbert Chen, *Rensselaer Polytechnic, USA*
Gabriele D' Angelo, *University of Bologna, Italy*
Xenofontas Dimitropoulos, *Georgia Institute of Technology, USA*
Martin Eklöf, *FOI Swedish Defence Research Agency, Sweden*
Boon Ping Gan, *Singapore Institute of Manufacturing Technology, Singapore*
Ashish Garg, *State University of New York, Buffalo, USA*
Talal Jaafar, *Georgia Institute of Technology, USA*
Nasser Kalantery, *University of Westminster, UK*
Cameron Kiddle, *University of Calgary, Canada*
Tobias Kiesling, *University Bundeswehr München, Germany*
Brian Logan, *University of Nottingham, UK*
James Nutaro, *Oak Ridge National Laboratory, USA*
Jari Porras, *Lappeenranta University of Technology, Finland*
David Prochnow, *The MITRE Corp, USA*
Dheeraj Reddy, *Georgia Institute of Technology, USA*
Regina Santana, *Univerity of San Paulo, Brazil*
Andrea Santoro, *University of Rome, Italy*
Charles Simpson, *Georgia Institute of Technology, USA*
Suiping Zhou, *Nanyang Technological University, Singapore*

20th Workshop – A Brief History of PADS

The PADS series of workshops began in 1985 as a track of the SCS Multiconference (later known as the SCS Western Multiconference) in San Diego. The second meeting was held in 1988 and thereafter the workshop became an annual event. Until 1990, the title of the conference was "Distributed Simulation", where *distributed* at that time referred to the distribution of the simulation model over a set of processors, usually tightly coupled. In 1991, the term *parallel simulation* had become more widespread and the conference name was changed to "Advances in Parallel and Distributed Simulation". This subsequently became "Parallel and Distributed Simulation", with the PADS acronym being used for the first time in 1992.

At this stage, the field of parallel and distributed simulation had grown to the point where it was felt that the PADS community was able to organize its own workshops. In 1993, PADS joined several other conferences at the first Federated Computing Research Conference (FCRC), which proved to be a great success. In 1994, PADS held its first European meeting in Edinburgh and this also proved to be highly successful. A cyclic pattern was established where PADS would hold two meetings in USA or Canada (one of which was with FCRC) and the third meeting in Europe.

In 2002, it was felt that the scope of the workshop should be expanded to include other aspects of advanced simulation technology in addition to the traditional focus on parallel and distributed simulation. However, there was strong support for keeping the PADS acronym, and the name "Principles of Advanced and Distributed Simulation" was approved at the 2003 Business Meeting, with the name first being used for the 2005 Workshop. PADS 2006 is therefore the 2nd Workshop under the new title, but the 20th Workshop in the PADS series, and for the first time, takes place outside North America and Europe in Singapore. A summary of the PADS series of Workshops is given below.

PADS 2006: 20th Workshop on Principles of Advanced and Distributed Simulation
Singapore, 24-26 May 2006
General Chair: Stephen J. Turner
Program Chair: Johannes Lüthi

PADS 2005: 2005 Workshop on Principles of Advanced and Distributed Simulation
Monterey, California, USA, 1-3 June 2005
General Chair: David M. Nicol
Program Co-Chairs: Christopher D. Carothers and Stephen J. Turner

PADS 2004: 18th Workshop on Parallel and Distributed Simulation
Kufstein, Austria, 16-19 May 2004
General Co-Chairs: Johannes Lüthi and Axel Lehmann
Program Co-Chairs: Ernest H. Page and A.L.M. Thom McLean

PADS 2003: 17th Workshop on Parallel and Distributed Simulation (with FCRC 2003)
San Diego, California, USA, 10-13 June 2003
General Chair: Katherine L. Morse
Program Co-Chairs: George F. Riley and Philip A. Wilsey

PADS 2002: 16th Workshop on Parallel and Distributed Simulation
Washington, D.C., USA, 12-15 May 2002
General Co-Chairs: Frederick Wieland and Philip A. Wilsey
Program Co-Chairs: Lorenzo Donatiello and Francesco Quaglia

PADS 2001: 15th Workshop on Parallel and Distributed Simulation
Lake Arrowhead, California, USA, 15-18 May 2001
General Co-Chairs: Rajive Bagrodia and Ewa Deelman
Program Chair: Philip A. Wilsey

PADS 2000: 14th Workshop on Parallel and Distributed Simulation
Bologna, Italy, 28-31 May, 2000
General Co-Chairs: Lorenzo Donatiello and Stephen Turner
Program Chair: David Bruce

PADS '99: 13th Workshop on Parallel and Distributed Simulation (part of FCRC '99)
Atlanta, Georgia, USA, 1-4 May 1999
General Chair: Richard Fujimoto
Program Chair: Stephen Turner

PADS '98: 12th Workshop on Parallel and Distributed Simulation
Banff, Alberta, Canada, 26-29 May 1998
General Chair: Brian Unger
Program Chair: Alois Ferscha

PADS '97: 11th Workshop on Parallel and Distributed Simulation
Lockenhaus, Austria, 10-13 June 1997
General Chair: Alois Ferscha
Program Co-Chairs: Rassul Ayani and Carl Tropper

PADS '96: 10th Workshop on Parallel and Distributed Simulation (with FCRC '96)
Philadelphia, Pennsylvania, USA, 22-24 May 1996
General Chair: Mary Bailey
Program Co-Chairs: Wayne Loucks and Bruno Preiss

PADS '95: 9th Workshop on Parallel and Distributed Simulation
Lake Placid, New York, USA, 14-16 June 1995
General Chair: Jason Yi-Bing Lin
Program Chair: Mary Bailey

PADS '94: 8th Workshop on Parallel and Distributed Simulation
Edinburgh, Scotland, U.K., 6-8 July 1994
General Chair: Rajive Bagrodia
Program Co-Chairs: Damal Arvind and Jason Yi-Bing Lin

PADS '93: 7th Workshop on Parallel and Distributed Simulation (with FCRC '93)
San Diego, California, USA, 16-19 May 1993
General Co-Chairs: Richard Fujimoto and Brian Unger
Program Co-Chairs: Rajive Bagrodia and David Jefferson

PADS '92: 6th Workshop on Parallel and Distributed Simulation
Newport Beach, California, USA, 20-22 January 1992
General Chair: Paul Reynolds
Program Chair: Marc Abrams

SCS Multiconference on Advances in Parallel and Distributed Simulation
Anaheim, California, USA, 23-25 January 1991
General Chair: David Nicol
Program Chair: Vijay Madisetti

SCS Multiconference on Distributed Simulation
San Diego, California, USA, 17-19 January 1990
General and Program Chair: David Nicol

SCS Multiconference on Distributed Simulation

Tampa, Florida, USA, 28-31 March 1989
General Chair: Brian Unger
Program Chair: Richard Fujimoto

SCS Multiconference on Distributed Simulation
San Diego, California, USA, 3-5 February 1988
General Chair: Brian Unger
Program Chair: David Jefferson

SCS Conference on Distributed Simulation
San Diego, California, USA, 24-26 January 1985
General Co-Chairs: Bernard Zeigler and Sallie Sheppard
Program Co-Chairs: Paul Reynolds and Horst Wedde

Principles of Advanced and Distributed Simulation

Session 1: Parallel Simulation

Aurora: An Approach to High Throughput Parallel Simulation

Alfred Park, Richard M. Fujimoto
Computational Science & Engineering Division
College of Computing, Georgia Institute of Technology
Atlanta, Georgia, USA 30332-0280
{park,fujimoto}@cc.gatech.edu

Abstract

A master/worker paradigm for executing large-scale parallel discrete event simulation programs over network-enabled computational resources is proposed and evaluated. In contrast to conventional approaches to parallel simulation, a client/server architecture is proposed where clients (workers) repeatedly download state vectors of logical processes and associated message data from a server (master), perform simulation computations locally at the client, and then return the results back to the server. This process offers several potential advantages over conventional parallel discrete event simulation systems, including support for execution over heterogeneous distributed computing platforms, load balancing, efficient execution on shared platforms, easy addition or removal of client machines during program execution, simpler fault tolerance, and improved portability. A prototype implementation called the Aurora Parallel and Distributed Simulation System (Aurora) is described. The structure and interaction of the Aurora components is described. Results of an experimental performance evaluation are presented detailing primitive timings and application performance on both dedicated and shared computing platforms.

1. Introduction

Recently, there have been several efforts to harness the massive potential computing power afforded by the Internet through large-scale public distributed computing projects. There have been many successful volunteer distributed computing projects such as distributed.net, World Community Grid, and SETI@home [1]. These projects operate on the principle of individuals donating spare processor cycles towards a common goal. The Aurora Parallel and Distributed Simulation System (Aurora) attempts to bridge the gap between general purpose distributed computing projects such as these and parallel discrete event simulations (PDES) through the use of web services. Like the other systems mentioned above, Aurora is designed as a vehicle for *high throughput computing* where the goal is to harness available computing cycles from large numbers of machines rather than strictly achieving high speedups on dedicated hardware.

Web services are built on a foundation of open-standards, protocols, and universally-readable files that allow them to be implemented on a wide range of computer systems. Consequently, through the use of web services, the Aurora system can be adapted to fit most programming languages and the generated Aurora server and Aurora clients can interoperate with a variety of operating systems and hardware architectures.

Traditional parallel simulation techniques involve creating simulators from scratch in a monolithic fashion or by federating existing simulators [2, 3] through standards such as the High Level Architecture (HLA) [4]. However, these executions are limited to structured simulations configured a priori with relatively low tolerance for dynamic client behavior and node failures. The latter is becoming increasingly problematic; as new machines emerge containing tens to hundreds of thousands of processors, the likelihood of a failure during a long simulation run is becoming a greater concern.

By contrast, the master/worker approach allows distribution of work to any clients that request it, greatly reducing the reliance on dedicating machine resources. Clients can be easily added or removed during the execution of the simulation as new resources become available, or must be removed for use by other computations. There are no restrictions placed upon the client other than proper configuration and the ability to contact the server to download simulation state and data. Client failures are easily handled by reissuing pending computations to other clients, and server failures can be handled by maintaining state information on secondary storage. Here, we focus attention on use of the master/worker paradigm in heterogeneous distributed computing systems.

2. Related Work

There has been a significant amount of work leveraging the web for simulations. Work in this area includes the Simulation Reference Markup Language [5], web-based simulations using Java RMI [6], self-managing web-based simulations [7], and use of Object Request Brokers for web-based simulation [8]. The Extensible Modeling and Simulation Framework is a collection of software and tools that promotes interoperability and the use of standards in the context of modeling and simulation [9]. There has been work done using grid-based technologies such as Globus [10] to execute HLA-compliant simulations over the grid through efforts such as

IDSim [11] and HLAGrid [12]. PIRS is an effort to speed up parallel simulation on machines with varying workloads using a scheduling policy [13]. The work presented here is fundamentally different than these efforts in that the Aurora framework utilizes a master/worker system over web services to allow parallel and distributed simulations to be run on a variety of clients but without guarantees that the client may ever return a result. Moreover, the Aurora system allows simulations to be run nearly anywhere, where resources do not have to be designated as part of a grid, a supercomputer, or a computational cluster.

Several distributed computing systems share similar goals as the Aurora system. Condor [14], Parallel Virtual Machine (PVM) [15], and Condor MW [16] are systems that pool processing power from various machines into a single computing resource. More recent work referred to as "public" or "volunteer" computing has attempted to harness computers on a massive scale. Examples include Unicorn [17], InteGrade [18], and Berkley Open Infrastructure for Network Computing (BOINC) [19]. The Aurora system utilizes a similar master/worker style of work distribution as employed by Condor MW combined with the features of BOINC-enabled projects like SETI@home. The important difference is that the Aurora system is specifically tailored for PDES execution, offering services such as time and logical process (LP) management.

3. Background and Motivation

Through the use of open standards, web services afford applications the ability to interoperate and provide a wide-range of services regardless of the language and architecture of the server and clients. The SOAP protocol is used as the underlying messaging framework to send XML-encoded messages between the server and clients. The Web Services Description Language (WSDL) describes the services provided by the server for the clients. SOAP messages are sent using HTTP. The advantage of using HTTP is that service requests can be provided through security measures such as firewalls, since HTTP access is usually unrestricted.

Node failure can be problematic with large-scale simulations over supercomputers or grids unless a checkpoint/recovery system is implemented. The Aurora system, through the master/worker design, allows a level of robustness for parallel and distributed simulations for dealing with node failure as well as distributing simulation load across the available client pool.

Another major feature of the Aurora system is the ability to run simulations in the "background." Machines with Aurora clients can be processing other jobs. This allows simulations to be run on non-dedicated or unreserved machines without significant overhead, while contributing to the overall distributed simulation computation.

Although the Aurora system permits flexibility with regard to simulation execution on different platforms and fault tolerance, the framework is not suitable for every type of simulation. Aurora is best suited for applications where a significant amount of computation can be handed to a client for execution. Tightly coupled simulations with much global communication or low amount of parallelism may be better suited for traditional PDES or sequential execution mechanisms. A goal of the research described here is to quantify these concepts to determine the range of applications where this paradigm is well suited.

The remainder of this paper is organized as follows. We next describe the Aurora system architecture and its current implementation to describe more concretely a specific master/worker PDES system. We then present results of an empirical performance evaluation study of the current implementation using various workloads on both dedicated and shared hardware platforms. This is followed by a discussion of future work and conclusions.

4. The Aurora Parallel and Distributed Simulation System

The emergence of web services has allowed applications to exploit open standards-based interoperable communications over the Internet. The Aurora system extends these principles to PDES. While conventional web services have emphasized interoperability over performance, the Aurora system was built with high performance as a priority while providing interoperability on the language and machine architecture levels. The Aurora system itself was constructed with extensibility in mind as different pieces of the system are modular and can be replaced or extended.

4.1. Conceptual Overview

The Aurora system applies a PDES execution to the master/worker paradigm while leveraging the advantages of web services. Following standard accepted practices, the parallel simulation program is assumed to consist of a collection of logical processes (LPs) that communicate exclusively by exchanging time stamped messages. LPs, with associated data structures, as discussed below, are clustered into *work units*. A work unit is the atomic unit transmitted between clients and servers. In a master/worker paradigm, the master controls the global available work pool and manages the overhead associated for each worker. Worker threads or processes perform the necessary computation on these work units and return results to the master. This cycle continues until all of the work units are exhausted or some other terminating condition is met. Additionally, the Aurora system must comply with requirements of PDES executions.

In traditional conservative PDES, the simulator must ensure that events are processed in strict time-stamp order to avoid violating the local causality constraint (LCC).

Consequently, synchronization algorithms are used to calculate guarantees such as lower bound on timestamp (LBTS) to regulate which events are safe to process. In optimistic PDES, the simulator may allow violations of the LCC to occur but must recover from such errors. The current design of Aurora includes a centralized conservative synchronization mechanism; an optimistic time management system is under development.

In addition to providing time management services, the Aurora system bridges the concept of work units and LPs. LPs generate messages for other LPs that may be local to it (i.e., residing within the same work unit) or destined for remote LPs (residing in other work units). In contrast to traditional massively distributed computing projects such as SETI@home, portions of work sent to client machines do not require communication between leased units of work. The Aurora system tracks messages that are generated and correctly distributes them to destination work units.

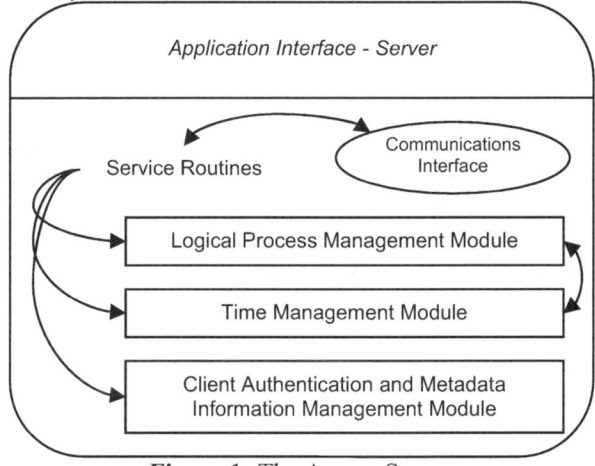

Figure 1: The Aurora Server

4.2. Aurora Communications

The default communication mechanism used in Aurora is based on SOAP, supporting interoperability among heterogeneous computing platforms. The Aurora system is designed to support different communication mechanisms. When used on a tightly coupled parallel computer, communications based on MPI may be used. Alternatively, sockets can be used in homogeneous networked environments. The communications interface shown in Figure 1 is a thin layer that is invoked when the client and server agree on a specialized transfer protocol other than the default SOAP transport during the handshaking phase of client initialization. The remainder of this paper assumes SOAP is used for communication.

One of the perceived disadvantages to developing a PDES framework under web services is low performance [20]. Due to the inherent nature of transmitting XML-encoded data, an optimized PDES engine should outperform any simulation framework based on web services. The gSOAP toolkit [21] is a mature, active, open source web services toolkit designed with performance as well as language and machine architecture interoperability as priorities. gSOAP is intended for applications in C/C++ but can be bridged to other languages. gSOAP supports many industry-standard web services protocols including SOAP 1.1/1.2, WSDL 1.1, and UDDI v2.

The gSOAP toolkit has shown low-latency and high performance by utilizing various techniques including streaming XML parsing, Base64/DIME encoding, HTTP chunking, compression, and Keep-Alive. gSOAP coupled with these techniques can outperform Java RMI for binary-encoded matrices with latencies under seven milliseconds [22]. gSOAP also exhibits good end-to-end performance in sending arrays of different primitives and low serialization and deserialization times [23] which are desirable attributes for the application-independent nature of the Aurora system.

4.3. Aurora Server

The Aurora server contains the control and management algorithms of the system that work together to form the master. Figure 1 shows the interaction between the web services routines and the various modules within the Aurora server.

The Aurora server architecture includes a module, currently under development, to support fault tolerant execution. This module allows the re-release of LPs if certain criteria defined within the module are met; mechanisms to manage duplicate results are also included. Other modules can be replaced or extended.

4.3.1. Logical Process Management

The Aurora logical process manager keeps track of application defined LPs. The simulation application may aggregate many LPs into one single Aurora work unit. An Aurora work unit is instantiated by the server-side application containing the initial state of the LP(s). Each work unit stored in the Aurora server includes one or more state vectors containing simulation variables, an event list, and an input and output message buffer associated with that work unit. Due to the application-independent nature of the Aurora system, the LP state vector is stored as a contiguous block of memory that is packed and unpacked by externally defined procedures. The input (output) buffer for each work unit is a table of messages destined for LPs contained within (beyond) the work unit that have been received from (sent to) other LPs. The event list contains locally scheduled messages. Each message is wrapped in a data structure providing information such as the message timestamp, destination, and size of the packed message.

A work unit includes an LP or collection of LPs with associated buffers and metadata such as the LBTS that is transmitted to a client as an atomic unit. When a work unit is executed and successfully returned to the server by the client, the Aurora LP manager first updates the state vector of the LPs contained in the work unit stored in the server. The messages packed in the output buffer for the returned work unit are binned to the correct input buffers of the destination work units. During this process, the Aurora LP manager re-organizes the input buffer of the returned work unit, freeing memory for any message buffers that can be released.

4.3.2. Time Management

The Aurora time management system provides support for conservative, optimistic, or a combination of both approaches to synchronization. Because time management computations are performed at the server, a simple, centralized algorithm for computing a LBTS of future messages that may be received by an LP is sufficient; distributed algorithms would be required for servers utilizing multiple processors. The LBTS value that is computed is equivalent to the Global Virtual Time value required for optimistic simulations. In Figure 1, the interaction between the time management module and the logical process module denotes the LBTS calculations each time a work unit is returned to the server after a client completes its execution.

There is significant potential for increased performance through an optimistic-style synchronization algorithm. Due to the inherent nature of the Aurora system, LPs can be leased at will to any client that is capable of execution. Furthermore, the results returned by any client do not have to be used. Depending upon how results are cached on the server to accompany an optimistic time management system, error recovery can be simplified to simply restore state from a known correct state instead of using a rollback recovery system.

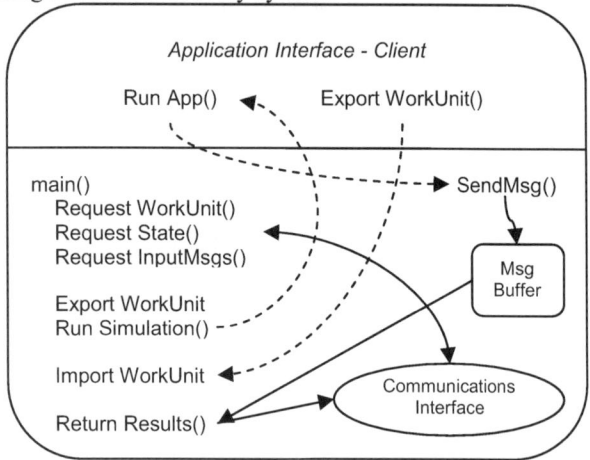

Figure 2: The Aurora Client

4.3.3. Client Authentication and Metadata Information Management

The Aurora system includes an authentication and metadata module to keep track of work units. Work units are designated as *available* or *leased*. An *available* work unit means that there are no clients currently performing computation on that work unit and is ready to be released to the next client request. Work units are marked as *leased* when the server releases it to a client. If a client is issued a work unit, a global unique key is assigned along with the work unit. This allows work units to be issued more than once for fault tolerance purposes, or in the case of abundant heterogeneous client machines, to issue the same work unit to multiple machines with the hope of receiving results more quickly if the relative execution speed among the different machines cannot be predicted, e.g., due to contention from other users.

4.4. Aurora Clients

The workers in the master/worker paradigm are implemented by the Aurora clients. Each Aurora client pulls the necessary information (work units) from the server through web service requests, executes the simulation implemented by the application developer, and uploads state vector and output message buffers back to the Aurora server (master) upon completing execution according to the specified time management scheme.

Figure 2 shows the interaction and data flow between different function calls and certain key data structures within the Aurora client. After initialization, the Aurora client performs a series of web service request procedure calls to the server. During the handshaking phase, the client requests an available work unit from the Aurora server as well as possible communication modes in addition to the default gSOAP transport. Once the client receives work unit availability confirmation from the server, the state vector and all of the incoming messages for the leased execution time window are downloaded from the Aurora server. Once this information has been received from the Aurora server, the client can operate autonomously from the master.

The incoming messages for the work unit are queued automatically for retrieval by the client in timestamp order. The state vector is uploaded to the application (data moving between the Aurora client and the actual simulation application are shown by dashed arrows in Figure 2), and the Aurora client invokes the application simulation loop. During the simulation, the application may generate messages that are destined for LPs residing in other work units. The Aurora client provides a message send interface where all messages which exceed the LBTS time of the work unit are buffered for upload to the server when the simulation completes. After the simulation completes, control is returned back to the Aurora client and the final state vector is imported back into the Aurora client and sent to the server using Base64 encoding.

5. Performance Evaluation

The current Aurora system was built using gSOAP 2.7.6c, compiled using gcc 3.4.3 with the –O2 flag. The

Aurora server was run in standalone mode. Machines designated as "Xeon" consist of two 2.8GHz Intel Xeon processors while "Pentium III" machines consist of eight 550MHz Intel Pentium III processors. Both machine types have 4GB memory using RedHat Linux with a Fast Ethernet interconnect. The Xeon and Pentium III machines do not reside on the same LAN.

5.1. Microbenchmark Timings

Table 1 shows the total time in milliseconds to invoke a web service routine using null message sizes for *Request State*, *Request InputMsgs*, and *Return Results* using Xeon machines. Without the extra payload of state vector or message data, these timings show the minimum amount of overhead incurred per web service call. It can be seen that each web service method exhibits sub-one millisecond latency when executed within a LAN environment.

XML and Base64 encoding of binary data is another source of overhead. As the size of binary data transformed for transmission over the network increases, so does the amount of overall time required for the web service method invocation. Table 2 shows the amount of time required for each web service call as the amount of data is increased. *Return Results* includes both state vector and output buffer transmission. Due to gSOAP's optimized Base64 routines and streaming XML techniques, the Aurora system exhibits good performance when sending small to large amounts of data from the client to the server and vice versa. Even at extreme amounts of data transferred, the Aurora system demonstrates a sustained transfer rate of 7.8 MB/sec for requesting 100 MB of state.

Table 1: Latency (ms) of Aurora Service Routines

	Null (0 KB) Messages
Request WorkUnit	0.56
Request State	0.53
Request InputMsgs	0.52
Return Results	0.61

Table 2: Transfer Time (ms) of Aurora Service Routines

	1 KB	100 KB	1 MB	10 MB	100 MB
Request State	0.77	14.19	129.45	1282.18	12814.65
Request InputMsgs	0.76	14.31	132.05	1308.92	13201.01
Return Results	0.93	26.67	262.50	2642.01	26638.82

5.2. PHOLD: Synthetic Workload

The *PHOLD* application was used to evaluate the performance of simulations running on the Aurora system using controlled workloads. The amount of computation performed by each execution of a work unit and the amount of state and message data transferred between clients and server were varied. In the following tests, a *linear PHOLD* model was used where generated messages are sent to an LP's immediate left and right neighbors. *PHOLD* was configured with 20 LPs, 500 KB of state, and lookahead of 1.0 seconds. The simulation was run over ten Xeon client machines with each client requesting 20 total work units.

Figure 3 shows the fraction of processor time at the client devoted to performing computation for the actual simulation for each work unit leased to a client. The different bars represent the amount of data transferred to the server. As the synthetic workload per work unit is increased, there is less overall wasted time in overhead due to less frequent web service calls. These results indicate that simulations should have a non-trivial amount of computation in order to achieve simulation application processor utilization that exceeds the overhead and idle request times.

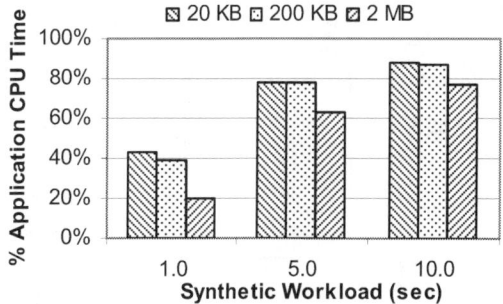

Figure 3: Effect of Workload on Performance

5.3. Execution on Shared Machines

One of the goals of the Aurora system is to have the ability to run simulations in the "background" on hardware of varying speeds and architectures that are shared with other users. Coupled with the fault tolerance features being developed, the Aurora system allows a simulation to run, in principle, virtually anywhere while tolerating node failure and automatically balancing workload among the available processors. For example, the Aurora server can be on a dedicated machine while the client machines are run from idle desktop machines or unreserved public computing clusters.

A torus queuing network is used for this evaluation. The servers can be aggregated into subnets which are mapped to a single work unit. The queuing network is configured as a 250,000 server 500x500 closed torus network partitioned into 625 20x20 torus subnets which can be leased as work units. The internal links within each work unit are set at a delay of 10 microseconds. The job generator creates 10,000 "local" jobs with random server destinations which exist within the work unit and an additional 10,000 "remote" jobs with random server destinations which are external to the work unit. Jobs reaching their destination server are assigned a new random destination according to their previous local or remote designation to keep the relative amount of local and remote jobs consistent. The service time for jobs is exponentially distributed with a mean of 5 microseconds.

There are a total of 78 clients, consisting of 14 Xeon machines and 64 Pentium III machines. The machines were unreserved and many were heavily loaded. No special priorities are given to the Aurora clients (e.g., `nice`). The Aurora server was run from a dedicated Xeon machine.

For the following figures, the overhead time includes state vector and input (server to client) or output (client to server) buffer data transmission and other various overheads such as server-side message binning and client-side input message queuing. The request time is the amount of time the client spends in the work unit request loop. If no work unit is available, the client sleeps for 1 second and tries again in order to avoid flooding the server with requests. All times are averages across all clients.

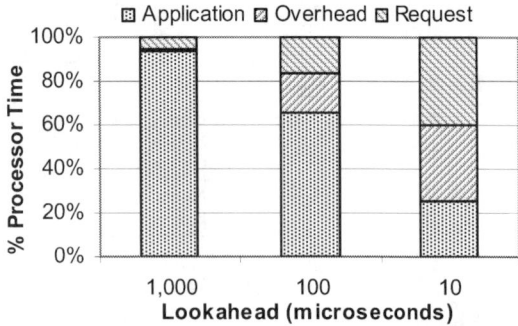

Figure 4: Effect of Lookahead on Performance

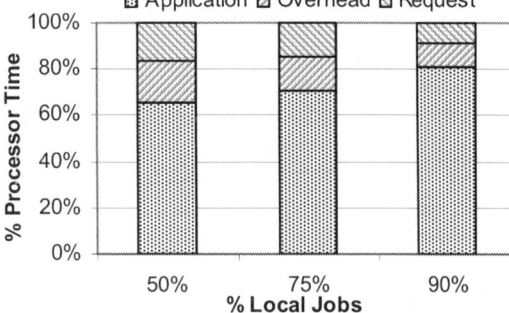

Figure 5: Effect of Relative Workload on Performance

The first scenario involves varying the delay on links between work units, thus varying the lookahead. Figure 4 shows the processor time used for running the simulation, overhead time, and request time. As lookahead decreases the number of messages that can be processed during the work unit lease decreases although the number of messages generated per work unit lease remains constant. Consequently, more messages will exceed the granted LBTS thereby increasing the number of output messages that must be buffered and sent to the server.

The next test modifies the percentage of jobs destined for servers local to the work unit. The delay between work units is held constant at 100 microseconds. As the relative number of jobs destined for local servers increases, the amount of processor time dedicated to the actual computation increases as well. Figure 5 shows increased computation at the clients resulting in less data transmission thereby reducing server load and overhead time.

This next test modifies absolute workload. The delay between work units is kept constant at 100 microseconds with 50% local and 50% remote jobs. Figure 6 shows that the efficiency remains stable as the number of jobs in the system increases. Although the raw overhead and request times increase for each case, the application run time increases as well due to the increased workload from doubling the number of jobs in the system. These experimental results suggest a proportional increase in each of the three areas contributing to the total execution time.

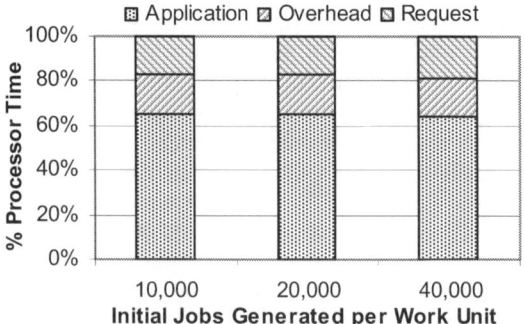

Figure 6: Effect of Absolute Workload on Performance

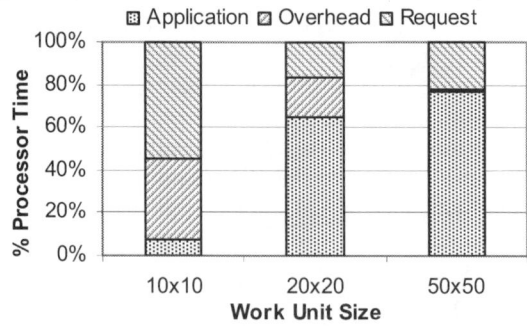

Figure 7: Effect of Partition Size on Performance

The final test evaluates the impact of varying the number of partitions of the torus network. The link delay between work units is 100 microseconds across all tests. The number of jobs generated is set at 10,000 local and remote server destinations. The torus network is partitioned into toroidal subnets of size 10x10 (2500 work units), 20x20 (625 work units), and 50x50 (100 work units).

As partition sizes increase, the number of local links a remote job must traverse increases significantly. Since the internal links between servers are 10 microseconds, a remote job may potentially traverse up to approximately 9 times within a work unit before either the LBTS limit is reached or the job reaches the partition boundary. Figure 7 shows that as the job route length to reach a partition boundary increases as partition size increases, the amount of local computation for larger partition sizes increases.

The large overhead and request times for the 10x10 subnet case can be attributed to high server load as there is relatively little computation performed at the clients compared to the time taken to transfer data. There is more server contention for smaller partition sizes as the work unit return rate is higher for smaller partition sizes increasing server load, thus, the decreasing *Overhead Time* as the partition sizes increase as shown in table 3. Increased server load contributes to increased request time as the server currently is not multi-threaded or distributed.

Table 3: Total Average Overhead and Request Times (sec)

	10x10	20x20	50x50
Overhead Time	1036.396	32.710	14.474
Request Time	1528.394	30.055	210.766

The 20x20 subnet case shows a reduced percentage of overhead and request times compared to the 10x10 case as there is more computation performed at the clients. The 50x50 subnet size does not follow a decreasing *Request Time* trend. Due to the conservative synchronization method used in the current implementation of Aurora, there must be approximately twice the number of work units as there are clients. Under conservative synchronization, the simulation application must be partitioned to accommodate enough work units for the anticipated number of clients to avoid the increased *Request Time* shown in the 50x50 case.

5.4. Hybrid Shock Discrete Event Simulation

An existing physics simulation modeling one-dimensional hybrid shock using the piston method [24] was ported to the Aurora system. This simulation models shockwave propagation using electromagnetic hybrid algorithms with fluid electrons and kinetic ions. The simulation space is partitioned into cells which initially contain a set amount of ions. Each Aurora work unit can contain many cells. For these performance tests, there were 20 LPs of 100 cells each, where ten Xeon clients were used. The lookahead is kept constant at 0.11 for these tests. The amount of state is non-trivial as each cell and ion requires 180 and 140 bytes of memory respectively to save.

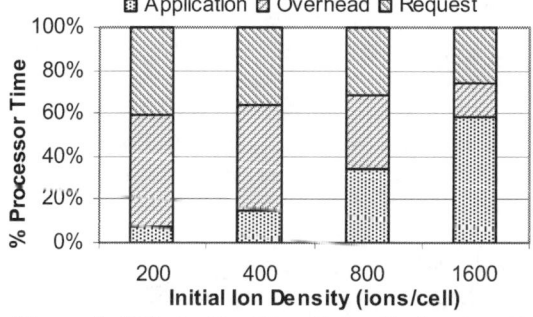

Figure 8: Effect of Ion Density on Performance

The cell width is held constant while the number of initial ions was varied from 200 to 1600 per cell. Figure 8 shows that if event computation per cell is sparse, the relative amount of processor time dedicated for simulation progress is low. Request and overhead times accounted for a large percentage of the total overhead as the single-threaded, single-process server must block for large amounts of incoming and outgoing state. Even with the current limitations in the Aurora server implementation, performance of this real-world application illustrates that Aurora can be an acceptable platform for PDES, however, the master/worker paradigm is not suitable for all applications, such as simulations with low concurrency.

6. Future Work

Work on the Aurora system and master/worker systems for PDES applications in general is in its infancy, and can be expanded in a variety of ways. As mentioned in previous sections, the Aurora time management system may benefit by using optimistic synchronization. Fault tolerance is another area that is currently under development to allow the simulation to work through node failure or even through a server-side crash by writing data to a secondary storage system such as a database. Since the clients only contain ephemeral information, the simulation can be restarted using saved information at any time.

The Aurora server can be improved to reduce client request wait times through multi-threading or partitioning the server itself into smaller server processes run over many machines with proper load-balancing techniques when there is high a work unit return rate. DIME over Base64 encoding can help improve performance through streaming for instances where large amounts of data is sent between server and client. Specialized communication mechanisms can be used to augment the current SOAP communications in use. These specialized communication modes can bypass Base64 and XML encoding required for web services calls.

The Aurora system can be extended to include a caching and pre-fetch system, where state vectors can be saved on the client side and the server can release work units that the client has seen recently. If the state vector has not changed from the previous execution, the client can bypass the download, reducing overhead. The server could issue a pre-release of a work unit that is "not ready" under a conservative time management system by allowing the client to download work unit data while clients await forward progress of the LBTS. Any invalid work units could be re-downloaded from the server when the LBTS is incremented.

7. Conclusions

The Aurora system provides a new technique for PDES by utilizing the master/worker paradigm and leveraging the interoperability of web services. The Aurora system delivers an application-independent simulation framework that can be run using various languages and on a variety of different hardware architectures. Through the use of gSOAP, the Aurora system provides good performance using open-standards built upon a stable, active, and mature toolkit for future improvements. The Aurora system is extensible, and can be expanded to enhance performance, fault tolerance, and security. However, the Aurora system is not suitable for every simulation. Fine-grained simulations that do not exhibit good concurrency and lookahead are better suited for conventional PDES executions.

We demonstrated Aurora's strength with running simulations in the "background." The Aurora system affords simulation application developers the ability to create and run simulations without having to worry about client failures, varying machine architectures, processor speeds, and load on unreserved machines.

Acknowledgements

The authors thank Kalyan Perumalla for contributing a high performance priority queue implementation.

References

1. Anderson, D.P., et al., *SETI@home: an experiment in public-resource computing.* Commun. ACM, 2002. **45**(11): p. 56-61.
2. Nicol, D. and P. Heidelberger, *Parallel execution for serial simulators.* ACM Trans. Model. Comput. Simul., 1996. **6**(3): p. 210-242.
3. Riley, G.F., et al., *A federated approach to distributed network simulation.* ACM Trans. Model. Comput. Simul., 2004. **14**(2): p. 116-148.
4. *IEEE standard for modeling and simulation (M&S) high level architecture (HLA) - framework and rules.* IEEE Std 1516-2000, 2000: p. i-22.
5. Reichenthal, S.W., *Re-introducing web-based simulation*, in *Proceedings of the 34th conference on Winter simulation: exploring new frontiers.* 2002, Winter Simulation Conference: San Diego, California.
6. Page, E.H., J. Robert L. Moose, and S.P. Griffin, *Web-based simulation in Simjava using remote method invocation*, in *Proceedings of the 29th conference on Winter simulation.* 1997, ACM Press: Atlanta, Georgia, United States.
7. Huang, Y., X. Xiang, and G. Madey, *A Self Manageable Infrastructure for Supporting Web-based Simulations*, in *Proceedings of the 37th annual symposium on Simulation.* 2004, IEEE Computer Society: Arlington, VA.
8. Cholkar, A. and P. Koopman, *A widely deployable Web-based network simulation framework using CORBA IDL-based APIs*, in *Proceedings of the 31st conference on Winter simulation: Simulation---a bridge to the future - Volume 2.* 1999, ACM Press: Phoenix, Arizona, United States.
9. Pullen, J.M., et al., *Using Web services to integrate heterogeneous simulations in a grid environment.* Future Gener. Comput. Syst., 2005. **21**(1): p. 97-106.
10. Foster, I. *Globus Toolkit Version 4: Software for Service-Oriented Systems.* in *IFIP International Conference on Network and Parallel Computing.* 2005: Springer-Verlag LNCS 3779.
11. Fitzgibbons, J.B., et al. *IDSim: an extensible framework for Interoperable Distributed Simulation.* in *Proceedings of the IEEE International Conference on Web Services.* 2004. San Diego, CA.
12. Xie, Y., et al., *Servicing Provisioning for HLA-Based Distributed Simulation on the Grid*, in *Proceedings of the 19th Workshop on Principles of Advanced and Distributed Simulation.* 2005, IEEE Computer Society: Monterey, CA.
13. Lin, Y.-B., *Parallel independent replicated simulation on a network of workstations*, in *Proceedings of the eighth workshop on Parallel and distributed simulation.* 1994, ACM Press: Edinburgh, Scotland, United Kingdom.
14. Litzkow, M.J., M. Livny, and M.W. Mutka. *Condor - A hunter of idle workstations.* in *Proceedings of the 8th International Conference on Distributed Computing Systems.* 1988. San Jose, CA.
15. Sunderam, V.S., *PVM: a framework for parallel distributed computing.* Concurrency: Pract. Exper., 1990. **2**(4): p. 315-339.
16. Goux, J.-P., J. Linderoth, and M. Yoder, *Metacomputing and the Master-Worker Paradigm.* 2000, Mathematics and Computer Science Division, Argonne National Laboratory.
17. Ong, T.M., et al., *Unicorn: voluntary computing over Internet.* SIGOPS Oper. Syst. Rev., 2002. **36**(2): p. 36-51.
18. Goldchleger, A., et al., *InteGrade: object-oriented Grid middleware leveraging the idle computing power of desktop machines.* Concurr. Comput. : Pract. Exper., 2004. **16**(5): p. 449-459.
19. Anderson, D.P. *BOINC: a system for public-resource computing and storage.* in *Proceedings of the Fifth IEEE/ACM International Workshop on Grid Computing.* 2004. Pittsburgh, PA.
20. Chiu, K., M. Govindaraju, and R. Bramley, *Investigating the Limits of SOAP Performance for Scientific Computing*, in *Proceedings of the 11th IEEE International Symposium on High Performance Distributed Computing.* 2002, IEEE Computer Society.
21. van Engelen, R.A. and K.A. Gallivan. *The gSOAP toolkit for Web services and peer-to-peer computing networks.* in *Proceedings of the 2nd IEEE/ACM International Symposium on Cluster Computing and the Grid.* 2002. Berlin, Germany.
22. van Engelen, R.A. *Pushing the SOAP Envelope with Web Services for Scientific Computing.* in *Proceedings of the International Conference on Web Services.* 2003. Las Vegas, Nevada.
23. Govindaraju, M., et al. *Toward characterizing the performance of SOAP toolkits.* in *Proceedings of the fifth IEEE/ACM International Workshop on Grid Computing.* 2004. Pittsburgh, PA.
24. Perumalla, K., R. Fujimoto, and H. Karimabadi. *Scalable Simulation of Electromagnetic Hybrid Codes.* in *International Conference on Computational Science.* 2006. University of Reading, UK.

Improving Lookahead in Parallel Multiprocessor Simulation Using Dynamic Execution Path Prediction

Moo-Kyoung Chung
Dynalith Systems Co., Ltd.
CHiPS KAIST Daejeon Korea
mookyoung@dynalith.com

Chong-Min Kyung
Department of EECS
CHiPS KAIST Daejeon Korea
kyung@ee.kaist.ac.kr

Abstract

Simulation performance is dominated by lookahead in null message-based conservative time management of parallel discrete event simulation (PDES). This paper proposes a scheme for software execution path prediction to extend lookahead in parallel multiprocessor simulation. Templates for predicting program execution path are generated by software analysis, then, a processor model gets lookaheads by evaluating the templates at simulation time. We reduced the amount of null messages by a factor of 10 to 50 in parallel simulation with eight clustered workstations and, as a result, achieved a speedup factor of 4 to 7 compared to a conventional method having constant lookahead.

1. Introduction

A multiprocessor-based system is used not only for a parallel computer but also for a today's complex system-on-chip (SoC) by increasing the computational demands of embedded systems. For architecture exploration of the multiprocessor systems, it is necessary to simulate the whole system concurrently by running multiple processor models with their clock synchronized. One of the most important factors in evaluation of the complicated multiprocessor system is simulation speed.

There are three important choices one should make decision about to simulate the multiprocessor system. The first is a choice of two processor modeling methods, namely, direct execution or Instruction Set Simulator (ISS). In direct execution, i.e., host execution or native code execution, software from the target processor is compiled for host processor and runs on the existing host machine. It gives the best simulation performance but is inaccurate due to architecture differences between the target and host processor. Accurate processor modeling is possible by using ISS, if some performance degradation can be allowed. The second option is which time management method will be better for scheduling multiple processor models. In synchronous (or centralized-time) method, all models synchronize with the global clock. It makes system debugging easier by providing better visibility of whole system as a snapshot, but excessive amount of messages for synchronizing among different models can lower simulation performance. On the other hand, asynchronous methods strive to improve simulation performance by removing the global clock synchronization. The last option is about the host machine. One can use single processor-based host machine with the advantages of low cost and fast inter-model message passing. Parallel computing environments, such as SMP (symmetric multiprocessor) or clustered workstations are better for simulation performance, but the speedup according to the number of simulation engines is often limited due to a number of messages and the long message passing delay.

Many multiprocessor simulators have been introduced to evaluate the memory architecture of parallel computers. To speed up the simulation, processor models (direct execution or ISS) are usually running on parallel simulation environment with synchronous or asynchronous time management methods [8-14]. On the other hand, multiprocessor simulators or co-simulation tools for SoC verification usually use ISS's for accurate processor modeling and run on multiple processes or threads of host operating systems in a single workstation [25, 26, 27]. Synchronous time management methods, such as lockstep simulation are tolerated since the communication overhead is relatively small over the distributed simulation environment.

In our multiprocessor simulator, multiple ISS's work together in parallel simulation environment with asynchronous time management for both accurate simulation and better performance. In this case, a large amount of message passing between the models lowers the simulation performance. Various studies on asynchronous time management to reduce the message passing overhead in PDES have been conducted for the last a few decades. (Section 2 describes the algorithms in detail.) Many multiprocessor simulators taking advantages of the algorithms have also been implemented [8-14]. In spite of those asynchronous time management algorithms, the simulation speed is still affected by a number of the messages. Among various asynchronous time management algorithms, we focused on *null* message-based conservative method, where *lookahead* dominates the simulation performance. The proposed method further reduced the amount of the messages by improving lookahead.

The rest of this paper is organized as follows. Section 2 describes previous works related to the asynchronous time management and multiprocessor simulation. The proposed methods are presented in section 3. Section 4 discusses experimental results of the proposed method.

2. Previous works

2.1. PDES

In PDES, simulation consists of a collection of event-driven simulators (*LP: logical process*) that have message queues for each in-degree from other LP's. Each LP asynchronously runs by consuming timestamped messages in its queue and produces timestamped messages to other LP's as shown in Fig. 1. The goal of the synchronization mechanism is maximizing simulation speed while satisfying *local causality constraint*[1].

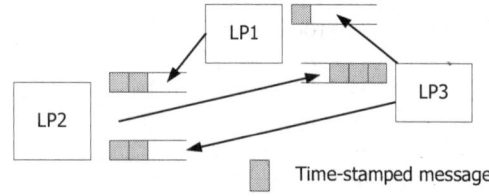

Figure 1. Parallel simulation is performed by exchanging timestamped messages among LP's.

The asynchronous time management algorithms can be classified as *conservative* and *optimistic*. Conservative methods strictly avoid local causality errors by making each LP consume messages in non-decreasing order of timestamp. A message having the smallest timestamp is selected for processing among the first events of all event queues. An LP can be blocked by empty queues and, as a result, deadlock occurs by a cycle of empty queues. To avoid the deadlock null messages are used, which guarantees there are no events until the timestamp of the null message [15, 16]. After processing a message, an LP sends a null message to each of connected LP. Although the null messages

[1] It guarantees that each LP consumes messages in timestamp order.

prevent deadlock, simulation performance is degraded by numerous null messages. For example, suppose two LP's whose local clocks (L) are 100 are blocked and waiting for a message from each other. If timestamp of a null message is ($L+1$) and the next ordinary message occurs at clock 200, one hundred null messages must be exchanged between the two LP's [19]. To reduce the overhead of the null messages, it is necessary to increase the timestamps of the null messages closer to the timestamp of the next ordinary message, which introduced *lookahead* algorithm where an LP having lookahead L produces a null message with timestamp $T + L$ at simulation time T. A large lookahead reduces the number of null messages and accordingly increases simulation performance. Another method to solve the deadlock problem is deadlock detect and recovery algorithm [18]. However, additional overhead to get the global view of the whole simulation system is required to detect and recover deadlocks.

Optimistic methods, on the other hand, allow local causality errors to occur but later detect and correct them [17]. An LP consumes input messages and produces output messages even if there are empty queues. If an LP receives messages with timestamp prior to current local simulation time (*straggle messages*), the LP rolls back to the error point and produces messages to cancel the previously produced messages (*anti-messages*). Although this method can exploit greater degrees of parallelism, there is an additional requirement for storage and computation for state saving and rollback. Also, rollback is not applicable to many commercial ISS due to the requirement of free access to the internal states of the model. Fujimoto gives a good overview of different approaches on the asynchronous time management algorithm of PDES in [19, 20].

2.2. Improving Lookahead

Null message-based conservative asynchronous method usually sets lookahead based on the computation delay of the simulated component and message delivery time that is necessary for a message to reach the destination component. However, it is not enough to reduce the null message when simulating a system having short computation delay and message delivery time. Some previous works strive to improve lookahead of a specific simulation model using its properties. Meyer extended lookahead by analyzing data flow dependency, so-called *path lookahead* [1]. Null message of an output queue is dealt with separately for each data flow path, i.e., only the input events dependent on the output is considered to get the optimized lookahead. Deelman improves lookahead by exploiting computation delay in direct-execution parallel simulator [2, 3]. Compiler finds the local code whose results do not effect program performance and replaces it with analytic performance model that calculates the execution time of the local code. The calculated execution time is added to the computation delay to consequently extend lookahead. On the other hand, Solcany introduces a calculation method of the computation delay when a submodel mapping to an LP is composed of a group of entities [4]. The computation delay of each entity is accumulated according to the data flow.

This paper presents another novel method to improve lookahead in ISS-based parallel multiprocessor simulation. Templates for predicting program execution path are generated at static time by software analysis, then, the extended lookahead is obtained by evaluating the prediction templates at simulation time.

3. Proposed Method

3.1. Parallel Multiprocessor Simulation

The multiprocessor simulation framework in this paper is based on the null message protocol of conservative simulation whose LP's are processor simulators. Each simulator has a processor model (ISS) with its local and shared memory, and slave component models can be attached to the simulator if necessary. Each ISS generates ordinary timestamped messages (events), which are accesses to shared memory or slave components on other simulators. We added a *Predictor* for each output queue in each ISS, which extends lookaheads using processor register values and local memory contents and generate null messages with lookaheads as illustrated in Fig. 2.

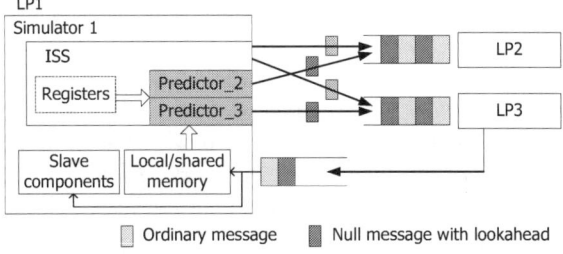

Figure 2. Processor models with predictors: Predictors generate null messages with lookaheads.

3.2. Execution Path Prediction

Because a processor executes program code sequentially and only the IO instructions (load/store) cause the processor to access external components, we can find a lookahead for a destination LP by selecting the execution path consuming the smallest number of clock cycles among all the paths reaching the IO instructions that access external components simulated in the destination LP, which is denoted by I_{EIO}. Accordingly, it is guaranteed that the processor does not produce any events to the destination LP within the lookahead.

A static method to find the shortest path from an address to another is introduced in [22]. Fig. 3 shows a simple example. First, from the binary code (a), control flow graph (CFG) is generated and cycle consumption of each instruction is annotated as shown in (b). If there are instructions that have variable cycle consumption, the minimum value is selected. Assume that IO instructions at address $0x28$, $0x30$ and $0x3c$ are I_{EIO}'s and denoted by $I_{EIO}0$, $I_{EIO}1$ and $I_{EIO}2$, respectively; Destination LP of $I_{EIO}0$ and $I_{EIO}1$ is LP2 and that of $I_{EIO}2$ is LP3. It is possible to find the shortest path from a certain node to another using "*Dijkstra's* shortest-path algorithm" [23], and the minimum cycle consumption from an address to an I_{EIO} is also found with the algorithm. A table in Fig. 3(c) lists the minimum cycle consumptions from address 0 to I_{EIO}'s. A lookahead for an LP is the minimum value among the cycle consumptions to the I_{EIO}'s whose destinations are the LP. Accordingly, we can make a constant lookahead table by performing this calculation for all program addresses as shown in Fig. 3(d).

Because a larger lookahead further reduces the null messages, we need to find a large lookahead close to the actual 'no-event' period. However, in many cases the static calculation method finds a smaller value than the optimal one because the execution path cannot be determined at static time but only at run time. For example, cycle consumption to the next ordinary message to LP2 at address $0x0$ can be larger then the constant lookahead 9, which is the cycle consumption of the shortest path from basic block A to D. If the program goes through the block B at address $0x10$ in Fig. 3(b), it is required to exchange additional null messages to synchronize with LP2. This overhead can be removed, if the ISS is able to predict the correct execution path.

We construct the lookahead table with prediction templates instead of constant values. The prediction templates are numerical expressions to calculate lookaheads using the contents of the data memory and register values as their operands. The calculation is performed at run time with the current values of the operands. The prediction templates are extracted from the CFG and data flow information. In this paper, we obtained larger lookaheads by predicting branch path and loop iteration counts.

3.2.1. Branch Path

To maximally extend lookaheads, the ISS needs to find the correct path at each of the succeeding conditional branch as early as possible at run time. Fig. 4 is the generation procedure of the prediction templates considering the branch

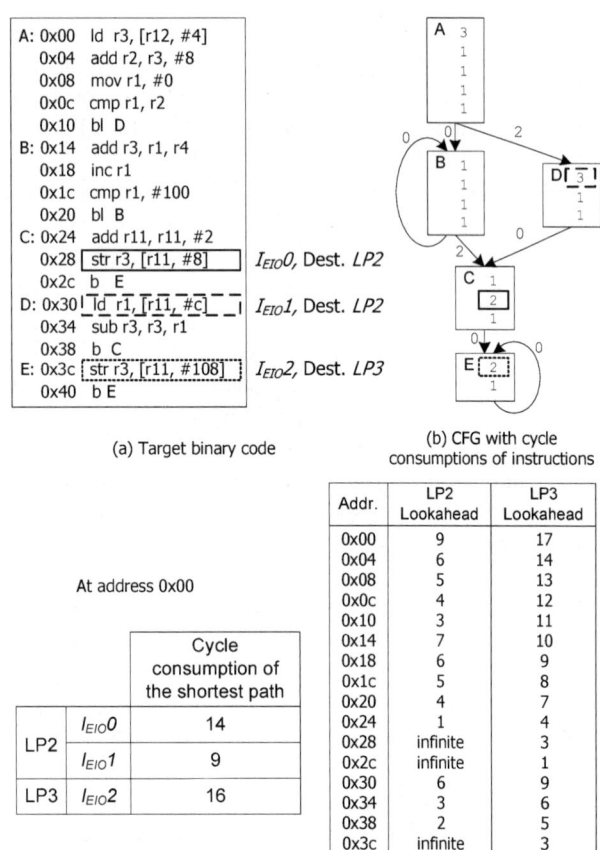

(a) Target binary code

(b) CFG with cycle consumptions of instructions

(c) Minimum cycle consumptions to the I_{EIO}'s at address 0x00

(d) Constant lookahead table

Figure 3. A simple example of finding constant lookahead by static analysis of software execution path

First, the branch condition and target addresses are extracted from a conditional branch instruction, $(r1 < r2)? D : B$ for the *bl* instruction at address $0x10$ in this example. In this case, prediction templates are generated in the form of
$$T() = C_{ToBranch} + ((Cond.))? C_{FromD} : C_{FromB}$$
, where $C_{ToBranch}$ is cycle consumption to the branch instruction; C_{FromD} and C_{FromB} are cycle consumption to I_{EIO} from basic block D and B, respectively. See Fig. 5(a).

The second step is to find the so-called *in-time expressions* for each operand ($r1$ and $r2$) of the branch condition, which represent the values of the operands using the registers and memory contents at that instance. This step is completed by repeating 1) searching the upper bound of *life region* and 2) deriving the in-time expression. For example, the upper bound of life region of the operand $r1$ of the branch condition, $(r1 < r2)? D : B$ at address $0x10$ is address $0x0c$, because the definition of the operand $r1$ is at address $0x08$. The in-time expression of $r1$ in this life region is $r1$, which is registered at address $0x0c$ to $0x10$ in the in-time expression table. The in-time expression for $r1$ at address $0x08$ is 0, which is derived from the instruction at the address, i.e., the value of the operand ($r1$) is propagated by the *copy* instruction ($mov\ r1, \#0$). The in-time expression table can be obtained by repeating these two sub-steps, 1) and 2), as shown in Fig. 5(b) for the operand $r1$ and $r2$.

The repetition of the two sub-steps is terminated according to the terminations rules as follows:

Termination Rule 1. *In the case of a Memory-Store instruction where the instruction stores something to local memory when the current in-time expression refers to local memory content, the upper bound of life region is determined by the address of the Store instruction and further repetition is terminated.*

Termination Rule 2. *In the case of a Constant-Operand where the new in-time expression is a constant, the upper bound of life region is unlimited and further repetition is terminated.*

If an in-time expression refers to memory, we should track the memory contents with addresses. However, it is difficult to track various types of indirect memory accesses and calculate the relevant indices. For the sake of fast prediction and simple implementation we did not track memory contents, as termination rule 1 indicates. Termination rule 2 means that there is no need to track the in-time expression any longer if it equals a constant, as it cannot be changed by other instructions. This second step is continued over basic block boundaries. If the in-degree of a basic block is two or more, this second step has to be performed for all paths.

Third, we can obtain expressions composing the looka-

prediction, and Fig. 5 shows the procedure step by step applied to the above example in Fig. 3.

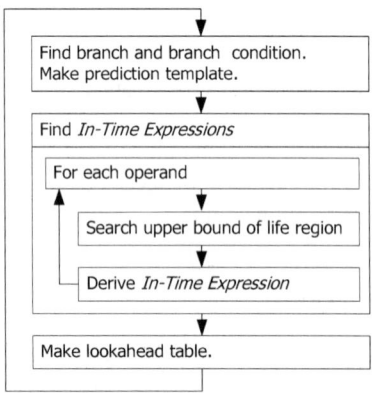

Figure 4. Branch prediction process

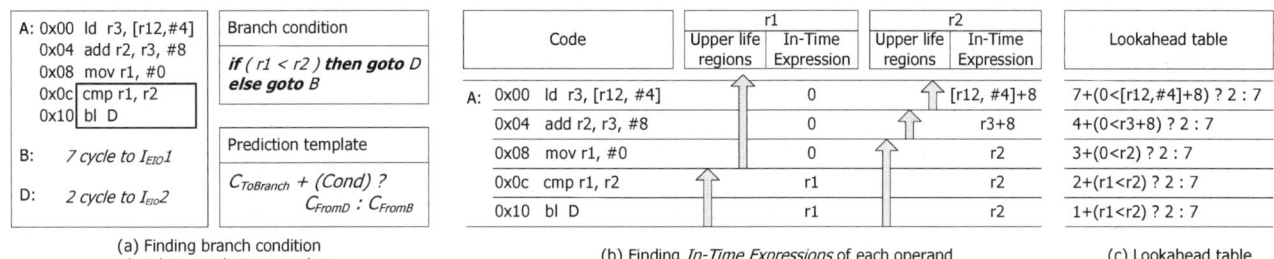

Figure 5. Process for generating a prediction table with branch prediction

head table for each code address by replacing the operands of the prediction template with the in-time expressions corresponding to the address. Lookahead table of this branch prediction example is shown in Fig. 5(c). Now, the ISS obtains the larger lookaheads through the evaluation of the expressions in the lookahead table. Because the in-time variables are extended over basic block boundaries, the two or more predictions can be overlapped, and the prediction templates are nested as in

$T2() = C_{ToBranch} + ((Cond.)? T1() : C_{FromX}$

for two adjacent branches. We can predict two or more succeeding branches taking advantage of the nested prediction templates.

3.2.2. Loop Iteration Count

Predicting loop iteration count is very effective at improving lookaheads. (More than 90% of CPU time is consumed within loops in typical numerical code.) Fig. 7 is the generation procedure of the prediction templates considering the loop iteration prediction.

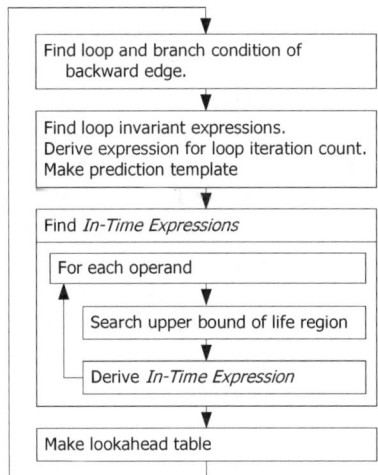

Figure 7. Loop iteration count prediction process

Loop iteration count prediction is as follows (refer to Fig. 6): First, we find loops that do not have I_{EIO} and branch instructions with conditions for the loop exit. Basic block B in the above example forms a self-loop and does not have I_{EIO}. Fig. 6(a) shows the branch instruction for the loop exit and its condition. The operands of the branch condition are the loop indices.

Second, we find loop-invariant expressions associated with the loop indices, as shown in Fig. 6(a). From the loop-invariant expressions, an expression to calculate the loop iteration count is derived. For example, if the branch condition turns out to be $r1 \leq C1$ and the loop-invariant expression associated with $r1$ is $r1 = r1 + C2$, where $C1$ and $C2$ are constant values. Then the loop iteration count is derived as follows: the value of loop index is $r1_n = r1_{n-1} + C2$, where subscript n denotes loop iteration count up to now. The loop exit condition is $r1_n + \sum^{Iter} C2 > C1$, where $Iter$ is remaining iteration count. $Iter$ is computed by $Iter = (C1 - r1_n)/C2$. Loop iteration prediction templates are generated in the form

$T() = C_{ToBranch} + Iter \cdot C_{Loop}$

, where C_{Loop} is the time consumed for the single iteration of the loop.

In the third step, the in-time expressions for the loop indices are found in the same way as in the second step of the above branch prediction procedure, as shown in Fig. 6(b). Finally, we can obtain expressions to calculate lookahead including loop iteration count by replacing the operands with the in-time expressions appropriate to the address. This step is similar to the third step of the branch prediction. Fig. 6(c) shows the prediction table for loop iteration count. In the address range from $0x0$ to $0x10$, the predictions are overlapped with the previous branch prediction (Fig. 5(c)). Fig. 8 shows the final lookahead table for both predictors of output queues to LP2 and LP3 in the example.

If a loop has multiple exits, each loop exit instruction (i.e., branch) has its own prediction template generated by this procedure. We take the minimum value among the templates for evaluating a lookahead. For instance, a loop can have two exits whose templates are $T1()$ and $T2()$, then $T() = min\{T1(), T2()\}$. Two or more predictions can also

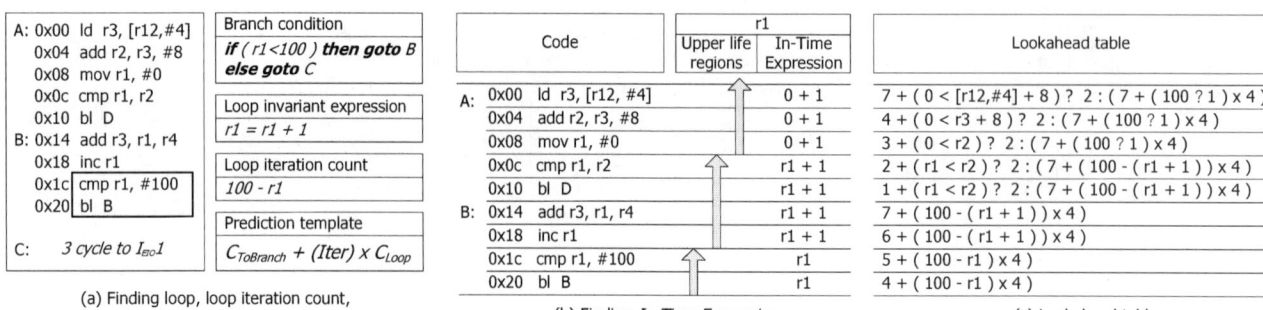

Figure 6. Generation process of prediction table with loop iteration prediction

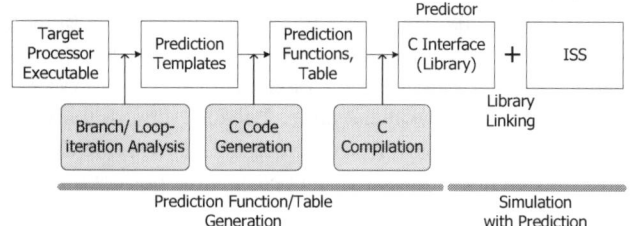

Figure 8. Lookahead table

Figure 9. Generation process of the predictors

be overlapped. For the disjoint loops, the template forms itself into $T() = Const. + Iter1 \cdot C_{Loop1} + Iter2 \cdot C_{Loop2}$; for the nested loops, $f() = Const. + Iter1 \cdot \{Const. + iter2 \cdot C_{Loop2}\}$. Prediction becomes simpler by handling only the loops that have *add*, *sub*, *inc* or *dec* instructions for their loop-invariant expressions associated with the indices.

3.3. Implementation

Fig. 9 shows the generation process the predictors. *Branch and Loop-iteration Analysis* step in the figure is explained in the previous subsections. Because the predictions are expressed by the combination of some fixed forms of prediction templates, *C Code Generation* step is simple and trivial; we exclude the details in this paper. The prediction C code is compiled into a C/C++ library and linked to an ISS by C linker. Hence, we can take advantage of the powerful optimization of the C compiler; there is no need for an additional step for the optimization of the expressions in the lookahead table. All these processes are automated and the only user responsibilities are to select the IO variables in the target C code with their destination LP's.

Some possible concerns with the proposed prediction method can be removed or reduced as follows. First, the prediction templates and table are generated at static time but the ISS obtains lookahead values at run time by evaluating the templates, so we cannot avoid prediction overhead. However, the overhead is insignificant. Although several hundreds of host instructions are typically executed for a single instruction simulation of the target processor, the prediction templates can be realized with a few lines of C code, usually not exceeding several tens of instructions. Moreover, the lookahead evaluation is performed only when it is necessary, which is also less often as lookahead increases.

Second, this approach is based on the analysis of the executable file, and it is difficult to manually appoint all I_{EIO}'s and their destinations. To automate this task without compiler modification, we made a so-called *BinMapper* that searches the executable file for instructions appropriate to C statements. We can find the instructions corresponding to a C statement accessing the variables that are mapped to external LP's. The input to the *BinMapper* is the list of the IO variables in the target C code and their destination LP's, and the output is the code addresses of the IO access instructions with the destination LP's. The mapping information from C to executable code is obtained from debugging information of *ELF*[2], which is described in detail in our previous work [21].

---

[2](Executable and Linkable Format) is the most widely used file format for the executable and linkable.

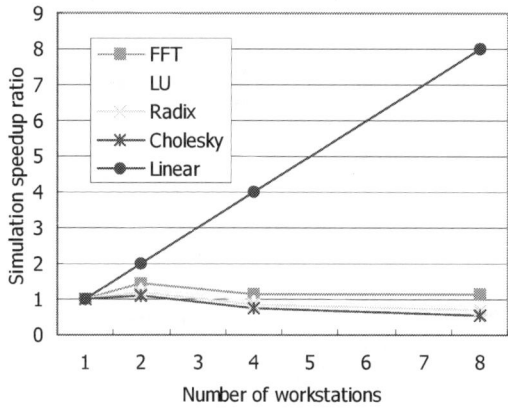

Figure 10. Parallel simulation speedup of conventional method with constant lookahead, eight clock cycles

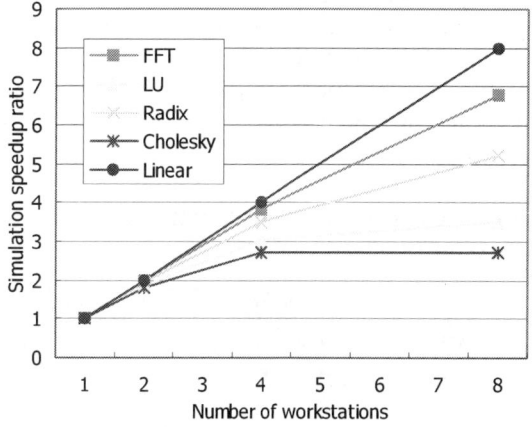

Figure 11. Parallel simulation speedup of proposed method

4. Experiment

We compared the proposed method with the existing one that uses constant lookahead based on message delivery time. The multiprocessor simulation platform is made up of two, four or eight workstations clustered with Ethernet (100 Mbps), each of which having a processor simulator as depicted in Fig. 2. We assume that the target multiprocessor system does not have cache and directories for the sake of simple implementation. For testbenches, we modified kernel programs of SPLASH-2 parallel applications suite [24] to suit for our target multiprocessor system with distributed shared memory.

Fig. 10 shows the simulation speedup ratio of the existing one depending on the number of simulators (workstations) while assuming that the constant lookahead (message delivery time) is eight clock cycles of the target processor. We can see that the simulation speed decreases instead as the number of simulators increases. This is because the latency of the Ethernet is too long, typically more than 0.5 msec. It means that there are few advantages to parallel simulation in this Ethernet clustered workstation, if the number of messages between the simulators does not decrease. Fig. 10 also shows that there are a few differences in simulation speedup between Cholesky, which requires short intervals of synchronization, and FFT, which requires long intervals. It is because the lookahead is a small constant value and the null messages should be continuously exchanged even when there is no need of synchronization and communication between the processor simulators. In other words, one cannot expect speedup even for the application generates a few ordinary messages due to the enormous null messages between the ordinary events.

Fig. 11 shows the simulation speedup ratio of the proposed method, where lookahead is improved through the dynamic execution path prediction. By reducing the null messages, we can get the speedup close to the ideal values (linear scale) for FFT, which requires relatively small number of ordinary messages, and also get fair performance for Cholesky requires large number of ordinary messages. Table 1 shows the details of the comparison including the improved lookahead, number of null messages and simulation time for the case of eight workstations (simulators). We can see that the null messages dominate the total number of messages and simulation time in the conventional method. The proposed method extends lookahead to several tens or hundreds clock cycles of the target processor (see *Average Lookahead* column). Simulation time and speedup ratio shows that the null message reduction through the proposed lookahead extension method is highly effective in simulation speedup.

5. Conclusion

Parallel simulation is a promising method for the fast simulation of a large system including today's complex SoC design. However, the simulation speed is limited due to a number of messages and its long latency, especially for the low-cost clustered workstations with Ethernet. We focused on the ISS-based multiprocessor simulation in the clustered workstations with the asynchronous time management, which is most suitable for the fast, accurate and cost-effective simulation of multiprocessor system. Simulation performance can be much improved by large lookahead closer to the timestamp of the next ordinary message in null message-based conservative time management. The proposed method aggressively extends lookaheads of null messages by dynamic execution path prediction of software running on each ISS. Experimental result shows the null message reduction by a factor of 10 to 50 and simulation speedup by a factor of 4 to 7 compared to the conventional method having constant lookahead.

Table 1. Details of improvement with eight workstations

	# of Ordinary Messages (x100)	Average Lookahead (clock cycles)	# of Null Messgaes (x100)		Simulatoin Time (sec)		Speed -up Ratio
			Conventional	Proposed	Conventional	Proposed	
FFT	71	224	6,274	121	1,484	266	5.58
LU	522	59	8,662	783	2,041	432	4.72
Radix	197	147	10,469	335	2,332	340	6.68
Cholesky	642	46	11,311	1,124	2,574	585	4.40

References

[1] R. A. Meyer, R. L. Bagrodia, "Path Lookahead: a Data Flow View of PDES Models," in *Proceedings of Workshop on Parallel and Distributed Simulation*, pp. 12-19, 1999.

[2] V. S. Adve, R. Bagrodia, E. Deelman, T. Phan, R. Sakellariou, "Compiler-supported simulation of highly scalable parallel applications," in *Proceedings of Conference on Supercomputing*, 1999.

[3] E. Deelman, R. Bagrodia, R. Sakellariou, V. Adve, "Improving Lookahead in Parallel Discrete Event Simulations of Large-Scale Applications Using Computer Analysis," in *Proceedings of Workshop on Parallel and Distributed Simulation*, pp. 5-14, 2001.

[4] V. Solcany, J. Safarik, "The lookahead in a user-transparent conservative parallel simulator," in *Proceedings of Workshop on Parallel and Distributed Simulation*, pp. 11-16, 2002.

[5] P. M. Dickens, J. Reynolds, P. F., "SRADS With Local Rollback," in *Proceedings of SCS Multiconference on Distributed Simulation*, pp. 161-164, 1990.

[6] L. M. Sokol, B. K. Stucky, "MTW: Experimental Results for a Constranied Optimistic Scheduling Paradigm," in *Proceedings of SCS Multiconference on Distributed Simulation*, pp. 169-173, 1990.

[7] R. L. Bagrodia, M. Takai, "Performance Evaluation of Conservative Algorithms in Parallel Simulation Languages," in *IEEE Transactions on Parallel and Distributed Systems*, Vol. 11, No. 4, pp. 395-411, 2000.

[8] S. S. Mukherjee, S. K. Reinhardt, B. Falsafi, M. Litzkow, M. D. Hill, D. A. Wood, S. Huss-Lederman, J. R. Larus, "Wisconsin Wind Tunnel II: a fast, portable parallel architecture simulator," in *IEEE Parallel and Distributed Technology*, Vol. 8, No. 4, pp. 12-20, 2000.

[9] C. J. Hughes, V. S. Pai, P. Ranganathan, S. V. Adve, "Rsim: simulating shared-memory multiprocessors with ILP processors," in *IEEE Computer*, Vol. 35, No. 2, pp. 40-49, 2002.

[10] D. Sunada, D. Glasco, M. Flynn, "ABSS v2.0: a SPARC Simulator," in *Technical Report: CSL-TR-98-755* Stanford University, 1998.

[11] M. Rosenblum, E. Bugnion, S. Devine, S. A. Herrod, "Using the SimOS machine simulator to study complex computer systems," in *ACM Transactions on Modeling and Computer Simulation*, Vol. 7, No. 1, pp. 78-103, 1997.

[12] S. Prakash, E. Deelman, R. Bagrodia, "Asynchronous parallel simulation of parallel programs," in *IEEE Transactions on Software Engineering*, Vol. 26, No 5, pp. 385-400, 2000

[13] P. M. Dickens, P. Heidelberger, D. M. Nicol, "A distributed memory LAPSE: parallel simulation of message-passing programs," in *Proceedings of Workshop on Parallel and Distributed Simulation*, pp. 32-38, 1994.

[14] U. Legedza, W. E. Weihl, "Reducing synchronization overhead in parallel simulation," in *Proceedings of Workshop on Parallel and Distributed Simulation*, pp. 86-95, 1996.

[15] R. E. Bryant, "Simulation of Packet Communication Architecture Computer Systems," Technical Report TR-188, Massachusetts Institute of Technology, Cambridge, 1977.

[16] K. M. Chandy, J. Misra, "Distributed Simulation: A Case Study in Design and Verification of Distributed Programs," *IEEE Trans. Software Engineering*, SE-5, 5, pp. 440-452, Sep. 1978.

[17] David R. Jefferson, "Virtual time," *ACM Trans. Programming Languages and Systems*, vol. 7, no 3, pp. 404-425, July 1985.

[18] K. M. Chandy, J. Misra, "Asynchronous Distributed Simulation via a Sequence of Parallel Computations," in *Communication of the ACM*, Vol. 24, No. 4, pp. 198-205, 1981.

[19] Richard. M. Fujimoto, "Parallel and distributed simulation systems," in *Proceedings of Winter Simulation Conference*, Vol. 1, pp.147-157, 2001.

[20] Richard M. Fujimoto, *Parallel and Distributed Simulation Systems*, Wiley InterScience, 2000.

[21] Moo-Kyoung Chung, Sangjun Yang, Sang-Heon Lee and Chong-Min Kyung, "System-Level HW/SW Co-Simulation Framework for Multiprocessor and Multithread SoC," *Proc. VLSI-TSA Design, Automation, and Test*, pp. 177-179, 2005.

[22] Jinyong Jung, Sungjoo Yoo, Kiyoung Choi, "Performance improvement of multi-processor systems cosimulation based on SW analysis," *Proc. Design, Automation and Test in Europe*, pp. 749-753, 2001

[23] E. W. Dijkstra, "A Note on Two Problems in Connexion with Graphs," *Numerische Mathematik*, pp. 269-297, 1989

[24] S. C. Woo, M. Ohara, E. Torrie, J. P. Singh, A. Gupta, "The SPLASH-2 Programs: Characterization and Methodological Considerations," *Proc. 22nd Symp. Computer Architecture*, pp. 24-36, 1995

[25] Seamless CVE, Mentor Graphics, product description available at http://www.mentor.com/seamless

[26] MaxSim, ARM Corporate, product description available at http://www.arm.com/products/DevTools/MaxSim.html

[27] ConvergenSC, CoWare, Product description available at http://www.coware.com/products/convergensc.php

The Distributed Open Network Emulator: Using Relativistic Time for Distributed Scalable Simulation

Craig Bergstrom Srinidhi Varadarajan Godmar Back

Department of Computer Science
Virginia Tech
Blacksburg, Virginia 24061
{cbergstr—varadarajan—gback}@cs.vt.edu

Abstract— In this paper, we present the design and implementation of The Distributed Open Network Emulator (dONE), a scalable hybrid network emulation/simulation environment. It has several novel contributions. First, a new model of time called relativistic time that combines the controllability of virtual time with the naturally flowing characteristics of wall-clock time. This enables a hybrid environment in which direct code execution can be mixed with simulation models. Second, dONE uses a new transparent object based framework called Weaves, which enables the composition of unmodified network applications and protocol stacks to create large-scale simulations. Finally, it implements a novel parallelization strategy that minimizes the number of independent timelines and offers an efficient mechanism to progress the event timeline. Our prototype implementation incorporates the complete TCP/IP stack from the Linux 2.4 kernel family and executes any application code written for the BSD sockets interface. The prototype runs on 16 processors and produces super-linear speedup in a simulation of hundred infinite-source to infinite-sink pairs.

I. INTRODUCTION

With the continuing exponential growth of the Internet and the ensuing rapid proliferation of network protocols, there is an urgent need for large-scale protocol development environments that can act as controlled experimental testbeds for protocol and interoperability testing, verification and validation. The last several years have seen the deployment of protocol development environments that allow users to create complex controlled experimental testbeds to verify and validate network protocols. Protocol development environments can be broadly classified into (a) Network simulators and (b) Direct code execution environments. Simulators such as NS [4], OPnet [7], SSFNet [8], MaRS [1], and GloMoSim [21] use an efficient, event-driven execution model, but they require that the protocol under test be expressed in that model. The simulated protocol must then be converted to a real-world code implementation before it can be deployed, raising the problem of how to guarantee the equivalence of simulated protocol and actual code implementation. In addition, such simulated models fail to accurately express the idiosyncrasies of real-world TCP/IP implementations, which can significantly affect performance [2].

By contrast, emulators such as Utah Emulab [20], dummynet [16], ENTRAPID [11], and ModelNet [18] directly execute unmodified real-world code in a network test-bed environment. As such, they cannot easily model virtual networks whose emulation would require resources that exceed the resources of the physical system used to perform the emulation. Additionally, direct code execution environments typically map each network application to a separate OS process, which limits their scalability. Finally, and most importantly, since direct execution environments work in real time as opposed to virtual simulation time, they suffer from an inherent lack of temporal determinism which impacts the controllability of experimental test-beds.

Consequently, we need an approach that combines the predictability and controllability of event-driven simulation with the ability of emulators to run unchanged network applications and their associated protocol code. Although the high degree of parallelism that is inherent to large-scale network lends itself to parallel or distributed implementations, creating efficient frameworks for large-scale, high-fidelity simulations has proved challenging for several reasons.

First, it requires a temporal model that can reconcile the real-time nature of direct code execution with the event-driven nature of simulation models. To reduce synchronization overhead, this temporal model should minimize the number of independent timelines the simulator has to track. Second, it requires a runtime support system that enables the use of unmodified applications within the emulation/simulation system. To be scalable, such a runtime system must accommodate multiple simulation entities within a single OS process.

In this paper, we present the Distributed Open Network Emulator, or dONE, a scalable, distributed emulation/simulation framework. dONE has several novel features. First, it deploys a new model of time called *relativistic time* that combines the controllability of virtual time models with the self-synchronizing, continuous nature of wall-clock time, without violating the model's consistency even for directly executed codes. Second, dONE uses a composition framework called Weaves that provides the ability to emulate multiple instances of an application or protocol stack inside a single OS process.

Weaves provides this support at the object code level, allowing emulated applications to be written in any programming language for which a compiler is available. Finally, dONE implements a novel parallelization strategy that minimizes the number of independent timelines and which offers a low-overhead mechanism to synchronize their progress with the timeline of simulated events.

To demonstrate the results of our approach, we present experimental results from a parallel implementation of dONE. The implementation incorporates the complete TCP/IP stack from the Linux 2.4 kernel family and executes unchanged application code written for the BSD sockets interface. We evaluated our prototype on a 16-CPU cluster and found that it scales to thousands of virtual hosts. It has produced superlinear speedup in a simulation of five-hundred infinite-source to infinite-sink pairs.

The rest of this paper is organized as follows. Section II reviews traditional approaches to modeling time in simulation environments. Section III presents the relativistic time model in detail. Section IV describes a distributed implementation of the relativistic time model in dONE. Section V presents experimental results and Section VI concludes.

II. RELATED WORK

Two broad classes of simulation algorithms have been widely cited in the simulation literature. Optimistic protocols such as the time warp protocol [12] allow simulation nodes to process events without bound until a causality error is detected. When this occurs, the simulation is rolled back to the time of the error so that it can be corrected. Although it is possible to rollback directly executed code, doing so would be prohibitive for a system that aims to support the embedding of thousands of unchanged protocol instances.

Conservative algorithms prevent causality errors from occurring in the first place. Algorithms such as Chandy-Misra-Bryant's [5], [6], [14] typically rely on information from other nodes about their simulation state before deciding whether it is safe to process an event without incurring a causality error (input-waiting-rule). This rule requires the nodes to pass NULL messages to explicitly synchronize their clocks and break deadlock conditions if necessary. A number of mechanisms have been proposed to improve the performance of the conservative NULL message algorithm. These include attempts to decrease the number of NULL messages passed between logical processes [17], attempts to use a conservative lookahead window [3], and the recognition that for certain application domains (i.e. Virtual Environments) the precise ordering of events is less important than efficient and highly responsive execution [9]. Despite these improvements, traditional conservative algorithms still incur high communication overhead, because the timelines of the different nodes must be synchronized with a global virtual timeline.

Temporal models provide another axis for comparison. Virtual time models rely on a counter that is forced by the progression of events to represent time. Although this model can provide a very high degree of controllability and precision, its rate of progress is intimately tied to the physics of the simulation. Real-time models prevalent in direct code execution use a naturally flowing clock that progresses independent of the simulation. While this enables real-time models to exploit the parallelism inherent in the simulation, it impacts both precision and controllability.

III. RELATIVISTIC TIME

The primary challenge in creating a hybrid emulation/simulation environment lies in reconciling two opposing requirements. Direct code execution of network applications runs in real-time or wall-clock time, which flows naturally (not forced by a progression of events), but is uncontrolled. Models of next generation network devices such as ultra high speed networks operate in highly controllable virtual time, but the virtual clock has to be forced by events occurring in the system.

To solve this problem, we developed a system of time called relativistic time, which borrows from the theory of relativity. Relativistic time reconciles real time and virtual time by creating a temporal model that flows naturally, and yet is highly controllable. Three basic properties underlie relativistic time. First, all physical measures of time are non-decreasing and ordinal in nature, rely on a periodic waveform, where the length of each period is controlled by the fundamental nature of space-time. Second, all clocks in a single frame of reference agree on the measure of time. Third, time is defined in terms of change of state.

To see how we use these properties, consider a network with two physical nodes that is used to model a virtual network with two virtual hosts (one per physical node). The physical nodes are connected over a network of bandwidth B. In this system, packets are sent from the virtual hosts to the simulator, which delivers it to the receiver at the appropriate time. If we model this network in a direct code execution environment, we are restricted to real time and hence cannot model a virtual network with bandwidth greater than B. Similarly, the latency of the virtual network we can model is restricted by the minimum latency of the physical network used in the emulation.

To emulate a virtual network that requires resources beyond the resources available to the physical system, we need to control how to stretch the amount of time given to the physical system so that it produces the virtual network's final state. This is similar to how a moving frame of reference's time is scaled relative to an inertial frame of reference.

In the above example control is achieved by (a) placing the virtual hosts in a new inertial frame of reference (I) (b) retaining the simulator in the original frame of reference (O), and (c) changing the velocity of I with respect to O. This brings us to the first operator of the relativistic time model—the time dilation operator. The ratio of the velocity of I with respect to O causes time to dilate in I. By judiciously selecting the velocity of I, we can dilate time sufficiently to enable the simulator in frame O to model a network of arbitrary

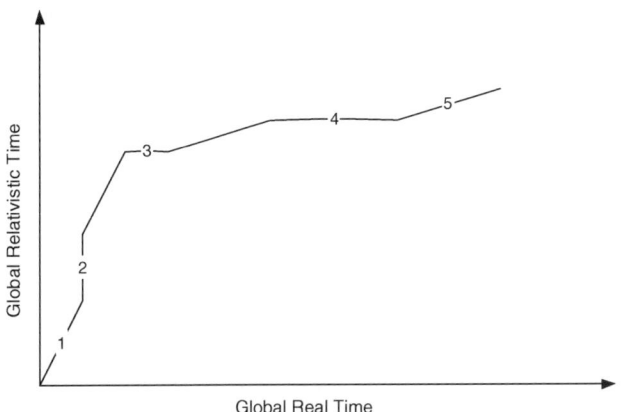

Fig. 1. Mapping of global real time to global relativistic time.

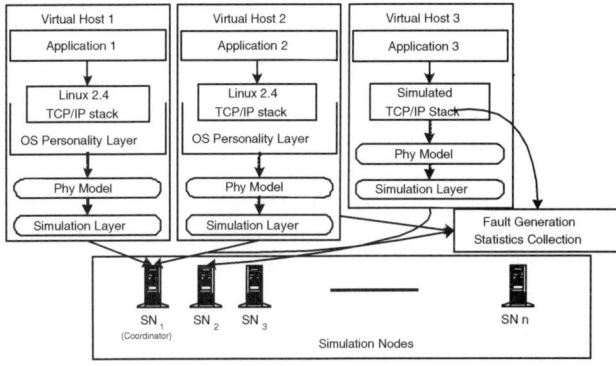

Fig. 2. The architecture of dONE.

bandwidth or latency, thereby achieving controllability. Intuitively, time dilation provides a mechanism to handle resource oversubscription.

While the example presented above handles the case of resource oversubscription, it is desirable to handle resource undersubscription efficiently as well. For instance, if the bandwidth of the virtual network is less than the physical network, it is desirable to run the simulation as fast as possible. This can be achieved in virtual time simulation systems, by warping over quiescent intervals. On the other hand, direct code execution engines use real-time delays to model undersubscription, which causes them to run at real-time or slower. Ideally, we desire a temporal model for direct code execution that can handle resource undersubscription efficiently.

Resource undersubscription can be divided into static undersubscription and dynamic undersubscription. Static undersubscription can be detected by analyzing the virtual network topology and statically setting the appropriate time dilation factor. Dynamic undersubscription occurs when there are global quiescent periods where all virtual hosts are waiting for an event to occur. To exploit quiescence, we use the third property of relativistic time. Since there is no change in the state of the system, time is not physically measurable. This leads to the second operator of the relativistic time model—time warp. If the simulator detects quiescence, it warps relativistic time to the next event in the system.

Relativistic time is thus a functional mapping between two frames of reference—the simulator's frame and the virtual network's frame. For simplicity, the simulator's frame of reference is chosen as real-time reducing relativistic time to a functional mapping of real-time. The functional mapping is kept consistent across all physical nodes in the simulation, thereby creating a single inertial frame of reference for the entire simulation. Since this functional mapping remains constant for the duration of a simulation, keeping timelines synchronized adds only minimal messaging overhead. The novel and advantageous aspect here is that the relativistic time simulator can apply a function to its local real-time clock and derive the current value of relativistic time with the assurance that all other physical nodes are at exactly the same instant of relativistic time. (In a distributed implementation, we assume that the physical real-time clocks of the participating nodes can be sufficiently tightly synchronized over short time intervals.) The result is that because nodes do not need to explicitly communicate to determine global time, messaging overhead is reduced.

Figure 1 depicts a sample mapping of relativistic time to real time. The inverse of the slopes of the lines represents the time dilation factor. Thus slopes greater than 1 (dilation factor less than 1) such as the line marked 1 imply static resource undersubscription, where relativistic time runs faster than real-time. Similarly the line marked 5 shows a resource oversubscription, where relativistic time runs slower than real-time. The line marked 2 shows the operation of a warp, where the simulator has detected global quiescence and warped relativistic time to coincide with the next event. The line marked 3 depicts a change in the functional mapping between relativistic time and real-time. In this case, the simulator stops the progress of relativistic time, broadcasts the new mapping to all physical nodes and resumes the progress of relativistic time with the new mapping. The line marked 4 shows a terminal case, where progress of relativistic time is stopped for an arbitrary amount of time. This is used to implement a pure simulation model where virtual time (in our case relativistic time) should not progress during an event handler.

IV. IMPLEMENTING RELATIVISTIC TIME

To implement the relativistic time model in a distributed environment, we had to design several components. First, we designed a mechanism to load multiple instances of a simulation entity into the simulation environment. Second, we designed a way to multiplex multiple virtual hosts onto a single physical node that kept their timelines in sync relative to each other and relative to the timeline imposed by the discrete event core. Third, we designed a method to separate a virtual host's state such that updates to internal state could be distinguished from updates with potential external effects. Fourth, we designed a coordinator-based mechanism to keep the timelines of virtual hosts executing on different physical nodes in sync. Figure 2 shows an overview of dONE's architecture.

A. Virtualizing the host environment

The Weaves [15] compositional framework provides a multi-threaded environment in which multiple virtual hosts, their network application and protocols, can run as separate threads within a single OS process. Unlike a traditional multi-threading framework, however, Weaves provides each virtual host with a separate namespace for its global and static variables. Weaves uses a binary rewriting process that transparently redirects accesses to those variables to a local copy for the current virtual host. This process is similar to how multiple instances of a shared library can exist in multiple processes, with a similar and small overhead.

B. Virtualizing Time

In addition to virtualizing a physical node's CPU and address space, we must virtualize its notion of time. The relativistic time model requires that a virtual host's time progresses at the rate of real time, or a fraction thereof, while it executes. Consequently, we provide a way for a virtual host to ascertain the fraction of real time during which it used the CPU. This fraction forms the basis for a virtual host's local clock. To accurately measure the virtual time that has elapsed on each virtual host, we have modified the Linux kernel to keep track of the amount of time allocated to each virtual host with nanosecond precision.

To conservatively guarantee the consistency of our simulation and to synchronize the timelines of virtual hosts with the timelines imposed by the discrete event engine, we must control their progress in two ways. First, we must ensure that no virtual host's timeline falls behind the timeline shared among all virtual hosts, as expressed by global relativistic time. If a virtual host fell too far behind global relativistic time, events originating from that virtual host may not be delivered to other virtual hosts on time, leading to temporal inversion. Second, we must ensure that no virtual hosts advance too far ahead of global relativistic time. If a virtual host advanced too far ahead of global relativistic time, its state would not reflect all events, again causing a causality error.

To ensure that no virtual host falls too far behind, we rely on the round-robin behavior and fairness of the OS's scheduler. To ensure that no virtual host advances too far ahead, we use a combination of conservative lookahead window and voluntary yield. Our model estimates the size of the conservative lookahead window based on the minimum lag between events. For instance, when simulating a network with a minimum latency of λ, we must make sure that no virtual host's local clock advances past $GRT + \lambda$.

If we cannot guarantee that a virtual host's local clock stays within λ of GRT, we must make sure that it is *either* preempted from the CPU *or* that its thread does not access state that might depend on external events.

C. State Management

Because current operating systems do not provide the ability to preempt threads at a sufficiently precise granularity, we have resorted to a cooperative approach. Virtual hosts are allowed to

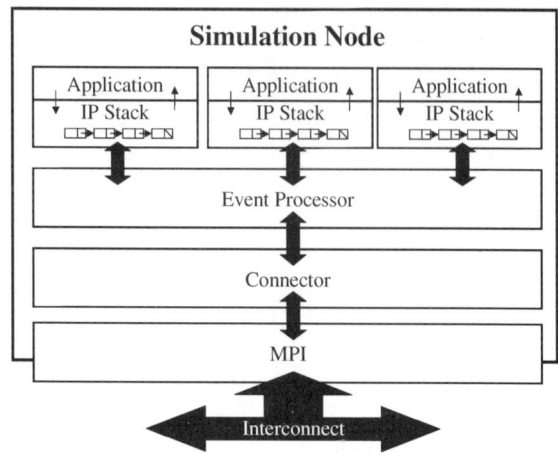

Fig. 3. Layers inside a simulation node in dONE.

progress as long as they access only internal state; they must yield the CPU if they are about to access state that might be influenced by the delivery of external events, or about to modify state whose modification might cause external events.

We exploit our knowledge of the modular structure of the software we are executing to identify when a virtual host might modify or depend on externally visible state. As an example, consider the interaction between a network application and its protocol stack shown in Figure 3. In this example, external events include the sending or receipt of packets. Because only the protocol code has access to the procedure used to send packets, a packet can only be sent while a thread executes inside the protocol stack. Since the stack exports a well-defined interface to the application, we can interpose on that interface and insert checks that ensure a thread's local time is not running too far ahead of global relativistic time. Should this situation occur, the thread is blocked. Similarly, a thread may enter the protocol code to receive data. Typically, such receive primitives are implemented by polling the state of a packet queue in which arriving packets are enqueued. We make sure that when a thread enters the stack, all packets that should have arrived by that point in time have been delivered, or else the thread will be blocked until such time has arrived. Note that we do not require intimate knowledge of the specific data structures that are used inside the stack to hold received packets, nor do we require changes to the protocol code being run. much more details we can afford here - we could talk about how the stack's about how we control when the

D. Global Relativistic Time & Warp

A physical host's connector layer performs a dual function. First, it is responsible for the distribution of events between the physical nodes in the simulation. Second, it cooperates with other connector instances and a global coordinator in synchronizing global relativistic time among all physical nodes. We use a variant of the two phase commit protocol [10] for this purpose.

TABLE I
OBSERVED TCP THROUGHPUT FOR TRANSMITTING 5MB OF DATA AT DIFFERENT SIMULATED BANDWIDTHS.

Link B/W	Throughput	Run Time	Simulated Time	Speedup	No of Warps
56kbps	54.842kbps	16.01s	764.637s	47.637	83,731
100kbps	95.638kbps	9.98s	438.474s	43.935	51,101
500kbps	478.182kbps	3.32s	87.696s	26.412	15,083
1Mbps	0.956Mbps	2.53s	43.849s	17.331	11,734
10Mbps	9.427Mbps	1.74s	4.448s	2.556	6,727
100Mbps	78.182Mbps	1.66s	0.536s	0.323	6,332

A coordinator starts a new epoch by choosing and announcing a dilation factor for this epoch. During the epoch, the progression of real time on each physical host advances the relativistic timelines of all virtual hosts it contains according to the chosen dilation. A local connector detects an opportunity for a warp if all virtual hosts are idle, or have exhausted their lookahead window and are blocked because they are about to access external state. When a connector detects such an opportunity, it signals its readiness to warp to the coordinator. Once the coordinator detects that all connectors are ready to warp, it decides whether to warp and instructs the participants accordingly.

When announcing a warp opportunity, the coordinator must compute and announce the relativistic time at which the next epoch starts. This value depends on the time stamp of the earliest undelivered event in the entire simulation. The coordinator is able to compute this time as the global minimum of all undelivered events. Each node sends the timestamp of the earliest event known to that node to the coordinator during the first phase of the commit protocol.

To ensure that all events are accounted for, we use a simple acknowledgement protocol. If an event originating at one physical host is destined for another host, the receiving host is required to send an acknowledgement to the originating host. Until the acknowledgement has been received, the originating host will report the event to the coordinator; after the acknowledgement has been received, this responsibility is transferred to the receiving host. While the acknowledgement is in transit, both hosts might report this event's timestamp to the coordinator. Should this occur, the outcome of the coordinator's computation does not change.

A node's connector implements the warp protocol in parallel with the normal processing of events. Warping merely presents an opportunity for "jumping ahead" in the simulation, relativistic time still passes until a warp is announced. Consequently, the coordinator may decide to forgo a warp opportunity should it judge that it would cost more to warp than to simply let time advance to the next event. In this case, the coordinator will poll nodes later to inquire whether they are ready to warp and what their current earliest event time is.

V. EVALUATION

We implemented a prototype of dONE based on a custom version of the Linux 2.6.11 kernel. We used MPI/LAM as the underlying transport layer. All our experiments were performed on a cluster of eight dual-CPU Opteron nodes for a total of sixteen processors with 2 GB of physical memory per node. The nodes were connected via a 10Gbps Infinicon Infiniband interface. Each node was configured based on Redhat Fedora Core 2 in a diskless configuration.

The software environment of the virtual hosts consists of clients written in the C language, linked against a BSD socket API that is implemented over a TCP/IP stack extracted from the Linux 2.4 kernel. Extracting the stack from the kernel was possible with only a small amount of changes to the code, which increases our assurance that our simulation closely models the behavior of an actual TCP/IP implementation [13]. We implemented glue code to link the protocol stack to the simulation environment. For instance, we provided virtual device drivers to link virtual nodes to the discrete event processor. We isolated its top-level interfaces through which applications enter the stack, as well as its bottom-level interfaces, which is entered during interrupt processing. We also redirected the interface a process uses when it is blocked on a wait queue to notify the simulator and yield the CPU.

A. Simulator Overhead

We used a simple file transfer-like application to evaluate the veracity of our simulation. This application opens a TCP connection to a well-known port, then sends a predetermined amount of data across the connection in chunks of 1KB each. After receiving the data, the receiver sends an acknowledgement and both sides close the connection. The receiving virtual host measures the achieved bandwidth using the time API provided to it by the simulator, which reports the virtual host's local time.

Table V shows our results for the nondistributed case, in which the two virtual hosts reside on the same physical host. It measures the overhead of event processing and warping. The throughput numbers match what one would expect from a physical link for each of the bandwidths modeled. The simulation can model links up to 10MBps with a speedup compared to emulating them, while a 100MBps network takes about 3-times as long to simulate as to emulate it.

B. Throughput vs Latency

Sliding window protocols such as TCP/IP can only send a limited amount of packets until the first packet that was sent is acknowledged by the receiver. The maximum amount of data that can be outstanding before an acknowledgement is received is known as the window size. The window size is influenced by the flow and congestion control mechanism used in the protocol. Without extensions that allow for larger windows (e.g., window scaling [19]), TCP's window size is restricted to 64KB. Consequently, achieved throughput drops off as the round trip time grows larger beyond a point. The theoretical maximum, without taking into account packet loss, is known to be $\frac{WMSS}{RTT}$ where W is the size of the window, counted in multiple of the maximum segment size MSS, and RTT is the round-trip time 2λ.

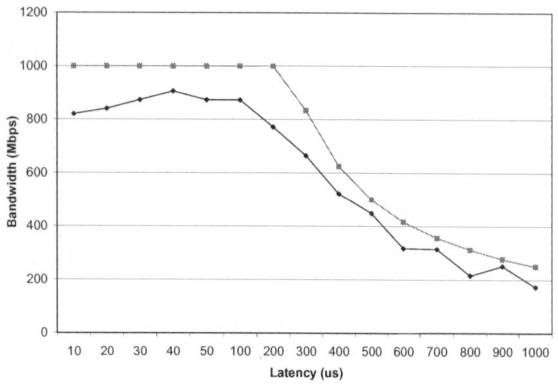

Fig. 4. Measured bandwidth for different simulated latencies. The top curve shows the theoretical maximum, the bottom curve shows the measured throughput. The simulation verifies the expected behavior of a sliding window protocol.

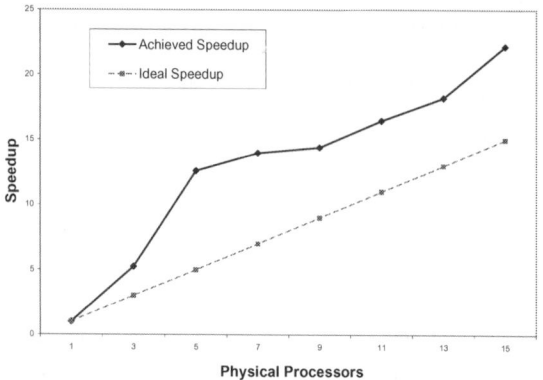

Fig. 5. Parallel speedup for different physical processor counts, assuming an optimal load balancing that minimizes communication. The bottom curve shows linear speedup; dONE achieves a superlinear speedup, shown in the upper curve.

To test if dONE could reproduce this phenomenon, we simulated a single 1Gbps link and varied the simulated latency of the link. The observed throughput when transmitting 10MB of data is shown in Figure 4. The upper line is the theoretical limit (neglecting the per packet header information, and TCP's startup cost). When the round trip time (twice the latency, shown on the X axis) is less than the time necessary to transmit a full window (488.273us), the observed throughput is about 80% of the link bandwidth. As the latency approaches the time to transmit a single window size, the observed bandwidth of the link drops off as expected. This demonstrates that the simulation is correctly modeling the bandwidth-limiting behavior of a sliding window protocol with a finite window size.

C. Scalability Results

To perform an initial evaluation of the scalability of dONE, we ran a simulation of one thousand simulated nodes transmitting 100KB of data over a 1Mbps link with short latencies. The same simulation was repeated for different numbers of physical processors. Each experiment was run four times, and the results were averaged and are plotted in the Figure 5. The same figure shows a theoretical, linear speedup, extrapolated from the single compute node case. All computations in this section ignore the cost of the coordinator node, so the single processor example involves two physical processors, the two compute node number really uses three processors, etc.. The simulation speeds up super-linearly as more physical processors are added, which we attribute to the greater overall cache capacity of the system. It should be noted that this speedup is achieved for a best case in which most virtual links do not cross physical node boundaries.

We also measured the how the accuracy of the simulation is affected as the number of virtual hosts increases. For a scenario of 50 source-sink pairs in which all virtual links crossed physical links, we found the measured throughput to be consistent and the variance negligible.

Although our initial results are encouraging, additional work remains to be done to validate the performance of the simulator on larger processor counts and with different network topologies and workloads.

VI. CONCLUSION

We have presented relativistic time, a novel model that supports the creation of hybrid emulation/simulation environments. We have prototyped a distributed network emulator, dONE, which shows the feasibility of implementing this model in a distributed environment. The core idea behind relativistic time is to rely on the continuous character of real time, but scale it to allow the simulating environment enough time to accomplish the tasks necessary for the emulation or simulation of the environment being modeled. Relativistic time is a conservative approach; careful management of the simulation state allows time to be stopped to avoid causality errors. Time can be fast forwarded in a time warp when it is safe to do so in order to achieve a speed up compared to emulation.

Our current prototype uses a composition framework that allows us to emulate actual network applications and protocol stack implementations rather than relying on abstract models. Initial experimental results indicate that our prototype correctly models the performance behavior of protocols such as TCP, and is able to scale to thousands of virtual hosts on a small cluster of 16 CPUs.

VII. ACKNOWLEDGEMENTS

This work is supported by National Science Foundation under grant number 0305644. The authors gratefully thank the NSF for all of its' support. Additionally, we thank Joy Mukherjee for his work on Weaves and Chris Knestrick for his work on LUNAR.

References

[1] C. Alaettinoğlu, A. U. Shankar, K. Dussa-Zieger, and I. Matta. Design and implementation of mars: A routing testbed. Technical Report UMIACS-TR-92-103, CS-TR-2964, Institute for Advanced Computer Studies and Department of Computer Science, University of Maryland, College Park, MD 20742, August 1992.

[2] Mark Allman and Vern Paxson. On estimating end-to-end network path properties. In *SIGCOMM '99: Proceedings of the conference on Applications, technologies, architectures, and protocols for computer communication*, pages 263–274, New York, NY, USA, 1999. ACM Press.

[3] Rassul Ayani and Hassan Rajaei. Parallel simulation using conservative time windows. In *Proceedings of the 1992 Winter Simulation Conference*, pages 709–717, 1992.

[4] Lee Breslau, Deborah Estrin, Kevin Fall, Sally Floyd, John Heidemann, Ahmed Helmy, Polly Huang, Steven McCanne, Kannan Varadhan, Ya Xu, and Haobo Yu. Advances in network simulation. *Computer*, 33(5):59–67, 2000.

[5] R. E. Bryant. Simulation of packet communication architecture computer systems. Technical report, Massachusetts Institute of Technology, Cambridge, MA, USA, 1977.

[6] K. Mani Chandy and Jayadev Misra. Asynchronous distributed simulation via a sequence of parallel computations. *Communications of the ACM*, 24(4):198–205, April 1981.

[7] Xinjie Chang. Network simulations with opnet. In *WSC '99: Proceedings of the 31st conference on Winter simulation*, pages 307–314, New York, NY, USA, 1999. ACM Press.

[8] Jim Cowie, Andy Ogielski, and David Nicol. The SSFNet network simulator, 2002. http://www.ssfnet.org/homePage.html.

[9] Richard M. Fujimoto. Parallel simulation: parallel and distributed simulation systems. In *WSC '01: Proceedings of the 33nd conference on Winter simulation*, pages 147–157, Washington, DC, USA, 2001. IEEE Computer Society.

[10] Jim Gray. *Notes on Database Operating Systems*, volume 60 of *Lecture Notes in Computer Science*, chapter Operating Systems: An Advanced Course, pages 393–481. Springer-Verlag, 1978.

[11] X. W. Huang, R. Sharma, and Srinivasan Keshav. The ENTRAPID protocol development environment. In *INFOCOM (3)*, pages 1107–1115, 1999.

[12] David R. Jefferson. Virtual time. *ACM Trans. Program. Lang. Syst.*, 7(3):404–425, 1985.

[13] Christopher C Knestrick. Lunar: A user-level stack library for network emulation. Master's thesis, Virginia Polytechnic Institute and State University, 2004.

[14] Jayadev Misra. Distributed discrete-event simulation. *Computing Surveys*, 18(1):39–65, March 1986.

[15] Joy Muhkerjee and Srinidhi Varadarajan. Weaves a framework for reconfigurable programming. *International Journal of Parallel Programming*, 33:279–305, 200.

[16] Luigi Rizzo. Dummynet: a simple approach to the evaluation of network protocols. *SIGCOMM Comput. Commun. Rev.*, 27(1):31–41, 1997.

[17] Wen-King Su and Charles L Seitz. Variants of the Chandy-Mistra-Bryant Distributed Discrete-Event Simulation Algorithm. In *Proceedings of the 1989 Distributed Simulation Conference*, December 1989.

[18] Amin Vahdat, Ken Yocum, Kevin Walsh, Priya Mahadevan, Dejan Kostic, Jeff Chase, and David Becker. Scalability and accuracy in a large-scale network emulator. In *Proceedings of the 5th ACM/USENIX Symposium on Operating System Design and Implementation (OSDI)*, Boston, MA, USA, December 2002.

[19] Mark West and Stephen McCann. Improved TCP Performance over Long-Delay and Error Prone Links. In *Proceedings of the IEEE Seminar on Satellite Services and Internet*, February 2000.

[20] Brian White, Jay Lepreau, Leigh Stoller, Robert Ricci, Shashi Guruprasad, Mac Newbold, Mike Hibler, Chad Barb, and Abhijeet Joglekar. An integrated experimental environment for distributed systems and networks. In *Proc. of the Fifth Symposium on Operating Systems Design and Implementation*, pages 255–270, Boston, MA, December 2002. USENIX Association.

[21] Xiang Zeng, Rajive Bagrodia, and Mario Gerla. Glomosim: a library for parallel simulation of large-scale wireless networks. In *PADS '98: Proceedings of the twelfth workshop on Parallel and distributed simulation*, pages 154–161, Washington, DC, USA, 1998. IEEE Computer Society.

Principles of Advanced and Distributed Simulation

Session 2: Performance Analysis

Performance Analysis of Shared Data Access Algorithms for Distributed Simulation of Multi-Agent Systems

Roland Ewald[1,3], Dan Chen[1], Georgios K. Theodoropoulos[1], Michael Lees[2],
Brian Logan[2], Ton Oguara[1], Adelinde M. Uhrmacher[3]

[1] School of Computer Science, University of Birmingham, Birmingham B15 2TT, UK
[2] School of Computer Science and Information Technology,
University of Nottingham, Nottingham NG8 1BB, UK
[3] Institut für Informatik, Universität Rostock, 18059 Rostock, Germany

Abstract

Distributed simulation is an important instrument for studying multi-agent systems (MAS). Such large scale MAS simulations often have a large shared state space. Moreover, the shared state and the access pattern of agent simulations both are highly dynamic and unpredictable. Optimising access to the shared data is crucial for achieving efficient simulation executions. PDES-MAS is a framework for distributed simulation of MAS, which uses a hierarchical infrastructure to manage the shared data. In order to enable agent simulations to access distributed shared data efficiently, this paper proposes two routing algorithms, namely the address-based routing and the range-based routing. The paper introduces a meta-simulation approach to evaluate the characteristics of both solutions and provides a quantitative comparative analysis of the proposed algorithms.

1. Introduction

The Logical Process Paradigm seeks to divide the simulation model into a network of concurrent *Logical Processes* (*LPs*), each of which models some object(s) or process(es) in the simulated system. Each LP maintains and processes a portion of the state space of the system and state changes are modelled as timestamped events in the simulation. In conventional distributed simulations, the shared state is typically small and the processes interact with each other in a small number of well defined ways. The topology of the simulation is determined by the topology of the simulated system and its decomposition into processes, and is largely static.

However, in the case of systems, which operate in a complex environment and interact with it in complex and dynamic patterns (such as multi-agent systems, battlefield simulations, ecological systems, games etc), it is often difficult to determine an appropriate simulation topology a priori. In such systems there is a very large set of shared state variables which could, in principle, be accessed or updated by the processes in the model [20]. Encapsulating the shared state in a single process (e.g. via some centralised scheme) introduces a bottleneck, while distributing it all across the LPs (decentralised, event driven scheme) will typically result in frequent all-to-all communication and broadcasting. This problem has received considerable attention in the context of Interest and Data Distribution Management for large scale distributed simulations [5, 13].

In [6] we have proposed an approach to manage the shared data in distributed simulations of multi-agent systems (MAS). Shared data management in distributed simulations needs to address two problems: data distribution and data accessing. In [15] we have addressed the first problem and have described data distribution algorithms for the PDES-MAS framework[1]. In this paper we focus on the second problem of data access.

Data accessing targets both individual data items (ID query) and selected data items overlapping given query windows (Range query). Although in the area of distributed data bases, range query strategies are increasingly used, e.g. [1, 14], this problem has received little attention in distributed simulations [4]. The issue becomes much more complicated when the value and the physical distribution of data items both are dynamic. Further problems arise when query sources are changing their positions, as in the context of location-dependent information services (LDIS) [7]. However, typically LDIS do not have to cope with highly dynamic data distributions, because the data can be distributed according to its geographical validity in a static manner.

---
[1] Synchronisation issues have been discussed in [8, 11].

In this paper, we propose two candidate algorithms for data accessing in the context of the PDES-MAS framework, namely the address-based and the range-based routing.

The rest of this paper is organized as follows: Section 2 provides a brief overview of the PDES-MAS system and states the problem. The candidate routing solutions are briefed in section 3. Section 4 introduce the simulation model used for the performance evaluation of the algorithms. The experimental results and their analysis are presented in section 5 while section 6 epitomizes the conclusions and suggests future work.

2. Background and Problem Statement

PDES-MAS is a framework for the distributed simulation of agent-based systems (figure 1). Each agent in the framework is modelled as an Agent Logical Process (ALP). An ALP has both private, which is maintained within the ALP, and shared state which is accessible to other ALPs.

The shared state is modelled as a set of Shared State Variables (SSVs), each of which is a tuple of the form $< SSVID, attributetype, value, timestamp >$, where type represents an attribute of the object's class.

ALPs interact with the shared state and other ALPs through read and write (update value) operations on SSVs. This operations can have the form of an ID query or Range query. To generate an ID query, an ALP needs to specify the SSV ID, and its new value in the case of update. A Range query requests a set of SSVs of a given type whose values match a designated range. Range queries are initiated to meet the need of an ALP to explore some portion of its environment, which it may not be aware of beforehand.

The SSVs are managed by a tree-shaped hierarchical structure of Communication Logical Processes (CLPs), which is dynamically reconfigured to reflect the shared data access patterns in the simulation [15]. SSVs are moved closer to the ALPs that access them most frequently, reducing the total access cost and thus contributing to the scalability of the framework. A CLP interacts with other LPs via *ports*. The queries from an ALP are modelled as timestamped messages, for which each CLP acts as a router responsible for forwarding them to the destination CLP(s). The ports are designed to maintain the distribution of the values of SSVs in the value space classified by the types of SSVs.

3. Two Routing Algorithms

In this section we propose two different algorithms to route ID and Range queries through the tree of CLPs. The two proposed algorithms dynamically adapt to different properties of the shared state and the system.

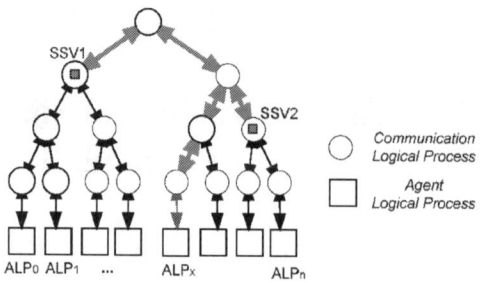

Figure 1. Illustration of PDES-MAS Framework

3.1. Address-Based Routing

The address-based routing scheme searches for SSVs according to their addresses, namely their exact location (host CLP) in the tree. Figure 2 illustrates an address-based routing scheme, which binds the ID of an SSV to its address. Each server CLP maintains a routing table which contains the addresses of SSVs. Furthermore, each CLP stores information about the values of SSVs that are hosted by its immediate neighbours. This information is obtained and refreshed when updates on those SSVs occur. To store the information efficiently, the overall value range of each SSV type is divided into a number of segments. Hence, only one bit per segment is needed to store information about the existence of SSVs with values covered by this segment. For example if a CLP contains a set of SSVs with values listed as: {20, 53, 56, 70, 80, 190, 310, 370}. Instead of using a simple range description like [Min(20), Max(370)], we segment the value space, such as Seg1: [0, 100], Seg2: [100, 200], Seg3: [200, 300], Seg4: [300, 400], Seg5: [400, 500], ... The approach logs the number of SSVs whose values fall onto each segment.

When an ALP issues a Range query (see figure 2), its server CLP propagates the request to all CLPs which host SSVs of that SSV type (in this example, CLP_1 and CLP_2). If the values of its SSVs are not within the segments covered by the Range query, the neighbours of a CLP can stop the query (unless there is another CLP that needs to be reached).

The algorithm for an ID query is straightforward. When an ALP issues an ID query, the server CLP determines the location of the SSV from its routing table and forwards the query to the corresponding host CLP.

3.2. Range-Based Routing

This approach uses information about the values of SSVs to locate them in the tree, in a fashion similar to associative memory. The algorithm matches the query window with

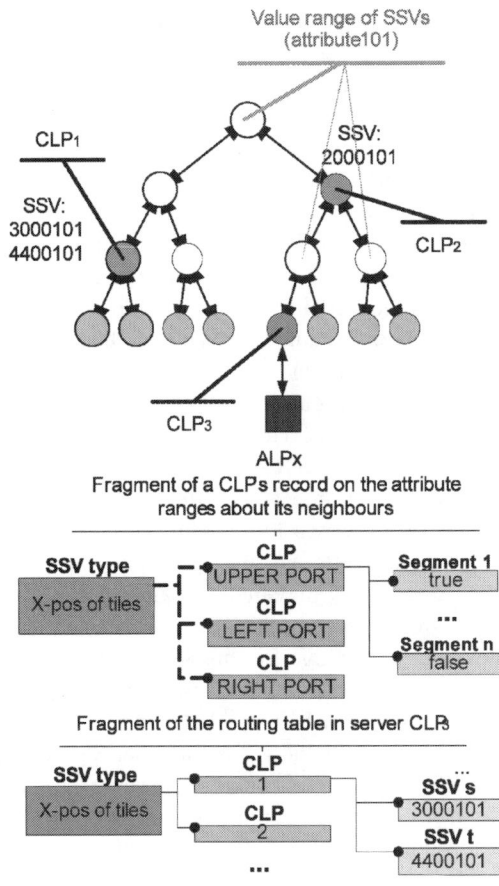

Figure 2. Address-based Routing

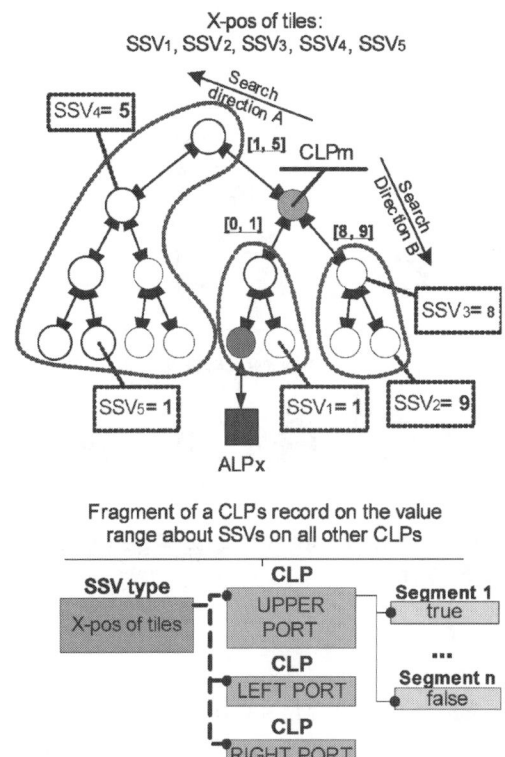

Figure 3. Range-based Routing

the value ranges along the searching paths to gradually approach the potential targets. Searching will stop at the directions where the query window and value ranges do not overlap. In the example shown in figure 3, CLP_m keeps a record of the SSV sets (denoted by the encirclings) behind its three ports.

When an ALP issues a Range query, this procedure starts from its server CLP. Suppose that a Range query for SSV type "X-pos" and range $[2, 6]$ reaches CLP_m: The CLP has two possible directions to propagate the query. Direction B will be omitted, as the value range $[8, 9]$ does not overlap the window $(2, 6)$. However, the query will be forwarded towards direction A, because the corresponding value range $[1, 5]$ matches the condition.

Like the address-based routing, the range-based routing stores the value range for each port by segmenting it. But instead of only considering the neighbour CLPs, each bit marks the existence of matching SSVs *somewhere* behind the port. The port information will be kept up to date according to returned messages from neighbours; if an empty message is returned, there are no matching SSVs behind the corresponding port and this information will be referred to in the future. Obviously, the port information may need to be updated when any SSV's value changes.

This approach can also be applied to access SSVs by ID. In this case, the ID number range is segmented as well, so that ID queries can be resolved in a similar way as Range queries.

4. Model of the Simulation System

A comparison of the two proposed algorithms is not trivial, as it involves the evaluation of efficiency in performing Range queries and ID queries, complexity for maintaining routing information, complexity for maintaining range information, design complexity etc. From the scale of CLP tree and number of SSVs, it is relatively straightforward to estimate the computational and communication complexity of the address-based routing solution using mathematical approaches. However, the evaluation of range-based routing needs to consider other complicated factors at both application level and simulation level.

For the sake of a quantitative analysis, one approach would be to directly implement and integrate the two so-

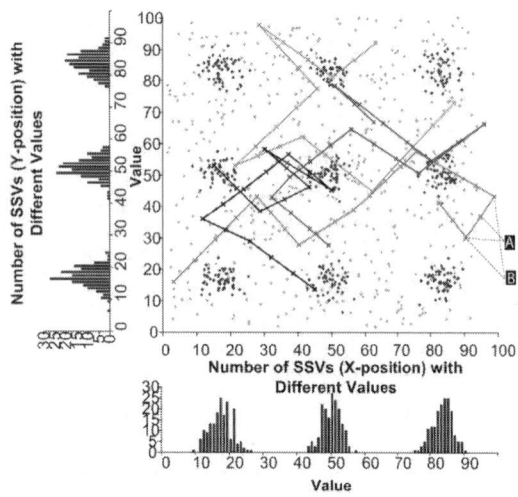

Figure 4. Environments and Agents' Behaviour Patterns

lutions into the PDES-MAS kernel. However, this would require considerable implementation efforts, and at least part of the implementation could be in vain, as the strategies may not meet the performance requirements. To avoid this, and to provide a generic framework for the study of dynamic data access in distributed systems in general, we have adopted a meta-simulation approach, as proposed for instance in [12, 18, 16].

For the meta-simulation we follow a layered approach similar to [3]. At the top layer we find the application model, which is responsible for generating realistic query patterns. The next layer is the middleware layer, where the routing strategies are described and the PDES-MAS framework is represented. The third layer, which typically is reserved for the network model, is implicitly represented in the performance measurements which are integrated by calculating the costs of queries in the second layer. Thus, similar to many simulations of P2P systems, the characteristics of the underlying network are abstracted away by only counting hops and messages.

Application Model. The application model focuses on the simulation of *situated* agents, namely, an agent has a position that determines its region of interest: only objects situated in the region can be accessed by the agent. In addition, situated agents are usually able to change their own positions.

This behaviour was modelled for a two-dimensional environment, as shown in figure 4. An agent moves step-wise towards a pre-selected target along the shortest path, and it randomly chooses a new target on arrival. The distance an agent can move in each step is referred to as *step size* (mark "A"). The distance of the new target, the *target distance* (mark "B"), is defined by the number of steps it takes the agent to reach it. The *step size* and *target distance* determine the activity scope and movement speed of an agent. After each step of movement, an agent generates ID or Range queries concerning its actual region of interest.

We assume that all SSV types within the MAS model have a *spatial* meaning, i.e. the value ranges for Range queries reflect the actual positions of the agents. Each SSV type represents a certain dimension of the environment, such as 'X-Pos' or 'Y-Pos'.

SSVs may have a uniform value distribution or multiple normal distributions. These are illustrated in figure 4 as light and dark dots respectively.

To investigate the impact of different SSV distributions within the CLP tree, a custom parameter has been defined: The *fluctuation* constraints the maximum difference between the largest and the smallest value of equally typed SSVs that are hosted on one CLP. It is defined as a ratio of the overall value range for this SSV type. For example, suppose $fluctuation_X = 0.05$ and SSVs of type X can have a value from 0 to 100: A CLP may host two SSVs of type X with values 80 and 82, but another SSV of type X, with value 75, cannot be hosted by the same CLP, because $82 - 75 > 5$. Since SSVs are not moved but have dynamic values, this condition holds only for the initial state.

PDES-MAS Model. The model of the PDES-MAS framework is formed by a set of SSVs. Each SSV consists of (unique) ID, type, value and position in the CLP tree. The modelled CLP tree is binary and complete and therefore its structure can be defined by its depth.

Another important parameter is the number of segments used by both routing algorithms, which determines the granularity of the description of the value distribution of SSVs.

To eliminate a possible source of bias, no load management mechanism has been modeled, i.e. the SSVs could not migrate (as proposed in [15]), although the SSVs' distribution pattern differs for different runs. Nevertheless, the mutual impact of routing and load management could be considerable and should be subject of future research. The model was simulated using discrete time steps.

5. Results and Analysis

In this section we present a quantitative comparative analysis of the two routing algorithms. Two main metrics are used to evaluate the algorithms:

- The *number of messages* is the number of all messages that are generated by the routing algorithm in order to resolve a query. Hence, the number of messages is a measurement of the overall bandwidth consumption.

- The *number of hops* is the maximum number of messages that had to be sent sequentially until the request could be resolved. This means, that the *number of hops* corresponds to the maximal path length from the ALP generating the request to a CLP which had to be contacted, multiplied by 2 (for the query and the corresponding response). Hence, the number of messages is a measurement of the overall latency.

In the experiments, the application model simulates 64 agents for 300 time steps, with 31 CLPs (i.e., a binary tree with depth 4) and each server CLP linking to 4 ALPs. There exists 12,400 SSVs of 16 different SSV types (775 SSVs per type, 8 types per dimension), which were uniformly distributed over the CLP tree. The initial SSV values are chosen from a uniform distribution of real numbers in $[0, 100)$. All agents move on a 100 x 100 torus. In other words, the scenarios represent a MAS operating in an environment with 8 different objects types, each of them consisting of two attributes defining their X and Y position.

The *step size* and *target distance* of an agent follow normal distribution with $\mu = 2.0$ and $\sigma = 1.0$ and $\mu = 5.0$ and $\sigma = 2.0$ respectively.

Each agent generates 8 random requests per time step. An agent's region of interest has a diameter of 2.0 for each dimension. For example, an agent at the position $X = 50$ could query a range of $[49, 51]$ for all types associated with this dimension. In the default setup, the fluctuation is 1.0 and value range is defined using 100 segments.

5.1. Evaluation based on SSV Properties

We have carried out a set of experiments to examine the effect of SSVs' value distributions and location constraints on the proposed routing algorithms.

In the first experiment, the initial SSV values have been assigned in a round-robin manner by one of three normal distributions, instead of being uniformly distributed. The mean values of these normal distributions were $16\frac{2}{3}$, 50 and $81\frac{1}{3}$. The deviation is varied from 0 to 10, making the SSV value distribution changing from highly concentrated to highly scattered.

As can be seen in figures 5 and 6, the results concerning hops and messages have a similar characteristic. The results indicate that the concentration of the SSV values has a huge impact on the routing performance of both algorithms ($\approx 500\%$): The more concentrated, the faster are both solutions, although the range-based approach adapts better to this parameter.

Another interesting study is how the configuration of the simulation infrastructure affects the performance of routing,

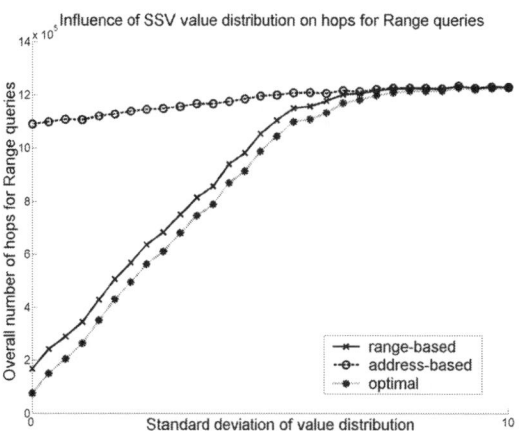

Figure 5. Hops traversed for Range queries, against different degrees of value concentration

such as a management policy regarding the SSVs' physical locations in the CLP tree. The policy is controlled by the $fluctuation$ parameter. Such a policy would, for instance, store SSVs with similar values on a single CLP. The effect can be reflected as in figure 7.

Given an arbitrary Range query, it is possible to calculate the probability of a single edge in the CLP tree to be used during a query. It assumes that the range-based approach has initialized all port information according to former queries, i.e. this is the best case. Let $ssvPerCLP_{type}$ be the number of SSVs each CLP is hosting per type.

Firstly, the edges from all server CLPs (except the one generating the query) to their parent CLPs in the tree are considered: These edges will only be used, if the CLP hosts an SSV of the specified type whose value is within the segments that cover the queried range. Let the probability that a single SSV is affected by a range query, given the number of segments (seg) and a query for the range (min, max), be $P_{min,max}^{type,seg}$. Hence, the probability that a link will *not* be used to resolve this query is:

$$P_{noFittingSSVs}^{serverCLP} = (1 - P_{min,max}^{type,seg})^{ssvPerCLP_{type}}$$

Clearly, this probability is very small if either $ssvPerCLP_{type}$ or $P_{min,max}^{type,seg}$ is significantly high. This equation holds true for both approaches.

The calculation of this probability for edges that are higher up in the tree demonstrates the major difference between the range-based and the address-based approach. The former considers the SSV values of all CLPs within the subtree to which the edge leads. In contrast, the address-based approach will propagate a query to any CLP whose subtree contains a CLP that hosts an SSV of the speci-

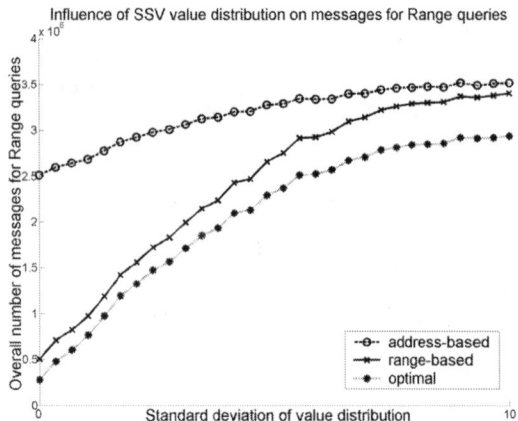

Figure 6. Messages generated for Range queries, against different degrees of value concentration

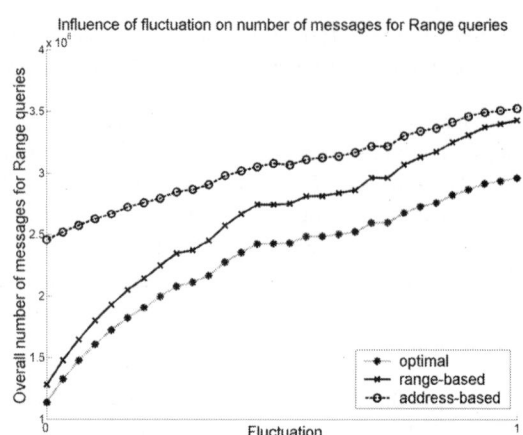

Figure 7. Messages generated for Range queries against different fluctuation values

fied type. For range-based routing, $P_{noFittingSSVs}^{upperlevel}$ depends on $P_{noFittingSSVs}^{serverCLP}$. For the address-based approach, $P_{noFittingSSVs}^{upperlevel}$ also depends on the probability of a CLP in the subtree hosting *any* SSV of this type.

The positive impact of concentrated SSV values (in figures 5 and 6) can be explained by the rather small $P_{min,max}^{type,seg}$ for all Range queries that did not cover high concentrations of SSV values. The same holds true for the experiment in figure 7, because introducing the fluctuation actually alters $P_{min,max}^{type,seg}$ on each individual CLP. For example, hosting only SSVs with higher values in the initial state would lead to a very small probability that this CLP is affected by Range queries covering lower values of this type.

The range-based approach benefits more from these situations, because its edge probabilities (between non-server CLPs) are more dependent on $P_{noFittingSSVs}^{serverCLP}$.

5.2. Evaluation based on Granularity

The experiments and results presented in this section mainly concern the granularity of segmenting value ranges. A larger number means a more precise attribute range description. The routing cost against segment number is reported in in figure 8. Increasing the number of segments leads to a reduction of generated messages. Although the performance of both routing algorithms are very similar for small segment numbers, range-based outperforms address-based routing when the number of segments is increased.

As mentioned above, both algorithms will show the same behaviour when accessing server CLPs for a Range query, but the range-based approach will save more communication between CLPs at higher levels. Of course, this is only possible if $P_{noFittingSSVs}^{serverCLP}$ is sufficiently high. One way of increasing this expression is to increase the number of segments, which explains the performance difference between both solutions (figure 8).

Consequently, it could be argued that the number of segments should be as high as possible, but a high number of segments also results in increasing storage and runtime requirements. Moreover, this way of optimization *only* increases the routing precision and can therefore only approximate an 'ideal' system, which would use a full list of SSVs instead of segments.

5.3. Evaluation based on Write Operations

In addition to routing Range queries efficiently, we have evaluated the performance of the routing algorithms for write operations (figure 9).

The number of update messages may strongly influence the speed of the PDES-MAS kernel, because the fast execution of write queries is crucial for optimistic simulations. If the write access to the shared state is too slow, this may provoke rollbacks [9].

Considering the nature of range-based routing, one could presume that the number of update messages it generates should be higher than that created by the address-based approach. However, this is not always the case, as illustrated in figure 9.

In the figure, the graphs of update messages and hops have very different characteristics, caused by the inherent properties of the solutions: An update message for the address-based approach will not be propagated further, since only the direct neighbours of a CLP need an update. On the other hand, *all* neighbours will receive a message in this case. Hence, given that the average degree of a node in

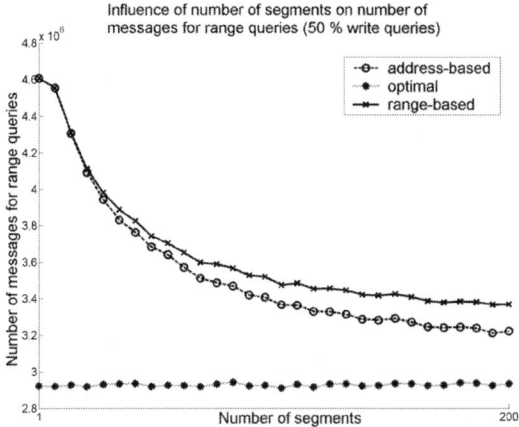

Figure 8. Number of messages generated for Range queries using different segment numbers

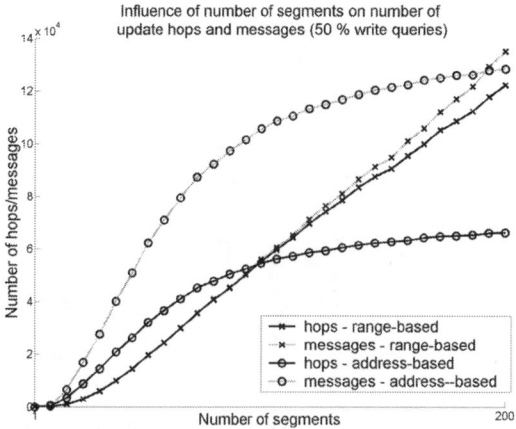

Figure 9. Number of update messages generated for write queries using different segment numbers

the CLP tree is ≈ 2, the message graph can be interpreted as the hop graph multiplied by the average degree of the CLP tree.

This is in contrast to the range-based approach, where the number of hops is very similar to the number of messages. This means that the message propagation is usually stopped after reaching the first neighbour, and often only one neighbour (instead of all) needs to be updated. This situation changes slowly when the number of segments is increased.

5.4. A Combined Comparison

Figure 10 illustrates a comparison of the two algorithms in terms of the difference in the total number of messages they generate (range-based minus address-based) and for different parameters.

Obviously, either algorithm may outperform the other one within certain regions of the parameter space. To facilitate an accurate comparison, we have also calculated the minimal number of hops and messages, as the optimal cost of each scenario. In this experiment, the probability for the occurrence of a Range query varies between 50% to 99% (with the rest being write queries) and the number of segments varies from 1 to 200. Each point is the result of a single simulation. A negative value means a better overall result for the range-based approach, whereas positive values show situations in which the address-based approach performed better.

6. Conclusions and Future Work

In this paper, we have identified efficient data accessing as a key issue to optimising the execution of MAS-based distributed simulations and we have described two different routing algorithms to achieve that in the context of the PDES-MAS framework.

The main conclusions drawn for the evaluation of the algorithms can be summarized as follows: (a) A highly ordered (low-fluctuation) system can significantly reduce (approx. 50%) the number of messages for Range queries. This fact needs to be considered in designing future data distribution mechanisms. (b) The address-based solution is superior to the range-based one when segments are very precise. When range-based routing is adopted, precise segmentation implies accurate routing, but this also leads to a large overhead in dealing with update queries. (c) The range-based solution with proper configuration can provide very efficient Range queries, whereas the address-based solution has an excellent performance for ID queries. A combination of both solutions would be desirable.

Future work will integrate the two proposed routing algorithms in the PDES-MAS kernel and evaluate their runtime performance. Another important issue is to analyse the impact of alternative load management mechanisms on the performance of the routing algorithms.

Acknowledgement

This work is part of the PDES-MAS project[2] and is supported by EPSRC research grant No. GR/R45338/01.

---
[2] http://www.cs.bham.ac.uk/research/pdesmas

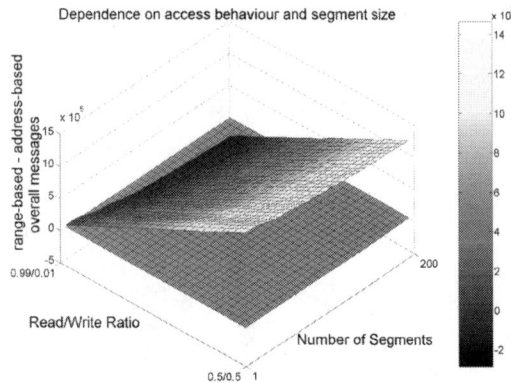

Figure 10. Overall message difference between range-based and address-based solution

References

[1] An, N., J. Jin, A. Sivasubramaniam. 2003. Toward an Accurate Analysis of Range Queries on Spatial Data. IEEE Transactions on Knowledge and Data Engineering 15(2):305-323.

[2] Chawathe, Y., S. Ramabhadran, S. Ratnasamy, A. LaMarca, J. Hellerstein, S. Shenker. 2005. A Case Study in Building Layered DHT Applications, ACM SIGCOMM Computer Communication Review, volume 35, Issue 4: 97-108.

[3] He, Q., M. H. Ammar, G. Riley, H. Raj, R. Fujimoto. 2003. Mapping Peer Behavior to Packet-level Details: A Framework for Packet-level Simulation of Peer-to-Peer Systems. 11th International Workshop on Modeling, Analysis, and Simulation of Computer and Telecommunication Systems, MASCOTS 2003

[4] Jang, M., G. Agha. 2005. Agent framework services to reduce agent communication overhead in large-scale agent-based simulations, G. K. Theodoropoulos, H. Karatza, Eds, Simulation Practice and Theory Journal, Special Issue on Distributed Systems Simulation.

[5] Kuhl, F., R. Weatherly, J. Dahmann. 1999. Creating Computer Simulation Systems: An Introduction to HLA. ISBN 13-022511-8, Prentice Hall, USA.

[6] Logan, B., G. K. Theodoropoulos. 2001. The distributed simulation of multi-agent systems. Proceedings of the IEEE 89(2): 174-186.

[7] Lee, D.L., Xu, J., Zheng, B., Lee, W. 2002. Data Management in Location-Dependent Information Services, IEEE Pervasive Computing: 65-72.

[8] Lees, M., B. Logan, and G. Theodoropoulos. Adaptive optimistic synchronisation for multi-agent simulation. 2003. In D. Al- Dabass, editor, Proceedings of the 17th European Simulation Multiconference (ESM 2003):77˙C82.

[9] Lees, M., B. Logan, R. Minson, T. Oguara, G. K. Theodoropoulos. 2004. Modelling Environments for Distributed Simulation, 1st International Workshop on Environments for Multi-Agent Systems (E4MAS), in conjunction with the 3rd International Joint Conference on Autonomous Agents and Multi-Agent Systems (AAMAS04).

[10] Lees, M., B. Logan, R. Minson, T. Oguara, G. K. Theodoropoulos. 2004. Distributed Simulation of MAS. Multi-Agent and Multi-Agent-Based Simulation: Joint Workshop MABS 2004: 25-36.

[11] Lees, M., B. Logan, D. Chen, T. Oguara, G. K. Theodoropoulos. 2005. Decision-Theoretic Throttling for Optimistic Simulations of Multi-agent Systems. Proceedings of the Ninth IEEE International Workshop on Distributed Simulation and Real-Time Applications: 179-186.

[12] Liu, J., D. Nicol, B. Premore, A. Poplawski. 1999. Performance Prediction of a Parallel Simulator, Proceedings of the 13th Workshop on Parallel and Distributed Simulation (PADS'99):156-164.

[13] Morse, K. L., M. D. Petty. 2001. Data Distribution Management Migration from DoD 1.3 to IEEE 1516, Proceedings of the Fifth IEEE International Workshop on Distributed Simulation and Real-Time Applications. August.

[14] Ndiaye, S., M. Tsangou, M. Seck, W. Litwin. 2003. Range Queries to Scalable Distributed Data Structure RP*. Proceedings of the Fifth Workshop on Distributed Data and Structures, WDAS 2003.

[15] Oguara, T., D. Chen, G. K. Theodoropoulos, B. Logan, M. Lees. 2005. An Adaptive Load Management Mechanism for Distributed Simulation of Multi-agent Systems. Proceedings of the Ninth IEEE International Workshop on Distributed Simulation and Real-Time Applications: 179-186.

[16] Perumalla, K. S. , R. M. Fujimoto, P. J. Thakare, S. Pande, H. Karimabadi, Y. Omelchenko, J. Driscoll. Performance Prediction of Large-Scale Parallel Discrete Event Models of Physical Systems. Winter Simulation Conference 2005

[17] Pollack, M. E., M. Ringuette. 1990. Introducing the Tileworld: Experimentally Evaluating Agent Architectures. AAAI

[18] Rajive, B., E. Deelman, T. Phan. 2001. Parallel Simulaiton of Lage-Scale Parallel Applications, The International Journal of High Performance Computing Applications, Volume15, No.1:3-12.

[19] Sycara, K. P. 1998. Multiagent Systems, AI Magazine: The American Association for Artificial Intelligence Volume 19, Issue 2: 79-92.

[20] Wyens, D., H. Parunak, F. Michel, T. Holvoet, J. Ferber. 2005. Environment for Multi-agent Systems, State-of-art and Research Challenges, Volume 3374, Lecture Notes in Computer Science: 1-48.

Analysing the Performance of Optimistic Synchronisation Algorithms in Simulations of Multi-Agent Systems

Michael Lees, Brian Logan,
School of Computer Science and Information Technology
University of Nottingham, UK
{mhl,bsl}@cs.nott.ac.uk

Chen Dan, Ton Oguara and Georgios Theodoropoulos
School of Computer Science
University of Birmingham, UK
{cxd,txo,gkt}@cs.bham.ac.uk

Abstract

In this paper we present a detailed analysis of the performance of the Decision Theoretic Read Delay (DTRD) optimistic synchronisation algorithm for simulations of Multi-Agent Systems. We develop an abstract characterisation of the access patterns found in MAS simulations based on the simulation's degree of coupling and skew. Using this characterisation, we generated stereotypical test cases which we used to compare the performance of the DTRD algorithm with that of Time Warp and time windows. To determine if the test cases reliably predict performance in a real agent simulation, we compared the predictions made by the test cases with performance results from the Boids agent simulation benchmark for a range of simulation parameters. The results indicate that DTRD adapts to the mixtures of coupling cases found in real agent simulations and is capable of tracking changes in coupling during the simulation.

1. Introduction

The simulation of agent systems has traditionally played an important role in agent research and development. Simulation allows a degree of control over experimental conditions and facilitates the replication of results in a way that is difficult or impossible with a prototype or fielded system, freeing the agent developer or researcher to focus on the key aspects of a system. Simulation has been applied to a wide range of MAS research and design problems from models of complex individual agents employing sophisticated internal mechanisms to models of large scale societies of relatively simple agents which focus more on the interactions between agents, e.g., [1, 13, 4, 12].

However, despite its wide application, the most appropriate simulation technique for different kinds of MAS simulation problems is often unclear. There are many different degrees of variation in MAS, and an algorithm or simulator which works well in one case may not work well in others. The work reported in the MAS simulation literature has employed a wide range of benchmark problems, e.g., Tileworld in [13], a distributed workflow framework in [4] and a simple 'bouncing ball' benchmark in [12], making it difficult to compare performance across approaches. In addition, the particular properties of simulations of situated MAS means that the performance of algorithms on standard PDES benchmarks may not be a good indicator of their performance on MAS simulations.

In this paper we take a first step towards characterising the performance of optimistic synchronisation algorithms in simulations of situated MAS. We present a detailed analysis of the performance of the Decision Theoretic Read Delay (DTRD) algorithm presented in [6]. To better understand the performance of the algorithm, we developed an abstract characterisation of the access patterns found in MAS simulations based on the simulation's degree of coupling and skew. Using this characterisation, we generated stereotypical test cases which we used to compare the performance of the DTRD algorithm with that of Time Warp and time windows. To determine if the test cases reliably predict performance in a real agent simulation, we compared the predictions made by the test cases with performance results from the Boids [11] agent simulation benchmark for a range of simulation parameters. The results indicate that DTRD is capable of adapting to the mixtures of coupling cases found in real agent simulations and tracking changes in coupling during the simulation.

The remainder of this paper is organised as follows. In section 2 we outline our model of MAS simulation and briefly describe the DTRD optimistic synchronisation algorithm. In section 3 we present a characterisation of access patterns in situated MAS simulations in terms of their coupling and skew. We show how an arbitrary MAS simulation can be decomposed into instances of three coupling cases and argue that performance on these three cases is indicative of performance on a real agent simulation. In section 4 we present a comparative evaluation of three optimistic synchronisation algorithms on two test cases generated using our characterisation of access patterns. In section 5 we extend our analysis to include comparisons on data from the Boids agent benchmark, before concluding in section 6

2. Distributed simulations of MAS

The simulation of situated agents (e.g., robots situated in a physical environment, or characters in a computer game situated in a virtual environment) presents particular challenges for standard parallel discrete event simulation (PDES) models and techniques as described in, e.g., [3, 2]. In a conventional decentralised event-driven distributed simulation the simulation model is divided into a network of Logical Process (LPs). Each LP maintains its own portion of the simulation state and LPs interact with each other in a small number of well defined ways. The topology of the simulation is determined by the topology of the simulated system and is largely static. In many cases we know the lower bound on the timestamp of an event generated by an LP in response to an input event.

In contrast, a defining characteristic of agents is their autonomy [19]. In a parallel discrete event simulation of a multi-agent system, agents may spontaneously generate an event at any point without there being a preceding input event. As a result, simulations of MAS typically have zero lookahead [18]. In addition, an agent's interaction with other agents and its environment is hard to predict in advance; indeed discovering how the agents interact with each other and their environment is often a primary goal of the simulation. For example, what a mobile agent can sense is a function of the actions it performed in the past which is in turn a function of what it sensed in the past. This makes it hard to determine an appropriate topology for a MAS simulation a priori, and simulations of MAS typically have a large shared state which is only loosely associated with any particular process [8].

To address these issues, we developed the PDES-MAS framework [8]. PDES-MAS adopts an optimistic approach to synchronisation in which agent logical processes (ALPs) interact with one or more shared state logical processes (SSLPs) which are responsible for maintaining the shared state of the simulation. ALPs interact with the shared state by reading and writing shared state variables (SSVs). We assume that agents execute a *sense–think–act* cycle, in which they obtain information from the environment (shared state) and compute an action which changes the environment. Sensing gives rise to read events, and acting gives rise to write events.

Within this read/write model, only certain patterns of access can cause a rollback [7]. Reads are the only inputs to an ALP and only the reading of incorrect values can cause a rollback. Agents which only write and never read can never be rolled back (though they can roll back other agents). For example, an ALP which simulates the weather within a virtual environment can never be rolled back by the actions of other agents (assuming there is no causal link between the agent's actions in the environment and the weather). Conversely, only agents which write can cause a rollback. For example, an agent which only reads and never writes, e.g., an LP which monitors the simulation, can never cause a rollback (though it can itself be rolled back by writes from other agents). More precisely, a rollback occurs when a SSLP receives a late or straggler write with timestamp t_w from an ALP a_i to a state variable which has previously been read with timestamp t_r by some ALP a_j, such that $t_w < t_r$ and $a_i \neq a_j$. We call a read *premature* if it is later rolled back by a straggler write.[1]

In [6] we presented DTRD, a synchronisation algorithm for PDES-MAS. DTRD attempts to avoid rollbacks by delaying the processing of read events which are likely to be premature, i.e., if there is reason to believe that the read is likely to be rolled back by a straggler write.[2] The algorithm uses a decision theoretic model to derive a optimal time to delay a read event so as to minimise the expected overall execution time of the simulation. The possible delay times are chosen from a finite set of delay times $\{0, 1, 2, \ldots\}$, where "delay for 0" means "commit this event immediately". Each delay time has an associated cost, namely the amount of real time the read is delayed and hence the ALP which generated the read must spend blocked waiting for the value returned by the read. If we prefer delay times with lower cost, we would therefore always choose to "delay for 0" which has zero cost. However, for each delay time we may have to pay an additional "rollback cost"—the real time spent rolling back if the read subsequently turns out to have been premature. We assume that the probability of paying this

---

[1] This scheme is similar to the query event tagging proposed in [15] and has similar advantages in reducing the frequency and depth of rollback and the state saving overhead.

[2] Write events can always be processed immediately: a write event by an ALP, a_i with a time stamp t_w can only be rolled back if a read by a_i with timestamp $t_r < t_w$ is rolled back.

rollback cost is lower for some delay times than others, i.e., the longer we delay, the lower the probability of a straggler write and hence of paying the rollback cost.

This gives us a simple trade-off which can be formulated in decision theoretic terms: delaying for less time costs less (in real time) but has a higher likelihood of incurring a rollback cost. The probability that the next write of a particular state variable will be a straggler, i.e., will have a virtual time earlier than that of the read being processed and will arrive after a given delay, is computed from the history of previous writes to the variable. The cost of rollback is computed by adding the cost of rolling back the ALP to the estimated cost of replaying the rolled back events by the ALP.

The DTRD algorithm is adaptive in the sense that it attempts to track changes in the access patterns by the ALPs during the simulation. Ideally it should reduce rollbacks and hence execution time across a wide range of MAS simulations (e.g., simulations in which agents interact frequently vs. simulations in which agents interact infrequently) and execution environments (e.g., environments in which all ALPs advance virtual time at the same rate vs. environments in which some ALPs run much faster than others). However assessing the performance of the algorithm in absolute terms is difficult: even if we know what the optimum performance (in terms of execution time) is for a particular simulation, the algorithm is unlikely to achieve it, given that it has only limited information. To better understand the performance of the algorithm we therefore developed an abstract characterisation of the access patterns found in MAS simulations and used this to investigate the performance of DTRD relative to that of two other optimistic synchronisation algorithms.

3. Characterising access patterns in MAS simulations

We can model the agents' interaction with the shared state at any given point in time in terms of an *access graph*. An access graph is a graph with two kinds of nodes, SSVs and ALPs, and two kinds of edges, corresponding to read and write events. A read edge from a variable v_i to an ALP a_j denotes a read of v_i by a_j, and a write edge denotes that v_i was written by a_j. Each edge has both a real and virtual timestamp, indicating the real and virtual time of the corresponding event. The access graph evolves in real time as edges are added (indicating read and write operations by agents on the shared state), and removed (as a result of rollback).

At any given point in the execution of a MAS simulation, a set of ALPs in the access graph can be characterised by their degree of coupling and their skew. *Coupling* refers to how the ALPs interact with the SSVs and the resulting potential for causality violations (rollback). By *skew* we mean the difference in the 'natural' rate of local virtual time (LVT) progression between the ALPs, in the absence of rollback or any throttling mechanism. Imbalances in the rate of LVT progression may be a result of different agent architectures requiring different amounts of real (CPU) time to advance by a single unit of simulation time, differing processor loads, differing network latencies between parts of a geographically distributed simulation etc. A given set of ALPs may vary between high and low degrees of coupling throughout the execution of the simulation. Similarly, depending on the execution environment (system loads etc) the degree of skew may vary throughout the simulation.

In an optimistic simulation of a highly coupled MAS, a high degree of skew will tend to result in frequent causality violations and rollbacks. In contrast, in a system with low coupling, a high degree of skew can be tolerated, at least from a correctness point of view, since the agents can't roll each other back. To avoid an excessive number of rollbacks, the skew of highly coupled ALPs should be minimised. This can be achieved either by balancing the load in the system to reduce the difference in the rate of LVT progression of the ALPs, or by constraining the optimism of the ALPs with positive skew, or both. While load balancing is desirable in general,[3] it is not always possible, for example, where the computational requirements of the ALPs are intrinsically very different, or where frequent process migration would result in unacceptable overhead, and in this paper we focus on constraining the optimism of the ALPs.

We can identify three stereotypical coupling cases characteristic of situated multi-agent simulations, and the degree of optimism appropriate for each:

uncoupled a set A of ALPs is uncoupled if for any variable v_i read (resp. written) by an ALP $a_i \in A$, for all $a_j \in A, i \neq j$, a_j does not write (resp. read) v_i. In an uncoupled set of ALPs, no matter how skew varies, there can be no causality violations.

fully-coupled a set A of ALPs is fully-coupled if for any ALP $a_i \in A$ there is a variable v_i written by a_i and read by an ALP $a_j \in A, i \neq j$, such that there is a sequence of ALPs $a_1 \ldots a_k$ and variables $v_1 \ldots v_{k-1}$, where a_1 writes v_1, a_2 reads v_1 and writes $v_2 \ldots a_k$ reads v_{k-1} and $a_j = a_1$ and $a_i = a_k$. With full coupling, the agent with the highest negative skew (slowest rate of LVT advance) constrains the rest.[4]

half-coupled a set A of ALPs is half-coupled if the ALPs are neither uncoupled or fully coupled. Informally, a

---
[3] We may also want to use load balancing in an uncoupled simulation, e.g., if the skew is due to an uneven distribution of processor loads.
[4] A fully-coupled set of ALPs is equivalent to a strongly connected component of the ALP nodes in the access graph, where reachability is defined in terms paths consisting write and read edges to and from SSV nodes. Full coupling is also similar to the notion of a *strong group* introduced in [17] in the context of load balancing in distributed optimistic simulations.

set of ALPs is half-coupled if there is a directed acyclic subgraph of the access graph, in which the leaves are linked to the subgraph by either read or write edges and the internal nodes are linked by both read and write edges. If the writing agents have negative skew (relative to the reading agents), then the optimism of the reading agents must be constrained, but not vice versa.

A fully-coupled set of ALPs may contain half-coupled or uncoupled subsets. Similarly, a half-coupled set of ALPs may contain uncoupled subsets. An ALP is constrained by the most constraining subgraph of which it is a member. For example, an ALP which is in both a half-coupled and fully-coupled subgraph of the access graph is constrained by the subgraph containing the writing agent with the highest negative skew.

An optimistic synchronisation algorithm for a MAS simulation should be able to cope with each of these three cases, and ideally should adapt as the degree of coupling and skew of the ALPs changes during execution. In the next section, we compare the performance of DTRD on the uncoupled and fully-coupled cases for differing degrees of skew, with that of two established optimistic synchronisation algorithms, Time Warp [5] and a windowing algorithm similar to Moving Time Windows [16].

4. Analysing the performance of optimistic synchronisation algorithms using access patterns

We created simple test cases consisting of instances of the uncoupled and fully coupled subgraph types in which we controlled the degree of skew of the ALPs.[5] In the uncoupled test case, two agents read the same state variable (see Figure 1(a)). In the fully-coupled test case, each agent reads a state variable which the other agent writes (see Figure 1(b)).

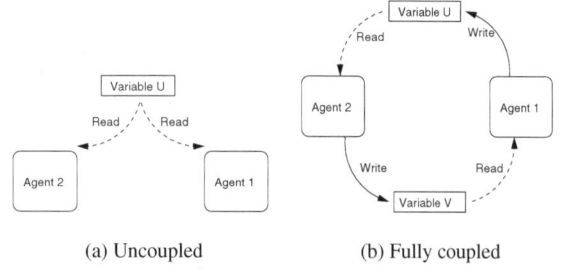

(a) Uncoupled   (b) Fully coupled

Figure 1. Two coupling test cases

We compared the performance of the DTRD algorithm with that of Time Warp and time windows in these two test cases. All experiments were performed using the ASSK simulation kernel [6] developed for parallel discrete event simulation of multi-agent systems. An ASSK simulation consists of one or more agent ALPs and a single shared state LP (SSLP) which maintains the shared state of the simulation. Each ALP processes an event trace from an agent in the original agent simulation and asynchronously sends read and write events from the trace to the SSLP. The ALPs execute asynchronously and inject real and virtual time delays into the event sequences to model the real and virtual time spent by an agent in the 'think' part of its cycle. An ALP blocks while waiting for the response to a read event from the SSLP containing the requested value.[6] Upon receiving an event the SSLP applies the appropriate access to the relevant state variable and generates any necessary responses. If the SSLP receives a straggler event from an ALP, it triggers rollbacks on all the ALPs which accessed the variable at times after the timestamp of the straggler. Rollbacks cause the ALPs to delay for a time (representing the time required to rollback the ALP and here assumed to be 5 msecs) and then rewind and replay their event traces from the time of the rollback. ASSK uses a form of incremental state saving, and in the experiments reported here no fossil-collection mechanism was used. Although deterministic in that the events generated by the ALPs are entirely determined by the input traces, ASSK provides a flexible framework for synchronisation experiments.

All three simulations used the same ASSK infrastructure—only the implementation of the synchronisation algorithm was varied. The Time Warp implementation is essentially the ASSK kernel without the read/write optimisation (i.e., all straggler events cause rollback). Our implementation of time windows used a single window size, w, for the simulation. ALPs can only send events which have a timestamp t_e, such that $t_e < GVT + w$. When an ALP reaches the end of its window, it repeatedly issues requests for GVT computation until GVT advances, allowing it to process its next event. While this adds an extra computational overhead for the blocked ALP, it ensures that the ALP's LVT advances as fast as possible.[7] ASSK uses Mattern's GVT algorithm [10], which may require each ALP to process two GVT messages per GVT calculation.

We generated a synthetic access trace for each test case consisting of 100 simulation cycles. The pattern of vari-

---

[5]In previous work [6] we have reported results for DTRD on the half-coupled case.

[6]While read events from ALPs are serialised at the SSLP, only the ALPs are delayed by the DTRD algorithm, and the loss of potential concurrency is bounded by the time required to process the events in the SSLP's receive queue.

[7]This is essentially the same as the moving time windows implementation [15] with the polling parameter set such that LPs do not wait for inactivity before initiating GVT calculation.

able access was constant for all 100 cycles in both traces. For the first set of runs, the difference in virtual timestamps between successive agent cycles was taken from a normal distribution with mean 15 and standard deviation 4, and the mean real cycle times were 50 msec for one agent and 200 msec for the other. The standard deviation of real timestamps was 0.05 of the mean. The mean real cycle times are typical of many real agent systems (e.g., 5–20 fps video) and are similar to those used in other agent simulations; for example, the results reported in [12] are for agents with cycle times in the range 95–105 milliseconds. In the fully coupled trace, all read and write events at the same cycle are assumed to occur at the same virtual time. For the time windows implementation we used a window size, w, of 30; this allows on average 2 events to execute optimistically.

Algorithm	Uncoupled		Fully Coupled	
	Comp.	Replayed	Comp.	Replayed
Time Warp	27.78	0	42.51	224.90
Time Windows	42.13	0	43.14	192.90
DTRD	27.78	0	30.50	25.80

(a) Mean cycle times of 50, 200 msecs (skew 4)

Algorithm	Uncoupled		Fully Coupled	
	Comp.	Replayed	Comp.	Replayed
Time Warp	12.63	0	14.54	27.90
Time Windows	12.64	0	14.53	27.70
DTRD	12.63	0	13.54	12.80

(b) Mean cycle times of 50, 50 msecs (no skew)

Algorithm	Uncoupled		Fully Coupled	
	Comp.	Replayed	Comp.	Replayed
Time Warp	47.98	0	82.40	528.20
Time Windows	81.66	0	83.15	203.90
DTRD	47.98	0	52.46	42.40

(c) Mean cycle times of 50, 400 msecs (skew 8)

Table 1. Performance on uncoupled and fully-coupled access traces

Table 1(a) shows the raw performance data for the three algorithms. For each algorithm, we report the computation time and number of replayed cycles averaged over 10 runs of both the uncoupled and fully coupled trace files. The computation time is defined as the total amount of CPU time required for all ALPs. The number of replayed cycles is the total number of cycles repeated by all agents as a result of rollback. This value indicates the frequency and depth of rollbacks within the system.

The first two columns of table 1(a) show the computation time and replayed cycles for each algorithm for the uncoupled test case. As can be seen, the computation time required by Time Warp and DTRD is significantly less than that required for time windows. The number of replayed cycles is 0 for all three algorithms as there are no rollbacks in the uncoupled case. The uncoupled case tests the ability of the algorithms to exploit parallelism within the simulation. As might be expected, the unconstrained optimism of Time Warp outperforms time windows in such a case. With time windows the faster agent is constrained to run at the speed of the slower agent, and must perform frequent GVT computations to advance its window. The results show how the adaptive nature of the DTRD algorithm exploits the parallelism inherent in the uncoupled case—by executing optimistically, DTRD achieves the same computation time as Time Warp.

Table 1(a) also shows the computation time and replayed cycles for each algorithm for the fully-coupled test case. As can be seen, the computation time required by Time Warp is proportionately greater in this case, and is similar to that required by time windows. However the number of replayed events is less with time windows than with Time Warp. With Time Warp, the last event generated by the slower agent is guaranteed to roll back the faster agent, effectively constraining it to run at the speed of the slower agent. With time windows, although the window reduces the number of rollbacks and hence replayed cycles, the resulting reduction in computation time is offset by the frequent GVT computations necessary to advance the window of the faster agent. The DTRD algorithm outperforms both algorithms for replayed cycles (by 87%) and computation time (by 30%). DTRD trades off rollback time and/or GVT computation time for delay time, reducing the computation time required by the ALPs.

We also investigated the effect of skew on the performance of the algorithms. Tables 1(b) and 1(c) show the computation time and replayed cycles for both the uncoupled and fully coupled cases when the difference between the mean cycle time of the faster and slower agents is 0 (mean cycle time of 50 msecs for both agents) and 350 msecs (mean cycle times of 50 and 400 msecs). With no skew (Table 1(b)), all three algorithms have similar computation times in both the uncoupled and fully coupled cases. However, DTRD is more effective in reducing the number of replayed cycles in the fully coupled case, by about 50% compared to both Time Warp and time windows. With a skew of 0, the window is ineffective in reducing the number of rollbacks in the fully-coupled system, as nearly all premature events fall within the window. As a result time windows and Time Warp have a similar number of replayed cycles in this case. Increasing the amount of skew in the simulation to 8 (Table 1(c)) does not affect the pattern of results for computation time (compared to a skew of 4), with both Time Warp and DTRD requiring significantly less computation time than time windows in the uncoupled case and Time Warp and time windows having the same computation time with full coupling. However, the reduction in replayed cycles achieved by time windows relative to Time

Warp is significantly greater with increased skew. With full coupling, the increase in skew also highlights the ability of DTRD to convert time spent in replaying computation (Time Warp and time windows) and/or GVT computation (time windows) into delays, resulting in a reduction in computation time of 37%. DTRD also prevents rollbacks more effectively than a static window, reducing the number of replayed cycles by 92% compared to Time Warp and 79% compared to time windows.

The DTRD algorithm performs well in both test cases, and appears to adapt to varying differing degrees of coupling and skew. However real simulations contain mixtures of uncoupled and fully-coupled access patterns and the degree of coupling (and skew) changes during the simulation. To investigate whether DTRD is capable both of coping with mixtures of coupling cases and tracking changes in coupling during the simulation, we tested its performance on traces from a real agent simulation.

5. Analysing the performance of optimistic synchronisation in intermediate coupling cases

In this section we compare the performance of the DTRD algorithm with that of Time Warp and time windows on traces taken from a standard agent simulation benchmark, Boids [11]. Boids was originally developed as a model of coordinated animal motion such as flocking birds or schools of fish. Each boid has its own local viewpoint of the flock and computes its own motion based on information it collects about other boids within its sensor range. While the Boids testbed is very simple, it captures key characteristics of situated multi-agent systems.

The Boids simulation was implemented using the SIM_AGENT toolkit [14]. Each boid is represented as a single agent and executes a sense–think–act cycle. In the sensing phase the agent reads the x and y position of the other boids within its sensor range (assumed to be 50 units in these experiments). It then computes its motion for this cycle (think phase) and finally writes its own x and y positions (act phase). The simulation is parameterised by the number of agents and the size of the agent's environment.[8] For a given number of agents, by varying the size of the environment we are able to control the average degree of coupling of the simulation. Higher density environments (measured as the number of boids per unit area) increase the likelihood of flocking. With optimistic synchronisation, runs where the agents manage to form a flock should have a larger number of rollbacks on average, whereas runs where little or no flocking occurs should have fewer rollbacks.

[8]The environment wraps around, e.g., a boid moving off the right edge of the environment reappears on the left edge.

We tested the DTRD, Time Warp and time windows algorithms using traces from the Boids simulation. For the experiments we varied the size of the environment from 200 × 200 to 1000 × 1000 in 200 × 200 increments. For each environment size, we collected trace files of accesses to the shared state by each agent for five runs of the simulation. The trace files record access events, each of which represents a single operation on a shared state variable. Each trace consisted of 500 cycles for each boid. To allow comparison with the synthetic test cases, all environments contain 2 agents and the mean difference in agent cycle times is in the range 50–200 msecs. For the time windows implementation we used a window size of 30.

While these traces are very simple, they allow us to investigate performance in mixed coupling situations and in situations where the degree of coupling varies during the simulation.[9] For example, even in low density environments it is rare for the agents to remain completely uncoupled for 500 cycles. Similarly, even in a small environment, the agents will not necessarily be fully coupled for the whole run. However, in general, as the density and hence average degree of coupling increases, we would expect to see the computation time and number of replayed cycles increase for Time Warp. Similarly, we would expect to see the computation time for time windows become proportionally lower and the number of replayed events increase more slowly (relative to Time Warp). Finally, we would hope to see DTRD adapt both across simulations and within a simulation run as the degree of coupling varies.

	Environment size				
Algorithm	200	400	600	800	1000
Time Warp	159.00	149.27	140.98	134.08	132.37
Time Windows	158.63	156.30	156.62	155.85	155.63
DTRD	140.09	147.17	136.66	133.82	132.58

(a) Computation Time

	Environment size				
Algorithm	200	400	600	800	1000
Time Warp	331.46	229.52	141.48	61.48	36.62
Time Windows	229.90	52.22	76.74	15.92	0.26
DTRD	97.80	198.24	75.22	60.74	52.50

(b) No. of Replayed Cycles

Table 2. Performance on the Boids benchmark for varying environment sizes

Tables 2(a) and 2(b) show the computation time and number of replayed cycles as the environment size is increased in 200 × 200 steps from 200 × 200 to 1000 × 1000. The values reported represent an average over 10 runs

[9]The uncoupled and fully coupled test cases represent all the access patterns seen in the Boids simulation. Since the boids have omni-directional sensors, there are no half-coupled subgraphs in the Boids access graph.

of the 5 trace files for each environment size for each algorithm. As can be seen, for small environments, Time Warp and time windows require similar amounts of computation time. However, while the time required by time windows remains essentially constant, the time required by Time Warp drops in the larger, less coupled, environments, and in the largest environments Time Warp outperforms time windows by about 15%. In the 200×200 environment, DTRD requires 12% less computation time than both Time Warp and time windows and in the 1000×1000 environment its performance is equivalent to that of Time Warp. The reason for this becomes apparent when we consider the number of replayed cycles (Table 2(b)). In the smaller, more highly coupled, environments DTRD significantly reduces the number of replayed cycles (by about 70% compared to Time Warp and 57% compared to time windows in the 200×200 environment), and this reduction in replayed cycles is converted into a reduction in computation time for DTRD. In the larger environments (800×800 and 1000×1000) time windows is more effective than Time Warp and DTRD in reducing the number of replayed cycles. However in these cases, the agents rarely interact, and the reduction in replayed cycles is more than offset by the GVT computation overhead of time windows.

	Environment size				
Algorithm	200	400	600	800	1000
Time Warp	777.08	177.7	263.8	54.86	0.74
Time Windows	440.56	99.44	148.00	30.46	0.40
DTRD	92.68	32.48	33.44	9.78	1.68

(a) No. of Rollbacks

	Environment size				
Algorithm	200	400	600	800	1000
Time Warp	0.43	1.29	0.54	1.12	49.49
Time Windows	0.52	0.53	0.52	0.52	0.65
DTRD	1.06	6.10	2.25	6.21	31.25

(b) No. of Replayed Cycles per Rollback

Table 3. Rollback frequency and depth in the Boids benchmark

While the DTRD algorithm requires less computation time than both Time Warp and time windows for all environment sizes, it performs better in some cases than in others. For example, the computation time and number of replayed cycles for DTRD increases from the 200×200 environment to the 400×400 environment. To probe the reasons for this, we investigated the relationship between rollbacks and replayed cycles in more detail. Table 3(a) shows the average number of rollbacks for each environment size for each algorithm. As can be seen, DTRD is successful in reducing the number of rollbacks in the 400×400 environment. However, as shown in Table 3(b), the relationship between the depth of rollbacks and environment size is complex and different for each algorithm. For Time Warp and DTRD, in smaller, more tightly coupled environments, the average number of replayed cycles per rollback is smaller than in larger, less coupled environments. With frequent rollbacks the difference between the LVTs of the ALPs is bounded, resulting in shallower rollbacks and hence fewer replayed cycles per rollback. In medium size environments, rollbacks become less frequent and hence deeper. For example, the average depth of rollback for both Time Warp and DTRD for an environment of size 400 is greater than for an environment of size 200. As the environments become even larger, with less coupling, the agents can execute farther ahead of each other and so each rollback tends to be deeper still, resulting more replayed cycles per rollback. However this is more than offset by the reduced frequency of rollbacks in these environments. In contrast, with time windows, which constrains the depth of rollback by the window size, the average depth of rollback remains more or less constant for all environment sizes. These results are similar to the theoretical predictions of differences in LVT for highly coupled and uncoupled groups of LPs in [17]. Indeed, the relationship between frequency and depth of rollback has been exploited by some optimistic algorithms which force rollbacks to prevent over optimistic execution and reduce the overall cost of rollback (e.g., [9]).

We hypothesised that the performance on the test cases presented in section 4 is a good indicator of performance in real agent simulations. We should therefore expect to see good agreement between the relative performance of the algorithms on the uncoupled and fully-coupled synthetic traces and the Boids simulations with the lowest and highest degrees of coupling. In the Boids traces, the degree of coupling is lowest in those traces with large environments. As expected, DTRD and Time Warp outperform time windows in these traces (though to a lesser extent than in the uncoupled test case). In the smaller environments with higher coupling, we would expect time windows to outperform Time Warp, and in these cases Time Warp does result in more replayed cycles than time windows (even though the degree of coupling is still relatively low in these environments), though again to a lesser extent than in the fully-coupled test case. The performance of DTRD in terms of computation time is at least as good as Time Warp and time windows in all cases, and often significantly better.

6. Conclusions and further work

In this paper we have presented a more detailed characterisation of the DTRD optimistic synchronisation algorithm for simulations of situated MAS originally presented in [6] and compared its performance to that of Time Warp and time windows. To better understand the performance of the algorithm, we characterised the problem of optimistic simulation of a situated MAS in terms of patterns of access in an access graph describing the shared state. By analysing the performance of the algorithms on stereotypical cases, we predicted where the algorithms should perform well and where they should perform badly in real agent simulations. We then extended our analysis by comparing the performance of the algorithms on a simple agent benchmark, which allowed us to investigate performance on time-varying combinations of the stereotypical test cases.

Our analysis gives us greater confidence about the performance of the decision theoretic approach to synchronisation in general and our specific algorithmic implementation in particular. More generally, we believe our characterisation of the problem is a first step towards a deeper understanding of the difficult problem of optimistic synchronisation for MAS simulation, which complements existing results from benchmark problems and testbeds. We hope that this characterisation of the problem may be useful to others investigating different algorithms for the simulation of situated MAS.

In future work we plan to investigate test cases for half-coupling and quantitative measures of the degree of coupling in an agent simulation based on the notion of critical accesses [7]. We also plan to test our predictions against results from large-scale agent simulations.

Acknowledgements

This work is part of the PDES-MAS project[10] and was partially supported by EPSRC research grant No. GR/R45338/01.

References

[1] J. Anderson. A generic distributed simulation system for intelligent agent design and evaluation. In *Proceedings of the Tenth Conference on AI, Simulation and Planning, AIS-2000*, pages 36–44, Tucson, 2000. Society for Computer Simulation International.

[2] A. Ferscha. *Parallel and Distributed Computing Handbook*, In A. Y. Zomaya, editor, Parallel and Distributed Simulation of Discrete Event Systems, pages 1003–1041. McGraw-Hill, 1996.

[3] R. Fujimoto. Parallel discrete event simulation. *Communications of the ACM*, 33(10):31–53, 1990.

[4] L. Gasser and K. Kakugawa. MACE3J: Fast flexible distributed simulation of large, large-grain multi-agent systems. In *Proceedings of the First International Joint Conference on Autonomous Agents and Multiagent Systems (AAMAS 2002)*, pages 745–752, Bologna, 2002. ACM Press.

[5] D. R. Jefferson. Virtual time. In *ACM Transactions on Programming Languages and Systems*, volume 7, pages 404–425, 1985.

[6] M. Lees, B. Logan, C. Dan, T. Oguara, and G. Theodoropoulos. Decision-theoretic throttling for optimistic simulations of multi-agent systems. In *Proceedings of the Ninth IEEE International Symposium on Distributed Simulation and Real Time Applications (DS-RT 2005)*, pages 171–178, Montreal, Canada, 2005. IEEE Press.

[7] M. Lees, B. Logan, and G. Theodoropoulos. Adaptive optimistic synchronisation for multi-agent simulation. In D. Al-Dabass, editor, *Proceedings of the 17th European Simulation Multiconference (ESM 2003)*, pages 77–82, Delft, 2003. Society for Modelling and Simulation International.

[8] B. Logan and G. Theodoropoulos. The distributed simulation of multi-agent systems. *Proceedings of the IEEE*, 89(2):174–186, 2001.

[9] V. K. Madisetti, D. A. Hardaker, and R. M. Fujimoto. The MIMDIX environment for parallel simulation. *Journal of Parallel and Distributed Computing*, 18(4):473–483, 1993.

[10] F. Mattern. Efficient algorithms for distributed snapshots and Global Virtual Time approximation. *Journal of Parallel and Distributed Computing*, 18(4):423–434, 1993.

[11] C. W. Reynolds. Flocks, herds and schools: A distributed behavioral model. *Computer Graphics*, 21(4):25–34, 1987.

[12] P. Riley. MPADES: Middleware for parallel agent discrete event simulation. In G. A. Kaminka, P. U. Lima, and R. Rojas, editors, *RoboCup-2002: The Fifth RoboCup Competitions and Conferences*, LNAI Vol. 2752, pages 162–178. Springer, Berlin. 2003.

[13] B. Schattenberg and A. M. Uhrmacher. Planning agents in JAMES. *Proceedings of the IEEE*, 89(2):158–173, 2001.

[14] A. Sloman and R. Poli. SIM_AGENT: A toolkit for exploring agent designs. In M. Wooldridge, J. Mueller, and M. Tambe, editors, *Intelligent Agents II: Agent Theories Architectures and Languages (ATAL-95)*, pages 392–407. Springer, Berlin. 1996.

[15] L. Sokol, J. Weissman, and P. Mutchler. MTW: An empirical performance study. In *Proceedings of the 1991 Winter Simulation Conference*, pages 557–563, 1991.

[16] L. M. Sokol, D. P. Briscoe, and A. P. Wieland. MTW: A strategy for scheduling discrete simulation events for concurrent simulation. In *Proceedings of the SCS Multiconference on Distributed Simulation*, pages 34–42, July 1988. Society for Computer Simulation.

[17] T. K. Som and R. G. Sargent. Model structure and load balancing in optimistic parallel discrete event simulation. In *Proceedings of the Fourteenth Workshop on Parallel and Distributed Simulation (PADS'00)*, pages 147–154, Washington DC, 2000. IEEE Computer Society.

[18] A. M. Uhrmacher and K. Gugler. Distributed, parallel simulation of multiple, deliberative agents. In *Proceedings of the Fourteenth Workshop on Parallel and Distributed Simulation (PADS'00)*, pages 101–110, Washington DC, 2000. IEEE Computer Society.

[19] M. Wooldridge and N. R. Jennings. Intelligent agents: Theory and practice. *Knowledge Engineering Review*, 10(2):115–152, 1995.

---

[10]http://www.cs.bham.ac.uk/research/pdesmas

Predicting Performance of Resolution Changes in Parallel Simulations

Dhananjai M. Rao
CSA Department
Miami University
Oxford, OH – 45056, USA.
raodm@muohio.edu

Philip A. Wilsey
Department of ECECS
University of Cincinnati
Cincinnati, OH 45221–0030, USA.
philip.wilsey@uc.edu

Abstract

Multi-resolution models can be statically (i.e., before simulation) or dynamically (i.e., during simulation) abstracted to accelerate the simulations without compromising the analysis goals. However, abstractions must be carefully chosen because not all abstractions improve performance. Unfortunately, identifying performance enhancing transformations, particularly in parallel simulations, is a complex task. We have been investigating this bottleneck using a component-based, Time Warp synchronized modeling and simulation environment called WESE in which static and dynamic abstractions are performed using a methodology called Dynamic Component Substitution (DCS). Our ongoing research has resulted in further advances to a novel DCS Performance Prediction Methodology (DCSPPM). DCSPPM combines and compares platform-specific performance characteristics of components via static analysis of the model to predict performance changes due to DCS transformations. This paper presents the enhanced version of DCSPPM and experiments. Empirical evidence obtained using diverse models indicates that DCSPPM provides good estimates (error < 5%) of the performance impacts of DCS transformations.

1 Introduction

Simulation of large, high resolution models is a time consuming task even when parallel simulation techniques are employed [6]. Furthermore, if analysis deals with specific subsystems or selected scenarios, processing voluminous data from inconsequential scenarios exacerbates analysis [6]. Consequently, multi-resolution modeling and simulation techniques are used to obtain more optimal tradeoffs between analysis requirements, accuracy, fidelity, and performance [6, 10]. In our research, we have enabled multi-resolution simulation using hierarchical, component-based models and a novel methodology called Dynamic Component Substitution (DCS) [6]. In DCS a set of components called a *module* is substituted with an equivalent component or vice versa to enable abstraction and refinement [6]. DCS transformations may be performed statically (*i.e.*, prior to simulation) or dynamically (*i.e.*, during simulation) to change the resolution of the model [6]. A more detailed overview of DCS is presented in Section 2.

Typically, abstractions are used to improve simulation performance while trading-off observability and possibly some fidelity. Unfortunately, in many scenarios abstraction negatively impacts performance and simulation times increases [6]. In other words, DCS transformations, to parts of a model, that seemingly improve performance have counterintuitive impacts on the model as a whole. Several examples in which abstraction deteriorates performance are discussed in the literature [6]. In addition, similar transformations to different parts of a model have different and often converse results [6]. Consequently, the effects of a transformation on simulation performance must be known apriori in order to enable effective use multi-resolution models. A conventional approach to determine the impacts is to use short test simulations. However, numerous test simulations need to be performed for each transformation to obtain reliable estimates. The scenario is exponentially complicated in the case of parallel simulation that are conducted using varying number of workstations.

We have been investigating approaches to predict performance impacts of DCS transformation and ease effective use of multi-resolution models. Initially, we explored the use of a more parsimonious approach for performance prediction [8]. However, the earlier approach had significant errors (sometimes > 50%) and could not be effectively used. Our continued research have resulted in the development of a DCS Performance Prediction Methodology (DCSPPM) that uses simulation-platform specific estimates and static analysis of a model to predict the performance impacts of DCS transformations. For example, given two DCS transformations, say τ_1 and τ_2, DCSPPM yields quantitative estimates, say $4.5 \pm 1\%$ and $-2.3 \pm 0.5\%$. Positive estimates indicate improvements in performance while negative values indicate degradation in performance. Using the estimates a modeler can scientifically choose suitable model transformations to improve overall efficiency of simulation-based analysis. Note that several studies related to performance prediction of parallel simulations have been reported [2, 3, 4]. Unlike earlier investigations, the focus of this study is to predict the change in performance due to resolution changes rather than the performance of the simulation as a whole.

This paper presents the latest results and numerous enhancements to DCSPPM conducted over a period of two years after our earlier publication [8]. A brief background on WESE and DCS is presented in Section 2. A detailed description of DCSPPM is presented in Section 3. The experiments conducted to evaluate the accuracy of DCSPPM are presented in Section 4. Section 5 concludes the paper summarizing contributions from this work.

2 Background

The performance prediction algorithm proposed in this paper has been implemented as part of a component-based modeling and simulation environment called WESE. WESE is an acronym for Web-based Environment For System Engineering. Model development in WESE involves two phases. First, a set of components involved in the model are developed using WESE's Application Program Interface (API) and bundled into a WESE factory. A WESE factory is a repository of components with additional capability for parallel simulation. Each component is associated with a *stub* object that is responsible for creating the object on demand. In addition, the stubs have also been used to store behavior and performance characteristics that play a central role in the proposed methodology. The WESE factories are deployed on various workstations to be used for parallel simulation. Interactions with a factory are performed via TCP/IP sockets using a custom protocol. Next, multi-resolution models are developed by suitably interconnecting a set of modules via ports that constitute the interface to a module. A module is a set of port-interconnected components (present on a given factory) and submodules. It also has a more abstract, Equivalent Component (EC) associated with it. An EC has an identical interface and similar functionality (as defined by the modeler) as that of the corresponding module. The model includes all the information and parameters to setup a parallel simulation using a given set of WESE factories.

Abstraction or refinement of the model is implemented by substituting a module with its EC or vice versa using a methodology called Dynamic Component Substitution (DCS) [6]. Substituting a module with its equivalent component is synonymous to abstraction. DCS also involves appropriately mapping the states of the components participating in the transformation. Strategies used for triggering DCS during simulation are broadly categorized into *proactive* (DCS scheduled in future) and *reactive* (scheduled in the recent past) strategies. A combination of proactive and reactive DCS transformation have been employed to accelerate parallel simulations in diverse applications such as: logic simulation, VLSI power estimation, rare phenomena simulation, mobile ad hoc network simulations, and simulation of Eco systems. The core constructs and several optimizations underlying DCS have been rigorously defined using a discrete mathematics algebra. DCS provides a flexible, scalable, and performance-predictable strategy for enabling dynamic multi-resolution simulations thereby improving overall efficiency of simulation studies [6]. A detailed description on DCS and its aforementioned usage is available in the literature [6].

In WESE, an event-driven approach has been utilized to sequence the various phases involved in enabling DCS. The event-driven approach has been developed by extending the backbone provided by the underlying simulation kernel called WARPED. WARPED is a general purpose, Time Warp synchronized parallel simulation kernel. WESE leverages the Time Warp infrastructure of WARPED in an unique manner to enable proactive and reactive DCS transformations. WESE also provides an API for mapping states of components during DCS. It is the responsibility of the modeler to utilize the API and suitably map states of components during DCS transformations. Care has been taken to ensure that WESE and the model implementations preserve scalability and linearity (with respect to number of ports) to enable predictable performance characteristics. A more detailed description of WESE, WARPED, and DCS implementation are available in the literature [5, 7, 9].

3 Performance Prediction Methodology (DCSPPM)

DCSPPM aims to provide a quantitative measure of the *change* in simulation time due to a given set of DCS transformations for a given partition of the model. An overview of the DCSPPM is shown in Figure 1. As shown in the figure, component-based models are parsed into an object oriented, in-memory intermediate format called SSL-IF. The SSL-IF is partitioned by logically assigning components to a given set of WESE factories. Currently, the partitioning is random and assigns equal number of components to each factory used for simulation. The partitioned SSL-IF is utilized by the DCSPPM module for further processing. As shown in the Figure 1, DCSPPM proceeds in four distinct but overlapping phases. A discussion of the four phases is presented in the following subsections.

3.1 Phase 1: Collating behavior tables for components

The first phase of DCSPPM involves collating the data for generating the Behavior Table (BT) for each component. A BT indicates the input-output characteristics of the component. Each row specifies the probability of output vectors (or events) being generated at each output port for a given combination of input vectors (or events) at a component's input ports. Components that do not have any inputs or outputs are treated as a special case and are described using a NULL input or output vectors. The set of I/O vectors are implicitly ordered to reflect the logical port numbers of a component to minimize size of BTs. Each BT entry contains a set of I/O vectors that are grouped based on simulation timestamp values. The I/O vectors at each port is represented using a 3-tuple consisting of $< I/O Probability, RealTime, Factory-ID >$, where

I/O Probability: The probability value associated with an I/O vector essentially indicates the probability with which an event occurs at a port. Probability of 0 indicates absence of an event. In WESE, the I/O probability value maybe empirically determined using test simulations (see Figure 1). Such test simulations are effective for components with few input and output ports (2 to 5 ports). All possible combinations of input vectors are fed to the component and the resulting output is analyzed to determine I/O probability. However, such an approach does not scale for large components. In such cases, the BT entries are computed on-the-fly as needed. In this case, the stubs associated with the components, provides BT entries on demand, once the actual input vectors to be analyzed is known. Furthermore, it computes output probabilities based on model specific knowledge provided by the modeler.

Real Time: This field indicates the real time (or wall clock time) at which the I/O events occur. Alternatively, this value indicates the time taken to process the given input vector and generate outputs. For example, the first row of the BT shown in Figure 1 indicates that if an input vector is presented to the component at real time 0, it generates output at 4.75 ± 0.1 μsec. This value also includes the simulation kernel overheads for processing the event such as: event scheduling costs, time spent for state saving, and garbage collection overheads. However, it does not include communication overheads or any synchronization overheads. It is the responsibility of the modeler to specify the set of "*typical*" events to be used for granularity estimation via suitable API calls. Typical events are those events that would be most commonly processed by the component and represent its average or characteristic behavior. Typical Event Granularity (TEG) is assumed to follow a Normal distribution in concordance with statistical theories [1]. Prior to usage of DCSPPM, it is suggested that the assumption of normality be verified [1] as illustrated in the literature [6]. The primary motivation for normality verification is to ensure that sufficient number of samples have been collated to yield a good representative statistic.

Factory-ID: The third value in the tuple indicates the logical WESE factory ID to which the component has been assigned by the partitioner. The ID value is used (in Phase 3) to detect and track interactions between components on different factories which requires communication over the network. Tracking such network centric communication points serves the following two purposes in DCSPPM: *(i)* It enables appropriate inclusion of communication latencies that impact the overall TEG of a model; and *(ii)* it is used to identify points where potential for rollbacks exist in order to account for synchronization overheads in Time Warp simulations.

3.2 Phase 2: Estimating Network Latencies

Estimation of communication latencies is performed by a pair of WESE factories. One WESE factory acts as a server while the other acts as a client. Communication latency is estimated by exchanging a large number of messages between the two factories and measuring the round trip time for the messages. A number of the round trip times are measured and averaged to obtain the mean latency and variance. Similar to component granularities, the average latency value is assumed to follow a normal distribution. The estimation process is suitably coordinated by the DCSPPM Module (see Figure 1). The estimated values are stored in the DCSPPM Module and reused as necessary during Phase 3.

3.3 Phase 3: Estimating Granularity of a Module

The overall TEG of a module is estimated in a recursive, top-down manner using the TEG of each component (estimated in Phase 1) and submodule constituting the module. The estimation is performed by propagating the BTs of components from inputs to outputs of

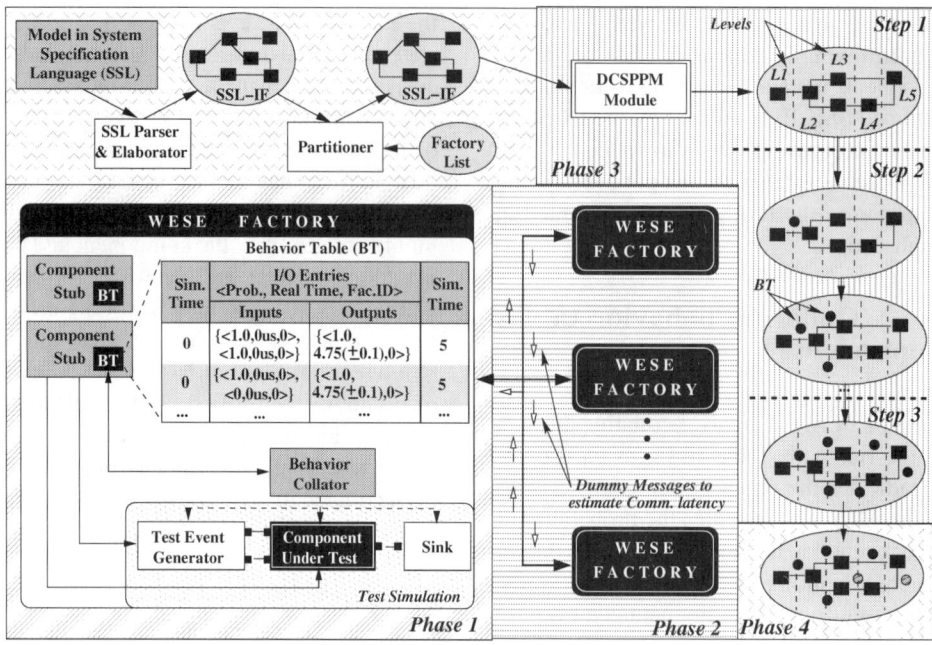

Figure 1. Overview of DCSPPM

the model. As the BTs are propagated they are suitably transformed to include the behavior and characteristics of the components constituting a module. As shown in Figure 1, this process proceeds in the following steps:

Step 1: Levelization: The objective of levelization is to capture the natural flow of events from inputs to outputs of a module. Accordingly, in this step, each component or submodule is assigned a level number such that inputs of a component are at a lower level. Cycles in a module are arbitrarily resolved. Currently, DCSPPM does not effectively account for cycles in a model. Levelization results in updates and minor reorganization of the SSL-IF representation of the module.

Step 2: Propagation of BTs: In this step, the BTs of components are propagated from the lowest level (input) to the highest level (output) of a module. Every component in a level utilizes the set of input BT records (IBTRs), its own BT, and generates output BT records (OBTRs) at its output ports. For each IBTRs, the OBTRs are computed in the following manner:

1. First, the probabilities in an IBTR are used to detect the presence or absence of inputs at each port which yields an input pattern. The components BT entry corresponding to the input pattern is obtained from the appropriate WESE factory. For example, consider a scenario in which an input BT entry $\{<0.5, 10\pm 1\mu s, 0>, <0.75, 12\pm 1\mu s, 1>\}$ at simulation time 35 is presented to component whose BT is shown in Figure 1. In this case, the component has inputs on both ports and uses the corresponding entry from the BT. In this case, the first row is obtained from the WESE factory.

2. The output simulation time is computed by adding to the IBTR simulation time to the value in the component's BT entry. In the aforementioned example, the output simulation time of the BR would be $35 + 5 = 40$.

3. Next, the maximum probability value from the IBTR is multiplied with the probability values in the component's BR entry to determine probability of OBTR. In the above example, the output probability would be: $1.0 * max(0.5, 0.75) = 0.75$.

4. If vectors arrive from different factories (identified using factory-id in IBTR entries) the communication latency between the pair of factories is added to the real time value of the corresponding input vector. For example, assume that the component being analyzed is assigned to factory 1. Given the earlier input vectors, the first vector ($< 0.5, 10\pm 1\mu s, 0 >$) is from factory 0. In this case the communication latency say $40 \pm 7\mu s$ is added to the real time (resulting in $< 0.5, 50 \pm 8\mu s, 0 >$). Note that the real time operations use statistical arithmetic based on the fact that these values represent normal distributions with a given mean and variance.

5. The real time at which the outputs are generated is determined by adding the maximum real time value of the IBTR vectors to each OBTR vector. Based on earlier example, the real time for the output

event would be: $4.75 \pm 0.1 + max(10 \pm 1, 12 \pm 1) = 16.75 \pm 1.1$.

6. Next, the following two heuristics are used to account for synchronization overheads in the simulation. Since the simulations are based on Time Warp, the heuristics estimate the probability of rollbacks. The heuristics are based on the fact that, in WESE rollbacks occur only when inputs are received from multiple factories. Rollbacks require reprocessing of events that requires additional wall clock time. Accordingly the probability of rollbacks is used to suitably scale the overall real time value of the output vectors. In addition, the rollback probabilities are propagated through the model to account for cascading rollbacks. Cascading rollbacks occur even though all events are received from the same factory because some component in the input chain rolls back.

7. *Heuristic 1*: This heuristic is based on the fact that if inputs at the same simulation time arrive at different real times from different factories, there is a probability for rollback. Accordingly, the real time values of various input vectors from different factories are statistically compared and for each pair that is different the rollback weight is increased by one. The real time values for each output vector is then suitably scaled using the rollback weight value for the component, *i.e.*, $realTime = realTime + (realTime * rollback\_weight)$.

8. *Heuristic 2*: This heuristic uses the fact that if inputs at earlier simulation times arrive at a later real time when compared to one another, then rollbacks occur. For example, if inputs at simulation time 30 arrive at real time $25 \pm 1\mu s$ while inputs at simulation time 40 arrive at real time $10 \pm 1\mu s$, then a rollback will most likely occur. The real time values of successive input BR entries are statistically compared to determine rollback probability. Similar to earlier heuristic, the real time values for each output vector is suitably scaled to reflect synchronization overheads.

Step 3: Overall Granularity: In order to determine the granularity of a module, first, the components in a module are grouped based on the factory in which they reside. Next, the granularity contributed to each factory by the module is determined by adding the granularity of components in each group.

Estimation of granularity of components proceeds in a recursive, top down manner until the top level module as been analyzed. At the end of analysis, the overall granularity contribution to each factory involved in the simulation is collated in the SSL-IF node corresponding to the top level module. Since each factory simulates in parallel, the maximum of these values is used as an estimate of the overall, typical event granularity (TEG) of the model as a whole. For example, the result of this phase would be a TEG in the form $4567 \pm 38\mu s$. This TEG is retained as the reference for further comparisons in Phase 4.

3.4 Phase 4: Estimating performance changes due to DCS

In this phase, parts of the model that undergo DCS transformations are located and Phase 3 is repeated starting with that part of the model. However, rather than using the BT for the module, the BT for the corresponding equivalent component is used. This results in a TEG value that indicates the overall estimated granularity with the new component in place. For example, say the result is $4238 \pm 42\mu s$. The new TEG is compared with the reference TEG from Phase 3 do determine the change in performance due to a DCS transformation. Using earlier example, the difference in performance would be $(4567 \pm 38 - 4238 \pm 42)/4567 \pm 38 = 7.2 \pm 1.9\%$.

4 Experiments

The experiments conducted to evaluate the fidelity of the performance estimates generated by DCSPPM were conducted using a diverse set of models. Some of the salient characteristics of the models used in the experiments is shown in Table 1. The first three models, namely Adder, Multiplier, and pASIC were digital logic circuits with diverse characteristics. The circuits were modeled in a hierarchical fashion using basic logic gates such as AND, OR, and NOT gates. The column titled Atomic in Table 1 indicates the number of atomic components in the models. The models also included more abstract components such as exclusive-or gates and FullAdder components. The column titled Abstract in Table 1 indicates the number of such abstract components in a model. These models also included components that generated primary inputs and captured outputs. The number of such auxiliary components in each model is shown in the column titled Others in Table 1. The Adder model does not have any loops and experiences negligible rollbacks. It can be considered an ideal candidate for DCSPPM. The Multiplier is a large model with complex interconnections between components. Although this model does not have loops in it, the inherent design causes numerous rollbacks and is a stress test for both Time Warp and DCSPPM. The pASIC model has numerous loops in it and does not have a deep hierarchical organization.

| Model | Number of components | | | |
Name	Atomic	Abstract	Others	Total
Adder	482	96	2	580
Multiplier	16360	3096	2	19458
pASIC	825	25	2	852
ATM-Net	126	3	0	129
MANET	88	4	0	92

Table 1. Characteristics of models

Model (#DCS)	#CPU	Change due to DCS		Err In Esti.
		Esti.	Obs.	
Adder (4)	1	10.95±0.01%	10.966%	0%
	2	19.77±0.8%	23.06%	2.49%
	6	17.47±1%	17.35%	0%
Adder (1)	1	-4.52±0.01%	-4.87%	0.35%
	2	-5.62±0.72%	-5.02%	0.6%
	6	-7.85±1.68%	-6.75%	1.1%
Mul32 (4)	1	-3.08%	-3.06%	0.02%
	2	-6.72±0.03%	-8.64%	1.92%
	6	-4.27±0.5%	-4.256	0%
Mul32 (8)	1	3.9%	4.87%	0.97%
	2	2.81±0.04	4.64%	1.83%
	6	6.9±1.2%	5.13%	0.57%
pASIC (8)	1	-1.27%	-1.09%	0.175%
	6	-4.53%	-4.10%	0.43%
pASIC (12)	1	4.38%	3.41%	0.97%
	6	3.21±0.08%	3.64	0.35%
ATM-Net (1)	1	15.27±0.01%	14.54%	0.73%
	4	10.23±0.97%	10.26%	0%
ATM-Net (3)	1	41.58±0.01%	40.8%	0.78%
	4	30.35±1.22%	30.16%	0%
	6	30.35±1.22%	30.16%	0%
MANET (4)	1	59.95%	59.89%	0.05%
	2	17.47±1.45%	17.0%	0.47%
	4	5.4±2.07%	5.47%	0%
	6	3.35±2.57%	3.5%	0%

Table 2. Statistics from experiments

Unlike the earlier models, this model requires 2-phase analysis to resolve the loops and additional complexity to handle cascading rollbacks.

The ATM-NET model is a detailed, cell-level model of an Asynchronous Transfer Mode (ATM) network utilizing the Private Network-to-Network Interface (PNNI) signaling and control protocol that provides scalable, QoS-based, dynamic link-state routing. The ATM-NET model had 9 ATM switches organized into 3 hierarchical ATM clouds. An ATM cloud is an abstraction of a given number of ATM switches. DCSPPM was used to analyze the performance impact of abstracting three ATM switches using an ATM cloud. The last model shown in Table 1 is a spatially explicit model of a Mobile Ad Hoc Network (MANET) based asset tracking system. The model involves 80 mobile assets tracked by 8 fixed base stations using ad hoc networking techniques. Dynamic Source Routing (DSR) protocol has been employed for ad hoc packet routing. All communication messages are routed to other assets via a hierarchical area composed of sub-area components. The spatially-explicit, hierarchical area is aggregated or de-aggregated using DCS into larger or smaller units depending on the overlap of the communication range of the wireless assets. The objective is to minimize the overhead of routing packets by dynamically adapting the logical partition of overlapping wireless assets. A detailed description of these models is available in the literature [6].

In concordance with the modeling strategy utilized by WESE, first a set of basic components were developed and bundled into suitable WESE factories. Next, multi-resolution models were developed by suitably interconnecting components from the appropriate factories and providing necessary parameters. The WESE factories were deployed on a dedicated network of workstations for empirical evaluation. Each workstation consisted of two Athlon processors (1 GHz) with 1 Gigabyte of main memory running Linux (kernel 2.4.2). The workstations were networked using a Gigabit Ethernet. Some of the statistics collated from the experiments is shown in Table 2. The columns titled #DCS, #CPUs, Esti, Obs Change, and Err in Esti. indicate the number of abstractions, number of CPUs (or WESE factories) used for simulation, DCSPPM estimate of change in performance, observed change in performance, and the percentage error between the estimate & observation respectively. The No DCS and DCS sub-columns under the Sim Time column indicate the time for simulating the model without any abstractions and with the indicated number of modules abstracted, respectively. Additional experimental configurations and data is available in the literature [6].

As illustrated by the last column in Table 2, DCSPPM generates good estimates of the change in performance due to abstraction of parts of a model using DCS. Refinement using DCS has the inverse effect of abstraction. Positive estimates indicate improvement in performance or decrease in simulation time when abstractions are applied. Conversely, negative estimates indicate decrease in performance. For example, in the case of the Mul32 model, a set of 4 modules were abstracted at different spots in the model in the two different cases shown in Table 2. In one case, performance improves while in another case performance degrades highlighting the dilemma involved in using multi-resolution models. The time durations for which the models were simulated was set by trial-and-error to the shortest duration after which valid performance comparisons could be made. The graph in Figure 2(a) shows the percentage change in simulation time due to a given abstraction in the various models. As indicated in the graph different models require different number of input vectors in order to obtain stable, average observations. The experimental observations in Table 2 were made at the knee point in the curves indicated by gray circles in Figure 2. This graph in Figure 2(a) also highlights the issues involved in using trial-and-error experiments to determine the impact of a DCS transformation.

As illustrated in Table 2, the estimates generated by DCSPPM have some errors. The source of errors include minor skew in model behavior, nonlinearities in the simulation kernel, changes in characteristics of the communication network, and operating system activities. Amongst the aforementioned factors, the following were found to be the most dominant ones in our experiments:

- *Nonlinearities in the simulation kernel*: The dominant source of nonlinearity in the kernel arises from Global Virtual Time (GVT) computations and fossil collection overheads that are necessary in a Time Warp simulation. The graph in Figure 2(b) illustrates the impact of GVT on simulation time. The data shown in the figure is the simulation time of the `Adder` model using 1000 input vectors approximated using Bezier curve fitting algorithm. It was noted that if the GVT period is not set in the linear region, then the observations significantly skew.
- *Nonlinearities in the network*: The next dominant source of error arises from the underlying Gigabit network. The nonlinearities are conspicuous due to bursty communication behaviors of a Time Warp simulations, particularly during rollbacks. The graph in Figure 2(c) illustrates the average message latency with different burst sizes. As illustrated by the graph, the average latency significantly skews depending on the total number of messages exchanged. This behavior in-turn skews the simulations and the DCSPPM estimates thereby introducing errors.

The accuracy of he estimates generated using DCSPPM is sensitive to the simulation platform characteristics. The DCSPPM estimates are valid as long as the load on the workstations and network do not change. The sensitivity of DCSPPM to GVT period, extraneous CPU load, and extraneous network load are shown by the graphs in Figure 3. The sensitivity experiments were conducted using the `Mul32` model because it is a large and complex model. As illustrated by the graph in Figure 3(a), the estimates are not sensitive to the GVT period which introduces some nonlinearities in the kernel. The graph in Figure 3(b) illustrates the deviations due to extraneous network load. The extraneous network load on each workstation was generated using an exter-

Model	Time spent for (sec)			
	Gran. Est.	Comm. Latency	DCSPPM Analysis	Fastest Test Sim.
Adder	6.23	15.48	0.457	36.86
Mul32	6.23	15.48	4.73	242.8
pASIC	6.23	15.48	3.72	45.83
ATM-Net	11.23	15.75	0.031	27.5
MANET	2.23	15.42	0.0025	11.93

Table 3. Time for DCSPPM vs. simulation

nal client-server program that exchange data at a fixed rate. As shown by the graph, the estimates are sensitive to network load but the deviations are influenced by the nonlinear characteristics of the network. The impact of extraneous CPU load on the estimates are shown by the graph in Figure 3(c). The CPU load was generated by running an extraneous process that performed a finite amount of dummy processing thereby consuming CPU time. The volume of processing was varied to generate different loads on the CPU. As illustrated by the graph in Figure 3(c), the estimates are very sensitive to CPU load. In other words, DCSPPM estimates are least sensitive to GVT period changes but are more sensitive to changes in network and CPU load.

The time taken for performing various phases in DCSPPM is tabulated in Table 3. The time for the fastest running test simulation is also shown for comparisons. Note that the granularity estimation and communication latency measurement is an one time task. On the other hand, DCSPPM analysis maybe repeated several times for different combinations. As illustrated in Table 3, DCSPPM analysis phase runs orders of magnitude faster than the fastest test simulation! A much broader spectrum of experimental observations and analysis of the empirical data is available in the literature [6]. As illustrated by the experiments DCSPPM provides a rapid approach for estimating the performance impacts of DCS transformations, thereby providing a more scientific approach to enabling effective use of multi-resolution, parallel simulations.

5 Conclusion

This paper presented a novel methodology called DCSPPM that can be applied to component-based, multi-resolution models to predict the performance impacts of changing the resolution using Dynamic Component Substitution (DCS). Empirical evaluation of DCSPPM conduced using diverse models were presented. The experiments indicate that the DCSPPM generates good estimates with errors less than $\pm 3\%$ in our experiments. Sources of errors in the estimates were presented and

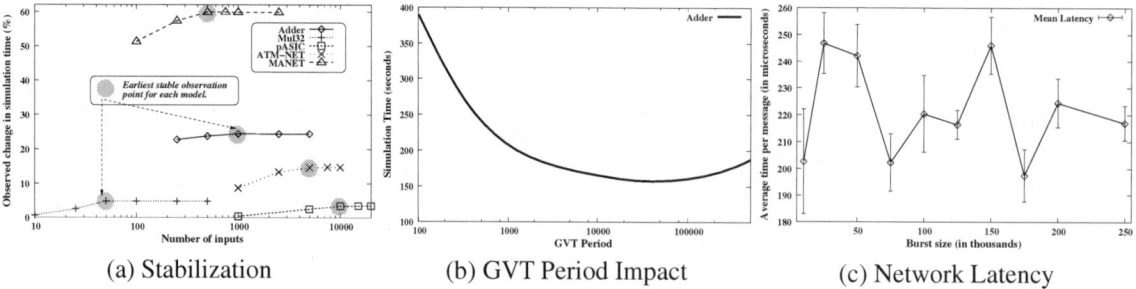

(a) Stabilization　　(b) GVT Period Impact　　(c) Network Latency

Figure 2. Observation points and sources of errors

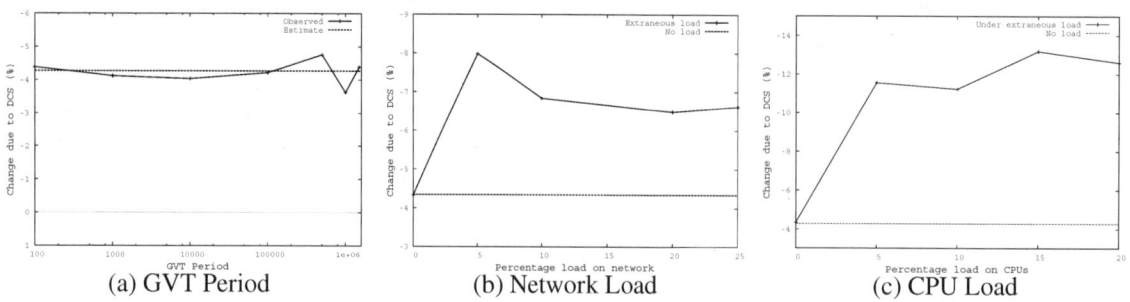

(a) GVT Period　　(b) Network Load　　(c) CPU Load

Figure 3. Sensitivity analysis of DCS$_{PPM}$ to extraneous loads

their influences were empirically explored. The estimates hold as long as the characteristics of the model and simulation platform do not significantly skew during simulation. The sensitivity of DCS$_{PPM}$ to external factors was also presented in the paper. The paper pitched the timing for DCS$_{PPM}$ analysis against the shortest possible simulation time for different models to highlight the speed of DCS$_{PPM}$. Since DCS$_{PPM}$ runs very fast, it can be used to explore numerous model configuration to identify the most optimal candidate for a given analysis. We are continuing our pursuit to enhance DCS$_{PPM}$ and apply it for diverse problem domains and synchronization methodologies. The objective of our investigations is to eliminate "guess work" involved in effective use of parallel, multi-resolution simulations.

References

[1] R. V. Hogg and A. T. Craig. *Introduction to Mathematical Statistics*. Prentice Hall, Englewood Cliffs, New Jersey, 1995.

[2] J. Liu, D. M. Nicol, B. J. Premore, and A. L. Poplawski. Performance prediction of a parallel simulator. In *Workshop on Parallel and Distributed Simulation*, pages 156–164, 1999.

[3] K. S. Perumalla, R. M. Fujimoto, P. J. Thakare, S. Pande, H. Karimabadi, Y. Omelchenko, and J. Driscoll. Performance prediction of large-scale parallel discrete event models of physical systems. In *In Proceedings of the 2006 Winter Simulation Conference (WSC'06)*, pages 356–364, Dec. 2006.

[4] S. Prakash and R. Bagrodia. MPI-SIM: Using parallel simulation to evaluate MPI programs. In *Winter Simulation Conference*, pages 467–474, 1998.

[5] R. Radhakrishnan, D. E. Martin, M. Chetlur, D. M. Rao, and P. A. Wilsey. An Object-Oriented Time Warp Simulation Kernel. In D. Caromel, R. R. Oldehoeft, and M. Tholburn, editors, *Proceedings of the International Symposium on Computing in Object-Oriented Parallel Environments (ISCOPE'98)*, volume LNCS 1505, pages 13–23. Springer-Verlag, Dec. 1998.

[6] D. M. Rao. *Study of Dynamic Component Substitution*. PhD thesis, University of Cincinnati, 2003.

[7] D. M. Rao and P. A. Wilsey. Dynamic component substitution in web-based simulation. In *In Proceedings of the 2000 Winter Simulation Conference (WSC'2000)*. Society for Computer Simulation, Dec. 2000.

[8] D. M. Rao and P. A. Wilsey. Performance prediction of dynamic component substitutions. In *In Proceedings of the 2002 Winter Simulation Conference (WSC'02)*, Dec. 2022.

[9] D. M. Rao, P. A. Wilsey, and H. W. Carter. Optimizing costs of web-based modeling and simulation. In *Proceedings of the First International Workshop on Internet Computing and E-Commerce (ICEC'01)*. IPDPS, Apr. 2001.

[10] A. F. Sisti and S. D. Farr. Model abstraction techniques: An intuitive overview. *Publication of the AFRL/IF*, 1998.

Principles of Advanced and Distributed Simulation

Session 3: Keynote Presentation

What comes after the Semantic Web - PADS Implications for the Dynamic Web

Andreas Tolk
Virginia Modeling Analysis & Simulation Center (VMASC), Old Dominion University
atolk@odu.edu

Abstract

The Internet started as a web of documents. The Semantic Web is targeting a web of data, enabling efficient machine-to-machine data exchange. In order to utilize the Internet for distributed simulation, procedures are needed for migration, alignment, and orchestration of the execution, which means higher levels of interoperation. This paper introduces related concepts leading to the idea of the Dynamic Web, which will be a web of composable services.

This paper is a concept paper written to encourage discussion. It summarizes related ideas and contributions in a loose style and doesn't claim to be complete or inclusive. Contributions are more than welcome.

1. Introduction

The Internet started as a *"web of documents"* to be displayed on request for use by humans. As long as this display was limited to pure text, it was mainly used by academics to easily exchange ideas on publications. With the advent of Internet browsers, the web became a medium used by many users so much so that the current use of Internet resources has become a standard for middle schools in technology driven countries.

The introduction of XML has produced dramatic changes: the Internet became a *"web of data"* instead of documents and it moves currently towards the Semantic Web. This has enabled new concepts, like machine-to-machine information exchange via the web without a human-in-the-loop. Web services allow web-based applications that are truly distributed in a way that has never before been possible.

However, when looking at the Principles of Advanced Distributed Simulation (PADS), the promise of the Semantic Web falls short. While the Semantic Web targets data to describe situations and common pictures, PADS drives towards the orchestration and alignment of highly agile and dynamic interdependent applications. Higher levels of interoperation are required to capture not only the semantics of data to be exchanged, but also the possible compositions of these data into business objects (pragmatics). Also affected is how the information exchange will influence the sending and receiving systems (dynamics) and the constraints for such compositions (concepts). In order to enable this, a vision beyond the Semantic Web is needed. Such a vision deserves the name *Dynamic Web* and it will be a *"web of composable services."*

2. Interoperation of Advanced Distributed Simulation Systems

The Internet is used by simulation experts on a daily basis: email is one of the main communication devices; literature research is initiated with an Internet browser; proceedings are published via the web; etc. Yet, while the Internet is such a commonly used piece of infrastructure for document and information exchange, the use of it as an M&S runtime infrastructure has yet to meet its potential use envisioned by the web-based simulation enthusiasts participating in early conferences, such as Web-based M&S [1]. More recent approaches on Web-enabled M&S conducted under a consortium of the Object Management Group (OMG), Open GIS Consortium (OGC), Simulation Interoperability Standards Organization (SISO), and the Web 3D Consortium also fall short in producing fertile ground for real web-enabled applications. The question is: Why is this happening? What is so special about web-based simulation applications? Why is the Internet being used for on-line shops, bank accounts, literature research, and thousands of other application domains, while Internet use for most of the advanced distributed simulations is still employing other infrastructure specifications?

The Society for M&S International (SCS) defined web-based simulation as *"representing a convergence of computer simulation methodologies and applications within the World Wide Web (WWW). There are many possible bridge areas between the web and the simulation field. Web-based simulation does not mean only "distributed simulation" or "simulation documentation." The introduction and widespread use of the web suggests that there are many areas where web science and technology will meet simulation to provide impetus to both fields."* [1]

As discussed in the introduction, the web changed from a web of documents to a web of data. The advent of XML in general and of web services in particular enabled its use for a variety of net-centric applications. In principle, every application based on data exchange and remote procedure calls can easily migrate using XML and web services, and it can play a role on the web [2]. Pullen et al. applied these principles showing a possible migration path for M&S applications [3]. Nonetheless, M&S on the Internet remains to be the exception.

In the author's opinion, the reason for this exception is rooted in the fact that interoperation for advanced distributed simulation systems is based on much more than data exchange and remote procedure calls. While the Internet, in its current form and even as the envision Semantic Web [4], focuses on implementation issues, meaningful interoperation of M&S applications requires the alignment and harmonization of underlying conceptual ideas as well: *Interoperability of Simulation Systems requires Composability of Conceptual Models!*

This result summarizes the findings of several researchers on composability of M&S systems. Page et al. [5] state that, at least within the military simulation domain, composability has arisen as a cousin of the longstanding U.S. Department of Defense objective of interoperability. Page et al. also support the view of Petty and Weisel [6], whose research resulted in the view that interoperability covers the technical aspects and composability the conceptual aspects. The conclusions drawn by Page et al. [5] suggest defining composability as the realm of the model and interoperability as the realm of the software implementation of the model. In addition, their research introduces integratability coping with the hardware-side and configuration side of connectivity. The author supports this categorization and recommends the following distinction when dealing with issues of simulation system interoperability, to include meaningful simulation-to-simulation system interoperation:

- *Integratability* contends with the physical/ technical realms of connections between systems, which include hardware and firmware, protocols, etc.

- *Interoperability* contends with the software- and implementation details of interoperations, including exchange of data elements based on a common data interpretation, etc.

- *Composability* contends with the alignment of issues on the modeling level. The underlying models are purposeful abstractions of reality used for the conceptualization being implemented by the resulting simulation systems.

This recommendation is consistent with ideas promoted by other researchers. During a recent panel discussion on Priorities for M&S Standards, Zeigler explicitly stated that *standardization must be aimed at the modeling level* to ensure interoperability between systems, i.e., the standardized level must be higher than the programming level standards currently applied [7]. For "meaningful interoperability" the sharing of standardized data via standardized protocols, such as the Distributed Interactive Simulation [8] protocol or the High Level Architecture [9] standard is necessary, but it does not complete what is necessary for meaningful interoperability. Also needed is the coordination of the underlying conceptual models and the harmonization of the operational ideas simulated, as they are the real crux to create interoperable solutions. Instead of only standardizing the information exchange requirements, the underlying modeled cause-effect-chains must also be coordinated.

Sarjoughian et al. [10] proposes a framework for a general modeling formalism comprising the system formalism describing the model, the abstract simulator, a platform independent description of implementation ideas interpreting the formulism, the simulation algorithm computing the formalism and correctly implementing the abstract simulator, and finally the computational platform. The general model formalism manages the conceptual issues. Abstract simulator and simulation algorithms deal with the implementation layer, and the computational platform contends with technical levels.

Yilmaz [11] formulates the requirements for contextualized introspective simulation models to address the fact that models are driven by intent when they are created. Yilmaz suggests that this intent is the basis for the purposeful abstraction of reality resulting in the model, which is implemented by the simulation system. If the intent differs too much, the models cannot be aligned. Similarly, Hofmann [12] identified the need to capture the intent of a simulation application in a communicable layer as a conceptual model independent from its implementation.

In summary, there are three main challenges to applying the Internet for M&S as an enabler:

- *Migration:* existing solutions must migrate to this new infrastructure. In order to use the Internet as the backbone for advanced distributed simulation, the migration to supporting protocols and standards must be easy and supported by commercial products.

- *Alignment:* the information exchange must be unambiguously defined to ensure the correct data interpretation and use within the participating system and/or services.

- *Orchestration:* the execution of the distributed simulation systems must be choreographed and observed, and it must be ensured that all relevant cause-effect chains are executed in the right order.

All three aspects must be supported for the composition of models, the interoperability of implementing simulation systems, and the technical layers used for the execution. The Levels of Conceptual Interoperability Model (LCIM) was introduced to answer the question, what additional support is needed from the Internet to support these efforts effectively?

3. The Levels of Conceptual Interoperability Model

The LCIM evolved from observations and results of several composability and interoperability efforts, going back to the beginnings of the High Level Architecture [9]. During a NATO M&S Conference on High Level Architecture applications, Judith Dahmann introduced the idea of distinguishing between substantive and technical interoperability [13]. In his research on composability, Mikel Petty enhanced this idea [14]. He distinguished between the implemented model and the underlying layers for protocols (such as the IEEE1516 protocols), the communication layers, and hardware. Realizing the need to explicitly address the conceptual layer, Tolk and Muguira published the first version of the LCIM in [15]. The discussions initiated by [15], in particular the work of Page et al. [5] and

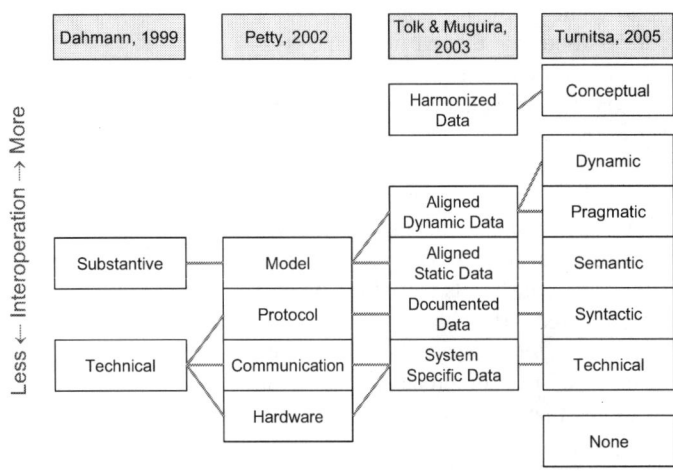

Figure 1: Evolution of Layered Interoperability Models

Hofmann [12], resulted in the currently used version, first published by Turnitsa [16]. Figure 1 shows the development.

The current version of the LCIM distinguishes eight layers, starting with stand-alone systems. The underlying approach was driven by bottom-up ideas.

- Level 0: Stand-alone systems have *No Interoperability*.

- Level 1: On the level of *Technical Interoperability*, a communication protocol exists for exchanging data between participating systems. On this level, a communication infrastructure is established allowing exchanging bits and bytes, the underlying networks and communication protocols are unambiguously defined.

- Level 2: The *Syntactic Interoperability* level introduces a common structure to exchange information, i.e., a common data format is applied. On this level, a common protocol to structure the data is used; the format of the information exchange is unambiguously defined.

- Level 3: If a common information exchange reference model is used, the level of *Semantic Interoperability* is reached. On this level, the meaning of the data is shared; the content of the information exchange requests are unambiguously defined.

- Level 4: *Pragmatic* Interoperability is reached when the interoperating systems are aware of the methods and procedures that each other are employing. In other words, the use of the data – or the context of its application – is understood by the participating systems; the context in which the information is exchanged is unambiguously defined.

- Level 5: As a system operates on data over time, the state of that system will change, and this includes the assumptions and constraints that affect its data interchange. If systems have attained *Dynamic Interoperability*, then they are able to comprehend the state changes that occur in the assumptions and constraints that each other is making over time, and are able to take advantage of those changes; the effect of the information exchange within the participating systems is unambiguously defined.

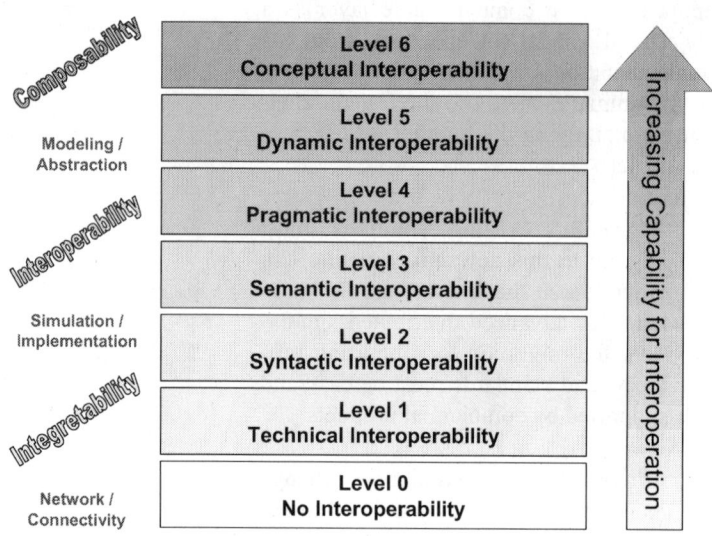

Figure 2: Levels of Conceptual Interoperability Model

- Level 6: Finally, if the conceptual model – i.e. the assumptions and constraints of the purposeful abstraction of reality – are aligned, the highest level of interoperability is reached: *Conceptual Interoperability*. This requires that conceptual models will be documented based on engineering methods enabling their interpretation and evaluation by other engineers. In other words, on this we need a "fully specified but implementation independent model" as requested in Davis and Anderson [17] and not just a text describing the conceptual idea.

Figure 2 shows the current LCIM including the relation to the ideas described in Page et al. [5], and showing the layers for modeling/abstraction, simulation/implementation, and network/connectivity.

4. The Dynamic Web: A Web of Composable Services

The Semantic Web initiative described in [4] changes the Internet by transforming it from a web of documents into a web of data. Daconta et al. identify multiple layers for the support of unambiguous information exchange, which they call the Ontology Spectrum, reaching from weal semantics to strong semantics.

- *Taxonomies* ensure the syntactic interoperability. Taxonomy is a semantic hierarchy, a partially ordered set. The main purpose is the classification of terms.

- *Thesauri* ensure structural interoperability. Thesaurus is a controlled vocabulary arranged in a known order and structured so that equivalence, homographic, hierarchical, and associative relationships among terms are displayed clearly and identified by standardized relationship indicators. The main purpose is the classification of relations of defined terms with each other.

- *Conceptual Models* as defined in [4] target the semantic interoperability. These models seek to model a portion of a domain to which a system must perform work by providing users with the type of functionality they require in that domain. They are closely connected to *Logical Theory*. In order to ensure strong semantics, frame-based or axiomatic logical theories are needed. The main purpose is machine-interpretability of description, which is more than machine processing of information.

This ontology spectrum can help to ensure that data exchanged can be unambiguously defined, but this is only sufficient for levels up to semantic interoperability in the LCIM. The data must also be exchanged and the systems orchestrated. The currently used implementing technology for this task is the use of web services.

The fundamental idea behind web services is integration of software applications as services within a service-oriented architecture. The concept represents a defined set of industry supported open standard technologies that work together to facilitate interoperability between heterogeneous systems, whether within an organization or across the Internet. In other words, web services can web-enable applications to communicate with other applications according to web services standards. This is potentially a tremendous opportunity to build bridges between legacy stove-piped developed systems. At its core, web services are another approach to distributed-computing with application resources provided over networks using standard technologies. Because web services are based on standard interfaces, they can communicate even if running on different operating systems and being written in different languages. They are widely supported by industry and already successfully applied in a wide range of different domains. For this reason they are a valuable approach to building distributed applications that must incorporate diverse systems over a network.

Web Services, as seen within the actual M&S research, are a set of operations, modular and independent applications that can be published, discovered, and invoked by using industrial standard protocols, such as Simple Object Access Protocol (SOAP), Web Service Description Language (WSDL) and Universal Distribution Discovery and Interoperability (UDDI). However, it should be noted that WSDL is not sufficient to describe M&S services, as pointed out in the recent report of the Extensible M&S Framework (XMSF) Group [18], which evaluated the applicability in detail. The use of web services is a distributed computing model that represents the interaction between program and program, instead the interaction between program and user, yet is part of the "web of data" idea. Web services can also be defined as discrete web-based applications that interact dynamically with other web services. In order to make this happen, several sub-functions are necessary, namely

- providing self-description of the service functionality,
- publishing the service descriptions using a standardized format,
- locating the service with the required functionality,
- establishing Communications with the service,
- requesting the required data to initiate the service, and
- exchanging data with other web services, including delivering the results.

The web service vision contends that services will work together seamlessly because they are developed by the same standards for self-description, publication, location, communication, invocation, and data exchange capabilities. As all the standards concerned are open, the technologies chosen for web services are inherently neutral to compatibility issues that exist between programming languages, middleware solutions, and operating platforms. As a result, applications using web services can dynamically locate and use necessary functionality – whether available locally or from across the Internet.

The studies conducted by the XMSF group [18] show the potential of web services in combination with the technologies defined in the ontology spectrum of [4]. Nonetheless, even a combination only satisfies the levels up to pragmatic interoperability: basic web standards, such as the Internet Protocol (IP), take care of the technical layers; the ontology spectrum supports the following levels up to semantic interoperability; and, the XML definitions of WSDL identify the methods and procedures that can be used. How to apply these ideas that enable XMSF based mediation services to translate dynamically between different dialects has been shown in [19, 20].

The next step of related research must focus on the dynamic and conceptual interoperability. Several ideas are currently evaluated. One of them is the use of OMG's Model Driven Architecture (MDA) [21]. For some M&S related ideas see [22]. The MDA defines three levels of abstraction used to describe systems and services. These models are Computation Independent Model (CIM), Platform Independent Model (PIM), and Platform Specific Model (PSM). To document these artifacts, MDA uses the following standards: the Meta-Object Facility (MOF), the Unified Modeling Language (UML), and the XML Metadata Interchange (XMI). Specifically, the community is evaluating the use of UML and capturing the information using XMI to generate the necessary metadata [23]. The relation of MDA and ontology is captured in [24]; the application of MDA for web services is described in [25]. Xie et al. [26] generalize these ideas, including the earlier version of the LCIM [15], for grid computing applications. Some examples for the military domain on applying these principles are given in Morse et al. [27].

A final domain directly related to the topic of this paper is the choreography and composition of web services, as these results are directly applicable to supporting standards for dynamic interoperability. Srivastava and Koehler conclude in their overview on current solutions for web service composability that the functionality of a web service needs to be described with additional pieces of information, either by a semantic annotation of what it does or by a functional annotation of its behavior [28]. Furthermore, they show that current solutions based on the Resource Description Framework (RDF) or the

Business Process Execution Language for Web Services (BPEL4WS) are not sufficient. Tosic et al. come to similar conclusions in [29]. Lopes and Hammoudi describe how the use of CIM, PIM, and PSM could support the composition of web services [25]. Alternatively, concepts such as the Web Service Conversation Language (WSCL) could enable services to negotiate their composition, as discussed in Banerji et al. [30]. However, in order to support such negotiations, a semantically rich environment for orchestration is needed. Agerval et al. summarize similar results and recommend a framework to represent the underlying concepts in the form of a common ontology [31].

In summary, all evaluated reports are pointing towards the necessity of capturing the meaning of services in order to compose them correctly. Technically, the composition of web service is solved, but the challenge remains to connect only functions being conceptually compatible with each other. As stated earlier, substantive interoperability on the implementation level requires composability of models on the abstraction level.

5. Principles of Advanced Distributed Simulation Implications for the Dynamic Web

In order to support M&S application, a web of composable services is needed. What layers of interoperation are needed for such a dynamic web has been derived from the LCIM: technical, syntactic, semantic, pragmatic, dynamic, and conceptual.

In summary, the technical layer of the LCIM is well covered by applicable standards. The current work on the semantic web is primarily focusing on unambiguity of exchanged data. As such, the levels of syntactic and semantic interoperability are supported.

Current research focuses on pragmatic and dynamic layers capturing the use of data and information within the system. The research on composition of web services contributes to recommendations for metadata and standards capturing the result in machine-interpretable form.

Nonetheless, M&S is a special domain, because the modeling part of M&S creates a *purposeful abstraction of reality* as the basis for the simulation implementation. In order to enable composable M&S services, conceptual models based on engineering methods are required that capture the assumptions and constraints. While the layers below the conceptual level cope with what we model in detail, only the conceptual level can express what we exclude from a model. For substantial interoperability, this information is as important as how the simulation system itself works. Even many established methods, such as DEVS [32] or completely UML documented models, fall short in this respect; they only document WHAT and HOW something is implemented, but not what has been cut in the process of purposeful abstracting the domain. Some first ideas on how to cope with this challenge are considered in [33], but this is just a start.

The special challenges of M&S applications must be met and captured in standards for the Dynamic Web. Among these topics requiring research are

- Migration of existing solutions and capturing their assumption and constraints in standardized metadata;

- Alignment of Data, in particular solving the issues of standardized description of scope and resolution, which includes the domain of aggregation and disaggregation of data between different levels of resolution [34];

- Orchestration of M&S service execution, including the domain specific aspect of time-management, such as described in [35].

Another important aspect not dealt with in the necessary detail so far is the topic of how to use bottom-up driven ontologies – such as described in the approach of this paper – and top-down driven ontologies – such as described by Sousa-Pousa in [36] – are two sides of one medallion. The research group around the author is convinced that both approaches are necessary and should be aligned, as sketched in [33]. How this should be done, however, is topic of ongoing research.

After focusing successfully for decades on solving the simulation challenges of PADS, it is now time to seriously think about standardization requirements and engineering-driven solutions for the modeling side of M&S. The community needs to agree on how to capture assumption and constraints so that intelligent software applications, such as intelligent software agents, can understand the assumptions and use this knowledge to compose services in support of the immediate needs of users. This will be beneficial in particular when they use operational systems supporting the ideas of service-oriented architectures, such as the Global Information Grid (GIG) currently envisioned by the US Department of Defense [37].

References

[1] *IEEE Proceedings of the 1998 International Conference on Web-based Modeling & Simulation,* January 1998, Catamaran Resort Hotel, San Diego, California, Part of the 1998 SCS Western Multi-Conference on Computer Simulation

[2] Tilley, S., Gerdes, J., Hamilton, T., Huang, S., Muller, H., and Wong K. (2002). "Adoption Challenges in Migrating to Web Services." *Proceedings Fourth International Workshop on Web Site Evolution* (WSE02)

[3] Pullen, J.M., Brunton, R., Brutzman, D.P., Drake, D., Hieb, M.R., Morse, K.L., and Tolk, A. (2004). "Using Web Services to Integrate Heterogeneous Simulations in a Grid Environment." *Proceedings International Conference on Computational Science* 2004: 835-847

[4] Daconta, M., Obrst, L., and Smith, K. (2003). *The Semantic Web: The Future of XML, Web Services, and Knowledge Management.* John Wiley, Inc.

[5] Page, E.H., Briggs, R., and Tufarolo, J.A. (2004). "Toward a Family of Maturity Models for the Simulation Interconnection Problem." *Proceedings IEEE Spring Simulation Interoperability Workshop,* IEEE CS Press

[6] Petty, M.D., and Weisel, E.W. (2003). "A Composability Lexicon." *Proceedings Spring Simulation Interoperability Workshop,* IEEE CS Press

[7] Simulation Interoperability Standards Organization (SISO) / Society for Modeling and Simulation (SCS) Panel Discussion on Priorities for M&S Standards; *IEEE Spring Simulation Interoperability Workshop* in Orlando, Florida, March 2003.

[8] IEEE Standard Group 1278: *Distributed Interactive Simulation* (Revision 2002)

[9] IEEE Standard Group 1516: *High Level Architecture* (Revision 2000)

[10] Sarjoughian, H.S., Zeigler, B.P., and Hall, S.B. (2001). "A Layered Modeling and Simulation Architecture for Agent-Based System Development." *IEEE Proceedings,* 89 (2), pp. 201-213

[11] Yilmaz, L. (2004). "On the Need for Contextualized Introspective Simulation Models to Improve Reuse and Composability of Defense Simulations." *Journal of Defense Modeling and Simulation* 1 (3): 135-145

[12] Hofmann, M. (2004). "Challenges of Model Interoperation in Military Simulations." *SIMULATION,* Vol. 80, pp. 659-667

[13] Dahmann, J.S. (1999). "High Level Architecture Interoperability Challenges." Presentation at the *NATO Modeling & Simulation Conference,* Norfolk VA, October 1999, NATO RTA Publications

[14] Petty, M.D. (2002). "Interoperability and Composability." *Modeling & Simulation Curriculum* of Old Dominion University, Old Dominion University

[15] Tolk, A., and Muguira, J.A. (2003). "The Levels of Conceptual Interoperability Model (LCIM)." *Proceedings IEEE Fall Simulation Interoperability Workshop,* IEEE CS Press

[16] Turnitsa, C.D. (2005). "Extending the Levels of Conceptual Interoperability Model." *Proceedings IEEE Summer Computer Simulation Conference,* IEEE CS Press

[17] Davis, P.K., and Anderson, R.H. (2003). *Improving the Composability of Department of Defense Models and Simulations.* RAND Corporation

[18] Blais, C.L., Brutzman, D.P., Drake, D., Moen, D., Morse, K.L., Pullen, J.M., and Tolk, A. (2005). *Extensible Modeling and Simulation Framework (XMSF) 2004 Project Summary Report.* NPS-MV-05-002, Naval Postgraduate School, Monterey, CA

[19] Tolk, A. (2004). "XML Mediation Services utilizing Model Based Data Management." *IEEE Proceedings of the 2004 Winter Simulation Conference,* IEEE 04CH37614C, pp. 1476-1484

[20] Tolk, A., and Diallo, S.Y. (2005). "Model-Based Data Engineering for Web Services." *IEEE Internet Computing,* Vol. 9, Nr. 4, 2005

[21] Object Management Group (OMG) (2005). *Model Driven Architecture (MDA) Resource Page* at http://www.mda.org

[22] Tolk, A., and Muguira, J.A. (2004). "M&S within the Model Driven Architecture." *Proceedings Interservice/Industry Training, Simulation, and Education Conference (I/ITSEC)*

[23] Morse, K.L. (Chair). (2005). *XMSF Profile Study Group Final Report.* SISO-REF-014-2005, Proceedings IEEE Fall Simulation Interoperability Workshop, IEEE CS Press

[24] Arpinar, B., Zhang, R., Aleman-Meza, B., and Maduko, A. (2005). "Ontology-driven Web services composition platform." *Journal on Information Systems and E-Business Management* 3 (2): 175 - 199

[25] Lopes, D., and Hammoudi, S. (2003). "Web Services in the Context of MDA." *Proceedings International Conference on Web Services,* IEEE CS Press

[26] Xie, Y., Teo, Y.M., Cai, W. and Turner S.J. (2005). "Towards Grid-Wide Modeling and Simulation." Sin-

gapore-MIT Alliance (SMA). *Computer Science*, MIT Libraries

[27] Morse, K.L., Drake, D., and Brunton, R. (2004). "Web Enabling HLA Compliant Simulations to Support Network Centric Applications." *Proceedings of the 2004 Symposium on Command and Control Research and Technology,* San Diego, CA, 2004

[28] Srivastava, B., and Koehler, J. (2003). "Web Service Composition - Current Solutions and Open Problems." *Proceedings ICAPS 2003 Workshop on Planning for Web Services*

[29] Tosic, V., Pagurek, B., Esfandiari, B., and Patel, K. (2001). "On the Management of Compositions of Web Services." *Proceedings Object-Oriented Web Services (OOPSLA 2001)*

[30] Banerji, A., Bartolini, C., Beringer, D., Chopella, V., Govindarajan, K., Karp, A., Kuno, H., Lemon, M., Pogossiants, G., Sharma, S., and Williams, S. (2002). *Web Services Conversation Language (WSCL).* W3C Note Mar 2002

[31] Agarwal, S., Handschuh, S., and Staab, S. (2005). "Annotation, Composition and Invocation of Semantic Web Services." *Journal on Web Semantics* 2 (1): 1-24

[32] Zeigler, B.P., Praehofer, H., and Kim, T.G. (2000). *Theory of Modeling and Simulation.* 2nd Edition, Academic Press

[33] Tolk, A., Turnitsa, C.D., and Diallo, S.Y. (2006). "Ontological Implications of the Levels of Conceptual Interoperability Model." *Proceedings of WMSCI 2006,* IEEE Press

[34] Tan, G., Ngee Ng, W., and Moradi, F. (2001). "Aggregation/Disaggregation in HLA Multi-Resolution Distributed Simulation," *Proceedings 5th IEEE International Workshop on Distributed Simulation and Real-Time Applications (DS-RT),* p. 76 ff., IEEE CS press

[35] Fujimoto, R. (2001). "On-Line Simulation Techniques for Real-Time Management of Systems." *Proceedings 9th International Symposium on Modeling, Analysis and Simulation of Computer and Telecommunication Systems*

[36] A.A. Sousa-Poza, A.A. (2005) "Pragmatic Idealism as the Basis for Understanding." *Proceedings of the International Conference on Systems, Man and Cybernetics,* IEEE Press

[37] Tolk, A. (2005). "An Agent-based Decision Support System Architecture for the Military Domain." In G.E. Phillips-Wren and L.C. Jain (Eds.), *Intelligent Decision Support Systems in Agent-Mediated Environments*, Volume 115 Frontiers in Artificial Intelligence and Applications, IOS Press

Principles of Advanced and Distributed Simulation

Session 4: Advanced Techniques and Applications

SOAr-DSGrid: Service-Oriented Architecture for Distributed Simulation on the Grid

Xinjun Chen, Wentong Cai, Stephen J. Turner, and Yong Wang
Parallel and Distributed Computing Center
School of Computer Engineering
Nanyang Technological University
Singapore 639798
{chen0081, aswtcai, assjturner, wang0065}@ntu.edu.sg

Abstract

Simulation is a low cost alternative to experimentation on real-world physical systems. Grid technology enables coordinated use of and secure access to distributed computing resources and data sources. The service-oriented architecture (SOA) is an ideal paradigm for next generation computing. The loose coupling among services in the SOA relieves service consumers from detailed knowledge of implementation, implementation language, and execution platform of the services to be consumed. In this paper, we propose a framework for developing a component-based distributed simulation and executing the simulation in a service-oriented architecture on the Grid. This framework consists of the schemas for developing simulation components and simulation applications, and underlying base component service modules for constructing a simulation component as a service. The use of component interfaces and schemas enables collaborative development of simulation applications, and the deployment of simulation components as services takes advantage of the SOA (e.g., loose coupling, heterogeneity, and transport neutrality). This paper discusses the motivation for developing such a framework and describes the details of its development.

1. Introduction

Simulation permeates many areas such as production, business, education, and science and engineering. It is a low cost alternative to experimentation on real-world physical systems. With the advance of computer networks and prevalence of low-cost commodity computers, distributed simulation becomes a favorable technology to reduce simulation time, to enable the execution of simulation components at different geographical locations, and to increase fault tolerance [8]. The High Level Architecture (HLA) for Modeling and Simulation (M&S) [13], the standard for distributed simulation, has been approved by US DoD and standardized as IEEE 1516. It facilitates interoperability among simulations and promotes reuse of simulation components (i.e., federates in HLA's terminology). Federates communicate with each other through the Runtime Infrastructure (RTI), which provides the implementation of the HLA standards.

Grid computing was proposed by Ian Foster as secure and coordinated resource sharing and problem solving in dynamic, multi-institutional virtual organizations [6]. Grid technology enables coordinated use of geographically distributed computing resources and facilitates access to geographically distributed data sources. The Globus Toolkit has become the de facto standard platform for Grid computing. The advantages of Globus middleware lie in its functionalities which are defined in Open Grid Services Architecture (OGSA) [7], such as resource management, data management, service discovery, security, service lifecycle, and notification. The latest Globus Toolkit version 4 (GT4) [11] implements Web Service Resource Framework (WSRF) [15] and Web Service Notification (WSN), and utilizes Web Service Addressing (WS-Addressing).

The early work on executing HLA-based distributed simulation on the Grid [4, 17, 18] aims to take advantages of both Grid computing middleware (e.g., Globus Toolkit) and the HLA/RTI. The Grid middleware is employed to perform the task of resource management (including scheduling, load-balancing and monitoring), coordination of simulation execution, and security. The HLA/RTI is used to perform simulation related tasks such as synchronization, time management and data distribution management. However, the dependency on the HLA/RTI requires that the simulation component developers must have a profound knowledge and skill of HLA/RTI programming and that the execution of the simulation federation must follow the conventions of the HLA/RTI. In addition, the simple integration of the Grid middleware and the HLA/RTI cannot fully exploit the benefits brought by the Service Oriented Architecture (SOA). Under the SOA, simulation components are loosely coupled. They can be discovered and composed to form a simulation application. Components can be deployed to heterogeneous resources and communicate via standard SOAP messages . But, how they communicate (i.e., the underlying transport layer protocol) need not be fixed till deployment.

To make natural progress over the work we have done and to address the problems mentioned above, in this paper we propose a Service Oriented Architecture for executing Distributed Simulation on the Grid: SOAr-DSGrid. In this architecture, different views are presented for the simulation development and simulation execution. The component-based view is used in the simulation development. To expose the operations implemented in a simulation component and to facilitate the composition of a simulation, schemas are defined for the component developers to publish component interfaces and for the simulation application developers to describe the constituent components and their interactions in a simulation.

The service-oriented view is presented during the simulation execution. Each simulation component is implemented as a GT4 service by extending some base component service modules. To hide the details of service and simulation management implementation, the base component service modules provide the underlying simulation management such as event scheduling and time advancement in addition to the basic service implementations. Component services communicate with each other through pre-defined service interfaces and they are configured according to the component interactions specified in the simulation description.

The separation of component interface from service interface makes the development of a component as a service easier. Component providers just need to describe the operations of a component using the component interface schema and implement the component operations accordingly. They do not need to worry about how a service is implemented, how a service interface is defined, and how services communicate with each other. Simulation application developers can then use the component interfaces and simulation description schema to compose a simulation application. They do not need to worry about how the component services are located and how they are deployed and invoked.

The use of component schema and the simulation description schema enables collaborative development of simulation applications, and the deployment of simulation components as services takes advantage of the SOA (e.g., loose coupling, heterogeneity, and transport neutrality). Using the component-based view, a simulation application developer can search for the required simulation components, and describe the composition of the components. Under our service-oriented architecture, simulation component services can be dynamically deployed to the heterogeneous resources and communicate via various transport layer protocols. They work in a peer-to-peer manner: a component service can be a service provider and a service consumer at the same time.

The rest of this paper is organized as follows: Section 2 describes related work on service-oriented architecture, composition, and distributed simulation on the Grid. In Section 3, we present the system architecture and components of SOAr-DSGrid. Section 4 details the interfaces and schemas in the framework. Section 5 explains the component development and application development, component runtime, and the organizer. We conclude the paper and look into future work in Section 6.

2. Background and related work

The Service Oriented Architecture (SOA) evolves from component technology such as DCOM and CORBA. It reorganizes software applications into a set of interacting services, each accessible through a standard interface (e.g., WSDL) and messages (e.g., SOAP). The most significant advantage of the SOA is the loose coupling among services. The consumer of a service is not required to have a detailed knowledge of implementation, implementation language, or execution platform of the service. The only concern of the consumer is how a service can be invoked according to the service interface. Exposing applications as services enables reuse of applications. Standards (e.g., WSDL, SOAP, and WS-I basic profile) ensure interoperability between services. Low dependency between loosely coupled services improves the scalability of a system. However, the basic SOA lacks support for simulation management, service orchestration, and security. Although GT4 incorporates comprehensive security mechanisms, it does not solve the problem of service orchestration, nor does it provide simulation management.

Composition can be categorized into composition in time and composition in space [14]. Composition in time, commonly known as workflow, specifies a series of tasks to be executed in a logical sequence. Composition in space refers to the inherent relationship between components. In this kind of composition, the services are composed based on their intrinsic properties (e.g., compatible ports), and independent of execution order.

In the web service community, various specifications are proposed to address the service composition (or orchestration). WSFL and XLANG are earlier work from IBM and Microsoft respectively. They are no longer active and are superseded by BPEL4WS [2]. These workflow specifications, in general, address only composition in time.

Indiana University's XCAT [1, 5, 12, 14] supports both composition in time and composition in space. Krakow's Application Flow Composer (AFC) [3] is a component-based system for Grid workflow composition based on CCA technology [5]. The contribution of AFC lies in its capability of reading incomplete application information and generating a complete description of a Grid application.

We cannot directly adopt BPEL4WS, XCAT or AFC for the following reasons. BPEL4WS was developed for stateless web services; whereas our simulation components are implemented as GT4 services. In addition, composition in space, rather than composition in time, is more appropriate to specify the composition of simulation components. Although XCAT and AFC provide support for composition in space and can be used to develop Grid workflow compositions, they do not address our requirements. They do not provide any simulation oriented services and they compose the components according to their service interfaces exposed. In our architecture, component interfaces are used in the composition. Simulation components are implemented as services. The simulation service interfaces are meant for communication between simulation component services. They are different from the component interfaces and are not exposed to the simulation application developers.

All of our previous work on the execution of distributed simulation over the Grid are based on the HLA/RTI [4, 16, 17, 19]. In [4], we described a Load Management System (LMS), implemented on top of GT2, to manage and coordinate geographically distributed resources for HLA-based simulation. The LMS has a resource management subsystem to acquire resource information, and a job management subsystem to monitor job execution and to perform load balancing. A federate migration algorithm was described in [17]. Our recent work based on GT3 was reported in [16] and [19]. We implemented a Federate-Proxy-RTI framework called HLAGrid [16]. Under this framework, simulation application developers develop simulation federates using the HLA/RTI interface as usual. But, the federate code is compiled with the HLAGrid library instead. Federates run on the resources at the client site, and proxies and the RTI, running on the resources available over the Grid, provide a backbone to support distributed simulation. There is one proxy for each federate and HLAGrid relays the federate initiated and RTI initiated services between federates and proxies. This framework provides the federate developer with a familiar interface and decouples the execution of simulation federates and the backbone that provides distributed simulation services. Apart from the benefits from the Grid, the framework also supports secure execution of simulation federate, flexibility and heterogeneity [16]. To support the execution of large-scale HLA-based distributed simulations over the Grid, we also developed federate factory services to dynamically map Grid services to computing resources and a centralized index service to support dynamic discovery of federation and federates [19].

The architecture described in this paper differs from our previous work in the following aspects (as discussed in Section 1): a component-based view is provided to the component and simulation application developers; whereas a service-oriented view is adopted in the execution of simulation components. To fully exploit the advantages of the SOA, instead of using the HLA/RTI, we integrate simulation execution (e.g., time management) as part of a component service.

3. Architecture overview

As shown in Figure 1, there are five roles in the architecture: the component provider (i.e., simulation component developer), the client (i.e., the simulation application developer), the repository, the organizer, and the index service. The component provider develops simulation components. The client builds simulation applications.

The repository stores the relevant files including component interface files, entity type files, and rule type files. Component interface files and entity type files which contain descriptive information about components and entities, are used during the development of a simulation application.

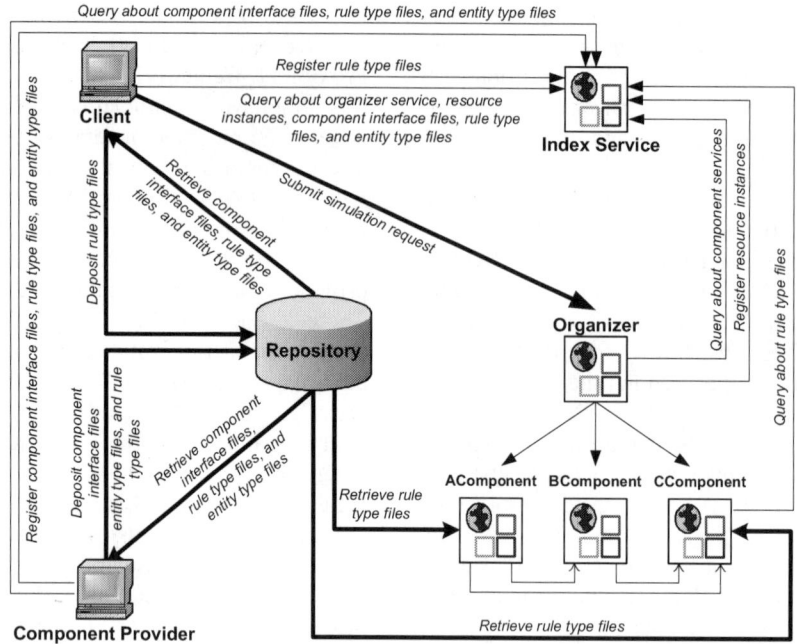

Figure 1. SOAr-DSGrid architecture overview

A rule type file, which provides rule logic to determine the target simulation operation or next component, is retrieved and used at runtime. They will be further explained in Section 4.

In this service-oriented architecture, the organizer, the index service, and every simulation component are implemented as GT4 services. The organizer acts as an agent to the client. It receives simulation description files submitted by the client, executes the simulation application, and returns the simulation results to the client. A centralized index service provides directory information on components, component interface files, entity type files, and rule type files. This directory information is required for component development and application development.

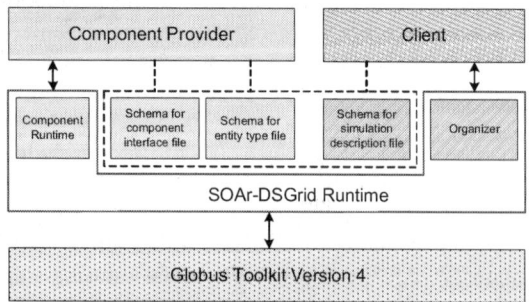

Figure 2. Layered structure of SOAr-DSGrid

Figure 2 illustrates the layered structure of the entire framework. SOAr-DSGrid is a layer residing between the users and GT4. The parts contained in the dotted box in the middle represent the schemas provided to the component providers and clients. The solid parts are used by the component providers, and the striped parts are used by the clients. The details about the interfaces and schemas are covered in Section 4. Other parts in the middle layer form the SOAr-DSGrid runtime. The component runtime includes base modules for generating simulation component services and tools for configuring and deploying component services. Section 5 elaborates the component runtime and addresses the issue of how the runtime links to the interfaces.

4. Interfaces and schemas

A simulation scenario used in SOAr-DSGrid is depicted in Figure 3. A simulation *component* processes certain types of *entities*. An entity is associated with a set of *attributes* (e.g., a1). A component has a set of *public variables* (e.g., v2) and *private variables*. Public variables are also referred to as *shared variables*, as they can be read by other components. There are two types of private variables: one receives setup values at component initialization time (e.g., v3); the other is internal to the component with no setup values (e.g., v1).

A simulation component (e.g., CA) starts simulating by receiving a processible entity (e.g., e1). It processes the entity by updating the attributes of the entity and/or variables of itself. It can also generate new entities (e.g., e2). It then routes the processed or generated entity to one of the possible next components based on the *routing rule* (e.g., r1).

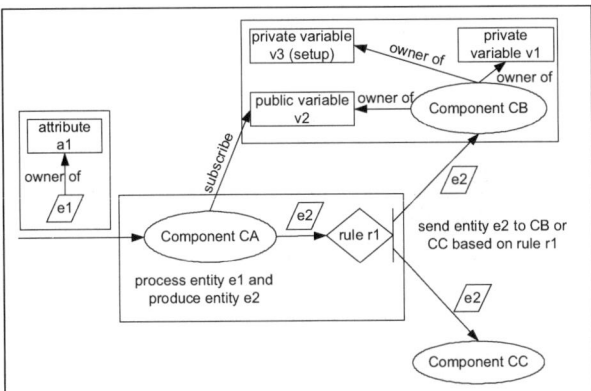

Figure 3. Definitions and relationships

The component interface file is defined by the component provider and is used during the development of a simulation application. The clients refer to these files to determine whether the corresponding component is suitable for building a specific simulation application.

The component interface contains information about variables, operations, and the entity types involved. Figure 4 is the pictorial representation of the component interface schema.

Clients develop simulation applications using the schema for simulation description files. As depicted in Figure 5, the schema requires clients to specify the participating component instances involved in a simulation application with relevant setup values. The entity flows, variable flows, operation rules and routing rules, and simulation results to be collected are also specified.

An entity flow comprises a set of entity links. Each entity link denotes a set of possible routes from one source component to a set of target components. Routing rules are used by the source component to determine the specific target component at runtime. A variable flow specifies one publisher component and a set of subscriber components. Simulation results are values of specified variables of participating component instances returned at the end of a simulation session.

The main features of the design are summarized as follows. First, a component does not invoke another component's simulation operation directly. Components are linked with each other through entity and variable flows. For components with multiple operations, operation rules are used to determine which operation should be performed on a received entity.

Second, unlike conventional workflow which requires the client to define a static route, SOAr-DSGrid allows the client to specify multiple possible routes for an entity during application development, and the exact route is determined automatically at runtime according to the routing rules prescribed. Third, the routing of entities is determined by an individual component without the need of a centralized component.

5. Simulation development and runtime support

The operations defined in the component interface will be implemented as component-specific operations in the component service. These operations are internal to a component service. In addition to the component-specific operations, a component service also implements a set of common service operations. These are the operations defined in the corresponding WSDL file and are exposed to other component services.

5.1. Component development

As described in Section 1, the component development and application development use the component-based view. Figure 6 shows the sequence diagram that illustrates the process of developing a simulation component. To develop a simulation component, a component provider first writes a component interface file using the component interface schema shown in Figure 4. New entity type files are defined if the simulation logic in the component involves new types of entities. If the simulation component contains multiple operations and the necessary rule type files are not available, new rule type files will be defined by the component provider. Subsequently, the component developer implements each operation defined in the component interface as a class. After that, the component provider requests the SOAr-DSGrid's service generator to generate a GT4 service corresponding to the component specified. The service generator takes in the simulation operation classes and entity type files, combines them with some predefined base component service modules, and creates the code of a component service. The service generator also builds and deploys the service on behalf of the component provider. Finally, the component provider deposits the component interface files and entity type files into the repository, and registers them with the index service.

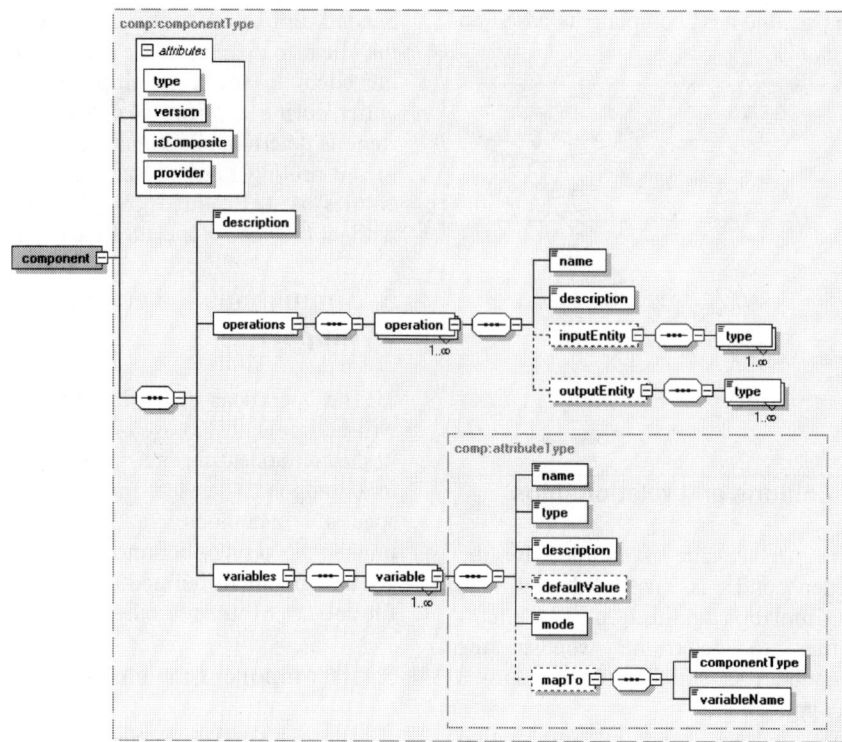

Figure 4. Component interface schema

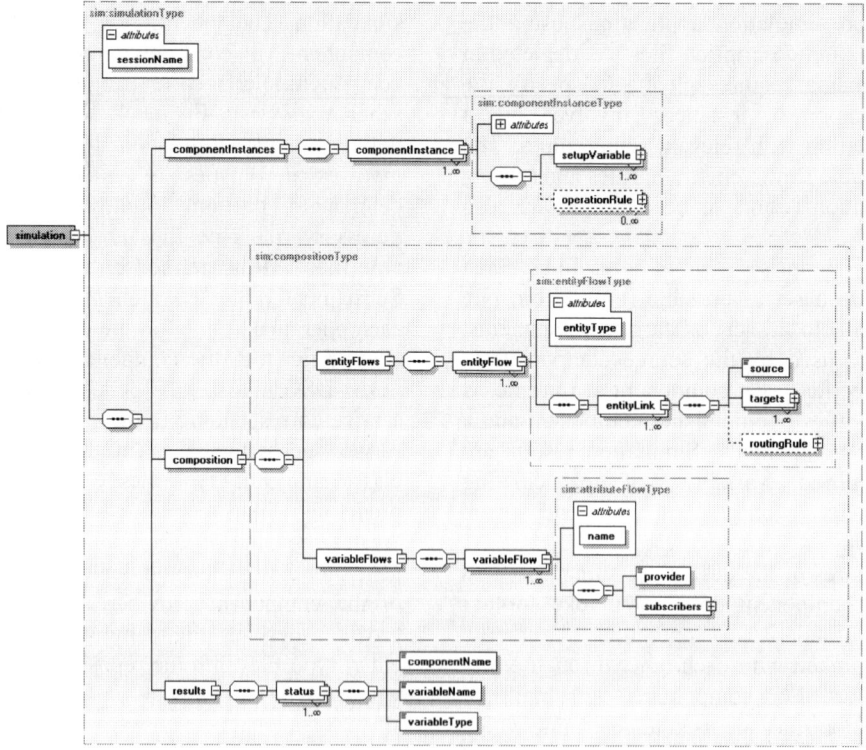

Figure 5. Schema for simulation description files

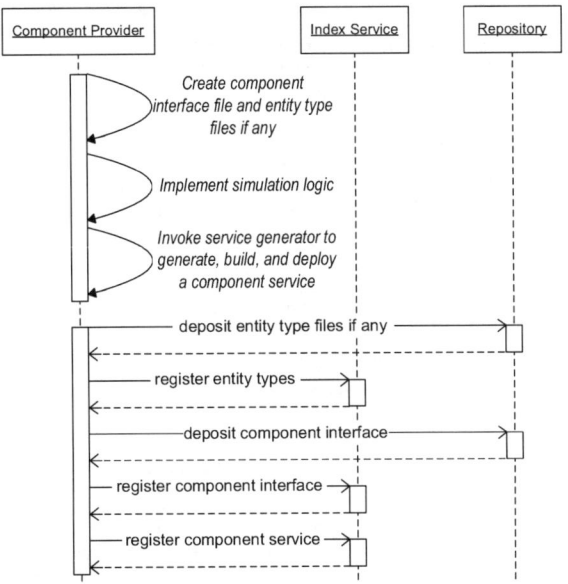

Figure 6. Implementing a simulation component

During the entire process of component development, the component provider only deals with the component interface file definition, component operations implementation, entity type files definition, and rule type files definition. The advantages of this design are obvious. The component providers are relieved from not only simulation management (e.g., time management an event scheduling) but also the complexity of service development and deployment.

As for the service generator, it combines the operations implementation with the base component service modules to generate a component service class. According to WSRF, a GT4 service also includes a resource class and a resource home class. The resource class includes both component-specific variables specified in the component interface file, and component-general variables that are common to all the component services. All component services have a similar resource home.

5.2. Simulation application development

The development of simulation applications is carried out by simulation application developers (or clients in SOAr-DSGrid terminology). As described in Section 1, a client builds an application in a component-based manner. He/She selects appropriate components by investigating published component interfaces. The directory information about the component interface files can be obtained through the index service. The client then builds a simulation description file according to the schema shown in Figure 5.

In the case where the simulation description file involves new rule types other than those available in the repository, the client creates new rule type files. The new rule type files will be deposited to the repository and registered with the index service (for reuse by other simulation application developers).

The execution of a simulation application is initiated by submitting the simulation description file to the organizer. The detailed runtime operation of the organizer is described in subsection 5.4.

As can be seen, if all the required simulation components could be found from the index service, the development of a simulation application is quite straightforward, as the client only needs to produce a correct simulation description file with necessary rule type files. The execution of a simulation application is handled by the organizer.

5.3. Component runtime

The component runtime (or the base component service modules) implements some component-general elements including input entity queue, output entity queue, output queue manager, message queue, message manager, time manager, and rule engine, as shown in Figure 7. The component manager, output queue manager, and message manager are active threads. The rule engine and time manager are passive objects invoked on demand. Common service operations (i.e., service interfaces) are defined to manipulate the input entity queue and message queue. At runtime, the output queue manager and message manager take the responsibility for the communication among components. SOAr-DSGrid packages all these common elements into a base component from which every component extends.

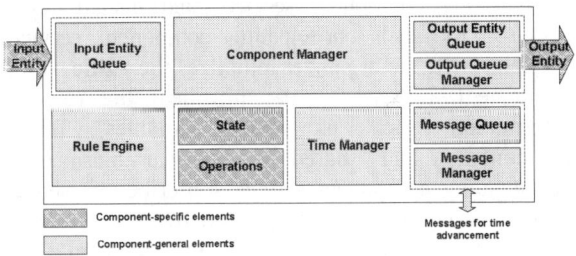

Figure 7. Component structure

A component service is activated by the organizer. The activation of a component service involves starting the three abovementioned threads. The component manager removes the first entity from the queue, and consults the rule engine to find the appropriate simulation operation to invoke. After processing the entity, the component manager invokes the time manager to advance simulation time. It also consults the rule engine to determine the next component for the processed entity. The processed entities are stored temporarily in the output entity queue, from which the output queue manager dispatches processed entities to their respective next components.

Time management is very important to the correct execution of distributed simulations. It is a great challenge especially when we implement the time management in a distributed manner like that in SOAr-DSGrid. We utilize an algorithm similar to that presented in [9] for time management. However, the use of shared variables in SOAr-DSGrid renders the safe time algorithm insufficient. Shared variables can be updated at any unexpected time. So, it is difficult to determine a lookahead for a component that has a shared variable. To implement the shared variables, we adopt an approach described in [10] and introduce a history list for each shared variable. To obtain the value of a shared variable, the consumer components *pull* the shared variable from the provider component.

5.4. Organizer

The organizer is the agent for the clients to execute simulation applications. It is a GT4 web service responsible for processing simulation description files. It initializes a simulation session, but does not intervene in the execution of simulation components.

The simulation initialization process is shown in Figure 8. Clients locate the existing organizer service by querying the index service. They create a resource instance (according to WSRF) for the organizer and submit a simulation request. The organizer parses the simulation description file and creates a simulation session accordingly.

The organizer queries location information of participating component services and instantiates a resource for each participating component service. Subsequently, the organizer initializes the participating component services by passing them the relevant information such as setup variables, linked components, and shared remote variables. Each participating component service subscribes its shared remote variables of the respective owners. If a rule type file is not available locally, it should be downloaded from the repository using the directory information obtained from the index service. After finishing all the setup procedures, the organizer activates all the participating component services to start simulation.

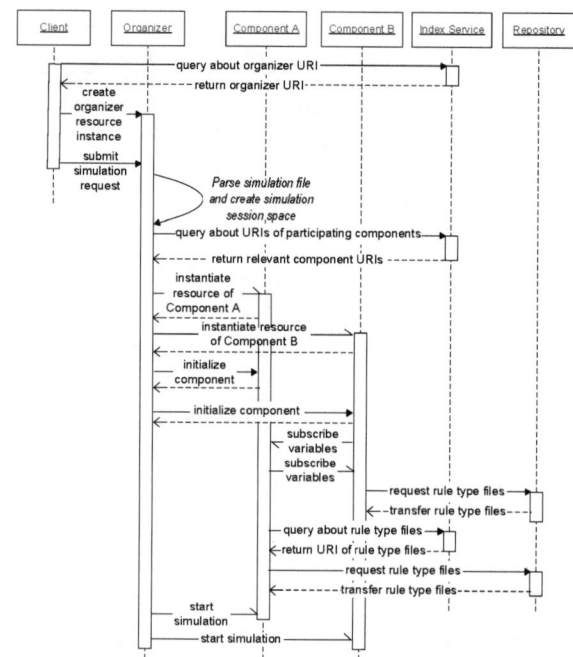

Figure 8. Simulation initialization

6. Conclusions and future work

This paper presents the SOAr-DSGrid, a service-oriented architecture for executing distributed simulation on the Grid. SOAr-DSGrid presents simulation component developers and simulation application developers with a component-based framework for ease of component development and simulation development. Its underlying runtime infrastructure uses a service-oriented architecture to ensure the interoperability between simulation components. In SOAr-DSGrid, every simulation component is exposed as a component conforming to a component interface schema, and implemented as a GT4 service. A simulation application is developed by creating a simulation description file using the simulation description schema. The execution of a simulation application is handled by the organizer. SOAr-DSGrid allows flexible dynamic service orchestration by employing rule type files and a rule engine. The runtime communication in SOAr-DSGrid is conducted in a peer-to-peer manner.

Performance is always a critical success factor to an architecture. From the results reported in [19], we note that the initial simulation setup cost is high. The performance improves when the workload increases. This also applies to SOAr-DSGrid. As discussed in subsection 5.4, when a client submits a simulation request to the organizer, the organizer parses the simulation description file, creates a simulation session for it, and initializes the simulation component services. As a result, the cost of the initialization process is comparatively high. However, the organizer does not intervene in the simulation execution after activating the simulation component services. The communications between simulation component services are in a fully distributed peer-to-peer manner. During runtime, there is no need to rediscover service endpoints and the runtime communication overhead will be mainly contributed by the time spent on generating and interpreting SOAP messages. Therefore, it is obvious that the greater the simulation workload, the better the performance will be.

To evaluate the performance of SOAr-DSGrid, a prototype of distributed simulation of wafer manufacturing will be developed. With the increase of simulation scale, the index service may need to be implemented in a distributed manner (e.g., one index service for each Virtual Organization). The time management may also need to be refined to effectively tackle the zero-lookahead issue. In addition, mechanisms will be developed to support hierarchical composition of simulation applications. Multi-level time management protocols will be investigated accordingly for the hierarchical composition.

7. References

[1] R. Armstrong, D. Gannon, A. Geist, K. Keahey, S. Kohn, L. McInnes, S. Parker, B. Smolinski, Toward a Common Component Architecture for High-Performance Scientific Computing, in *Proc. of High Performance Distributed Computing Conference*, 1999, pp.13-22.

[2] BPEL4WS, Business Process Execution Language for Web Services Version 1.1, http://www-128.ibm.com/developerworks/library/specification/ws-bpel/.

[3] M. Bubak, K. Gorka, T. Gubala, M. Malawski, K. Zajac, Component-based System for Grid Application Workflow Composition, in *Proc. of the 10th European PVM/MPI Users' Group Meeting*, 2003, pp.611-618.

[4] W. Cai, S. J. Turner, H. Zhao, A Load Management System for Running HLA-based Distributed Simulations over the Grid, in *Proc. of the 6th IEEE Intl. Symposium on Distributed Simulation and Real Time Application*, Oct 2002, pp.7-14.

[5] CCA, The Common Component Architecture Forum, http://www.cca-forum.org/glossary/index.html.

[6] I. Foster, C. Kesselman, S. Tuecke, The Anatomy of the Grid: Enabling Scalable Virtual Organizations, in *Intl. Journal of Supercomputing Applications*, 15(3), 2002, pp.200-222.

[7] I. Foster, H. Kishimoto, A. Savva, The Open Grid Service Architecture, Version 1.0, http://www.gridforum.org/documents/GWD-I-E/GFD-I.030.pdf.

[8] R. M. Fujimoto, Background and Applications - Why Parallel/Distributed Simulation, in *Parallel and Distributed Simulation Systems*, Wiley Interscience, 1999, pp.4-5.

[9] B. P. Gan, L. Liu, S. Jain, S. J. Turner, W. Cai, W. J. Hsu, Distributed Supply Chain Simulation Across Enterprise Boundaries, in *Proc. of the 32th Winter Simulation Conference*, 2000, pp.1245-1251.

[10] B. P. Gan, Y. H. Low, J. Wei, X. Wang, S. J. Turner, W. Cai, Synchronization and Management of Shared State in HLA-based Distributed Simulation, in *Proc. of the 35th Winter Simulation Conference*, 2003, pp.847-854.

[11] Globus, Globus Toolkit Version 4.0, http://www.globus.org/toolkit/.

[12] M. Govindaraju, S. Krishnan, K. Chiu, A. Slominski, D. Gannon, R. Bramley, Merging the CCA Component Model with the OGSI Framework, in *Proc. of 3rd Intl. Symposium on Cluster Computing and the Grid*, 2003, pp.182-199.

[13] IEEE, IEEE Standard 1516 (HLA Rules), 1516.1 (Interface Specification), and 1516.2 (Object Model Template), https://www.dmso.mil/public/transition/hla/.

[14] S. Krishnan, D. Gannon, XCAT3: A Framework for CCA Components as OGSA Services, in *Proc. of 9th Intl. Workshop on High-Level Parallel Programming Models and Supportive Environments*, April 2004.

[15] WSRF, The Web-Service Resource Framework Version 1.0, http://www.globus.org/wsrf/specs/ws-wsrf.pdf.

[16] Y. Xie, Y. M. Teo, W. Cai, S. J. Turner, Service Provisioning for HLA-based Distributed Simulation on the Grid, in *Proc. of the 19th Workshop on Principles of Advanced and Distributed Simulation*, 2005, pp.282-291.

[17] Z. Yuan, W. Cai, Y. H. Low, S. J. Turner, Federate Migration in HLA-based Distributed Simulation, in *Proc. of 1st Workshop on HLA-based Distributed Simulation on the Grid (in conjunction with Intl. Conference of Computational Science)*, 2004, pp.856-864.

[18] K. Zajac, M. Bubak, M. Ma-lawski, P. Sloot, Towards Grid Management System for HLA-based Interactive Simulations, in *Proc. of the 7th IEEE Intl. Symposium on Distributed Simulation and Real Time Applications*, 2003, pp.4-11.

[19] W. Zong, Y. Wang, W. Cai, S. J. Turner, Grid Services and Service Discovery for HLA-based Distributed Simulation, in *Proc. of the 9th IEEE Intl. Symposium on Distributed Simulation - Real Time Applications*, 2004, pp.116-124.

Discrete-event Execution Alternatives on General Purpose Graphical Processing Units (GPGPUs)

Kalyan S. Perumalla
perumallaks@ornl.gov
Oak Ridge National Laboratory
Oak Ridge, Tennessee, USA

Abstract

Graphics cards, traditionally designed as accelerators for computer graphics, have evolved to support more general-purpose computation. General Purpose Graphical Processing Units (GPGPUs) are now being used as highly efficient, cost-effective platforms for executing certain simulation applications. While most of these applications belong to the category of time-stepped simulations, little is known about the applicability of GPGPUs to discrete event simulation (DES). Here, we identify some of the issues & challenges that the GPGPU stream-based interface raises for DES, and present some possible approaches to moving DES to GPGPUs. Initial performance results on simulation of a diffusion process show that DES-style execution on GPGPU runs faster than DES on CPU and also significantly faster than time-stepped simulations on either CPU or GPGPU.

1. Introduction

Traditionally, graphics cards for workstations and personal computers have been designed to handle intensive graphics operations to enable high speed rendering of complex objects and scenes. More recently, the graphics cards of the past have been evolving to support more programmable interfaces for graphics operations. These interfaces eventually became sufficiently general to be able to map non-graphics computation in terms of graphics elements and achieve non-graphics computation on graphics processors. Evolution in hardware programmability together with software development platforms has transformed graphics cards into General Purpose Graphical Processing Units (GPGPUs). Their programmability has reached a point to make them suitable for more general-purpose computation[1, 2]. Computing that is generally targeted towards execution on CPUs could now be re-targeted for execution on GPUs. An application can use a GPGPU as either co-processor or core processor.

General-purpose computation using GPUs is, however, a relatively recent area of research. Several new applications of GPGPUs are being considered, and new algorithms are being developed that are demonstrated to be highly efficient for execution on GPGPUs. Certain applications have been shown to execute much faster on GPGPUs than on CPUs[2]. Generally speaking, applications that have more "arithmetic intensity" are more suitable for GPGPUs. GPUs have also been touted as low-cost alternative platforms for supercomputing, due to their high peak execution rates relative to comparable CPUs.

Among simulation applications attempted on GPGPUs, the majority use time-stepped execution, and have been shown to execute must faster on the GPGPUs than on CPUs[3]. This is mainly because time-stepped approaches tend to map relatively easily to the *streaming* paradigm of GPGPUs. However, little is known with respect to the applicability of GPGPUs to discrete event simulation (DES). It is unknown whether DES is relevant, practical and/or better on GPGPUs relative to CPUs. At the outset, it seems unclear as to how discrete event models could be mapped to the streaming model of execution of GPGPUs. For example, is a traditional event loop implementation applicable to GPGPUs? Is there a more suitable alternative DES implementation approach for GPGPUs? How much faster can GPGPU-based DES perform compared to an equivalent CPU-based DES? What types of DES applications are better suited for execution on GPGPUs? In this paper, we attempt to address and answer some of these questions, and highlight areas where additional research is needed for better understanding.

In section 2 we provide relevant background information on GPGPUs. In section 3, we present a case study in using GPGPUs for simulating a phenomenon (diffusion process) that has both TS and DES models, and show that a DES algorithm specially adapted for the GPGPU can outperform both a traditional DES algorithm on the CPU as well as time-stepped algorithms on CPU and GPGPU. Following the case study, in section 4, we sketch possible alternative algorithms and data structures for executing more general DES applications on the GPGPU platforms. We also outline the challenges and limitations that GPGPU platforms impose that constrain the types of DES applications that can be effectively realized. Finally, we conclude and discuss future work in section 5.

2. Motivation and Background

A considerable body of literature now exists on hardware, software and algorithmic details of graphics processors that are suitable for general purpose computation. The related literature and bibliography is now too large to be cited comprehensively here. Hence, we outline the main GPGPU features that are relevant in our immediate context of DES applications. The interested reader is referred to [1, 2, 4, 5] for literature surveys and detailed background on GPGPUs, and to some applications such as efficient line-of-sight calculations for battle-field simulations[6], and efficient tracking of pheromone diffusion effects in unmanned vehicle control[7].

2.1. GPGPU Architectures

A highly simplified functional view of a GPGPU is shown in Figure 1. A set of textures is fed as input to a bank of "fragment processors". User-specified code, called "kernel," can be loaded into fragment processors (FPs), which is executed for each and every element of the input textures. As and when computed values are generated by the fragment processors, the computed output is stored at appropriate locations in target textures. The generated output textures can then be fed back as input for additional processing, and so on. For performance reasons, it is desirable to perform as many operations as possible with the texture memory before the values in texture memory are transferred to/from the host CPU's main memory.

Many other details, such as the vertex processors and the rasterizer, are not discussed here for simplicity. The interested reader is referred to [8] for additional detail on GeForce 6800, which is a good representative of modern GPGPUs. Current GPGPUs even support conditional and looping constructs in FPs, as well as a few registers local to each FP. Parallelism is realized by processing multiple elements of input textures concurrently among all available FPs. Asynchronous memory fetches are supported by FPs, allowing computation on some elements to proceed even while other elements are being fetched from texture memory.

The pipelined flow of vertices and fragments through the graphics pipeline is the main reason why general purpose computation on GPUs is cast in the form of *stream computation*. Streaming applications map very well to GPGPU architectures, in which the same operation is applied to all elements in a stream of data elements (e.g., performing transforms on a stream of Cartesian positions & vectors).

In comparison to CPUs, the biggest constraint imposed by GPGPUs is a lack of scatter operations (i.e., "compute & store instructions" of the form a[i]=b). This is because the output address of fragment processor is automatically fixed by the hardware for each input element. This makes assignment to arbitrary location of an output texture difficult. But gather operations (i.e., "load & compute" instructions of the form b=a[i]) are supported by GPGPUs in the form of "dependent texture fetch" operations. Algorithms for achieving scatter in terms of gather have been proposed[1], but cannot always be applied without regard to increased runtime overheads.

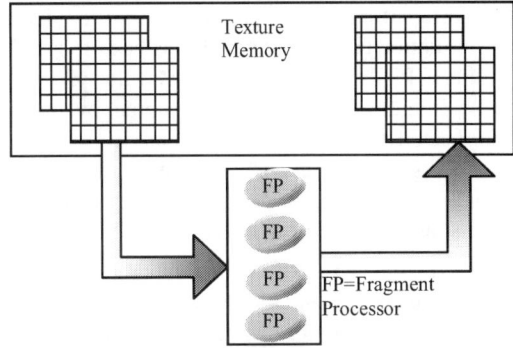

Figure 1: Highly simplified schematic of GPGPU operation. Textures are input to a bank of fragment processors (FPs). FPs "render" the results of their computation to target textures.

Another limitation of GPGPUs is the limit on the maximum size of a texture that can be allocated (e.g., 4096 x 4096 floating point values per 2-D texture). Floating point operations are typically single precision, although very recent GPGPUs are offering support for double (64-bit) precision.

2.2. GPGPU Programming Environments

Beyond traditional tools for graphics applications, special programming languages and environments have been developed for general purpose programming on GPGPUs. The Cg language[9] from NVIDIA provides C-like interface to graphics primitives. An optimizing compiler generates shader routines from Cg program fragments. Its high-level language interface helps shield the developer from low-level graphics programming, but demands some level of expertise with graphics concepts (e.g., colors, textures, etc).

Similar interfaces are supported by the `fxc` compiler of `DirectX` SDK from Microsoft. Higher-level languages, such as `Brook`[5], provide more generalized abstraction of "streams" and stream programming constructs. The `Brook` compiler generates code that maps all abstractions transparently to graphics primitives, and manages all runtime aspects automatically.

In the experiments reported here, we coded all GPGPU simulations in `Brook`, and we executed using the `DirectX 9 (dx9)` runtime. The CPU is an Intel 2.13GHz Centrino with 2 Gigabytes of memory. The GPGPU is an NVIDIA GeForce 6800 Go[8] with 256MB memory, and contains 16 fragment processors and 4 vertex processors. All CPU programs are compiled with Microsoft Visual C++ v7.

2.3. *Parallel Simulation "in the Small"*

A significant amount of parallel/distributed discrete event simulation (PDES) literature has been focused on traditional CPU-based execution. Parallel processing on these traditional platforms is enabled by multiple interconnected CPUs connected either by high-speed interconnects or by a network. However, the GPGPUs represent a different type of parallel simulation platforms that are emerging lately.

A way to consider GPUs is to view them as a means to perform parallel simulation "in the small". This is in contrast to traditional parallel simulation "in the large" using networks connecting a large numbers of CPUs. In traditional parallel/distributed simulation efforts, the simulation problem size is typically scaled in order to afford enough parallelism commensurate with the increase in the number CPUs. A modern GPGPU on the other hand contains a small number (e.g., 8 or 16) of fragment processors (parallel processing elements) built into the chip, which can be exploited for parallel simulation with minimal inter-processor communication penalty.

In fact, it is the performance/price ratio that is a key differentiating factor between parallel processors and GPGPUs. While conventional parallel processors (e.g., dual or quad-CPU shared-memory machines) could conceivably deliver performance comparable to GPGPUs on applications of interest, GPGPUs are extremely appealing due to their low cost. For example, the recent GeForce 7 series GPGPU with 24 fragment processors only costs less than $500, which *includes* its 256MB video memory. Thus CPU and GPGPU comparisons are based more on configurations with similar prices, rather than on those that are technically equivalent.

Other non-CPU platforms include Field Programmable Gate Arrays (FPGAs) and network co-processors. These non-conventional platforms also afford opportunities for realizing parts of simulation functionality, such as time synchronization[10], check-pointing[11] and data distribution[12]. The GPGPU approaches considered here, however, are intended to perform an entire simulation, and not just parts of it.

3. DES on GPGPU – Case Study

3.1. *Application*

We use a diffusion simulation as an application for a case study in initially exploring the DES methodology on GPGPUs. Simulation of the diffusion equation is a well-studied problem, and has many applications (e.g., heat transfer, dye spreading and gas diffusion). We chose this application as it easily affords both time-stepped as well as discrete-event formulations for its solution[13]. Our simulation uses the following two-dimensional version of the diffusion equation:

$$\frac{\partial Q}{\partial t} = \alpha_x \frac{\partial^2 Q}{\partial x^2} + \alpha_y \frac{\partial^2 Q}{\partial y^2} + \beta$$

The space is uniformly and constantly heated from outside, i.e., the temperature is held constant at the boundary, with the initial temperature of the interior being at a value lower than at the boundary. For discretization of the continuous function, the *spatial* dimension is discretized by partitioning the space as a grid in *x* and *y* dimensions. The choice of the method for *temporal* discretization is an important one, leading to different approaches to simulation.

We now outline the traditional time-stepped algorithm, followed by two other algorithms: discrete event and hybrid. For each of these algorithms, we present runtime performance results. The results are normalized against the runtime of the first algorithm (traditional time-stepped) running on a CPU. Thus, all speedup numbers are relative to time-stepped simulation performance on a CPU.

3.2. *Time-Stepped Algorithm*

In the time-stepped method of simulation (TS), time is discretized into a grid with equi-distant points, with the spacing fixed for all grid elements. Time-stepped simulation is schematically illustrated in Figure 2. The horizontal bars represent timelines of each logical process, while the solid vertical lines represent points in simulation time at which the logical processes are updated. The time step value (simulation time period between successive updates to the state) is determined by model-specific means to ensure stability along with sufficient accuracy.

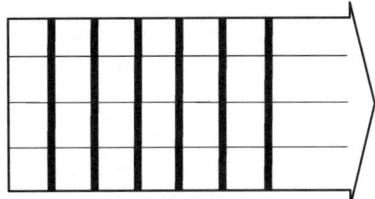

Figure 2: Schematic of timestepped simulation

In the diffusion process simulation, within each time step, the processing per (i,j) grid element in the 2-D grid can be performed by one of several known methods. We chose the following simple explicit method, where $q^{n+1}_{i,j}$ is the computed value of q_{ij} at timestep $n+1$:

$$q_{i,j}^{n+1} = q_{i,j}^{n} + \alpha_x \frac{q_{i,j-1}^{n} - 2q_{i,j}^{n} + q_{i,j+1}^{n}}{\Delta x^2} + \alpha_y \frac{q_{i-1,j}^{n} - 2q_{i,j}^{n} + q_{i+1,j}^{n}}{\Delta y^2} + \beta$$

The time-stepped algorithm for the diffusion grid is shown in Figure 3. Previous research on GPGPUs has, by and large, implemented simulations using such a time-stepped approach on GPGPUs, and compared their performance against that on CPUs[5]. We implemented this algorithm both on a CPU and on a GPGPU. The runtime performance of time-stepped algorithm is shown in Figure 4. Consistent with the level of speedups published in the literature, our implementation of the diffusion process simulation reflects more than 4-fold speed up of GPGPU over CPU, as shown in Figure 4.

1. **While not end of simulation**	
	/*Advance current simulation time*/
1.1	t_{now} += timestep
	/*Advance all grid elements to current time*/
1.2	For all (i,j): Q_{ij} += $Qdot_{ij}$ * timestep

Figure 3: Time-stepped algorithm

It is known from the GPGPU literature that, in general, when an application's working set fits mostly within the cache of CPU, the application executes sufficiently fast to exceed the speed of an equivalent version of the application on a GPGPU. This phenomenon is indeed reflected in the speedup on smaller problem sizes of the diffusion application, which are sufficiently small to fit well within the L2 cache size of 1MB. In problems with grid sizes 50x50 and 100x100, the GPGPU version experiences slowdown relative to the CPU-based time-stepped approach. When the working set of the problem no longer fits in the L2 cache, however, there is significant benefit to using the GPGPU. The fragment processors are kept busy on the GPGPU via asynchronous memory operations, resulting in over 4-fold speedup.

While the relative performance improvement of time-stepped algorithms is as expected, a logical question arises, namely, how GPGPU and CPU performance compares on discrete event algorithms. DES in general entails fewer, infrequent updates to the logical processes and hence performance can be expected on the CPU to equal the speed improvements afforded by GPGPU. We will now consider an equivalent discrete event formulation of the problem, and compare its performance on a CPU against the fast time-stepped performance of GPGPU.

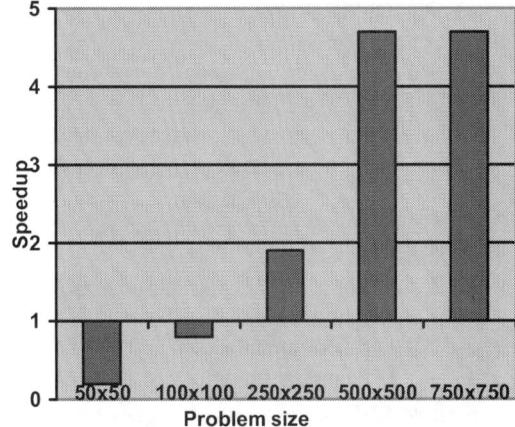

Figure 4: Speedup of GPU-based time-stepped algorithm relative to that on CPU

3.3. Discrete-Event Algorithm

In discrete event formulation, time is discretized on an individual basis for each grid element, independently and dynamically during the simulation. The discrete event formulation for the diffusion problem has been studied (see, for example, [13]). A schematic of updates is shown in Figure 5, and the pseudo code for the DES algorithm is shown in Figure 6. We used the ADEVS package[13] for a CPU-based implementation of the DES formulation.

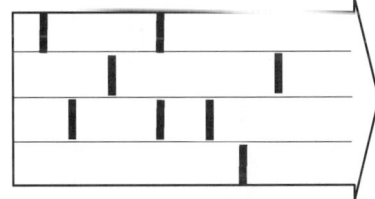

Figure 5: Schematic of DES execution

The main idea is that each grid element i,j computes the next latest time at which its state needs to be updated without violating a discretization of the effect of its own state value ($q_{i,j}$) on its neighboring elements.

In this CPU-based formulation, each element schedules an event to itself for its next update time. If nothing changes before the time at which the update occurs, the state gets advanced correctly. Otherwise, if the value of any of its neighboring elements changes "significantly", the update time of this element is recomputed and the self event is rescheduled accordingly. The correction and rescheduling of the update event of an element is accomplished by updating the event in the future/pending event list.

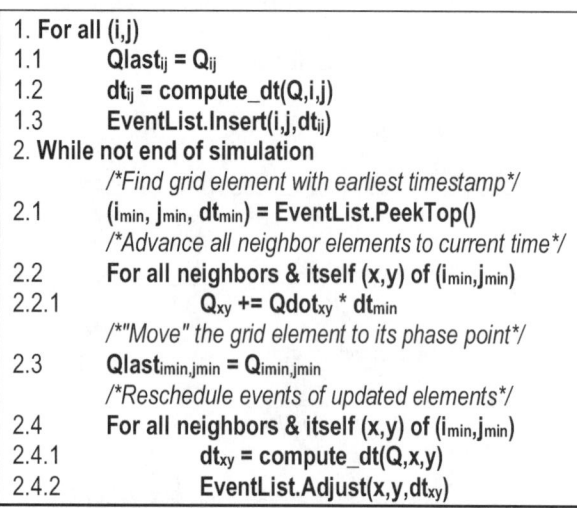

```
1. For all (i,j)
1.1     Qlast_ij = Q_ij
1.2     dt_ij = compute_dt(Q,i,j)
1.3     EventList.Insert(i,j,dt_ij)
2. While not end of simulation
        /*Find grid element with earliest timestamp*/
2.1     (i_min, j_min, dt_min) = EventList.PeekTop()
        /*Advance all neighbor elements to current time*/
2.2     For all neighbors & itself (x,y) of (i_min,j_min)
2.2.1        Q_xy += Qdot_xy * dt_min
        /*"Move" the grid element to its phase point*/
2.3     Qlast_imin,jmin = Q_imin,jmin
        /*Reschedule events of updated elements*/
2.4     For all neighbors & itself (x,y) of (i_min,j_min)
2.4.1        dt_xy = compute_dt(Q,x,y)
2.4.2        EventList.Adjust(x,y,dt_xy)
```

Figure 6: Discrete event algorithm

Clearly, the CPU-based DES algorithm (CPU-DES) outperforms the fast GPGPU-based time-stepped algorithm (GPU-TS), as shown in Figure 7. While GPU-TS is over 4 times faster than CPU-TS, CPU-DES is over 8 times faster than CPU-TS (for the 750x750 grid scenario). The natural question that follows is whether there exists an algorithm analogous to CPU-DES that can make the GPGPU perform better than GPU-TS and CPU-DES. The main challenge in addressing this question is the fact that the DES algorithm cannot be ported to the GPGPU architecture. As we discuss in more detail in section 4, selective individual updates to grid elements are not possible in the GPGPU's streaming paradigm. The challenge then is to find a suitable variant of the DES approach that is better suited and realizable on a GPGPU. We describe one such algorithm next.

3.4. Hybrid Algorithm

The key difference between the (CPU-based) DES algorithm and the traditional time-stepped algorithm is that time advances are permitted to be variable in length at runtime. On a CPU, it is possible to selectively vary this length on an individual element-by-element basis. An equivalent operation on a GPGPU would be to find the minimum timestamp among the next update times of all elements, and advance that particular element to its update time. However, it then becomes difficult to thereafter selectively modify the update times of that element's neighbors.

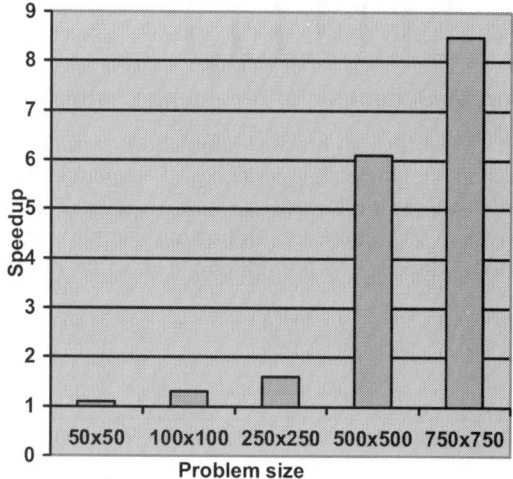

Figure 7: Speedup of CPU-based DES algorithm relative to CPU-based TS algorithm

To accomplish this, it becomes necessary to update *all* elements of the grid, not just the neighbors, since it is necessary to stream *all* the grid elements anyway, even if one wanted to only update the neighbors alone. Reasoning this way, a "hybrid" algorithm emerges naturally that combines the time-stepped nature of synchronous updates to all elements with the variable timestep support of DES. This is realized in the hybrid algorithm shown in Figure 8, which is surprisingly simple. Each individual element computes its next "safe" update timestamp in step 1.2. The minimum among all update times is chosen as the next timestep, and a synchronous update of state is performed across all elements in step 1.5. While the variability of minimum timestep mimics the DES nature of dynamic updates, the synchronous updates mimic the collective nature of state updates of the time-stepped method, thus giving the hybrid scheme. The schematic diagram corresponding to the hybrid algorithm is shown Figure 9. The schematic shows that global synchronous updates are performed at every discrete event point. Note that multiple discrete event points become merged into a single update step during synchronous updates (which turns out to be a key benefit with GPGPU).

Advantages: While the hybrid is surprisingly simple, it provides some non-intuitive advantages when executed on a GPGPU. First, a synchronous update can result in faster time advances globally, leading to faster evolution of state as compared to time-stepped method.

```
1. While not end of simulation
    /*Find next update times for all elements*/
1.2    For all (i,j): dt_ij = compute_dt(Q,i,j)
    /*Find minimum among all update times*/
1.3    dt_min = min(dt_ij) of all (i,j)
    /*Advance current simulation time*/
1.4    t_now += dt_min
    /*Advance all grid elements to current time*/
1.5    For all (i,j): Q_ij += Qdot_ij * dt_min
```

Figure 8: Hybrid algorithm

Secondly, simultaneous events are processed *in parallel* on the fragment processors of GPGPU. In a CPU-DES, simultaneous events are processed one at a time (i.e., grid elements that have the same update time are sequentially processed), where as such simultaneity is naturally processed in a single step (1.5) in the synchronous update in the hybrid algorithm. This effect is pronounced when many grid elements have the same value for their next update timestamps (which is often possible in initial stages of diffusion with large grid sizes). Thirdly, computing the minimum update time is logarithmic in time complexity on the GPGPU due to the availability of hierarchical reduction algorithms on streams[2]. This makes the overhead for computation of the minimum timestep to be comparable to that of event list management on a CPU.

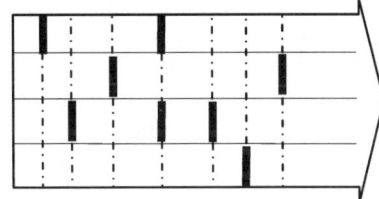

Figure 9: Schematic of hybrid simulation

Note that this algorithm differs from synchronous event processing algorithms such as described in [14]. The operation of the hybrid algorithm is somewhat akin to that of variable timestep algorithms, but differs from them in the fact that all elements are processed in parallel at each timestep, unlike on a single CPU. Moreover, the hybrid algorithm is akin to variable timestep algorithms only operationally, but retains the unique capability of advancing each element independently. In fact, the synchronous global update is a "free" operation for each local update, because of the stream processing nature of GPGPUs. Also, repeatability is not affected by parallel processing because the write operations on the input do not take affect (i.e., input is not affected by output) until all writes are completed.

The runtime performances of hybrid algorithm on a GPGPU (GPU-Hybrid) and on a CPU (CPU-Hybrid) are shown in Figure 10. The 16-fold speedup of GPU-Hybrid over CPU-TS makes it the fastest among all variants. In particular, it is more than twice as fast as the optimized CPU-DES approach which is the fastest sequential implementation on a CPU. The reason is that GPU-Hybrid not only reaps the advantages of leaps in time due to DES-style operation, but also benefits from fast parallel (stream) processing within each synchronous update. That parallel processing on the GPGPU (by fragment processors) contributes significantly to this speedup is reinforced by the low speedup of the same algorithm on a CPU (CPU-Hybrid).

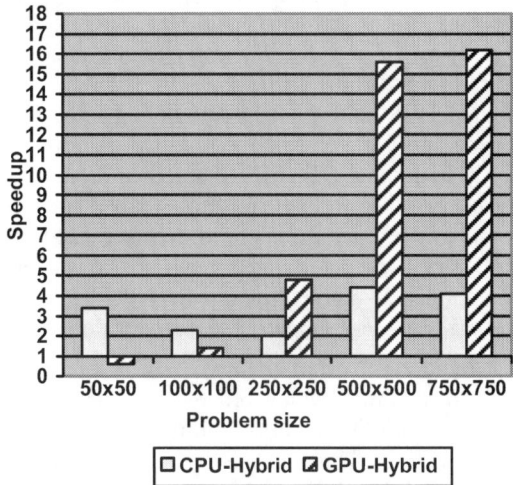

Figure 10: Speedup of CPU- & GPU-based hybrid algorithms relative to CPU-based time-stepped algorithm

3.5. *Additional Discussion on Performance*

It is clear that the CPU-based simulations are faster than GPGPU-based simulations for smaller problems sizes, presumably due to their containment in the CPU's L2 cache. This is in line with the well-known rule of thumb that the Intel Pentium 4 processor operating mostly off its L2 cache outperforms an ATI or NVIDIA GPU despite the GPGPU's concurrent processing and asynchronous memory operations. This explains the slow down (speed up less than 1.0) for 50x50 and 100x100 sized grids.

The real benefit of GPUs' streaming architecture in fact becomes truly evident on larger problem sizes that exceed the L2 cache size of the CPU (e.g., 500 x 500 x 8 bytes/variable x 3 variables = 6MB, which is more than the 2MB L2 cache of the Intel processor we used). In these scenarios, the GPGPU starts posting gains over CPU, and delivers performance almost equal to or greater than an optimized DES version executing on a

CPU. `Brook` documentation states that a kernel function can have any number of output streams. However, we found that the runtime is buggy when more than one output is generated by a kernel function. One reason for this discrepancy could be due to the fact that we used a NVIDIA GeForce 6800 Go, which is a portable version of the `Brook`-tested GeForce 6800 Ultra. Our implementation in `Brook` hence was constrained by a single output stream, and could be optimized to potentially run faster if multiple output streams were employed.

4. Generalized DES on GPGPU

We now turn our attention to extending these approaches to a more generalized set of DES applications. The GPGPU computation paradigm presents significant challenges to realizing the traditional DES application programming interface in full generality. We describe the typical event/LP model in traditional DES/PDES, and then discuss how such an interface relates to the GPGPU platform constraints. Here we focus on an event-oriented view [14] of DES. Process-oriented views are considerably more complex to implement on the GPGPU (due to lack of stack context support) and not considered here.

In traditional (event-oriented) DES, events are processed in time stamp order. In general, the simulation state is organized into multiple logical processes (LPs). Time-stamped events are sent from one (source) LP to another (destination) LP. During processing of an event, more new events could be generated by the source LP to any subset of LPs (including the source LP itself). The processed event is then noted as "consumed", which removes the event from the event list and makes its memory eligible for reuse. As part of event processing, the LP's state memory is modified. Unfortunately, this classical style of event processing simply does not carry forward to GPGPU platforms for the following reasons:

1. Since processing cannot be performed on events (or LPs) one at a time in von Neumann style, traditional event processing simulation loop does not apply to GPGPUs. Consequently, isolated, individual processing of events is extremely inefficient on GPGPU's streaming architecture.

2. The notion of sending events from one LP to another is straightforward to implement on the CPU. Conceptually if an event E is to be sent by LP i to LP j, it is realized as an assignment similar to: `Event[i][j]=E`. However, this is not easily implemented on a GPGPU either, because of lack of scatter operations as discussed in Section 2.1.

3. Also, the possibility of one event generating multiple events is relatively difficult to realize in the streaming paradigm of GPGPUs, due to significant performance overhead incurred by dynamic variability of stream sizes.

On the other hand, a GPGPU does help perform parallel processing of simultaneous events naturally. As we saw, the hybrid algorithm shown in Figure 8 naturally captures the availability of all simultaneous events and opens them up for parallel processing on the fragment processors of the GPGPU. The GeForce 6800, for example, has 16 fragment processors, which opens up 16-fold parallelism for processing simultaneous events. A CPU on the other hand processes simultaneous events sequentially, one at a time. Overall, it appears as though existing DES (and PDES) conceptual frameworks need to be rethought from scratch. The key to realizing DES on GPUs is to cast traditional events and LPs into a stream processing paradigm supported by GPGPUs.

4.1. GPGPU Usage Alternatives in DES

GPGPUs can be put to use in DES in more than one way. For example, one could use GPGPUs with a traditional CPU-based event scheduler as usual for DES. In this scheme, any intensive computation that is present in intra-event processing can be delegated to be performed on the GPGPU. The GPGPU is essentially used as a co-processor during each individual event processing. Somewhat similar to the line-of-sight calculations used in [6], this style of DES is particularly suitable for medium- to coarse-grained events that entail heavy arithmetic processing (such as linear algebra or transcendental function computations). Also, this approach is relatively easy to adapt an existing application to use GPGPU.

A more challenging approach is to use the GPGPU as a core processor rather than as a co-processor. In this "all-GPU approach," the entire DES event processing is performed on the GPGPU, with little mediation from the CPU. The GPU-Hybrid algorithm in Figure 8 is an example of this type of approach. In general, two streaming alternatives can be envisioned:

1) "Stream of events", in which the event list is stored as a stream of events, and the entire event stream is fed as input to an event processing kernel on the GPGPU. The kernel processes only those events in the input event stream whose timestamps are less than safe/allowed time, and leaves the others marked unprocessed.

2) "Stream of LPs", in which all the logical-processes are stored as a single stream, and fed through an LP-processing kernel, which processes all events of each LP that are eligible for processing. This kernel

processes only those LPs who have events whose event time is less than safe/allowed time.

Although event stream and LP stream schemes appear to be two distinct possibilities, they are in fact necessitated by the GPGPU's streaming and gathering architecture (and lack of scatter) to be one and the same approach. This is because, in order to process an event, the event's LP state must be updated as well. Also, in order to send/receive events, the source and/or destination LP state should be available at the time of an event processing. Thus, the only data structure that seems feasible is one in which an LP has a fixed number of events that it has sent to other LPs. This data structure allows events and LP state to be co-located, allowing them to be read and written in the event processing kernel. The resulting output stream will be an updated LP stream for use in the next iteration of simulation.

5. Conclusions and Future Work

GPGPUs offer a unique set of computational features that should prove useful for efficient execution of DES applications. Also, their mass market enables cost advantages via economies of mass manufacture. GPGPUs thus represent highly promising platforms for efficient (and cost-effective) execution of DES applications, but significant new research is needed to redesign traditional DES/PDES approaches into new stream-based paradigms for GPGPU platforms.

While time-stepped approaches have been studied in simulations using GPGPUs, to the best of our knowledge, this is the first work to explore DES using GPGPUs, and to properly compare the best sequential (DES-based) simulation on the CPU against a comparable technique on GPGPU. The results demonstrate the benefits of GPGPUs, showing two-fold improvement of GPGPU-based DES implementation over a traditional CPU-based DES execution. Discretization is thus helpful to speed up the simulation relative to time-stepped simulation. However, for more general DES applications, the traditional discrete event simulation loop seems inapplicable to GPGPU's stream processing style of computation, and hence a hybrid (discrete plus time-stepped) approach seems more appropriate. The performance results reflect this relative ordering of approach.

Additional research is needed to optimize DES variants on GPGPUs, both in terms of algorithms as well as optimized system implementations. For example, uncovering additional parallelism via lookahead across fragment processors could be explored. Similarly, optimized implementations directly over lower-level frameworks such as Cg language (as opposed to using Brook) can help achieve much higher performance for tuned DES applications. Simulations with greater arithmetic intensity are to be explored for even better suitability to the GPGPU platforms. We are also exploring the performance of physics models such as particle-in-cell models in this light.

References

[1] M. Pharr and R. Fernando, *GPU Gems 2: Programming Techniques for High-Performance Graphics and General-Purpose Computation*: Addison Wesley Professional, 2005.

[2] J. D. Owens, et al., "A Survey of General-Purpose Computation on Graphics Hardware," Eurographics, 2005.

[3] S. Tomov, et al., "Benchmarking and Implementation of Probability-based Simulations on Programmable Graphics Cards," *Computers and Graphics*, vol. 29(1), pp., 2005.

[4] General Purpose Computation Using Graphics Hardware, http://www.gpgpu.org.

[5] I. Buck, et al., "Brook for GPUs: Stream Computing on Graphics Hardware," *ACM Transactions on Graphics*, vol. 23(3), pp. 777-786, 2004.

[6] M. Verdesca, et al., "Using Graphics Processor Units to Accelerate OneSAF: A Case Study in Technology Transition," Interservice/Industry Training, Simulation and Education Conference (IITSEC), 2005.

[7] B. Walter, et al., "UAV Swarm Control: Calculating Digital Phermone Fields with the GPU," Interservice/Industry Training, Simulation and Education Conference (IITSEC), 2005.

[8] J. Montrym and H. Moreton, "The GeForce 6800," *IEEE Micro*, vol. 25(2), pp. 41-51, 2005.

[9] R. Fernando and M. J. Kilgard, *The Cg Tutorial: The Definitive Guide to Programmable Real-Time Graphics*, 1 ed: Addison Wesley Professional, 2003.

[10] M. Rosu, et al., "Supporting Parallel Applications on Clusters of Workstations: The Intelligent Network Interface Approach," IEEE Symposium on High Performance Distributed Computing, 1997.

[11] F. Quaglia and A. Santoro, "Non-blocking Checkpointing for Optimistic Parallel Simulation," *IEEE Transactions on Parallel and Distributed Systems*, vol. 14(6), pp. 593-610, 2003.

[12] A. Santoro and R. M. Fujimoto, "Off-Loading Data Distribution Management to Network Processors in HLA-Based Distributed Simulations," Distributed Simulations and Real-Time Applications, 2004.

[13] J. Nutaro, "Parallel Discrete Event Simulation with Application to Continuous Systems," thesis, University of Arizona, 2003.

[14] R. M. Fujimoto, *Parallel and Distributed Simulation Systems*: Wiley Interscience, 2000.

Progressive Time-Parallel Simulation

Tobias Kiesling
Fakultät für Informatik
Universität der Bundeswehr München
85577 Neubiberg, Germany
tobias.kiesling@unibw.de

Abstract

Parallel simulation techniques are designed to increase simulation model performance by exploiting model concurrency. Unfortunately, designing efficient parallel simulations is not always an easy task. Most existing techniques guarantee results identical to a corresponding sequential simulation. Other methods try to increase efficiency by relaxing causal constraints, leading to the calculation of approximate results. This work proposes to combine both approaches using the novel technique of progressive time-parallel simulation, where imprecise results are calculated rapidly and improved progressively later on until precise results are known. The user is allowed to cancel this process at any time if the accuracy is satisfying. Progressive time-parallel simulation is a specialized parallelization approach that is not applicable to every kind of simulation model. Possible application areas include simulation-based decision support or simulation-based scheduling and control of manufacturing systems. A successful application of the technique is illustrated with progressive queuing system simulation.

1. Introduction

Parallel simulation techniques are utilized to increase the performance of complex large-scale simulation models. Classical parallel simulation methods [7] preserve causal relationships between events, leading to simulation results identical to those of a corresponding sequential model. However, depending on the nature of the underlying model, the parallelism achievable with these approaches is limited in many cases. Therefore, several alternative approaches have been developed that increase the achievable parallelism at the cost of a loss of accuracy in the simulation results [1, 6, 17, 22, 26, 30].

These methods are comparable to the technique of *imprecise computations* [21] which has been developed for hard real-time systems. An imprecise computation is allowed to give imprecise (approximate) results if the precise results cannot be provided in time.

The concept of *progressive processing* is very similar to imprecise computations, with the exception that computations are continued after the initial determination of approximate results to improve these results *progressively*. One of the more prominent applications of this technique is *progressive image rendering* [2, 4, 13], where an imprecise (e.g. blurred) or incomplete representation of the image is provided to the user after a short answer time, after which the quality of the image is progressively improved until the best representation of the image has been produced or the user cancels the image rendering process. This is of renewed importance with the advent of the World Wide Web (e.g. progressive rendering of Scalable Vector Graphics files with SVG 1.2 [12]). Other applications are progressive information retrieval [32], progressive data stream processing [25], and progressive DBMS-based decision support [29].

Progressive processing can be utilized effectively in contexts where quick results are desirable, regardless of their accuracy, but more precise results might be needed later. The novel concept of progressive time-parallel simulation introduced in this paper is an application of the idea of progressive processing to the field of parallel and distributed simulation. The basic idea is to produce approximate simulation results as early as possible and increase their accuracy progressively afterwards. This is especially interesting in systems with real-time constraints. Possible application areas of progressive analytic simulation models (also known as constructive or as-fast-as-possible simulation models) include simulation-based military decision support, simulation-based traffic control, or simulation-based scheduling and control of manufacturing systems.

The central property of progressive time-parallel simulation is the repeated calculation of simulation results, which are refined progressively during the simulation execution. Unfortunately, this process of result computation in conjunction with time-parallel simulation cannot be applied to arbitrary simulation models, which results in a limited applicability of this technique. Nevertheless, models suitable for this specialized technique do exist.

A similar approach to progressive simulation can be performed with Genesis [27, 28]. In Genesis, the whole simulation domain (a communication network) is decomposed into a number of subdomains. Each subdomain is simulated concurrently with the other domains for a given time interval. After the simulation of a time interval, domain simulators exchange information about the simulation results, which is used to start another iteration over the same time interval to calculate more accurate results. This process is repeated until convergence of results can be observed. If Genesis is used with a single time interval comprising the whole simulation time, overall simulation results are calculated in a progressive way. The main difference between progressive time-parallel simulation and Genesis is the utilized parallelization strategy, i.e. temporal decomposition with the former and domain decomposition with the latter.

When studying progressive time-parallel simulation, the impression might occur that it is a special technique for parallel replicated simulation [8, 10], as every one of the parallel processes performs simulation independently from the other processes. However, due to the combination of results computed by each process in the progressive global result computation, this is not the case. The amount of information gained by each process during its simulation execution is exploited to provide the most accurate simulation results available at a specific time.

Before the method of progressive time-parallel simulation is introduced in Section 3, Section 2 gives an overview of basic time-parallel simulation. An application of progressive simulation to queuing systems is presented in Section 4 together with results of experiments with a prototypical progressive queuing simulator in Section 5. Finally, Section 6 concludes the work.

2. Time-Parallel Simulation

In classical parallel simulation [5], the set of state variables of a simulation model is decomposed into subsets, each of which is assigned to a logical process managing the corresponding part of the global state. Logical processes are then executed concurrently on paral-

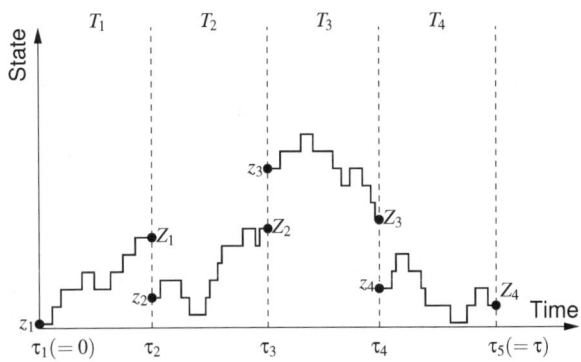

Figure 1. Time-parallel simulation.

lel processing nodes. The drawbacks of this approach are the introduction of an overhead for the synchronization between logical processes and the limited amount of achievable parallelism, which is restricted by the number of state variables and the decomposability of states in the model. Time-parallel simulation [3] is a different approach that decomposes the time axis and performs simulations of resulting time intervals in parallel. Afterwards, the results of all intervals are combined to create the overall simulation result. This has the potential for massive parallelism, as the maximum number of logical processes is determined by the number of possible time intervals, which is only restricted by the granularity of the time representation in the simulation implementation.

However, without further mechanisms, the final and initial states of adjacent time intervals do not necessarily coincide at interval boundaries, possibly resulting in incorrect state changes. Several different solutions of this problem have been proposed. Lin and Lazowska [20] introduce the notion of *regeneration points*, which are states that keep reoccurring throughout a simulation execution. If such a state can be identified a priori, a number of simulations can be executed concurrently, starting from the regeneration point and continuing until the regeneration point is reached again. Afterwards, the traces of the parallel simulations are concatenated to a correct trace of the simulation over the whole time period. The drawback of this approach is the difficulty to identify regeneration points, especially for models with complex states. Among other applications, this approach was used successfully for the simulation of cascaded statistical multiplexers [24].

Heidelberger and Stone [11] introduce another solution using *fix-up computations*, which has been used for the simulation of caching in computer systems [11], the simulation of Ethernet networks [31], and the simulation of communication switches with losses [23]. Fix-up computations are a more general construct than regeneration points, as they can be applied to almost any simulation model. Therefore, the rest of the paper is only concerned with time-parallel simulation using fix-up computations.

Let $T = [0, \tau]$ be the interval of the whole simulation time. T is decomposed into the *time intervals* $T_1, \ldots, T_m$, where $T_k = [\tau_k, \tau_{k+1}]$, with $\tau_1 = 0 < \tau_2 < \ldots < \tau_m < \tau_{m+1} = \tau$, such that every point in simulated time is contained in some interval and the intervals overlap only at boundaries $\tau_2, \ldots, \tau_m$. Simulations of time intervals are to be executed concurrently by corresponding processes $p_1, \ldots, p_m$ in the *initial simulation phase*. Unfortunately, the correct states at time interval boundaries $\tau_2, \ldots, \tau_m$ are unknown prior to the simulation. Therefore, these states are guessed and used as initial states $z_2, \ldots, z_k$ of the simulation processes. Now, the situation may occur, that the final state Z_k of a simulation execution for time interval T_k does not match the initial (probably incorrect) state z_{k+1} that has been used for the simulation of the following time interval T_{k+1}. Figure 1 illustrates these issues.

If it is the case that $z_{k+1} \neq Z_k$ for at least one time interval T_k, overall simulation results might be incorrect. Therefore, a *fix-up phase* is utilized after the initial simulation phase to amend these illegal state changes. Fix-up computations for an interval T_{k+1} (see Figure 2 for an illustration) are just a continuation of the simulation of the preceding interval T_k by process p_k until a time τ'_k, where the state of the initial simulation performed by process p_{k+1} matches the corresponding state calculated during the fix-up computations by process p_k. As can be noted in Figure 2, the correct sequence of states results from a concatenation of the sequences of states of intervals $T'_k = (\tau'_k, \tau'_{k+1}]$ calculated by process p_k for all $k \in \{1, \ldots, m\}$. An interval $[\tau_k, \tau'_k]$ can be interpreted in two ways: as the *fix-up phase* of process p_{k-1} and as a *warm-up phase* of process p_k.

A central aspect of fix-up computations is the detection of state matching. State matching might occur in both deterministic and stochastic simulation models, but in the latter case it is harder to anticipate and sometimes leads to obscure results. Fortunately, it is easy to transform a stochastic simulation model into an equivalent deterministic one by pre-sampling of random numbers. This leads to a trace-driven simulation, where the now *repeatable* simulation executions enable a direct comparison of the simulation states of initial simulation and corresponding fix-up computation. The details how this presampling can be performed depend on the specificities of the simulation model.

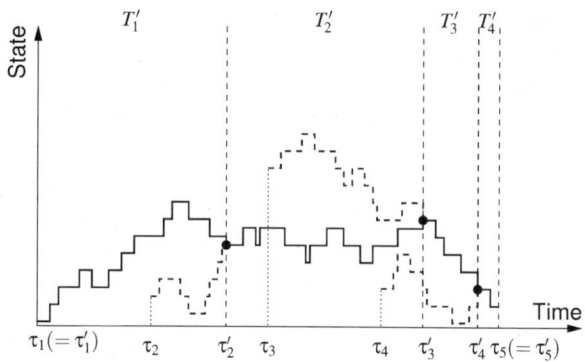

Figure 2. Fix-up computations.

3. Progressive Time-Parallel Simulation

In basic time-parallel simulation, results are available only after fix-up computations of all parallel processes are complete. The other alternative is to produce results as early as possible, viz. directly after the initial simulation phase is completed. As already discussed above, simulation results are imprecise at that time, but in many cases they might still serve as valuable indications on the precise results. Furthermore, instead of terminating the simulation at that time (having calculated approximate results), fix-up computations can be performed, while providing increasingly accurate simulation results to the user in the ongoing simulation execution. The accuracy of results should improve continually with runtime, reaching exact results upon completion of fix-up computations.

3.1. Simulation Progress

To capture the dynamic nature of such a system, a family of *progress functions* is introduced, indicating the local simulation time of a process at a point in wallclock time.

Definition 3.1. Let $\tau_0(t) := 0$ and $\tau_{m+1}(t) = \tau$. Furthermore, for all $k \in \{1, \ldots, m\}$, let $\tau_k : \mathbb{R}_0^+ \to [0, \tau]$ be a family of monotonic increasing functions with $\lim_{t \to \infty} \tau_k(t) = \tau$ and $\tau_{k-1}(t) \leq \tau_k(t)$. τ_k is the *simulation progress function* of p_k, where the local simulation time of process p_k at wallclock time t is given by $\tau_k(t)$.

For every process p_k, it is required that the corresponding progress function is monotonically increasing. Otherwise, processes might roll back their local time, which is not considered here. Further, it is assumed that processes make progress, eventually reaching the end of the simulation period and overtaking of processes is not

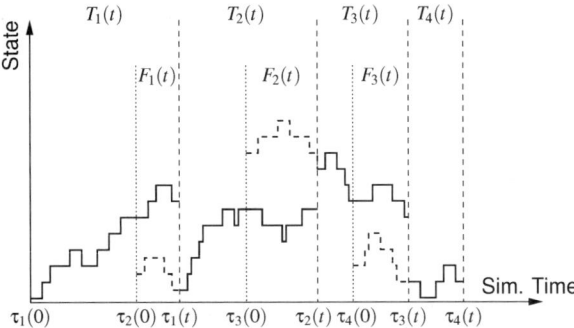

Figure 3. Progressive simulation at time t.

allowed. The latter assumption is not necessary in all cases, but is provided here to simplify the following definitions.

The processing of a progressive time-parallel simulation system can be divided in two phases. The *initial simulation phase* of a process p_k lasts until it has progressed to the start time of its following process, i.e. $\tau_k(t) = \tau_{k+1}(0)$. After that time instant, the process is in its *fix-up computation phase*. At wallclock time t, a process p_k has calculated the sequence of states of interval $[\tau_k(0), \tau_k(t)]$. At any time during the fix-up computation phase of a process, this interval can be divided in two different parts: one for which fix-up computations have already been performed by the preceding process, and the second part, where this is not the case and thus results have to be provided for this interval by the process.

Definition 3.2. For every $k \in \{1, \ldots, m-1\}$,

$$F_k(t) := [\tau_{k+1}(0), \tau_k(t)]$$

is the *fix-up region* of p_k and for every $k \in \{1, \ldots, m\}$, the *results region* of p_k is defined as

$$T_k(t) := (\tau_{k-1}(t), \tau_k(t)].$$

The results region of a process has a direct impact on the results generated by that process: Results and statistics are adapted to reflect only the computations performed inside the results region of the process (see Section 3.2). A snapshot of an example simulation system at wallclock time t is given in Figure 3.

3.2. Simulation Results

The notions of initial simulation phase and fix-up computation phase of a process p_k were introduced above. Now, similar terms are defined for the overall simulation. The overall simulation system is in the *initial simulation phase* if at least one of the processes is in the initial simulation phase, and in the *fix-up computation phase* afterwards. The identifier $t_0 := min\{t \geq 0 | \forall k \in \{1, \ldots, m\} : \tau_k(t) > \tau_{k+1}(0)\}$ is used in the rest of the paper to denote the time instant where the system finishes the initial simulation phase.

Simulation results are not available during the initial simulation, as only a part of the whole simulation interval has been processed. At any time t after t_0, preliminary simulation results are available by combining the local results computed by each process p_k in the time-interval $T_k(t)$. Let $\mathcal{R} = \mathbb{R}^n$, with an arbitrary $n \in \mathbb{N}$, denote the result space of the simulation (in general, the results of a simulation can be of an arbitrary type. However, in most practical cases, atomic results can be mapped to real numbers, so using $\mathbb{R}^n$ for the result space should be sufficient). Then the results calculated by the processes $p_1, \ldots, p_m$ are represented by a number of result functions.

Definition 3.3. For all $k \in \{1, \ldots, m\}$, let $R_k : [t_0, \infty) \to \mathcal{R}$ be the *local result function* of process p_k, where $R_k(t)$ is the result computed by p_k for interval $T_k(t)$ at wall-clock time t. Furthermore, let $\widehat{R} : [t_0, \infty) \to \mathcal{R}$ be the *global result function* which is an arbitrary combination of the R_k for all $k \in \{1, \ldots, m\}$. A requirement on $\widehat{R}$ is: If $T_k(t) = \emptyset$, then $R_k(t)$ should have no impact at all on $\widehat{R}(t)$.

The preliminary simulation results computed at time t are given by the global result function. The only requirement on the global result function is, that the local result of a process p_k should have no impact at all on the global result if the results region of p_k is empty, i.e. no results should be produced by the process. This also implies, that

$$\lim_{t \to \infty} \widehat{R}(t) = \lim_{t \to \infty} R_1(t), \quad (1)$$

i.e. if the parallel simulation is run for a sufficiently long time, the global result is completely determined by the first parallel process p_1.

The global result function $\widehat{R}$ is an estimation of the correct result R that would be provided by an equivalent sequential or basic time-parallel simulation execution. Guessing of initial states at time interval boundaries before start of the simulation is not performed for the first process p_1, because the same initial state can be used as for a sequential simulation. Therefore, the results calculated by process p_1 for its time interval $T_1(t)$ are always identical to those of a sequential simulation. Together with the assumption $\lim_{t \to \infty} \tau_k(t) = \tau$, it holds that

$$R = \lim_{t \to \infty} R_1(t). \quad (2)$$

These observations lead to the following important theorem, which indicates that the progressive parallel simulation eventually produces correct results.

Theorem 3.1. *Given a progressive time-parallel simulation execution with progress functions $\tau_1, \ldots, \tau_m$, local result functions $R_1, \ldots, R_m$, and global result function $\widehat{R}$. Then it holds, that*

$$\lim_{t \to \infty} \widehat{R}(t) = R.$$

Proof. Follows directly from (1) and (2). □

Theorem 3.1 settles the question, whether progressive time-parallel simulation eventually leads to correct simulation results. In practical cases, however, the rate of the convergence of $\widehat{R}$ and R, reflecting the development of the accuracy of the simulation, is of more interest. The *accuracy function* α is used to relate the value of the estimated result $\widehat{R}(t)$ at a time t with the correct simulation result. Different possibilities for the definition of α exist. For example α could be defined as the difference between estimated and correct result:

$$\alpha(t) := R - \widehat{R}(t),$$

or as the ratio between estimated and correct result:

$$\alpha(t) := \frac{\widehat{R}(t)}{R}.$$

The precise definition of α depends on the specificities of the result functions in the model. In most cases, the accuracy function is not available during the simulation execution, but it can be used to evaluate the feasibility of a specific progressive simulation application. Section 4.2 contains an exemplary definition of the accuracy function.

Another important aspect of the accuracy function is its monotonicity. In general, it cannot be guaranteed that α is a monotonic function. However, in such a case, the employment of progressive simulation is dangerous, as the user might cancel a simulation execution due to a sufficient accuracy of results, which would be misleading if the accuracy degraded with further simulation. Therefore, a necessary preliminary for the reasonable application of progressive time-parallel simulation to a model is that α is found to be a monotonic function. For example, in the specific model of single-server queuing systems, this property is shown in Theorem 4.2.

4. Application to Queuing Systems

Queuing Systems are an important modeling tool due to their simple nature, as well as the substantial work that has been done in the theory of queuing phenomena. The concepts discussed in Section 3 are applied to the simulation of queuing systems here. The representation of queuing system dynamics is based on the formal queuing system model presented in [16], which discusses efficient non-progressive queuing system simulation. The basic simulation model of [16] is extended here to investigate the impact of progressive result computation.

Alternative schemes for the parallel simulation of queuing systems and queuing networks with varying strengths and weaknesses have been developed earlier [9, 19, 30]. In order to apply the technique of progressive time-parallel simulation, repeatability of the simulation has to be assured (see Section 2). Otherwise, no guarantee regarding the progression of fix-up computations could be given. Fortunately, repeatability of a stochastic queuing system simulation can be achieved by sampling of random numbers prior to the simulation execution. In practice, no presampling of random numbers might be necessary, the same effect probably being achievable by the utilization of pseudo random number generators with fixed seeds. Furthermore, it is supposed that the sequence of job arrival instants is available instead of the job interarrival times. The determination of job arrival instants from interarrival times is a task that can be calculated easily and efficiently [9].

Before introducing approximate queuing simulation, some necessary preliminaries have to be provided. First, a mathematical definition of $G/G/1$ queuing system simulation is given. Then, basic time-parallel queuing simulation is presented.

4.1. Foundations

In the following, the problem of queuing simulation is reduced to the calculation problem of determining the departure times of a number of jobs with associated arrival instants and service times. Based on this sequence of departure instants, the trajectory of the number of jobs in the system over time can be reconstructed easily [9]. The calculation of the job departure instants of a $G/G/1$ queue can be represented by a recursive function that relates a job with its departure time [18]. The basic observation underlying this formulation is, that the departure instant $d(j)$ of job j is determined by its own service time $s(j)$ and either its arrival instant $a(j)$ or the departure instant of the previous job $d(j-1)$ (depending on which occurs later in time):

$$d(j) = max(a(j), d(j-1)) + s(j). \quad (3)$$

This recursive formula for the calculation of departure times is easily understandable and can be implemented efficiently as a sequential computer program. However, to allow for parallel queuing simulation, (3) is modified to support the parallel calculation of departure times, defined later.

Definition 4.1. Let $N := \{1, \ldots, n\}$ be the set of jobs to simulate. Let $s : N \to \mathbb{R}^+$ be a positive function of job service times. Let $a : N \to \mathbb{R}_0^+$ be a strictly monotonic increasing function of job arrival instants. The *departure function* $d_u^i : \{i-1, \ldots, n\} \to \mathbb{R}_0^+$ for $u \in \mathbb{R}_0^+$ and $i \in N$, is defined as

$$d_u^i(j) := \begin{cases} u, & \text{if } j = i-1 \\ \max(a(j), d_u^i(j-1)) + s(j), & \text{otherwise} \end{cases}$$

The parameter i is used to restrict the domain of the function to the interval $\{i-1, \ldots, n\}$, starting at job i, which is a part of the overall simulation domain. The function is defined for job $i-1$, as well, but this value is only to be used as the base case of the recursion. The parameter i is relevant in the context of time-parallel simulation of the queuing system, where the simulation of a parallel process is started with an initial job representing the time interval boundary. The parameter u of the departure function is used to indicate an *initial delay* for the queuing system. In a sequential queuing system which is typically empty at the beginning of the observed time, $u = 0$. However, if there is an initial load of the system, the queue starts with at least one existing job. This property can be captured by introducing an initial delay with $u > 0$ that must pass until the first job can be served. Later, this is used to represent the performance of fix-up computations in a time-parallel simulation. As can be seen easily, d_u^i is a strictly monotonic increasing function.

Based on Definition 4.1, it is now possible to specify time-parallel queuing system simulation.

Definition 4.2. Let $N := \{1, \ldots, n\}$ be a set of jobs with corresponding arrival instants $a : N \to \mathbb{R}_0^+$ and service times $s : N \to \mathbb{R}^+$. *Time-parallel queuing system simulation* is performed by m processes $p_1, \ldots, p_m$, assigning start job $j_k \in \{1, \ldots, n\}$ to every process p_k ($j_1 = 1 < j_2 < \ldots < j_m \leq n$). Furthermore, each logical process p_k is assigned a simulation interval $N_k := \{j_k - 1, \ldots, n\}$ and an initial delay $u_k := a(j_k)$.

The initial delay u_k of p_k is set to the arrival instant of j_k, the first job processed by p_k. This value of the initial delay represents an empty queue at the beginning of the simulation of each simulation interval, as the departure time of the first job j_k is in any case $a(j_k) + s(j_k)$ and the job is not influenced by any of the preceding jobs in the system.

The value $a(j_l)$ of the initial delay u_l of a process p_l is reasonable, as it leads to the domination of $d_{u_l}^{j_l}$ by $d_{u_k}^{j_k}$ for every $k < l$. This property is formalized in the following theorem.

Theorem 4.1. *Let $k, l \in \{1, \ldots, m\}$ with $k < l$. Then the following inequality holds for all $j \in N_l$:*

$$d_{u_k}^{j_k}(j) \geq d_{u_l}^{j_l}(j).$$

See [16] for the proof of Theorem 4.1.

4.2. Progressive Queuing Simulation

Time-parallel queuing simulation, as discussed in the preceding section, is extended to provide simulation results at any wallclock time instant in order to perform progressive queuing system simulation. To be able to do this, it is necessary to relate a wallclock time instant with the simulation progress of parallel processes. This is done in the following by introducing a family of simulation progress functions.

Definition 4.3. Let $\tau_0(t) := 0$ and $\tau_{m+1}(t) := n$ for all $t > 0$. For all $k \in \{1, \ldots, m\}$ let the *simulation progress function* $\tau_k : \mathbb{R}_0^+ \to N_k$ with $\tau_k(0) = j_k$ be a monotonic increasing function being complete (i.e. taking all values in N_k) and converging to n, i.e. $\lim_{t \to \infty} \tau_k(t) = n$. Further it is required that $\forall k \in \{1, \ldots, m\} : \tau_{k-1}(t) \leq \tau_k(t)$.

The simulation progress function τ_k returns the next job which is to be processed by p_k after wallclock time t. There are three requirements on the progress functions: (i) No jobs are skipped during the simulation, i.e. every value in N_k is taken by τ_k. (ii) Simulations realize progress, eventually calculating the departure time of the last job, which is expressed by the convergence to n. (iii) No passing of processes is allowed, which is expressed by the last sentence in Definition 4.3.

In Section 3.2, the result functions of a progressive time-parallel simulation are defined with a domain starting at a time t_0, after which estimations on the correct simulation results can be provided. With time-parallel queuing simulation defined above, it is possible to return result estimators even before every job has been processed once. Thus, the following definitions of the result functions have a domain starting at time 0. In queuing system simulation, the result and accuracy functions depend on the simulation goals, i.e. the result statistics to evaluate. In the following, it is supposed that the average job system time (i.e. the average time a job spends in the system) is to be determined. Many of the other statistics of interest in queuing simulation can be derived from this measure. Furthermore, in order to simplify the following definitions, only the calculation of the total system time (i.e. the total time all jobs spend in the system) is considered.

Definition 4.4. Let $\tau'_k(t) := \max(\tau_k(0), \tau_{k-1}(t))$. The *local cumulated system time* function $R_k : \mathbb{R}_0^+ \to \mathbb{R}_0^+$ of process k, the *global cumulated system time* function $\widehat{R} : \mathbb{R}_0^+ \to \mathbb{R}_0^+$, and the *total system time* of jobs $R \in \mathbb{R}_0^+$ are defined as

$$R_k(t) := \sum_{j=\tau'_k(t)}^{\tau_k(t)-1} d_{u_k}^{j_k}(j) - a(j),$$

$$\widehat{R}(t) := \sum_{k=1}^{m} R_k(t), \text{ and}$$

$$R := \lim_{t \to \infty} R_1(t) = \sum_{j=1}^{n} d_{u_1}^{j_1}(j) - a(j).$$

$\widehat{R}(t)$ is an estimation, available at wallclock time t, of the total system time R, which is defined as the cumulated system time which would be calculated by the first process. Some further remarks on Definition 4.4:

- After time t_0, as defined in Section 3.2, $\tau'_k(t)$ denotes the next job that is to be processed by p_{k-1} at time t, which is identical to the first job in the results interval of p_k at time t. To be able to calculate results before t_0, the result function is adapted not to consider jobs that have not been processed yet. This is achieved by choosing the maximum of $\tau_k(0)$ and $\tau_{k-1}(t)$ for the sum in the definition of $R_k(t)$.

- A sequential queuing simulation calculates departure times of all jobs $j \in \{1, \ldots, n\}$, which is exactly what is done by p_1 if its fix-up computations extend up to the last job n. Hence, simulation results calculated by the first process p_1 are assumed to be the correct results (cf. the related discussion in Section 3.2).

The *accuracy* of the simulation system at a time t is given by the accuracy function, which consists of the ratio between cumulated system time and total system time.

Definition 4.5. In the progressive queuing system simulation defined above, the *accuracy function* $\alpha : \mathbb{R}_0^+ \to [0,1]$ is defined as

$$\alpha(t) := \frac{\widehat{R}(t)}{R}.$$

The accuracy function is a theoretical construct and can, in general, not be determined during the runtime of the simulation. However, it can be used to evaluate the behavior of a progressive time-parallel simulation application, which is done in the following theorem for queuing system simulation.

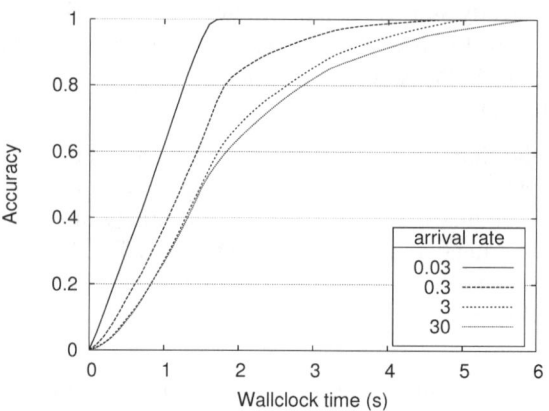

Figure 4. Accuracy function α with $\lambda - \mu = 0.001$ and varying λ using 4 processes.

Theorem 4.2. *In the progressive queuing system simulation defined above, $\alpha(0) = 0$, $\lim_{t \to \infty} \alpha(t) = 1$, and α is monotonically increasing.*

The theorem shows the normalization of α to the interval $[0, 1]$, the accuracy being minimal (a value of 0) at the beginning of the simulation and growing monotonically, converging to the maximum accuracy of 1 (representing precise results). The proof of Theorem 4.2 is provided in the appendix.

5. Experiments

To investigate the development of the accuracy of progressive queuing system simulation over time, a prototypical progressive queuing simulator has been implemented and a number of experiments have been performed on an SGI Origin multiprocessor machine. As a maximum of eight processors was available for the experiments, the number of processes was varied between one and eight. It has been shown that the expected overhead of basic time-parallel queuing simulation tends to grow proportionally to $\frac{\lambda}{(\mu-\lambda)^2}$ [16]. Hence, it is expected that the accuracy of a simulation execution tends to grow slower with an increasing arrival rate λ, as well as with an increasing distance $\mu - \lambda$. Therefore, experiments were conducted with varying parameters λ and μ in order to confirm that expected behavior. The results of the experiments are summarized in the following. Note that the values shown here are averages over 50 repetitions of the same experiment with different random numbers. All of the experiments consisted of the calculation of cumulated system times for 200,000 jobs.

Figure 4 summarizes the results of experiments with a varying arrival rate λ while keeping a fixed distance

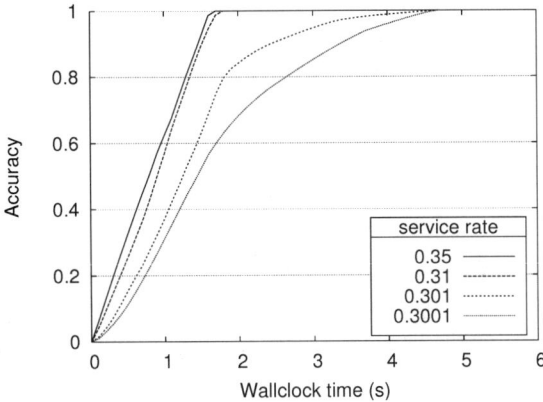

Figure 5. Accuracy function α with $\lambda = 0.3$ and varying μ using 4 processes.

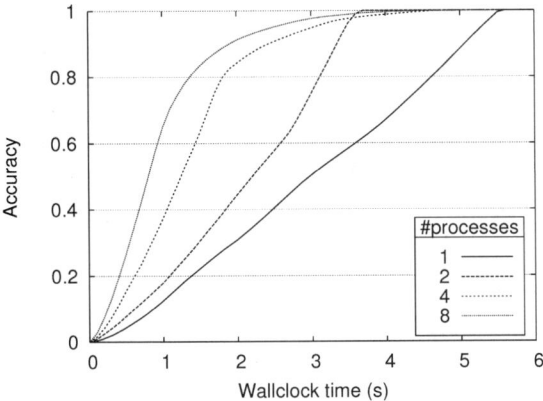

Figure 6. Accuracy function α with $\lambda = 0.3$, $\mu = 0.301$, using a varying number of processes.

$\mu - \lambda = 0.001$ and 4 processes. The accuracy function α is plotted against wallclock time measured in seconds. As expected, accuracy tends to grow slower with an increasing value of λ. Note also, that the accuracy grows faster in the beginning, with the growth slowing down afterwards. This is a desirable property with progressive simulation, as a reasonable accuracy can be achieved after a short runtime, although the calculation of the exact result might take much longer.

Figure 5 shows the results of experiments with a fixed arrival rate $\lambda = 0.3$ and varying service rate μ using 4 processes. Again, the expectation of a slower growth of the accuracy with increased distance $\mu - \lambda$ is met. Note that growth is nearly identical with the larger values of $\mu = 0.35$ and $\mu = 0.31$. However, as the distance between λ and μ decreases to 0.001 and further to 0.0001, the growth of the accuracy decreases significantly.

Figure 6 shows the results of experiments with fixed arrival rate $\lambda = 0.3$ and fixed service rate $\mu = 0.301$ with 1, 2, 4, and 8 parallel processes. As expected, the accuracy tends to grow faster with a higher number of processes, although the increase in growth lags behind the expectation. The reason for this is the significant overhead due to the computation of simulation results, which could be ameliorated by more infrequent result computations.

6. Conclusions

Progressive time-parallel simulation is a novel technique for rapid provision of approximate simulation results with continuous refinement of results by progressive fix-up computations. The process of progressive simulation is performed until correct results have been determined, but can be cancelled at any time before, if result accuracy is sufficient. The method is comparable to existing progressive techniques in various other fields of research, like progressive image rendering or progressive information retrieval.

Progressive time-parallel simulation is a specialized parallelization approach that is not applicable to every kind of model. However, it is supposed that there is a significant number of existing models being suitable for progressive simulation. One of those, queuing system simulation, is presented in more detail in this paper. Time-parallel Least-Recently-Used caching simulation [11] is another, as existing approximate cache simulation approaches [15, 14] can be modified easily to provide results progressively.

A formal model of progressive time-parallel simulation has been provided, with the central aspects of simulation progress and progressive calculation of simulation results. The accuracy of a progressive simulation is required to grow monotonically with time, which has to be ensured in an application of this technique.

The application of progressive time-parallel simulation on existing simulation models was illustrated by the example of queuing systems. The simple nature of basic queuing systems allows for a concise mathematical representation of model dynamics if the stochastic properties of queuing systems are removed by presampling of random numbers. Progressive time-parallel simulation can be used to shorten answer times of a simulation execution, providing estimations of the correct results early on. Result and accuracy functions of a progressive time-parallel queuing simulation have been defined and it has been shown that this is indeed a feasible application of progressive techniques, as the accuracy function is monotonically increasing, starts with the minimum accuracy at the beginning of the simulation, and converges to the maximum accuracy with growing simulation runtime. Furthermore, experiments have been performed to determine the rate of increase of the accuracy function. Depending on the arrival and service rates, as well as the number of parallel processes, these indicate a reasonable growth of accuracy with simulation runtime.

Appendix

A. Proof of Theorem 4.2

Before providing the proof of Theorem 4.2, the following lemma establishes some properties of the global cumulated system time, which are used later.

Lemma A.1. *In the progressive queuing system simulation defined above, it holds that $\widehat{R}(0) = 0$, $\lim_{t \to \infty} \widehat{R}(t) = R$, and $0 \leq \widehat{R}(t) \leq R$ for all $t \geq 0$.*

Proof. Due to Definitions 4.2 and 4.3, $\tau_k(0) \geq \tau_{k-1}(0)$. Hence,

$$\widehat{R}(0) = \sum_{k=1}^{m} \sum_{j=\tau_k(0)}^{\tau_k(0)-1} (d_{u_k}^{j_k}(j) - a(j)) = 0.$$

By definition, $\lim_{t \to \infty} \tau_k(t) = n$, whereby follows for all $k \in \{2, \ldots, m\}$,

$$\lim_{t \to \infty} \tau'_k(t) = \max(\tau_k(0), \lim_{t \to \infty} \tau_{k-1}(t)) = \max(\tau_k(0), n) = n$$

and thus $\lim_{t \to \infty} R_k(t) = 0$. This reduces $\widehat{R}(t)$ to $R_1(t)$ as t tends to infinity. Hence, $\lim_{t \to \infty} \widehat{R}(t) = R$.

Due to Definition 4.1, it holds that $d_{u_k}^{j_k}(j) \geq a(j)$ for all $k \in \{1, \ldots, m\}$ and all $j \in \{j_k, \ldots, n\}$. Therefore, for $t \geq 0$, $R_k(t) \geq 0$ and furthermore $\widehat{R}(t) \geq 0$.

For the proof of $\widehat{R}(t) \leq R$ for $t \geq 0$, first note that for all $k \in \{1, \ldots, m\}$,

$$R_k(t) \leq \sum_{j=\tau_k(t)}^{\tau_k(t)-1} (d_{u_k}^{j_k}(j) - a(j)) =: R'_k(t),$$

as $R'_k(t)$ is basically identical to $R_k(t)$, except that if $\tau_{k-1}(t) < \tau_k(0)$, then all elements between $\tau_{k-1}(t)$ and $\tau_k(0)$ are skipped in the sum of $R_k(t)$. Hence, it remains to be shown that

$$\widehat{R}'(t) := \sum_{k=1}^{m} R'_k(t) \leq R.$$

Due to Theorem 4.1, $d_{u_1}^{j_1}(j) \geq d_{u_k}^{j_k}(j)$ for all $k \in \{1, \ldots, m\}$ and all $j \in N_k$. Thus, for $t \geq 0$,

$$R'_k(t) \leq \sum_{j=\tau_{k-1}(t)}^{\tau_k(t)-1} (d_{u_1}^{j_1}(j) - a(j))$$

and furthermore

$$R = \sum_{k=1}^{m} \sum_{j=\tau_{k-1}(t)}^{\tau_k(t)-1} (d_{u_1}^{j_1}(j) - a(j))$$

leading to $\widehat{R}'(t) \leq R$ and thus $\widehat{R}(t) \leq R$. □

Proof of Theorem 4.2. $\alpha(0) = 0$ and $\lim_{t \to \infty} \alpha(t) = 1$ follow directly from Lemma A.1. As R is constant over time, it remains to be shown, that $\widehat{R}(t)$ is monotonically increasing.

For an arbitrary $t \geq 0$, choose $t' > t$, such that for all $k \in \{1, \ldots, m\}$

(i) $\forall t'' > 0$ with $t < t'' < t'$: $\tau_k(t'') = \tau_k(t)$ and

(ii) $\tau_k(t') \leq \tau_k(t) + 1$ and there exists at least one $k \in \{1, \ldots, m\}$ with $\tau_k(t') = \tau_k(t) + 1$.

Such a time t' can be found due to the monotonicity and completeness of τ_k (see Definition 4.3). Let $G := \{k \in \{1, \ldots, m\} | \tau_k(t') = \tau_k(t) + 1\}$, $G_1 := \{k \in G | \tau_k(t') \leq \tau_{k+1}(0)\}$, and $G_2 := \{k \in G | \tau_k(t') > \tau_{k+1}(0)\}$. Then for all $t'' > 0$ with $t < t'' < t'$, $\widehat{R}(t) = \widehat{R}(t'')$. Furthermore, with $\tau'_k := \tau_k(t') - 1$,

$$\begin{aligned}
\widehat{R}(t) = {} & \widehat{R}(t') + \\
& \sum_{k \in G_1} (d_{u_k}^{j_k}(\tau'_k) - a(\tau'_k)) + \\
& \sum_{k \in G_2} ((d_{u_k}^{j_k}(\tau'_k) - a(\tau'_k)) - (d_{u_{k+1}}^{j_{k+1}}(\tau'_k) - a(\tau'_k)))
\end{aligned}$$

Due to Definition 4.1, $d_{u_k}^{j_k}(\tau'_k) - a(\tau'_k) \geq 0$ for all $k \in \{1, \ldots, m\}$ and due to Theorem 4.1, $d_{u_k}^{j_k}(\tau'_k) \geq d_{u_{k+1}}^{j_{k+1}}(\tau'_k)$ for all $k \in \{1, \ldots, m\}$. Hence, $\widehat{R}(t') \geq \widehat{R}(t)$, and $\widehat{R}$ is monotonically increasing. □

References

[1] R. Beraldi and L. Nigro. A time warp based on temporal uncertainty. *Transactions of the Society for Modeling and Simulation*, 18(2):60–72, 2001.

[2] L. Bergman, H. Fuchs, E. Grant, and S. Spach. Image rendering by adaptive refinement. *ACM SIGGRAPH Computer Graphics*, 20(4):29–37, 1986.

[3] K. Chandy and R. Sherman. Space-time and simulation. In *Proceedings of the SCS Multiconference on Distributed Simulation*, pages 53–57, 1989.

[4] M. F. Cohen, S. E. Chen, J. R. Wallace, and D. P. Greenberg. A progressive refinement approach to fast radiosity image generation. *ACM SIGGRAPH Computer Graphics*, 22(4):75–84, 1988.

[5] R. M. Fujimoto. Parallel discrete event simulation. *Communications of the ACM*, 33(10):30–53, 1990.

[6] R. M. Fujimoto. Exploiting temporal uncertainty in parallel and distributed simulations. In *Proceedings of the 13th Workshop on Parallel and Distributed Simulation*, pages 46–53, 1999.

[7] R. M. Fujimoto. *Parallel and Distributed Simulation Systems*. John Wiley & Sons, New York, 2000.

[8] P. W. Glynn and P. Heidelberger. Analysis of parallel replicated simulations under a completion time constraint. *ACM Transactions on Modeling and Computer Simulation*, 1(1):3–23, 1991.

[9] A. G. Greenberg, B. D. Lubachevsky, and I. Mitrani. Algorithms for unboundedly parallel simulations. *ACM Transactions on Computer Systems*, 9(3):201–221, 1991.

[10] P. Heidelberger. Statistical analysis of parallel simulations. In *Proceedings of the 1986 Winter Simulation Conference*, pages 290–295, 1986.

[11] P. Heidelberger and H. S. Stone. Parallel trace-driven cache simulation by time partitioning. In *Proceedings of the 1990 Winter Simulation Conference*, pages 734–737, 1990.

[12] D. Jackson and C. Northway, editors. *Scalable Vector Graphics (SVG) Version 1.2*. World Wide Web Consortium (W3C), April 2005. W3C Working Draft. Available at http://www.w3.org/TR/SVG12/.

[13] A. K. Jain. *Fundamentals of Digital Image Processing*. Prentice-Hall, Inc., 1989.

[14] T. Kiesling. Achieving linear speedup in parallel LRU cache simulation. In *Proceedings of the 12th GI/ITG Conference on Measuring, Modelling, and Evaluation of Computer and Communication Systems*, pages 167–172, 2004.

[15] T. Kiesling. Approximate time-parallel cache simulation. In *Proceedings of the 2004 Winter Simulation Conference*, pages 345–354, 2004.

[16] T. Kiesling and T. Krieger. Efficient distributed simulation of queuing systems. Technical Report 2006-01, Fakultät für Informatik, Universität der Bundeswehr München, 2006.

[17] T. Kiesling and S. Pohl. Time-parallel simulation with approximative state matching. In *Proceedings of the 18th Workshop on Parallel and Distributed Simulation*, pages 195–202, 2004.

[18] N. K. Krivulin. Recursive equations based models of queueing systems. In *Proceedings of the 1994 European Simulation Symposium*, pages 252–256, 1994.

[19] Y. Lin. Parallel trace driven simulation for packet loss in finite buffered voice multiplexers. *Parallel Computing*, 19(2):219–228, 1993.

[20] Y. Lin and E. Lazowska. A time-division algorithm for parallel simulation. *ACM Transactions on Modeling and Computer Simulation*, 1(1):73–83, 1991.

[21] J. W. S. Liu, K.-J. Lin, W.-K. Shih, A. C.-S. Yu, J.-Y. Chung, and W. Zhao. Algorithms for scheduling imprecise computations. *Computer*, 24(5):58–68, 1991.

[22] P. Martini, M. Rümekasten, and J. Tölle. Tolerant synchronization for distributed simulations of interconnected computer networks. In *Proceedings of the 11th Workshop on Parallel and Distributed Simulation*, pages 138–141, 1997.

[23] A. S. McGough and I. Mitrani. Efficient distributed simulation of a communication switch with bursty sources and losses. In *Proceedings of the 14th Workshop on Parallel and Distributed Simulation*, pages 85–92, 2000.

[24] I. Nikolaidis, R. M. Fujimoto, and C. A. Cooper. Time-parallel simulation of cascaded statistical multiplexers. In *Proceedings of the 1994 SIGMETRICS Conference on Measurement and Modeling of Computer Systems*, pages 213–240, 1994.

[25] D. Olteanu, T. Kiesling, and F. Bry. An evaluation of regular path expressions with qualifiers against XML streams. In *Proceedings of the 19th International Conference on Data Engineering*, pages 702–704, 2003.

[26] D. M. Rao, N. V. Thondugulam, R. Radhakrishnan, and P. A. Wilsey. Unsynchronized parallel discrete event simulation. In *Proceedings of the 1998 Winter Simulation Conference*, pages 1563–1570, 1998.

[27] B. K. Szymanki, Y. Liu, A. Sastry, and K. Madnani. Real-time on-line network simulation. In *Proceedings of the 5th IEEE International Workshop on Distributed Simulation and Real-Time Applications*, pages 22–29, 2001.

[28] B. K. Szymanski, Q. Gu, and Y. Liu. Time-network partitioning for large-scale parallel network simulation under SSFNet. In *Proceedings of the Applied Telecommunications Symposium*, 2002.

[29] K.-L. Tan, P.-K. Eng, and B. C. Ooi. Efficient progressive skyline computation. In *Proceedings of the 27th International Conference on Very Large Data Bases*, pages 301–310, 2001.

[30] J. J. Wang and M. Abrams. Massively time-parallel, approximate simulation of loss queueing systems. *Annals of Operations Research*, 53:553–575, 1994.

[31] H. Wu, R. M. Fujimoto, and M. Ammar. Time-parallel trace-driven simulation of CSMA/CD. In *Proceedings of the 17th Workshop on Parallel and Distributed Simulation*, pages 105–114, 2003.

[32] S. Zilberstein and A.-I. Mouaddib. Reactive control of dynamic progressive processing. In *Proceedings of 16th International Joint Conference on Artificial Intelligence*, pages 1268–1273, 1999.

Developing An Hierarchical Simulator for Beta-binders

Jan Himmelspach*, Paola Lecca+, Davide Prandi+,
Corado Priami+, Paola Quaglia+, Adelinde Uhrmacher*
*Department of Computer Science, University of Rostock, Germany &
+The Microsoft Research - University of Trento Center of Computational and Systems Biology, Italy
jh|lin@informatik.uni-rostock.de & lecca|prandi|priami|quaglia@dit.unitn.it

Abstract

BETA-BINDERS *form a recently developed extension of stochastic* π CALCULUS *to describe micro-biological systems. It introduces special binders to wrap processes just as membranes enclose some living matter and hence to mimic biological interfaces. One means to define the operational semantics of a modeling formalism is by an abstract simulator description. In developing an abstract simulator for* BETA-BINDERS *concepts are adopted that have been developed in the context of* JAMES II. *Processors of the simulator are structured into a hierarchy and each of them is splitted into different methods. This design reflects the structure of* BETA-BINDERS *models and facilitates experimenting with different operational semantics. Two discrete event simulation schemes, the First-Gillespie method and Gibson-Bruck method, are combined to calculate the reactions that occur within and between the modeled bioprocesses, respectively. The functioning of the simulator is illustrated by processing step-wise the reaction of an immune cell to the occurrence of a virus.*

1 Introduction

Although continuous systems models are the dominant type of models being used in Systems Biology [5], stochastic discrete event models are recently gaining ground as well. They address specific constraints of continuous, deterministic models: concentrations do not necessarily change continuously. In addition, the dynamics of some biological systems can be best approached in a stochastic manner, e.g. if the gene regulation is to be described, where stochastic fluctuations are abundant.

For a discrete description of biological systems different general modeling formalisms for discrete event systems have been employed over the last years, e.g. DEVS [7], PETRI NETS [12], and stochastic π-CALCULUS [13]. Applications in Systems Biology have revealed deficiencies of the respective general modeling formalism [21], that are being addressed by extending the respective formalisms. E.g. recent developments like BIOAMBIENTS which is based on the stochastic π-CALCULUS, allow the description of spatial cell compartments, and entities moving from one compartment to the next [20]. The BRANE CALCULI [3] addresses the need for modeling constructs of cellular coordination via membranes. It forms an application specific refinement of the general modeling and simulation approach. In the PROJECTIVE BRANE CALCULI the membrane actions become directed thereby, moving the calculi even closer to the perception of the activities within biological membranes [4].

Similarly BETA-BINDERS introduce special binders, so called *bio-processes* (or simply in the following *boxes*), to wrap processes just as membranes enclose some living matter and hence to mimic biological interfaces. The concrete places of interaction (the sites where the molecules might dock) are called *sites* or *binder* whose type constrains the interaction with other bio-processes. The basic formalism of BETA-BINDERS has been introduced in [17] and a stochastic extension of BETA-BINDERS is being presented in [6].

Whereas some simulators for stochastic π-CALCULUS exist, e.g. BIOSPI [18], SPIM [15], and STOPI [1], the development of simulators for the various extensions, including BETA-BINDERS, has just started. Thus, currently, the diverse extensions of the stochastic π are only used for describing biological systems. No simulator implementations exist so far.

The current paper addresses this lack of simulators by defining an abstract simulator for BETA-BINDERS. The idea to define the operational semantics of a modeling formalism by an abstract simulator which can also serve as a basis for simulator implementations has been put forward by Bernard Zeigler in the context of DEVS [23]. Only recently Philips and Cardelli introduced an abstract simulator for stochastic π-CALCULUS [15] which forms the basis of the SPIM simulator.

The idea of BETA-BINDERS, i.e. grouping individual

processes into bio-processes and let them interact via binder but otherwise independently, leads to the idea to reflect this kind of interaction at the level of simulators by providing a simulator component for each bio-process (or box) and a coordinator for synchronizing the interaction between bio-processes respectively. The concepts are inspired by the hierarchical processor tree [10] and the handling of variable structure events in DEVS-type models in JAMES II [11]. In JAMES II the hierarchical design and the exploitation of template patterns have facilitated the development of a family of different simulators that can be easily combined. Although the DEVS and BETA-BINDERS formalism are very different, e.g. for a comparison of DEVS and stochastic π-CALCULUS see [21], adopting and adapting these concepts shall support also a flexible and convenient exploration of different simulators for BETA-BINDERS.

The paper is structured as follows. We will first shortly introduce the First-Gillespie method as a basis for discrete-event simulation in Systems Biology and afterward describe the basic concepts of BETA-BINDERS. Together with a simulator component for executing stochastic π-CALCULUS they form the basis for developing the abstract simulator for BETA-BINDERS which is structured bottom-up into simulators, coordinators, and root coordinator. Simulators are responsible for processing events within the boxes, a coordinator synchronizes the activities of and the interactions between the boxes, the root-coordinator advances the time. The functioning of the abstract simulator will be illustrated based on an example. Afterward the flexibility of the approach will be shown by changing the interpretation of individual activities in the BETA-BINDERS calculus and presenting the implied changes of the simulator.

2 Background

2.1 Introduction into Gillespie Algorithms

As most other work on discrete-event simulation in Systems Biology we will base our algorithms on the first reaction method introduced by Gillespie (FG) [9] and the next reaction method (GB) introduced by Gibson and Bruck [8].

Algorithm 1 First reaction method of Gillespie

```
1  //set initial numbers of molecules
2  initialize
3  while not done do
4    for each r in reactions do
5      a[r] := calculatePropensity(r)
6      tonie[r] := generatePTime(r, a[r])
7    end for
8    //get the reaction having the least time
9    nextReaction := getNextReaction (tonie)
10   numMolecules := execute(nextReaction)
11   time := time + tonie[nextReaction]
12 end while
```

First for each reaction (r) its propensity is calculated (a)

which takes the number of reactants available and the velocity of the reaction into account. The time span until the next event is calculated as an exponential distributed variate with mean $a[r]$. The reaction whose time is next, advances the current simulation time. As Gibson and Bruck noticed the original FG uses r random numbers per iteration, takes time proportional to r to update the propensities, and takes time proportional to r to identify the smallest time of next event [8].

In the solution Gibson and Bruck suggest, the tentative reaction times are computed for each reaction once during initialization. The reactions are stored in a priority queue with the smallest tentative execution time in root position. Then the first reaction is selected from the root position and executed. During update only the tentative execution time of the last executed reaction using a single random number and the priority queue have to be updated accordingly. Finally all reactions that are affected by the substrate and product changes of the executed reaction can be updated without using a new random number. The next reaction method only needs one random number per iteration. Events are scheduled in advance, and only those events that are affected by the current reaction have to be rescheduled. To identify them a dependency graph is used. The performance gain of GB is the larger the more sparse the dependency matrix of the reaction network is [8]. Little work has been done so far in evaluating the performance of different discrete event simulation algorithms in Systems Biology. Mostly they are offered as alternative to a processing by numerical integration [22]. However, the benefit in supporting different discrete-event simulators within one simulation system is slowly being acknowledged, e.g. [19].

2.2 Introduction into Beta-binders

BETA-BINDERS[17] is a formal language that merges the basic features of classical process calculi [14] with the intuition that, in order to better model biological entities, simple concurrent processes can be wrapped by borders with explicit interaction sites.

A process in BETA-BINDERS ("bio-process" for short) is defined as a box with a proper border and an internal machinery. The entities lying within the borders ("processes") are formally made up of a limited number of operators that allow to express, e.g., the high degree of parallelism of the activities of the living matter. Parallel internal processes can independently execute their input and output actions, or synchronize the one with the other on complementary actions (input and output on the same channel are meant to be complementary). The enclosing borders mimic biological membranes and are equipped with typed sites that resemble the motifs of molecules.

A set of parallel bio-processes forms a system, and the

language is provided with a formal operational semantics that describes the evolution of the specified system. We refer the reader to [17] for an introductory reading about the underlying mathematical model, and give just an informal presentation of the language.

The possible execution steps of a bio-process can be roughly classified into the following categories:

1. synchronization of an input and an output action by two processes internal to the same box (intra-communication);

2. modification of the enclosing interface of a certain box (hiding, unhiding, or exposing a site);

3. synchronization, through a matching pair of interaction sites, of an input and an output action distributed on distinct boxes (inter-communication);

4. structural modification of the set of boxes (join or split of boxes) driven by suitable functions.

In the stochastic extension of BETA-BINDERS [6], each execution step represents a *reaction* in Gillespie terminology, and propensity functions can be computed on the basis of rate reaction constants and of the number of entities competing to perform an analogous reaction. For the reactions described in (1-2) above, rate constants are associated with channel names (1) and with site names (2), respectively. For (3), rate constants are bound to the pair of interaction sites that allow information flow between boxes, and for (4) the constants are given by the functions applied to get the actual reactions. To give just a flavor of BETA-BINDERS semantics, we show below the representation of (part of) the Michaelis-Menten equation for competitive inhibition:

$$IE + S \underset{K_{EI}^{-1}}{\overset{K_{EI}}{\rightleftharpoons}} I + E + S \underset{K_{ES}^{-1}}{\overset{K_{ES}}{\rightleftharpoons}} I + ES \overset{K_P}{\rightharpoonup} I + E + P.$$

A competitive inhibitor I is a molecule that can occupy the catalytic site of an enzyme E. When this happens, the substrate S cannot be catalyzed by E and hence cannot transform into product P. The values K_X in the above equation represent the constant rate of the labeled reaction. Here we focus on the single reaction:

$$IE + S \overset{K_{EI}}{\rightharpoonup} I + E + S.$$

In BETA-BINDERS each of the reactants I, E and S is specified as a distinct box that executes in parallel with the others. Graphically:

$$\begin{array}{ccc} \Delta_I & \Delta_E & \Delta_S \\ \boxed{Q_I} & \boxed{Q_E} & \boxed{Q_S} \end{array} \quad (1)$$

where the leftmost box corresponds to I, the middle one to E and the rightmost to S. Each bio-process has an active site typed by Δ_X and an internal structure given by process Q_X. The operational semantics of the language is such that,

with the constant rate K_{EI} of the enzyme/inhibitor reaction, the system displayed in (1) performs a join-step and moves to the configuration

$$\begin{array}{cc} \Delta_I^h \quad \Delta_E^h & \Delta_S \\ \boxed{Q_I \mid Q_E} & \boxed{Q_S} \end{array}$$

where the leftmost box corresponds to the complex IE in the Michaelis-Menten equation. Therein, the two backbones Q_I and Q_E are put in touch (composed in parallel), and the sites Δ_I and Δ_E are hidden (written Δ_X^h) to mean that the sites of I and E are now occupied. This configuration can still be reversed, as expressed by $IE + S \overset{K_{EI}^{-1}}{\rightharpoonup} I + E + S$, depending on the behavior of the actual specification of $Q_I \mid Q_E$.

2.3 A Simulator for Stochastic π

As the internal processes Q_i of the bio-processes are typical stochastic pi-processes, we define a simulator for stochastic π as a first step toward developing a BETA-BINDERS Simulator. Thereby, we will adopt the idea proposed in [10] to split simulators into different parts, i.e. *postEvent* and *doEvent*. Whereas the *postEvent* is utilized for calculating the time of next event, the *doEvent* method is responsible for executing the event.

Algorithm 2 Pseudo Code of the *doEvent* simulator for Stochastic pi

```
1  when receive * message
2    toDo    := extractMin(pel)
3    selProc := randSelProcPair (getChan(toDo), term)
4    term    := reducePI (term, getChan(toDo), selProc)
5  end when
```

The *doEvent* method takes the first element of the pending event list *pel* (02), selects randomly a pair of processors waiting on channel *getChan(toDo)* (03) and reduces the current state *term* by applying the reduction rules, defined for stochastic π [16] according to the selected channel *getChan(toDo)* and the selected processes *selProc* (04). The *postEvent* method calculates what reaction is going to take place and when it is going to take place according to the approach suggested by Gillespie in his first reaction method (FG). In the first reaction variant of Gillespie the pending event list, contains exactly one element. If we were to realize the next reaction method by Gibson and Bruck, the pending event list would contain more than one element. One of the difficulties in stochastic π however is to maintain the dependency graph as inter dependencies are frequently changing. Therefore, simulators for stochastic π use FG rather than the method by Gibson and Bruck.

The developed simulator is rather similar to the simulation engine of BIOSPI, SPIM, or STOPI (for a detailed comparison of the three simulators see [15]). Unlike the other

Algorithm 3 Pseudo Code of the *postEvent* simulator (FG) for Stochastic pi

```
1  for each i in currentChannel(term) do
2    a[i]   := propensity(i, term)
3    tau[i] := exponentialRandom(a[i])
4    if t + tau[i] < getTime(first(pel)) then
5      pel := replaceFirst(pel,(i, tau[i]))
6  end for
7  send done(tonie) message to coord.
```

simulators its design is aimed at facilitating its adaptation and extension as will be shown by developing a simulator for BETA-BINDERS.

3 A Hierarchical Simulation Concept for Beta-binders

The above simulator handles the synchronization of an input and an output action by two processes internal to the same box (intra-communication). Now, the question is how the above algorithm has to be adapted if the other execution steps of a bio-process shall be supported, i.e.:

1. expose, hide, unhide
2. inter
3. join, split

Expose, hide, unhide change the interface of a box and are associated with a temporal delay. They can be initiated locally. *Inter*, the interaction between boxes and *join, split* are based upon and effect more than one bio-process. Therefore, we decide to schedule (1) within the individual simulators, whereas (2) and (3) shall be done on the next higher level, i.e. by the coordinator. Please note that join and split are defined as axiom schema at the level of the entire model. E.g. as soon as certain conditions are met, a join or split of bio-processes will be executed. A join defines typically the aggregation of boxes, renaming of the enclosed π processes, and the definition of the actual interface. We currently restrict the conditions to trigger a join or split to the knowledge about interfaces. This is not a true restriction as all bio-processes are able to change their sites and thus, trigger the join and split events respectively. In addition it seems intuitive that both are preceded by some changes at the binders of the bio-processes.

With each box a simulator is associated. We associate with the entire BETA-BINDERS model one coordinator responsible for coordinating the interactions between the boxes and checking whether joins and splits are to occur. Currently no nesting of boxes is supported. Therefore, directly above the coordinator the root coordinator is responsible for advancing the simulation time. The hierarchical processor tree will proceed by pulses of messages that propagate the tree structure down and up. The simulator components are based on FG [8]). The coordinator is based on an event scheduling approach according to the GB method.

3.1 A Simulator Component

Algorithm 4 Pseudo Code of the *doEvent* method of the Beta-binders simulator

```
1  when receive * or xy message
2    if * message then
3      toDo := extractMin(pel)
4      if toDo isA expose or hide or unhide or inter
           then
5        selProc := randSelOneProc (getType(toDo),
             getChan(toDo), term)
6      else
7        selProc := randSelProcPair (getChan(toDo),
             term)
8      end if
9    else
10     toDo   := xy
11     selProc := randSelOneProc (getType(toDo),
           getChan(toDo), term)
12   end if
13   term := reduceBeta (term, getChan(toDo),
           getType(toDo), selProc)
14   varStruct := getVarStruct (term,toDo)
15 end when
```

In contrast to the basic stochastic π simulator now * and *xy* messages are received by a simulator. In DEVS-like simulators *xy* messages announce the arrival of an external event as an input. In BETA-BINDERS an *xy* message announces an inter communication between boxes, i.e. *inter*, which might mean the arriving (input) or requesting (output) of an event. Please note that communication happens synchronously in BETA-BINDERS, as it does in stochastic π CALCULUS and not asynchronously, as it e.g. is the case in DEVS [21]. The simulator distinguishes between a normal *intra* interaction taking place (06,07) and an activity of type hiding, unhiding, exposing a site or an inter interaction (04,05). The former requires the random selection of a pair of processes to resume computing and corresponds to a normal stochastic pi processing. The latter implies that one of the internal processes waiting for an expose, hide, unhide, or inter event will be resumed. The simulator distinguishes box external events (09,10,11) that arrive at the simulator via an *xy* message and indicate an inter event, either an input or an output request. The *reduceBeta* follows the reduction rule specified in [17]. The reduction method has to take care that suspended processes are correctly resumed after a * or *xy* message has been received. The reduction will stop at the moment a time scheduled event is encountered and the according process will be suspended. The change of interface is handled by the simulator itself. However, it has to inform the coordinator about the newly available, or newly hidden binders, and it has to send a request for an inter-interaction to the coordinator. All this information is collected in *varStruct* (14):

- the execution of expose, hide, and unhide, which includes the name of the Beta-binders and the type,
- the request for an inter event, which includes all information required by the coordinator for a matchmaking

and a substitution

Whereas the coordinator has only to be informed about an already executed expose, hide, and unhide event, the inter event forms a request. The inter event shall be scheduled in the future, with a certain delay that depends on the rate of the binders. Thus, inter events are scheduled at the coordinator, and are competing with the events: intra, expose, hide, unhide of all boxes. Whatever is scheduled first, will win.

Algorithm 5 Pseudo Code of the *postEvent* method (FG) of the Beta-binders simulator

```
1   for each i in currentChannel(term) do
2     a[i]   := propensity(i, term)
3     tau[i] := exponentialRandom(a[i])
4     if t + tau[i] < getTime(first(pel)) then
5       pel := replaceFirst(pel,(i, tau[i], ''intra''))
6   end for
7   for each i in currentExpose(term) do
8     a[i]   := propensity(i, term)
9     tau[i] := exponentialRandom(a[i])
10    if t + tau[i] < getTime(first(pel)) then
11      pel := replaceFirst(pel,(i, tau[i], ''expose''))
12  end for
13  for each i in currentHide(term) do
14    ...
15  end for
16  for each i in currentUnHide(term) do
17    ...
18  end for
19  tonie := getTime(first(pel))
20  send done(tonie, varStruct) message to coord
```

Within the simulator the processes of intra communication (03,..), expose (09,..), hide, and unhide are competing who is first. Thereby, they will determine the time of next event of the box. For all current channels (reactions), the propensities are re-calculated, and the minimum is determined (06,07). This will determine the time of the next intra event to happen. Afterward events of type hide, unhide and expose are scheduled. Therefore, we take the propensity into account. Again the minimum is built and if the expose event has a time stamp less than the intra-interaction events, it will be scheduled as next event to happen (10,11). The same is done for hide and unhide respectively. The coordinator will receive the information when the time of next event is scheduled for this box and the information about variable structures (*varStruct*), which includes the information about changes of the interfaces, and current requests on inter-interactions (20). Please note that each expose implies that a new name is generated, however, for inter communication only the types are important. If we have n processes requesting an expose with the same type, successively expose events will be scheduled and executed resulting in a set of binders with different names but all with the same type. So after a time span we will likely have n binders being of the same type and thus will be able to respond to the same interaction request. The names of the binders themselves are only used in the context of the box.

3.2 A Coordinator for Beta-binders

Algorithm 6 Pseudo Code of the *doEvent* method of the Beta-binders coordinator (Join/Split without rates)

```
1   when receive * message
2     toDo := extractMin(pel)
3     if toDo isA inter then
4       selBoxes := randSelMatchingPair
                    (getBinderType(toDo), boxList)
5       binders := getBinders(getBinderType(toDo),
                    selBoxes)
6       send xy(sending(binders)) to sending(selBoxes)
7       send xy(receiving(binders)) to
                    receiving(selBoxes)
8     else
9       selBoxes := getBox(toDo)
10      send * message to simulator of selBoxes
11    end if
12    for each i in selBoxes do
13      wait for done from i
14      update tonie of i
15    end for
16    for each i in selBoxes do
17      boxList[i] := updateInterface(varStruct[i],
                      boxList[i])
18    if checkForJoinAndSplit(boxList, joinSplit) then
19      boxList := executeJoinSplit(boxList, joinSplit)
20  end when
```

The coordinator keeps a pending event list *pel* list where the time of next event of the different boxes are recorded. If an event that is scheduled "internally" within a box (which might be of type inter, hide, unhide, or expose) is the next to happen the simulator of the corresponding box is informed via a * message (07). Other events are also in the *pel* list of the coordinator: those are inter events (03) that signalize the interactions between two bio-processes. They are calculated in analogy to the intra interaction within the boxes, i.e. the propensities are considered (cp. the *postEvent* method). To the specification of a model belongs the specification of the f_{join} and f_{split} functions with which the reduction rule for a join or split is parametrized [17]. They define the new interface, the potential renaming and the merging and splitting of boxes. They are stored in *joinSplit*. In this version the join and split operations are assumed to be time less. If they were associated with a time delay, they would not directly be executed but be scheduled in the pending event list for being executed at a later time. The coordinator keeps also a list for variable structures, e.g. which also includes the information at which time an inter request is seen at the interface of an individual box.

After *done* messages have been received, the interfaces of the boxes possibly need to be updated. The information about current boxes, their interfaces, and the currently requested inter-interaction form the state that the coordinator works upon. A *checkForJoinAndSplit* is executed after all other processes have been completed to see whether the structure of the boxes has to be changed. In the *postEvent* method it is checked, whether a join or split has been executed by comparing the old and new boxes. If the structure

Algorithm 7 Pseudo Code of the *postEvent* method (GB) of the Beta-binders coordinator

```
1  for each i in compare(oldBoxList,boxList) do
2      boxList[i] := updateSimulator(boxList[i])
3  pel := updatePel (pel, boxList)
4  for each i in union(someMatchingBetaTypes(boxList),
          affected(toDo)) do
5      a[i]   := propensityBeta(i, boxList)
6      tau[i] := exponentialRandom(a[i])
7      pel    := updateAndSort (pel,(i, t + tau[i],
          ``inter'', a[i]))
8  end for
9  tonie := getTime (first(pel))
10 oldBoxList := boxList
11 send done(tonie) to (root)coord.
```

of the boxes changed, the structure of the simulator tree will change with it (1,2) and the time of next event of the new box(es) will be newly calculated. The pending event list will be updated. Afterward the propensities of matching binders that are effected by the last activity (*toDo*) are updated (04,..,08). Inter-interaction are affected by

- the removal and addition of binders they are referring to, that might be due to a hide, unhide, expose, join, or split
- a change of site types, and
- if a request is made at a binder where before was none of this type, or
- if no longer a request is associated with a certain binder.

Thus, the calculation of the propensity of Beta-binders is more complex than the calculation of propensities of channels in traditional stochastic π. For intra events the names of channels are used for counting. To schedule the inter communication, all possible combinations of matching binder types have to be taken into account (04,05). If the propensity has been calculated, the pending event list has to be changed and newly sorted (07). Afterward the time of next event can be determined and sent to the (root) coordinator. The root coordinator will simply advance the time, and will send a * message to the coordinator to continue.

4 An example - the virus attack

Let us go through a simple virus attack, that has been described in [17]. Three bio-processes characterize the example, i.e. a virus, a cell of our immune system (macrophage) which can engulf the virus by endocytosis, elaborate it, distill the antigen molecule and display the antigen on its surface, a lymphocyte which can recognize the antogene and then activate mechanisms of the immune reply. Let us take a look at Figure 1. In the top line the current situation is depicted, the bio-processes are from left to right, the cell, the virus and the lymphocyte. In the midth the currently active nodes of the processor tree are identified. At the right of the figure fragments of the introduced algorithms are listed to illustrate the corresponding activity of the simulators and coordinators.

At t_1 the cell has just changed its type of site to include the type v_1, so to be able to engulf the virus. At the level of the entire model it is now recognized that a join can occur.

$$f_{join}(B_1, B_2) =$$
$$\text{if } (B_1 = \beta(x, \Gamma) \, B_1^*) \text{ and}$$
$$(B_2 = \beta(y, \Delta) \, B_2^*) \text{ and } (\Gamma \cap \Delta)$$
$$\text{then } (\beta(x, \Gamma) \, B_1^*, \emptyset, \{x/y\}, \text{Basal Rate})$$

For its execution the coordinator signs responsible. The join is executed within the *doEvent* method of the coordinator. Thereby, the y occurrence within the original virus is replaced by x. Although the join is triggered by conditions referring to the interface, the join has an effect on the overall structure and the processes within the boxes. Within the *postEvent* method the simulator structure is updated, and times of next events are recalculated, and the pending event list is updated as well. Now the current simulation step is complete and the coordinator sends the time of next event to the root coordinator, which sends a * message to the coordinator with the time of next event, i.e. t_2. According to the coordinator's *pel* an event of the cell model is due, therefore a * message is forwarded to the simulator of the cell model.

At t_2 the simulator checks its pending event list and identifies the event to be of type intra. Thus the term is reduced: the output $\overline{x}(a_1)$ and the input x interact thereby replacing the occurence of w of the receiving stochastic π process by a_1. No further reduction can occur since expose has also delays associated with it. After the *doEvent* method of the simulator has completed the *postEvent* method is invoked and calculates the time of next event to be sent to the coordinator. The *varStruct* is empty. The done message propagates up the tree the coordinator updates the time of next events, and the root coordinator triggers a new pulse with t_3, which reaches again the simulator of the cell.

At time t_3 the simulator of cell has been activated again by a * message, an expose shall be executed now. This will be done by reducing the term. Afterward the simulator will calculate the *varStruct* which will now contain an expose, (expose $u:\{a_i\}$), and the information of inter, (inter $\overline{u}$). The simulator will send the information of time of next event and *varStruct* to the coordinator. The coordinator will change the interface of the box representing the cell accordingly and will schedule an inter event. Again the messages propagate the processor tree up and down.

At time t_4 the coordinator receives the * messages and identifies an inter event to be the next to be executed. It selects the corresponding bio-processes (in a normal model we would have many immune cells and many viruses) and sends * messages to both. Please note that therefore the types of the binders have to be compatible (which is the case

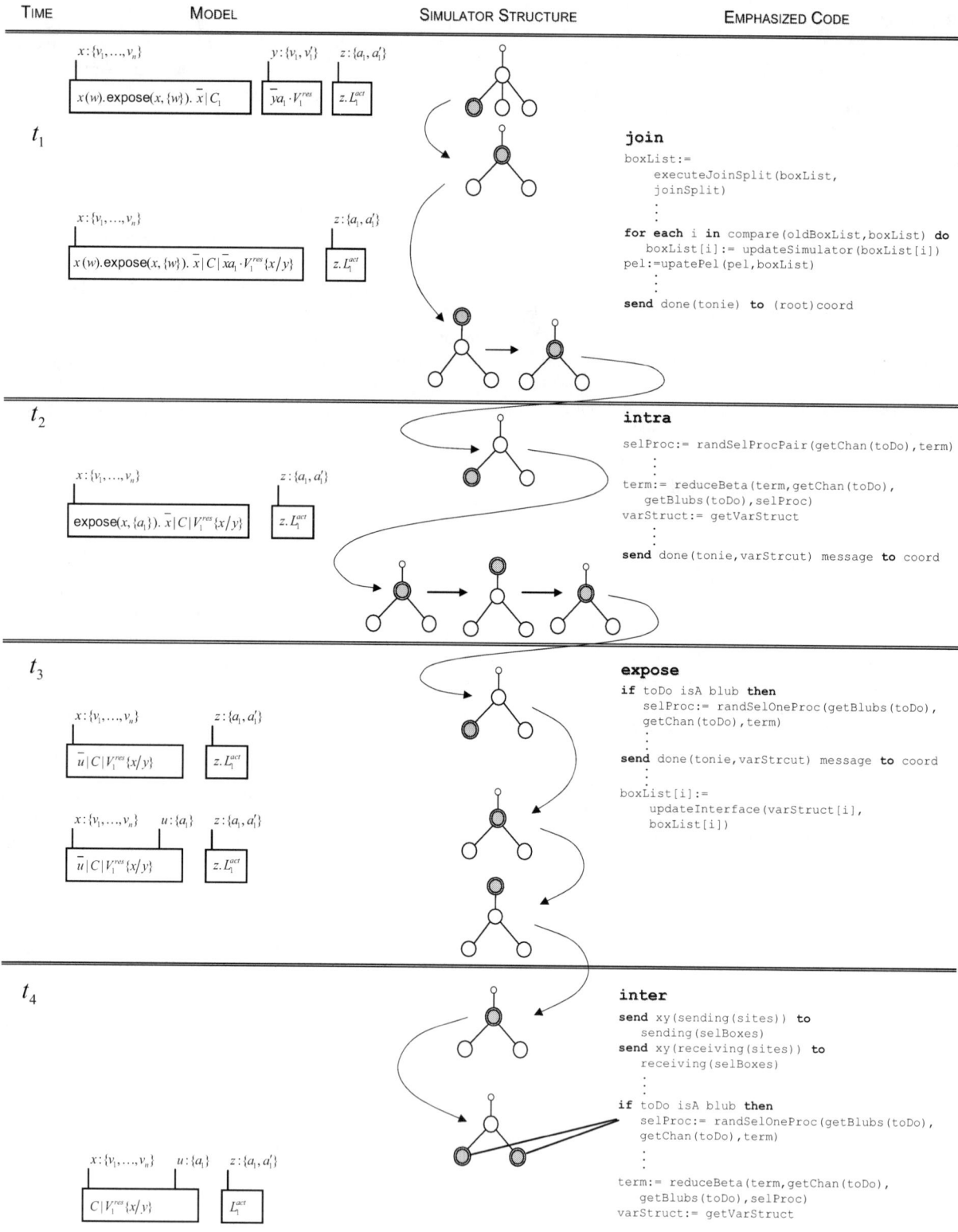

Figure 1. Virus attack - step wise

both types include a_1). The lymphocyte will be activated and can reduce to L_1^{act}, and the cell process is reduced to the processes $C|V_1^{res}x/y$.

5 Adaptability of the Concept

To illustrate the flexibility of the developed concept, let us assume two changes of interpreting a BETA-BINDERS model.

5.1 Join and Split with Rates

Algorithm 8 Pseudo Code of the *doEvent* method of the Beta-binders coordinator with delayed joins and splits

```
1  when receive * message
2    toDo    := extractMin(pel)
3    selBoxes := {}
4    if toDo isA inter or toDo isA intra then
5      if toDo isA inter then
6        selBoxes := randSelMatchingPair
                      (getBinderType(toDo), boxList)
7        binders := getBinders(getBinderType(toDo),
                      selBoxes)
8        send xy(sending(binders)) to sending(selBoxes)
9        send xy(receiving(binders)) to
                      receiving(selBoxes)
10     else
11       selBoxes := getBox(toDo)
12       send * message to simulators of selBoxes
13     end if
14     for each i in selBoxes do
15       wait for done from i
16       update tonie of i
17     end for
18     for each i in selBoxes do
19       boxList[i] := updateInterface(varStruct[i],
                      boxList[i])
20    else
21      if checkForJoinAndSplitToDo (boxList, toDo) then
22        boxList := executeJoinSplitToDo (boxList,
                      toDo)
23      endif
24  end when
```

The prior simulation engine assumes that join and split are being done instantly without delay. Now we assume that join and split have rates associated with them. In this case only the *doEvent* method of the coordinator has to be adapted, as now join and split are scheduled like the inter events by the coordinator. Please note that although the join or split has been scheduled for this time to happen, it might be that the original conditions that triggered the join and split are no longer true, in this case in the above example they will not be executed. The *postEvent* method does not need to be changed at all.

5.2 Expose without propensity

Another interpretation of expose is to calculate this without propensity. At execution time each request for an expose receives a different name. So we can also calculate

Algorithm 9 *postEvent* method of the Beta-binders simulator without expose Propensity

```
1  for each i in currentChannel(term) do
2    a[i] := propensity(i, term)
3    tau[i] := exponentialRandom(a[i])
4    if t + tau[i] < getTime(first(pel)) then
5      pel := replaceFirst(pel,(i, tau[i]))
6  end for
7  for each i in currentExpose(term) do
8    tau[i] := exponentialRandom(rate(i))
9    if t + tau[i] < getTime(first(pel)) then
10     pel := replaceFirst(pel,(i, tau[i], ''expose''))
11 end for
12 for each i in currentHide(term) do
13   ...
14 end for
15 for each i in currentUnHide(term) do
16   ...
17 end for
18 tonie := getTime(first(pel))
19 send done(tonie, varStruct) message to coord.
```

it without propensity. In this case only two lines in the *postEvent* method of the Beta Binder Simulator have to be changed. This time only the *postEvent* of the simulator is effected and the *doEvent* method remains the same. Thus different kinds of interpretation can easily be realized. This flexibility will not only help in testing the implications of different operational semantics of the modeling formalisms, which is important when developing new modeling formalisms. Over the last few years a series of algorithms have been developed to improve the performance of discrete event simulation in Systems Biology, e.g. either by splitting models into slow and fast processes, by approximating rather than exactly calculating future events, or by parallel executions [2]. As always an efficient simulation will depend on many aspects including the structure of the model. Thus, a flexible easily extendable simulation engine following the approach taken in JAMES II will support efficiently simulating diverse models and systematically comparing different simulation approaches.

6 Conclusion

Inspired by the work in JAMES II we introduced an abstract simulator for BETA-BINDERS. For each box a simulator signs responsible. The synchronization between boxes is done by the coordinator. The simulators are working based on the first Gillespie method and are responsible for scheduling *expose, hide, unhide* events. The *inter* events are scheduled by the coordinator. The coordinator is also checking whether the conditions for a *join, split* are given. Currently if more than one process is able to be processed only one will be resumed, and this one will be selected randomly. With this the simulator stands in the tradition of the traditional simulators for stochastic π like BIOSPI, SPIM, and STOPI. The structure of the developed abstract simulator facilitates realizing a family of simulators. As has been shown two further variants of BETA-BINDERS required only slight changes in the simulator code. The hierarchical structure and splitting each single simulator into *doEvent* and *postEvent* methods reduces significantly the effort required to conceptualize and realize different simulators as has been shown in the simulation system JAMES II [10, 11]. Future work will be dedicated to exploiting the developed concepts in concrete implementations. E.g. the different time scales at which events of type *inter, join, and split* on the one side and *intra* on the other side typically occur indicate a partitioning into logical processes that should allow an efficient parallel execution. Simulators supporting different interpretations, execution modes, and degrees of exactness are particularly important, if an area has as much momentum as the area of process calculi and their applications in Systems Biology. The realization of such a family of simulators will be facilitated by the presented design.

References

[1] A. Bloch, M. Hoyer, and S. Knudsen. The stopi-calculus and simulator. http://www.cs.auc.dk?~steffen/dat4/stopi, 2003.

[2] K. Burrage, P. Burrage, N. Hamilton, and T. Tian. Compute intensive simulations for cellular models. In A. Y. Zomaya, editor, *Parallel Computation for Bioinformatics and Computational Biology*. Wiley, 2005.

[3] L. Cardelli. Brane Calculi. In *Proc. of BIO-CONCUR'03*, Electronic Notes in Theoretcial Computer Science. Elsevier, 2003.

[4] V. Danos and S. Pradalier. Projective brane calculus. In *Computational Methods in Systems Biology: International Conference CMSB 2004*, volume 3082 of *Lecture Notes in Computer Science*, pages 134–148. Springer Verlag Heidelberg, 2004.

[5] H. de Jong. Modeling and Simulation of Genetic Regulatory Systems: A Literature Review. *Journal of Computational Biology*, 9(1):67–103, 2002.

[6] P. Degano, D. Prandi, C. Priami, and P. Quaglia. Beta-binders for biological quantitative experiments. Submitted for publication, 2005.

[7] D. Degenring, M. Röhl, and A. M. Uhrmacher. Discrete event, multi-level simulation of metabolite channeling. *BioSystems*, 75(1-3):29–41, 2004.

[8] M. A. Gibson and J. Bruck. EfficientExact Stochastic Simulation of Chemical Systems with Many Species and Many Channels. *Journal of Physical Chemistry A*, 104(9):1876–1889, 2000.

[9] D. T. Gillespie. Exact Stochastic Simulation of Coupled Chemical Reactions. *The Journal of Physical Chemistry B*, 81(25):2340–2361, 1977.

[10] J. Himmelspach and A. M. Uhrmacher. A component-based simulation layer for JAMES. In *Proc. of the 18th Workshop on Parallel and Distributed Simulation (PADS), May 16-19, 2004, Kufstein, Austria*, pages 115–122, 2004.

[11] J. Himmelspach and A. M. Uhrmacher. Processing dynamic PDEVS models. In D. DeGroot and P. Harrison, editors, *Proceedings of the 12th IEEE International Symposium on MASCOTS*, pages 329–336, Volendam, The Netherlands, October 2004. IEEE Computer Society.

[12] R. Hofestädt. Petri nets and the simulation of metabolic networks. *In Silico Biology*, 3, 2003.

[13] P. Lecca, C. Priami, P. Quaglia, B. Rossi, C. Laudanna, and G. Constantin. Language Modelling and Simulation of Autoreactive Lymphocytes Recruitment in Inflamed Brain Vessels. *SCS Simulation*, 80:273–288, 2004.

[14] R. Milner. *Communicating and mobile systems: the π-calculus*. Cambridge Universtity Press, 1999.

[15] A. Phillips and L. Cardelli. A correct abstract machine for the stochastic pi-calculus. In *BioConcur 2004*. Electronic Notes in Theoretical Computer Science, 2004.

[16] C. Priami. Stochastic π-calculus. *The Computer Journal*, 38(6):578–589, 1995.

[17] C. Priami and P. Quaglia. Beta binders for biological interactions. *Transactions on Computationa Systems Biology*, 2005.

[18] C. Priami, A. Regev, E. Shapiro, and W. Silvermann. Application of a stochastic name-passing calculus to representation and simulation of molecular processes. *Information Processing Letters*, 80:25–31, 2001.

[19] S. Ramsey, D. Oreell, and H. Bolouri. Dizzy: Stochastic simulation of large scale genetic regulatory networks. *Journal of Bioinformatics and Computational Biology*, 01(13), 2005.

[20] A. Regev, E. Panina, W. Silverman, L. Cardelli, and E. Shapiro. BioAmbients: An Abstraction for Biological Compartments. *Theoretical Computer Science*, 2004.

[21] A. M. Uhrmacher and C. Priami. Discrete event systems specification in systems biology – a discussion of stochastic PI calculus and DEVS. In *Proceedings of Winter Simulation Conference 2005*, 2005.

[22] K. Van Gend and K. U. STODE - Automatic Stochastic Simulation of Systems Described by [differential equations. In T.-M. Yi, M. Hucka, M. Morohasi, and H. Kitano, editors, *Proceedings of the 2nd International Conference on Systems Biology*, pages 326–333. Omnipress, Madison, USA, 2001.

[23] B. Zeigler. *Multifacetted Modelling and Discrete Event Simulation*. Academic Press, London, 1984.

Principles of Advanced and Distributed Simulation

Session 5: Distributed Virtual Environments

Greedy Algorithms for Client Assignment in Large-Scale Distributed Virtual Environments

Duong Nguyen Binh Ta, Suiping Zhou and Haifeng Shen
Parallel & Distributed Computing Centre
School of Computer Engineering
Nanyang Technological University, Singapore 639798
{pa0236892b, asspzhou, ashfshen}@ntu.edu.sg

Abstract

Distributed Virtual Environments (DVEs), such as online games, military simulations, collaborative design, etc., are very popular nowadays. To support large-scale DVEs, a multi-server architecture is usually employed, and the virtual world is partitioned into multiple zones for load distribution. The client assignment problem arises when assigning the participating clients to the servers. Current approaches usually assign clients to servers according to the locations of clients in the virtual world, i.e., clients interacting in the same zone of the virtual world will be assigned to the same server. This approach may degrade the interactivity of DVEs if the network delay from a client to its assigned server is large. In this paper, we formulate the client assignment problem, and propose two algorithms to assign clients to servers in a more efficient way. The proposed algorithms are based on the heuristics developed for the well-known Terminal Assignment problem. Simulation results with the BRITE Internet Topology Generator show that our algorithms are effective in enhancing the interactivity of DVEs.

1. Introduction

Recently, advances in high-speed networking technologies, computer graphics and CPU processing power have enabled the development of Distributed Virtual Environments (DVEs). DVEs are distributed systems that allow multiple geographically distributed clients to explore and interact with each other in real-time within a shared, 3D virtual world [1], in which each client is represented by an avatar. A client controls the behavior of his/her avatar by various user inputs, and changes in an avatar's behavior need to be propagated to other clients in the same interaction zone to support the interactions among clients. Applications of DVEs can be seen in many areas, such as collaborative design [4], military simulation [5], e-learning [3] and multi-player games [6, 2]. In practice, to support the high resource demands of DVEs, e.g., network bandwidth, CPU processing cycle, memory, etc., usually a *multi-server* communication architecture [7, 8, 9] is employed. In this architecture, multiple geographically distributed servers are connected to each other, usually via high-speed links, and each client is connected to one of these servers.

A popular approach to distribute the virtual world over the server network is the mirrored server architecture [14]. In this approach, the entire virtual world is replicated at *all* servers in the system, and a client may select to connect to its closest server (in terms of network delay) to reduce the communication delay. However, the mirrored server architecture is not scalable, and only suitable for small-scale virtual worlds with a few tens of clients. In order to deal with large-scale virtual environments with hundreds, or even thousands of clients interacting simultaneously, which is the focus of this paper, usually the virtual world is spatially partitioned into several distinct *zones*, with each zone handled by only one server, as in [18]. Clients only interact with other clients in the same zone, and may move to other zones. A server only needs to handle one or more zones instead of the entire world, thus the system becomes more scalable. In this paper, we refer to such a partitioning approach as the *zone-based approach*.

Traditionally, in the zone-based approach, all clients in a zone are connected to the same server. However, due to the fact that clients in DVEs are geographically distributed and the heterogeneous nature of the Internet, clients in a zone will have different network delays to the server of that zone. For a zone, we are interested

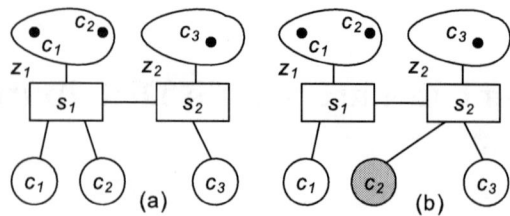

Figure 1. Multi-server architecture with zone-based approach

in the *maximum round-trip* client-to-server delay of all clients in that zone, since if the round-trip delay of a client in a zone is high, the interactivity of the DVE for *all* clients in that zone may be damaged [13].

The purpose of this paper is to find a good assignment of clients to servers in order to enhance the interactivity of DVEs. In this paper, this problem is termed the *client assignment* problem. We have proposed two simple yet effective algorithms to reduce the round-trip client-to-server delay, thus improving the interactivity of the application. Our algorithms are based on the greedy heuristics for solving the Terminal Assignment problem [19, 20], which is known to be NP-complete.

The rest of the paper is organized as follows. Section 2 discusses the client assignment problem and some related work. Section 3 describes our proposed algorithms. Simulation results are described in section 4, and section 5 concludes the paper.

2. The client assignment problem

2.1. System model and definitions

In this paper, we focus on DVEs that adopt a multi-server architecture and the zone-based approach. The servers are geographically distributed and interconnected via well-provisioned network links with low network delays. The connections between clients and servers may have high delays. We assume that network delays have known upper bounds.

Fig. 1(a) shows an example of DVE in which there are two servers s_1 and s_2 hosting two zones z_1 and z_2, respectively. The avatars of client c_1 and c_2 are in zone z_1, while the avatar of client c_3 is in zone z_2.

We define the following concepts:

Contact server: A *contact server* of a client is the server that this client directly connects to. Clients only send requests to their contact servers. The contact server may execute the request and respond to the client if it is hosting the client's zone, or it may forward the request to another server which is hosting the client's zone. For example, in Fig. 1(a), s_1 is the contact server of c_1 and c_2.

Target server: A *target server* of a client is the server that is hosting the client's zone. Requests from a client will be forwarded to its target server. The target server may respond to the client directly if it is also the contact server of the client, or it may respond indirectly via the client's contact server. All clients in a zone have the same target server (therefore, we may say "the target server of a zone"), while they may have different contact servers.

For example, in Fig. 1(a), s_1 is both the contact and target server of c_1 and c_2. In Fig. 1(b), we switch c_2 to server s_2 (but the avatar of c_2 is still in zone z_1), the target server of c_1 and c_2 is still s_1, the contact server of c_1 is s_1, while the contact server of c_2 is now s_2. Requests from c_2 are forwarded to s_1 by s_2.

Zone communication delay: The zone communication delay measures the interactivity provided by the DVE to all clients in a zone z_i, and is denoted as D_i^Z. To determine D_i^Z, we need to consider all the clients in z_i in order to ensure consistency and fairness among all clients interacting in z_i [13]. The target server s_k for z_i needs to wait for requests from the farthest (in terms of network delay) client in z_i before executing the requests of other clients in z_i. Then, the resulted responses must not be presented to any client in z_i until the farthest client receives its response [13]. Therefore, D_i^Z depends on the client with highest round-trip network delay in z_i, and is determined by:

$$D_i^Z = \max_{c_j \in z_i} d_{c_j s_k}$$

where $d_{c_j s_k}$ is the round-trip delay from a client $c_j \in z_i$ to its target server s_k.

For example, in Fig. 1(a), assume that $d_{c_2 s_1} > d_{c_1 s_1}$, D_1^Z can be calculated as $d_{c_2 s_1}$.

System communication delay: The system communication delay measures the maximum zone communication delay for all zones in the system, and is denoted as D^S:

$$D^S = \max_{z_i} D_i^Z$$

Delay bound: The delay bound D for a DVE indicates the requirement of D^S in order to maintain interactivity. For different types of DVEs, there are different delay bound requirements. For example, Multi-player Real-Time Strategy (RTS) games typically require a delay bound of $500ms$, while First-Person Shooter (FPS) games require a delay bound of $100ms$ [6].

Server load: The load of a server in the DVE can be divided into network-related load (receiving, sending packets) and application-related load (executing requests) [16]. In this paper, we measure the load of a server as its CPU load. The network bandwidth consumption is assumed to be proportional to the network-related load on CPU, hence it will not be considered separately. The target server of a client needs to handle both network-related and application-related load generated by the client, while a contact server of the client only needs to handle network-related load. In this paper, the load of a server s_i is denoted as L_{s_i}, and can be expressed as:

$$L_{s_i} = \sum \alpha_{c_j} + \sum \beta_{c_k}$$

where c_j is any client that has s_i as its target server, and c_k is any client that has s_i as its contact server but not the target server, α_{c_j} is the load on s_i for handling a client c_j with both network-related and application-related load, and β_{c_k} is the load on s_i for handling a client c_k with network-related load only.

For example, in Fig. 1(b), assuming $\alpha_{c_1} = \alpha_{c_2} = \alpha_{c_3} = 1$, and $\beta_{c_2} = 0.5$ we have $L_{s_1} = \alpha_{c_1} + \alpha_{c_2} = 1 + 1 = 2$, and $L_{s_2} = \alpha_{c_3} + \beta_{c_2} = 1 + 0.5 = 1.5$.

In this paper, due to the heterogeneous nature of DVEs, we assume that servers may have different capacities, and clients may also generate different processing loads on servers, which is referred to as the *weights* of clients. If the load of a server s_i exceeds its capacity T_{s_i}, the server is saturated, which may seriously affect the interactivity of DVE, as shown in [17].

2.2. Problem formulation

We have observed that a client which is far (in terms of network delay) from its target server will degrade the interactivity of the whole zone. Therefore, in order to meet the interactivity requirement of the application, we must seek some client assignment mechanisms that satisfies the delay bound D, and at the same time, avoids server saturation, i.e.,:

$$D^S \leq D \wedge L_{s_i} \leq T_{s_i}, \forall s_i$$

Note that in practice, sometimes we may not be able to find an assignment that satisfies the delay bound. In that case, we aim to find an assignment that minimizes D_S, and also avoids server saturation.

2.3. Related work

To our knowledge, there is not much existing work that directly addresses the client assignment problem. Instead, most of the existing work is based on the approach of assigning clients to servers according to clients' virtual locations [11, 10, 12], which is regarded as the Virtual Assignment (VA) approach in this paper. With VA, if a client in a zone is far from its target server, the communication delay for that zone may become very high, thus the interactivity of the application may be damaged.

In [15], the authors proposed a server selection algorithm that considers both the network delays and the virtual locations of clients. However, this work uses the average delay between clients and servers as the main performance metric. To ensure consistency and fairness, the maximum round-trip delay is a more appropriate performance metric.

In a more recent work [13], the authors proposed a distributed algorithm for clients to selects the best server in a mirrored architecture for online games, taking into account the network delays between clients and servers. However, the mirrored architecture replicates the entire virtual world at every server, thus is not suitable for large-scale DVEs.

3. Client assignment algorithms

In this section, we describe some simple yet effective assignment algorithms for assigning clients to servers. Our algorithms are based on the greedy algorithm which is originally proposed to solve the Terminal Assignment (TA) problem in designing communication networks. In general, TA is a NP-complete problem [19, 20]. The objective of TA is to determine the minimum cost links to form a network by connecting a given collection of terminals to a given collection of concentrators. Concentrators may have different capacities, and terminals may have different resource requirements, i.e., weights. The cost of linking a terminal to a concentrator is the distance between the terminal and the concentrator. Each terminal connects to only one concentrator, and any concentrator must not be overloaded by the total weight of its assigned terminals.

In this paper, we extend the greedy algorithm for TA problem in [19, 20] to two 2-phase algorithms to address our client assignment problem. The client assignment problem is similar to the TA problem where servers become the concentrators, and clients (or zones) become the terminals. Our proposed algorithms are centralized, and can be executed in a master server that manages the whole server system.

3.1. Virtual assignment algorithm (VA)

We describe the Virtual Assignment (VA) algorithm here for comparison purpose. The VA is widely used in DVEs [11, 10, 12]. However, it does not take into account the round-trip delay from clients to servers when assigning zones to servers. In this paper, we implement VA algorithm using a First-Fit-Decreasing heuristics, which is one of the simplest and most effective algorithms for the Bin Packing problem [21]. The pseudo-code is shown in Fig. 3.1. The VA algorithm sorts the list of zones by the total weight of clients in each zone in descending order, then assign the first zone z_i (with all of its clients) in the list to the first server s_j with sufficient capacity, i.e., $L_{s_j} + \sum_{c_k \in z_i} \alpha_{c_k} \leq T_{s_j}$, and so on. With VA, the target server and the contact server of all clients in a zone are the same.

```
begin
    sort the list of zones L^Z in descending order by
    the total weight of each zone;
    while L^Z is not empty do
        pick the first zone z_i in L^Z;
        find a server s_j such that
        L_{s_j} + \sum_{c_k \in z_i} \alpha_{c_k} \leq T_{s_j};
        set the contact server and target server of
        all clients c_k \in z_i to s_j;
        remove z_i from L^Z;
    end
end
```

Figure 2: VA algorithm

3.2. Greedy assignment algorithm 1 (GDA-1)

The proposed GDA-1 algorithm exploits the fact that the well-provisioned links between servers usually have much lower delay than the connections between clients and servers. Therefore, we may achieve a smaller communication delay if a client do not send requests directly to its target server. Instead, the client selects the closest server as its contact server, its and requests are forwarded to its target server via the low-delay link between its contact server and target server. However, this should be done with care, since allocating a client to a contact server which is different from its target server will increase the system load, due to the extra network-related load that the contact server has to handle. The GDA-1 algorithm is implemented in two phases: *initial assignment* and *refined assignment*.

3.2.1 Initial assignment

This phase is the same as the VA algorithm.

3.2.2 Refined assignment

In the refined assignment, we try to further reduce the D^S of the initial assignment. This is similar to the TA problem, where servers become the concentrators and clients become the terminals. The pseudo-code is shown in Fig. 3. First, we find a list of clients c_i whose communication delays to their current contact servers exceed the pre-specified delay bound D (which we refer to as delay-exceeding clients). The list is sorted in descending order according to the round-trip delay between each client and its target server. Then, the following procedure is repeated until the list is empty: remove a client c_i from the top of the list (i.e., the client with highest round-trip delay), and find a server s_j that satisfies the delay bound, i.e., $d_{c_i s_j} + d_{s_j s_k} \leq D$, where s_k is the target server of c_i, and $d_{s_j s_k}$ is the round-trip delay between s_j and s_k.

```
begin
    find list L^C of delay-exceeding clients c_i ;
    sort L^C in descending order by d_{c_i s_k}, where s_k
    is the target server of c_i \in L^C ;
    while L^C is not empty do
        pick the first c_i \in L^C ;
        find a server s_j such that d_{c_i s_j} + d_{s_j s_k} \leq D
        and L_{s_j} + \beta_{c_i} \leq T_{s_j};
        if such s_j can't be found then
            select a non-saturated server s_j with
            min(d_{c_i s_j} + d_{s_j s_k});
        end
        change the contact server of c_i to s_j ;
        remove c_i from L^C ;
    end
end
```

Figure 3: GDA-1 refined assignment algorithm

To find the new contact server s_j for c_i, we sort the list that consists of all servers in the system in ascending order according to the round-trip delay between c_i and each server. Then the first server s_j in the list (the closest server to c_i) is picked. If s_j will be saturated when assigning c_i to it (i.e., $L_{s_j} + \beta_{c_i} > T_{s_j}$), or if the delay bound cannot be satisfied by using s_j, we select the next server in the list and so on. If there's no server that satisfies the delay bound, a non-saturated server s_j that provides client c_i with the minimum round-trip delay to c_i's target server will be selected. The new contact server of c_i is now s_j, while the target server of c_i is unchanged. If there's no better contact server for c_i than its current contact server, no re-assignment will be done.

3.3. Greedy assignment algorithm 2 (GDA-2)

In the GDA-2 algorithm, we try to optimize the initial assignment in GDA-1 algorithm in order to reduce the number of re-assignments (which means to reduce the extra network-related load that contact servers have to handle due to the re-assignments) in the refined assignment process.

3.3.1 Initial assignment

The pseudo-code of the initial assignment is shown in Fig. 4. First we sorts the list of zones by the total weight of clients in each zone in descending order. Then, we repeat the following until the list is empty: remove the zone z_i that has the highest total weight from the list, and find a target server s_j that minimizes the number of delay-exceeding clients in z_i, i.e., find the server s_j that minimizes the number of re-assignments if z_i is assigned to s_j. In addition, s_j must not be saturated, i.e., $L_{s_j} + \sum_{c_k \in z_i} \alpha_{c_k} \leq T_{s_j}$. Then, the contact server and target server of each client in z_i are set to s_j.

```
begin
    sort the list of zones L^Z in descending order by
    the total weight of each zone;
    while L^Z is not empty do
        pick the first zone z_i in L^Z;
        find a server s_j such that the number of
        delay-exceeding clients in z_i is minimized
        and L_{s_j} + \sum_{c_k \in z_i} \alpha_{c_k} \leq T_{s_j};
        set the contact server and target server of
        all clients c_k \in z_i to s_j ;
        remove z_i from L^Z ;
    end
end
```

Figure 4: GDA-2 initial assignment algorithm

3.3.2 Refined assignment

This phase is the same as the refined assignment in GDA-1 algorithm.

3.4. Implementation considerations

In this section we address some practical considerations when implementing the proposed assignment algorithms. The first consideration is the dynamic property of DVEs. During the course of interactions in the virtual world, clients may move from one zone to another, new clients may join, existing clients may also leave the virtual world. An obtained assignment may not be good after some time. Thus, the proposed algorithms need to be re-executed to ensure good client assignments.

Another issue is how to obtain input data for the proposed assignment algorithms. The input data includes the client-server and inter-server round-trip network delays, and the server load generated by each client. The network delays can be obtained using scalable network measurement tools such as King [22] or IDMaps [23]. King uses existing recursive DNS queries to accurately estimate round-trip network delays between arbitrary Internet end hosts, while IDMaps relies on end hosts called *tracers* deployed at some strategic locations in the Internet. Both approaches are scalable and incur little estimation overhead.

In this paper, the load generated by each client on the server, i.e., client's weight, is measured as the server's CPU consumption. This can be obtained via actual measurements of existing multi-player game systems, as in a recent study of the well-known FPS game Quake [16]. In addition, [16] also showed that the network-related load and application-related load in Quake are approximately equal in terms of CPU consumption.

4. Performance evaluation

4.1. Simulation parameters

We evaluate our proposed algorithms via simulations. In the simulations, we use a two-level, Internet-like topology generated by the BRITE Internet Topology Generator [24]. The topology consists of 2000 nodes and 4040 links. Upper bound delay of each link is uniformly distributed in $[0, 25ms]$. We randomly select nodes in the set of 2000 generated nodes to be the servers and clients. To simulate well-provisioned inter-server connections which have lower delays than client-server connections, we reduce the network delays between any two servers to 50% of the actual delay values obtained from the topology generator.

The capacity of each server, number of clients in each zone and the weight of each client are uniformly distributed in $[70, 100]$, $[10, 20]$ and $[1, 3]$, respectively.

The network-related load and application-related load generated by a client is assumed to be equal, i.e., $\alpha_{c_i} = 2\beta_{c_i}$, as shown in [16].

4.2. Results and discussions

In this section, we discuss the simulation results to compare our proposed algorithms, GDA-1 and GDA-2, with the VA algorithm. The system communication delay D^S as well as the *system utilization* (measuring how much system resource is consumed, and is calculated as the total server load divided by the total server capacity) are of interest in the analysis. We have simulated a large number of DVE configurations, ranging from 10 servers to 50 servers, 10 zones to 60 zones. However, in this paper, due to space limitation, we only reports some typical results.

Table 1. System communication delay with $D = 300ms$

DVE configuration	VA	GDA-1	GDA-2
10s-15z-204c	357ms	301ms	300ms
20s-25z-386c	388ms	301ms	301ms
30s-40z-619c	406ms	315ms	313ms
40s-50z-709c	455ms	300ms	300ms

The D^S value for each algorithm with different DVE configurations is shown in Table 1. Note that the notation for a DVE configuration, as shown in Table 1, has the format: number of servers - number of zones - number of clients in all zones. For example, the notation 10s-15z-204c means that the DVE has 10 servers, 15 zones with 204 clients in total. From Table 1, it is observed that in all cases, our GDA-1 and GDA-2 algorithm are able to achieve an D^S which is within or close to the delay bound $D = 300ms$, while the VA algorithm fails to do so. This result indicates that our GDA-1 and GDA-2 algorithm can produce a client assignment with much better DVE interactivity than the traditional VA algorithm.

Table 2. Results for 40s-50z-709c with $D = 300ms$

Algorithm	Exceed	Reassign	Utilization	D^S
VA	88	0	43%	455ms
GDA-1	88	88	46%	300ms
GDA-2	39	39	44%	300ms

The simulation results for the DVE configuration 40s-50z-709c with different values of the delay bound

Table 3. Results for 40s-50z-709c with $D = 250ms$

Algorithm	Exceed	Reassign	Utilization	D^S
VA	238	0	43%	455ms
GDA-1	238	236	50%	276ms
GDA-2	126	126	47%	262ms

Table 4. Results for 40s-50z-709c with $D = 200ms$

Algorithm	Exceed	Reassign	Utilization	D^S
VA	451	0	43%	455ms
GDA-1	451	436	56%	276ms
GDA-2	311	296	52%	258ms

D are shown in Table 2, 3 and 4. In these tables, the *Exceed* column shows the number of delay-exceeding clients. The *Reassign* column shows the number of delay-exceeding clients that are re-assigned by the algorithms to another contact server in order to obtain smaller D^S. The *Utilization* column shows the value of system utilization for each algorithm.

From Table 2, 3 and 4, it can be seen that the GDA-2 algorithm always has a smaller number of delay-exceeding clients compared to the GDA-1 and VA algorithm. This is due to the initial assignment process in GDA-2, which greedily seek an initial assignment that minimizes the number of delay-exceeding clients. Therefore, the GDA-2 algorithm needs to re-assign a smaller number of clients compared to GDA-1. This helps GDA-2 to achieve a similar or better D^S with lower system utilization (resource consumption) than GDA-1. Note that in Table 3 and 4, our algorithms cannot find an assignment that has $D^S \leq D$, since the delay bound requirement is too tight. Instead, our algorithms can produce an assignment with D^S much closer to D than that of the VA algorithm.

In summary, our algorithms GDA-1 and GDA-2 are much better than the existing VA algorithm in enhancing the interactivity of DVEs. In addition, the GDA-2 algorithm yields better performance than GDA-1 algorithm, due to GDA-2's improved initial assignment process, which results in less number of delay-exceeding clients.

5. Conclusions and future works

Client assignment is an important issue in large-scale DVEs. A bad client assignment may greatly damage the interactivity of the system. In this paper, we have formulated the client assignment problem for DVEs. The main objective of this paper is to find good client assignment algorithms that are able to provide a system communication delay as close to the required delay bound as possible, and at the same time, avoid server saturations. We have proposed two algorithms, GDA-1 and GDA-2, to address the client assignment problem. Simulation results show that the GDA-2 algorithm consumes less system resources than the GDA-1 algorithm, and both of these two algorithms are much better than the traditional VA algorithm in enhancing the interactivity of DVEs.

Though the algorithms presented in this paper are still centralized, they provide the first step towards finding better algorithms for efficient client assignments. In our future work, we will investigate the feasibility of distributed algorithms for the client assignment problem.

References

[1] S. Singhal and M. Zyda, *Networked Virtual Environments*. Addison-Wesley, New York, 1999.

[2] Zona Inc. and Executive Summary Consulting Inc., "State of Massive Multiplayer Online Games 2002: A New World in Electronic Gaming". Available at http://www.zona.net, 2002.

[3] T. Nitta, K. Fujita and S. Cono, "An Application of Distributed Virtual Environment to Foreign Language", *IEEE Education Society*, 2000.

[4] J. Dias, R. Galli, A. Almeida, C. Belo and J. Rebordao, "mWorld: A Multiuser 3D Virtual Environment", *IEEE Computer Graphics* Vol. 17(2), 1997.

[5] D. Miller, J. Thorpe, "SIMNET: The advent of simulator networking", *Proc. of the IEEE* Vol. 83(8), 1995.

[6] J. Smed, T. Kaukoranta, and H. Hakonen, "Aspects of Networking in Multiplayer Computer Games", *Proc. of the International Conference on Application and Development of Computer Games in the 21st Century*, 2001.

[7] T. K. Das, G. Singh, A. Mitchell, P. S. Kumar, and K. McGee: NetEffect, "A Network Architecture for Large-Scale Multi-User Virtual Worlds", *Proc. of the ACM VRST*, 1997.

[8] M. Mauve, S. Fischer, and J. Widmer, "A generic proxy system for networked computer games", *Proc. of NetGames*, 2002.

[9] D. Bauer, S. Rooney, and P. Scotton, "Network infrastructure for massively distributed games", *Proc. of NetGames*, 2002.

[10] Duong N. B. Ta and S. Zhou, "A Dynamic Load Sharing Algorithm for Massively Multi-Player Online Games", *Proc. of the 11th IEEE International Conference on Networks*, 2003.

[11] J. Lui and M. Chan, "An Efficient Partitioning Algorithm for Distributed Virtual Environment Systems", *IEEE Transactions on Parallel and Distributed Systems* Vol. 13(3), 2002.

[12] W. Cai, P. Xavier, S. Turner and B. S. Lee, "A Scalable Architecture for Supporting Interactive Games on the Internet", *Proc. of the 16th Workshop on Parallel and Distributed Simulation*, 2002.

[13] K. W. Lee, B. J. Ko and S. Calo, "Adaptive Server Selection for Large Scale Interactive Online Games", *Proc. of NOSSDAV*, 2004.

[14] E. Cronin, B. Filstrup and A. Kurc, "A Distributed Multiplayer Game Server System", *Technical Report*, University of Michigan, 2001.

[15] K. Fujikawa, M. Hori, S. Shimojo and H. Miyahara, "A Server Selction Method based on Communication Delay and Communication Frequency among Users for Networked Virtual Environments", *Proc. of ASIAN*, 2002.

[16] A. Abdelkhalek, A. Bilas and A. Moshovos, "Behavior and Performance of Interactive Multiplayer Game Servers", *Special Issue of Cluster Computing: the Journal of Networks, Software Tools and Applications*, 2002.

[17] P. Morillo, J.M. Orduna, M. Fernandez and J. Duato, "On the Characterization of Distributed Virtual Environment Systems", *Proc. of Euro-Par*, 2003.

[18] Sony Online Entertainments, Everquest. Available at http://eqlive.station.sony.com.

[19] S. Khuri and T. Chiu, "Heuristic Algorithms for the Terminal Assignment Problem", *Proc. of ACM Applied Computing*, 1997.

[20] S. Salcedo-Sanz and X. Yao, "A Hybrid Hopfield Network-Genetic Algorithm Approach for the Terminal Assignment Problem", *IEEE Transactions on Systems, Man and Cybernetics* Vol. 34(6), 2004.

[21] A. Kershenbaum, *Telecommunications Network Design Algorithms*, McGraw-Hill, 1993.

[22] K. P. Gummadi, S. Saroiu, and S. D. Gribble, "King: Estimating Latency between Arbitrary Internet End Hosts", *Proc. of the ACM SIGCOMM IMW*, 2002.

[23] P. Francis, S. Jamin, C. Jin, Y. Jin, D. Raz, Y.Shavitt, and L. Zhang, "IDMaps: A Global Internet Host Distance Estimation Service", *IEEE/ACM Transactions on Networking* Vol. 9(5) (2001).

[24] BRITE Topology Generator. Available at htttp://www.cs.bu.edu/brite.

Interest Operators: Facilitating Attribute Interest Criteria for Formula-based Interest Management in Distributed Virtual Environments

Robert Bartlett
University of Western Sydney
Sydney, Australia
rbartlet@cit.uws.edu.au

Abstract

Interest Management (IM) schemes for Distributed Virtual Environments (DVEs) provide a means to scale-up the number of participants and objects in a DVE instance by reducing the amount of information DVE components send and/or receive across a communication network and reducing the amount of DVE state information a DVE component must keep. Formula interest expressions (IEs) coupled to a model for propagating formula IEs provide formula IM. This paper proposes an approach to specify interest criteria in a general way when using formula IM.

Formula IEs were traditionally constructed using geometric and object property value criteria. To evaluate formula IEs, interest managers accessed objects' attributes. Interest managers were also able to perform calculations upon these attributes (and determine the existence of interest). Before joining a DVE instance, Interest managers needed to be aware of the attributes available for IM and the calculations that could be performed upon these attributes. This requirement discouraged the dynamic addition of objects to a virtual world and resulted in interest managers becoming complex. To address this problem, this paper proposes Interest Operators (IOs): a basic building block for formula IEs that indicates whether an object satisfies the interest criteria. We argue that our IOs, which are not simply class methods, are a natural and comprehensive means to realise the concept of interest.

In the literature, syntax for expressing formula IEs does not exist. Formula IE designs have been tightly coupled to class attributes. Utilising IOs, we propose a general formula IE syntax to set out the criteria grammar for interest.

1. Introduction

Distributed virtual environments (DVEs) have historically been small in scale [1, 2]. The ability to scale up the number of participants and objects in a DVE instance (a uniquely identifiable running DVE) is desired [3]. A DVE's distribution impacts its scalability. Two predominant distribution types exist: client/server (C/S) and peer-to-peer (P2P).

In a C/S distributed DVE, virtual world state is maintained by a server (or multiple servers). The scalability of a C/S distributed DVE instance depends on the capacity and availability of its servers. In a P2P distributed DVE, virtual world state is maintained by each DVE component (where a DVE component is a set of programs executing at a host) participating in the DVE instance. In a traditional P2P distributed DVE instance, each of the n DVE components maintains a connection to every other DVE component (i.e. $(n-1)$ DVE components), resulting in $O(n^2)$ connections in total. If the frequency of state changes is high, a large number of state update messages will be sent. This results in a large amount of network traffic and requires a significant amount of processing from each DVE component. This is not scalable [4].

Techniques have been developed to improve P2P DVE's scalability. These techniques reduce network traffic, reduce the impact of delays between one DVE component sending and another DVE component receiving a message, or reduce the amount of processing DVE components must perform. Example techniques include: combining multiple state update messages into a single (large) update, which is sent less regularly; and predicting state changes [5]. Another technique is interest management (IM) [6]. IM reduces the amount of state information that passes between DVE components by filtering state information such that it only flows between DVE components that require it. Instead of a DVE component maintaining state information pertaining to an entire virtual world, a DVE component maintains information regarding sections of the virtual world that it is interested in. An interest expression (IE) is a representation of an interest that facilitates filtering, that is, it unambiguously states the selection criteria.

Three IM specificities exist: cell, extent and formula [7]. In a DVE using cell specificity the virtual world is divided into static or dynamic regions. Regions are defined and managed by separate logic in the DVE instance (often an IM server). All DVE components are aware of all regions. Extent specificity is similar to cell specificity except that the regions are defined and managed by DVE components. In both approaches DVE components subscribe to the regions they are interested in. In a DVE using formula specificity, DVE components construct algebraic expressions that represent their interests. A formula IE specifies *what is of interest*, unlike cell and extent IEs that specify *where what is of interest may be located*. Formula specificity is considered *conceptually clear, but complex to implement* [7] when compared to cell and extent specificities.

Research into formula specificities stopped around 1995 [8]. We believe that research into formula specificities stopped, as alternative IM models were simpler and better suited to the applications being developed at the time. P2P formula IM represents an interesting research area for two reasons. Firstly, due to recent growth in the amount of virtual world content per DVE instance, a precise specification of interest, to improve the granularity of filtering performed is required. Improving the granularity of filtering reduces the amount of network traffic and virtual world state that DVE components must process. Secondly, dynamic large-scale P2P systems (i.e. content sharing applications) have recently become popular due to their ability to scale without requiring additional resources (i.e. servers). Whilst some C/S DVEs are scalable, they are inherently not dynamic (i.e. server availability dictates whether new DVE components are able to join a DVE instance; and DVE components cannot introduce new virtual world content without firstly obtaining server support). It is therefore important to see whether P2P formula IM can facilitate the construction of such systems.

In formula IM, interest managers (a sub-component of a DVE component) supply formula IEs to other DVE components to allow them to perform filtering. The originator of a formula IE is referred to as the formula IE originator (FIEO). Filtering can either be performed by: a FIEO when it receives state updates; or a remote filterer (RF) before it sends a state update. The first type of filtering is referred to as receiver-based filtering and does not reduce network traffic. The second type of filtering is referred to as sender-based filtering and has the potential to reduce processing overheads and reduce network traffic.

In sender-based filtering FIEOs propagate their formula IEs to RFs to enable filtering. Currently only a single approach to propagating formula IEs exists: FIEOs send their formula IEs to all DVE components in a DVE instance. If the number of DVE components is large, or the rate at which DVE component's interest changes is high, then this approach does not scale. What is desired is for a FIEO to be able to quickly identify RFs likely to be responsible for virtual world objects of interest. A formula IE should only be sent to these DVE components.

Our research proposes a model for propagating formula IEs for use in P2P distributed DVEs. A goal of the model is to allow DVE instances to scale independently of resources beyond those supplied by participating DVE components (i.e. no servers). Not relying on static infrastructure allows virtual world content and DVE components to be dynamically added and removed from a DVE instance. Removing central control allows (and encourages) virtual world content to be developed by anyone (assuming adherence to a standard specification).

To support the proposed formula IE propagation model (the subject of [9]), this paper specifies the building blocks for formula IEs, referred to as interest operators (IOs). IOs are operations that indicate whether an object satisfies interest criteria. Building upon IOs, this paper also presents syntax for specifying formula IEs. In the remainder of the paper: section 2 introduces the different types of interest criteria; section 3 presents a summary of existing IM work; section 0 proposes and discusses IOs; section 5 presents the formula IE syntax; and section 6 concludes and discusses future work. All work has been verified by the construction of a fully operational proof of concept prototype.

2. Interest criteria

The aspects of objects that enable filtering are referred to as interest criteria. Several different interest criteria exist. As few DVEs use formula IM, in this section, we look at the interest criteria used by other specificities. Alone, this approach is not suitable, as it does not address issues specifically regarding formula IM. To address this deficiency, after introducing each interest criteria, a discussion framing each criterion in the context of formula IM is performed. Three criteria are discussed: spatial, class and attribute.

2.1. Spatial interest

In the most commonly used interest criteria, a particular unit of interest is spatially bound to a virtual world. In the real world, humans are often interested in what is happening in their immediate vicinity. The human sense of sight is the predominant sense (coupled with hearing) used to perceive an area in the real world. Spatial interest applies this real world concept to virtual worlds. Spatial interest differs slightly to human sight, in that it is not inhibited by visibility conditions such as transparencies or line-of-sight. This means that it is (often) able to capture more information than human sight (when applied to the same scenario).

Spatial interest may be defined relative to: the position of an object in a virtual world (e.g. *objects within distance X of object Y*); or the virtual world (e.g. *objects located within the bounds of points W, X, Y and Z*). Defining spatial interest relative to the virtual world is the most common approach. We believe that the reason for this relates to the predominant use of cell and extent IM and their use of regions.

We suggest that the main reason why spatial interest is used with cell and extent IM is that it is easy to implement. A region is a filtering space. Cell and extent IM set the boundaries of a region to a spatial area in the virtual world. The boundaries of a region are not limited to virtual world spatial information. Like a jigsaw puzzle, multiple regions may encompass the entire spatial area of a virtual world. Adopting spatial interest with formula IM is more complex than with cell or extent IM. Most objects in a virtual world are likely to possess position attributes. If a formula IE specifies spatial criteria, all DVE components with objects (that possess position attributes and are being made available for formula IM) must evaluate this formula IE and determine whether interest exists.

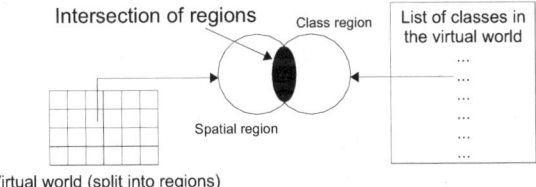

Figure 1. Combining regions

2.2. Class interest

In class interest, objects' class hierarchy is used as interest criteria. Resulting filtering is referred to as class-based filtering. Class interest is taxonomic, in that it groups objects based on class. Class interest is often used as secondary interest criteria to refine an (otherwise broad) interest domain. IEs that only use class interest are uncommon.

In cell or extent IM, a region may include a class (or classes) to facilitate class interest. When class interest is used as secondary interest criteria, (logical) regions encapsulating the primary and secondary criteria are logically *AND*ed to form a new region (see Figure 1).

When regions change in a DVE instance, cell and extent IM make all DVE components aware of region changes. Frequent region changes result in a high maintenance task. Class interest is not widely used in conjunction with cell and extent IM, as it often requires the creation of new regions (or changes to existing regions). Class interest is well suited to formula IM, as there are no predefined regions. Classes may be specified as interest criteria without penalty.

2.3. Attribute interest

In attribute interest, class attributes are interest criteria. Spatial interest is a subset of attribute interest. In spatial interest classes' position attributes (i.e. attributes pertaining to objects' positions in a virtual world) are interest criteria. Spatial interest was presented (in section 2.1) separate to attribute interest, as it is the most commonly used interest criteria.

Position attributes are not the only attributes that may be used as interest criteria. Other applicable attributes may include (but are not limited to): colour; shape; other distinguishing features; heading; composition; and age (in regards to the amount of time an object has existed in a virtual world). In DVEs there are usually more class attributes then there are classes. This implies that attribute interest has more ways to specify interest than class interest.

Excluding spatial interest, attribute interest has not been widely used in conjunction with cell or extent IM. When using attribute interest a potentially large number of regions may be created/modified, as the filtering space may be subdivided in numerous ways. The overhead of dynamically creating/modifying regions (i.e. informing all DVE components) can negate the benefit of using IM.

Formula IM significantly differs to cell and extent IM in regards to attribute interest. In formula IM, incorporating different attributes in formula IEs does not introduce region overheads (i.e. the creation and management of regions), as regions are not employed. Formula IEs are distinct. Equivalent formula IEs may exist (in different FIEOs), but are processed separately.

In the real world, humans are often aware of an attribute (or attributes) of an object they are interested in, before they become aware of the class of the object that they are interested in. Humans specify interest by listing desired attributes. Interest is determined by filtering out objects that do not support all of the required attributes. Humans specify class interest when they are already familiar with the area. In software, attributes can only be accessed via classes. As a result, the real world approach to specifying interest cannot be directly applied to DVEs. To facilitate equivalent attributes that possess no common class ancestry other than the hierarchy root (i.e. to decouple interest criteria from virtual world objects' classes) and allow interest to be specified in a more human-like manner, we propose IOs.

Table 1. Summary of the use of IM in DVEs

DVE	Year	Interest criteria	Specificity	Distribution	Messaging
SimNet [11]	1983-1990	Spatial, class	Formula	P2P	Broadcast
NPSNET [12] NPSNET II NPSNET III NPSTEALTH [13]	1990-1995	Spatial, class	Formula	P2P	Broadcast
DIVE [14-18]	1993-2003	*Undefined*	*Undefined*	P2P	Multicast
NPSNET IV [19] [20] [21]	1995	Spatial	Cell	C/S hybrid	Multicast
MASSIVE [22]	1995	Spatial, *"attribute"*	Extent	C/S	Unicast
SPLINE [23]	1996	Spatial	Cell	C/S	Multicast
MASSIVE-2 [24-26]	1997	Spatial	Extent	C/S hybrid	Multicast
NetEffect [27]	1997	Spatial	Cell	C/S hybrid	Unicast
DEE [28]	1998	Spatial	Cell	C/S hybrid	Unicast
MASSIVE-3 [29, 30]	1999	Spatial, class	Extent	C/S hybrid	Unicast/multicast
ATLAS [31, 32]	2000	Spatial	Cell	C/S hybrid	Multicast
Urbi et Orbi [33]	2000	Spatial	Cell	P2P	Multicast
DEVA3 [34] & MAVERIK [35]	2000	Spatial	Extent	C/S hybrid	Multicast
GISA [36]	2001-2003	*Undefined*	Extent	C/S hybrid	Unicast
VELVET [37]	2002	Spatial	Cell	C/S hybrid	Multicast
MaDViWorld [38]	2002	Spatial	Extent	P2P	Unicast
Mercury [39, 40]	2002	*"Attributes"*	Extent	P2P	Unicast
NPSNET V [41]	2003	Spatial, class	Extent	C/S hybrid	Multicast
SCORE [42]	2004	Spatial	Cell	P2P	Multicast

3. Related Work

As mentioned in section 1, little formula IM research has been performed over the last decade, whilst comparatively, a significant amount of research on cell and extent IM has been performed. Furthermore, existing research has focused primarily on spatial interest criteria. To provide context for this paper's work on formula IM and interest criteria, we provide a chronologically ordered tabularised summary of nineteen existing research initiatives that employ IM (see Table 1). The summary is not intended to be definitive, but rather indicative of research trends. Entertainment applications are omitted from the summary as they significantly outnumber the number of research initiatives, and they all employ IM in a similar manner (i.e. spatial interest criteria, a cell-based specificity, a hybrid C/S distribution, and unicast messaging). DVEs, such as the *Joint Precision Strike Demonstration* (JPSD), are omitted from the comparison, as first-hand published documentation is not publicly available. Similarly, the *Aggregate Level Simulation Protocol* (ALSP) (upon which JPSD was built), whilst noteworthy due to its work on attribute-based filtering using formula specificity, is not discussed, due to a lack of available literature (much of the work was contracted by the American Department of Defense and is not available to the public). From the little available literature, we believe that ALSP's support for attribute interest criteria was implementation dependent and not run-time extensible [10]. In Table 1, we comment on the: year when the DVE started development; supported interest criteria; specificity; distribution; messaging.

DIVE, a DVE toolkit, supports IM but leaves the definition of specificity and interest criteria to the implementer of a system. MASSIVE supports interest criteria that are "a function of position, and *possibly of other object attributes*" [22]. Despite this, documented MASSIVE examples have exclusively used spatial interest criteria. GISA leaves the definition of supported interest criteria to the implementer of a system, although, unlike DIVE, specificity is defined. Mercury's specifications dictate the attributes that are interest criteria.

Of the nineteen compared DVEs: sixteen support spatial interest criteria, twelve utilise a C/S or C/S hybrid distribution, and sixteen use cell or extent specificity. As can be seen, both formula IM and attribute interest criteria are supported by none of the research initiatives presented in Table 1 (with the potential exclusion of DIVE).

4. Interest operators

This section proposes IOs: an approach to facilitate attribute interest in formula IM. A straightforward, though simplistic approach to attribute interest, is to make all class attributes public and available for IM (for classes that are used to instantiate virtual world objects). There are three problems with this approach. Firstly, if all class attributes are interest criteria, interest managers need to be able to process all attributes, in order to determine the existence of interest (making interest managers complex). Secondly, many attributes should not (or may not be desired to) be available for IM. The designer of a class should be able to specify the attributes being made available for IM. Thirdly, equivalent attributes in classes with no common class ancestry other than the hierarchy root, need to be identified and resolved.

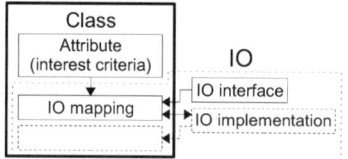

Figure 2. IO interface, mapping and implementation

What is desired is to decouple attribute interest criteria from virtual world objects' classes. To do this, we propose: the definition of interfaces for accessing interest criteria; a mapping between interfaces and implementations of interfaces; and implementations (of attribute interest criteria) able to compute the existence of interest. Each interface may be used as an operator in formula IEs. The combination of the interface, the mapping to an implementation and the implementation is referred to as an IO (see Figure 2).

4.1. Defining IOs

An IO is an operator that accepts parameters, performs a calculation (using the parameters) and returns results. Results are whether interest criteria are met. IOs are conceptually similar to remote procedure calls (RPCs) and web services (and XML-RPC), in that they represent an abstract interface that may be mapped to various implementations, in the DVE case implementations provided by different classes. They may be invoked (by a RF), perform a calculation and return results. Parameters may be sourced from either: parameters local to an object that a FIEO is responsible for; or parameters local to an object that a RF is responsible for. Most IOs employ a combination of both types of parameters. A RF's interest manager instructs an object to invoke an IO to determine whether a unit of interest with another object is satisfied. IOs were designed for use with sender-based filtering (i.e. RFs invoke IOs – not FIEOs).

An IO interface specifies the name of an IO and all its parameters. Parameters possess a type, a name and information indicating whether the FIEO or RF supplies it. An example IO interface is presented in Figure 3.

IO implementations do not need to be tightly coupled to a class (although an IO may be implemented as a class method or a method of some other utility class). Equivalent IOs may be used in classes with no common ancestry other than the hierarchy root (as depicted in Figure 4). An IO implementation accepts parameters (specified in the corresponding IO interface), performs a computation on the parameters and returns results indicating the existence of interest. Different implementations of equivalent IOs should produce the same results when supplied with the same parameters.

Each class, that when instantiated creates a virtual world object, may possess IO mappings. IO mappings provide a transparent means for IM to access private class attributes. An interest manager invokes an IO mapping and supplies parameters local to the FIEO. IO mappings access (and obtain copies of) class attributes local to the RF. The IO mapping then invokes the corresponding IO implementation, passing all required parameters (both those local to the FIEO and to the RF) as specified in the IO interface. The IO mapping passes results returned by the IO implementation to the interest manager.

Formula IEs comprise (in part) any number of IOs. IOs facilitate the evaluation of formula IEs and determine the existence of interest. Evaluating a formula IE requires that each IO contained within a formula IE first be evaluated. IOs perform calculations using supplied parameters. Calculations are able to possess varying degrees of complexity. In a simple example, an IO may perform a comparison upon attributes of a simple type. In a more complicated example, an IO may determine whether one point (a complex type) is within a certain distance of another point. IOs provide a generic framework for defining comparative operators. Even simple comparisons, such as equality, differ based on the data types of values being compared.

Figure 5 presents an example of evaluating an IO. In this example the FIEO is responsible for object X, RF1 is responsible of object Y and RF2 is responsible for object Z. Object Y and object Z are not necessarily of the same type. The FIEO's interest manager constructs a formula IE that specifies the IO *colourEqualsIO*. In this example, the IO *colourEqualsIO* requires two parameters: a desired colour (provided by the FIEO) and the colour to which it is compared (provided by the RF). If these two colours are the same, the IO returns true. In this example, the IO at RF1 would return true, whilst the IO at RF2 would return false (as blue is not the same colour as red). In this example the IO, *colourEqualsIO* uses a simple equality check. IOs with more elaborate complicated calculations may be constructed.

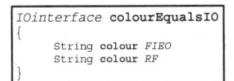

Figure 3. Example IO interface

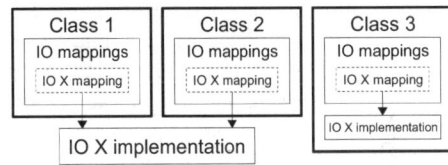

Figure 4. Alternative implementations of an IO

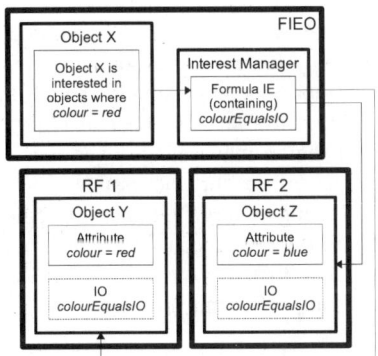

Figure 5. IO example

4.2. IO advantages and disadvantages

This section discusses the advantages and disadvantages to the IO approach for facilitating attribute interest in formula IM. There are four primary advantages to using IOs:

- IOs can be easily indexed based on their name. This is useful for the purposes of designing a propagation model (for formula IEs) [9].
- Different classes may support the same IO. This can reduce development time (as designers are able to draw from a pool of available IOs). An effect similar to regions (employed in cell and extent IM) is also created. This effect is different to cell/extent regions, in that a large number of unique IOs may be present, but DVE components are not required to possess knowledge about all IOs.
- IOs provide a class independent framework for performing calculations on class attributes. Interest managers are not required to be aware of attributes available to IM (and thus do not need to be aware of the calculations that may be performed on these attributes).
- IOs may be dynamically added and removed from a DVE instance during runtime, providing IM extensibility.

Adopting IOs (to handle attribute interest criteria) instead of spatial or class interest criteria adds complexity to an implementation, as more interest criteria are available for IM (with each IO requiring an interface, mapping, and implementation). However, having more interest criteria allows a finer-grained specification of interest, which, after filtering, can result in a reduction in network traffic (if additional objects that are not of interest are found). Apart from this added complexity, which is manageable, there are no tangible drawbacks to using IOs. An aspect of IOs that requires further research is how to ensure that IOs are unique and are defined global to a DVE. A registry containing IO interfaces may prove to be beneficial to facilitating this.

DVEs with cell or extent specificity cope poorly with IOs. Each IO may have a corresponding region defined (with each region encompassing a small number of objects), resulting in a large number of regions. Objects contained in a region may change over time. As region information needs to be accessible by all DVE components, having a large number of regions makes keeping region information consistent and available to all DVE components difficult. As formula IM does not use regions, it does not suffer this problem.

5. Formula IE syntax

Having discussed interest criteria and proposed IOs (a means for expressing attribute interest in formula IM), this section proposes syntax for specifying formula IEs (abstracted from implementations). The syntax is presented in an eXtensible Markup Language (XML) document type declaration (DTD). Later in this section, an example formula IE is constructed as an XML document. Formula IEs do not need to be bound to XML. However, in a proof of concept system encompassing this work, XML was adopted as: XML is platform independent; and XML processors have been developed for many different operating systems in a range of different programming languages. Using XML simplified the task of developing interest managers for DVE components, as an existing XML processor was adopted. In our proof of concept, interest managers employed an XML processor. The XML processor mapped (platform independent XML document) formula IEs to a particular DVE component implementation.

A formula IE is a proposition. The elementary formula IE involves a single IO and its associated parameters. More complicated formula IEs may associate a class with an IO, and include many IOs. *AND* and *OR* logical operators connect IOs in a formula IE. Using the *OR* operator means that an IO's results are independent of other IO results. Using the *AND* operator means that IO results depends on the results of subsequent IOs (in the formula IE). Interest managers evaluate logical operators. The formula IE syntax DTD is presented in Figure 6.

```
<!DOCTYPE FormulaInterestExpression [

<!ELEMENT FormulaInterestExpression (InterestOperator+)>
<!ELEMENT InterestOperator (IOParameter+, Class*)>
<!ELEMENT IOParameter (#PCDATA)>
<!ELEMENT Class (EMPTY)>

<!ATTLIST InterestOperator name CDATA #REQUIRED>
<!ATTLIST InterestOperator operation (OR|AND) "OR">
<!ATTLIST IOParameter name CDATA #REQUIRED>
<!ATTLIST IOParameter dataType CDATA #REQUIRED>
<!ATTLIST Class name CDATA #REQUIRED>

]>
```

Figure 6. Formula IE syntax DTD

In the formula IE syntax an *operation* is a logical AND or OR operation that is applied to the IO that specifies the operation and the subsequent IO. Any operation in the final IO of a formula IE is ignored (this scenario occurs due to a limitation with DTDs). *Data* is a serialised copy of the corresponding IOParameter's data. *Data* is supplied by a FIEO. IOParameters match the IOParameters local to a FIEO (for each IO). Any number of classes may be specified as secondary interest criteria.

Figure 7 presents an example formula IE represented in XML. The formula IE specifies two IOs: the *colourEqualsIO* and the *distanceFromIO*. On line 4, an *OR* operation is specified. In this formula IE, interest may either exist in objects of class book that support the IO *colourEqualsIO*; **or** objects of any class that support the IO *distanceFromIO*. In this context the **or** is inclusive. The first IO (lines 4 through 9) requires a single parameter from a FIEO (a colour) and specifies the class interest criteria *book*. The second IO (lines 11 through 18) requires two parameters (the first of which is not a simple type) and specifies no class interest criteria. The data for the first parameter in the second IO (line 13) has been simplified for exposition in this example.

A propagation model is responsible for sending a formula IE to the DVE components responsible for an object (or objects) able to satisfy the interest criteria it contains. Interest managers evaluate formula IEs (i.e. they determine whether interest exists). The steps for a RF interest manager to evaluate a formula IE are presented in Figure 8 (efficiencies made possible through logical short cutting are not detailed).

```
01  <?xml version="1.0"?>
02  <FormulaInterestExpression>
03
04      <InterestOperator name="colourEqualsIO" operation="OR">
05          <IOParameter name="colour" dataType="String">
06              red
07          </IOParameter>
08          <Class name="book" />
09      </InterestOperator>
10
11      <InterestOperator name="distanceFromIO">
12          <IOParameter name="point" dataType="point">
13              [X, Y, Z]
14          </IOParameter>
15          <IOParameter name="distance" dataType="Integer">
16              8
17          </IOParameter>
18      </InterestOperator>
19
20  </FormulaInterestExpression>
```

Figure 7. XML formula IE example

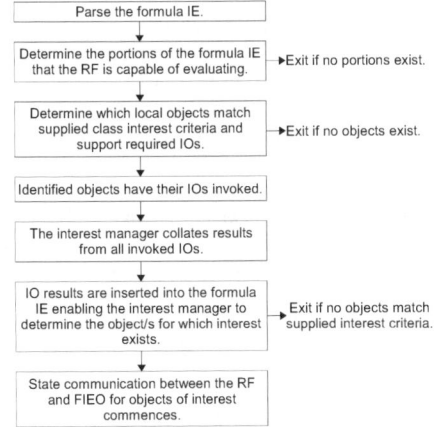

Figure 8. Steps in evaluating a formula IE

6. Conclusion

This paper explored the problem of how to specify formula based interest. IOs, a basic building block for formula IEs that indicate whether an object satisfies interest criteria, were proposed to allow the specification of interest criteria at an abstract level, independent of class hierarchy. Whilst IOs possess many similarities with object-oriented methods there is a key difference: an IO may appear in different classes (with no common class ancestry other than the hierarchy root). IOs allow designers to establish criteria that may be of interest to objects or users. An IO implementation may be implemented in specific class methods or separate code.

Having addressed the problem of capturing interest criteria, this paper proposed syntax for expressing formula IEs using IOs as the basic building blocks. In this syntax a formula IE is a proposition. The elementary formula IE involves a single IO and its associated parameters. More complicated formula IEs may associate a class with an IO, and include many IOs. *AND* and *OR* logical operators connect IOs in a formula IE. Using the *OR* operator means that an IO's results are independent of other IO results. Using the *AND* operator means that IO results depend on the results of subsequent IOs (in the formula IE). The syntax provides a standard means for constructing a formula IE. It was demonstrated that this relatively simple syntax could capture the essential interest criteria and could leverage XML processing tools. The function and viability, with satisfactory performance, of this IO based approach has been verified in a proof of concept system executing on 3 PCs, encompassing 50 DVE components, 100 classes and 300 IOs.

Whilst IOs and the formula IE syntax allow the specification of interest criteria and formula IEs, they do not facilitate the scalability benefit of IM. To provide scalability, a propagation model is also required. A propagation model has been designed and developed to a proof of concept level (in tandem with the work in this paper) [9].

7. Acknowledgements

The author would like to acknowledge the feedback and advice provided by Mr. C. Linn and Dr. M. Cook whilst constructing this article.

8. References

[1] Jarett, A., et al., *IGDA Online Games White Paper*. 2003.

[2] Bartlett, R. *A Categorisation Model for Distributed Virtual Environments*. in Parallel and Distributed Processing Symposium, 2004. Proceedings. 18th International. 2004. Santa Fe, New Mexico, United States: IEEE.

[3] Day, G., *Online Games: Crafting Persistent-State Worlds*. IEEE Computer, 2001. **34**(10): p. 111-112.

[4] Chia-Hao, L., W. Chen-Hsing, and C. Hsing-Lung. *Tracking-needless grouping: an efficient and scalable grouping scheme in networked virtual environments*. in Consumer Communications and Networking Conference. 2004. Las Vegas, Nevada, United States: IEEE.

[5] Zhang, X., D. Gracanin, and T.P. Duncan. *Evaluation of a pre-reckoning algorithm for distributed virtual environments*. in Parallel and Distributed Systems, 2004. ICPADS 2004. Proceedings. Tenth International Conference on. 2004. Newport Beach, California, United States: IEEE.

[6] Morse, K.L., et al. *An Architecture for Web-Services Based Interest Management in Real Time Distributed Simulation*. in Distributed Simulation and Real-Time Applications. 2004. Budapest, Hungary: IEEE.

[7] Morse, K.L., *An Adaptive, Distributed Algorithm for Interest Management*. 2000, University of California, Irvine. p. 216.

[8] Morse, K.L., *Interest Management in Large-Scale Distributed Simulations*. 1996, University of California. p. 16.
[9] Bartlett, R. *A Peer-to-Peer Formula Interest Expression Propagation Model for Distributed Virtual Environments*. in Distribution Simulation and Real-time Applications. 2005. Montreal, Canada: IEEE.
[10] Wilson, A.L. and R.M. Weatherly. *New Traffic Reduction and Management Tools for ALSP Confederations*. in Elecsim 1994 Internet Conference. 1994.
[11] Miller, D.C. and J.A. Thorpe, *SIMNET: The Advent of Simulator Networking*. Proceedings of the IEEE, 1995. **83**(8): p. 1114-1123.
[12] Zyda, M., et al. *NPSNET: Constructing A 3D Virtual World*. in Symposium on Interactive 3D Graphics. 1992. Cambridge, Massachusetts, United States: ACM.
[13] Singhal, S. and M. Zyda, *Networked Virtual Environments: Design and Implementation*. 1999: Addison-Wesley. 331.
[14] Carlsson, C. and O. Hagsand. *The Distributed Interactive Virtual Environments - Architecture and Applications*. in Distributed Virtual Reality. 1993. London, United Kingdom: IEEE.
[15] Carlsson, C. and O. Hagsand. *DIVE - a Multi-User Virtual Reality System*. in Virtual Reality. 1993. Seattle, Washington, United States: IEEE.
[16] Frecon, E. and A. Nou. *Building Distributed Virtual Environments to Support Collaborative Work*. in Virtual Reality Software and Technology. 1998. Taipei, Taiwan: ACM.
[17] Frecon, E., C. Greenhalgh, and M. Stenius. *The DiveBone - An Application-Level Network Achitecture for Internet-Based CVEs*. in Virtual Reality Software and Technology. 1999. London, United Kingdom: ACM.
[18] Frecon, E. *Dive: A generic tool for the deployment of shared virtual environments*. in Telecommunications, 2003. ConTEL 2003. Proceedings of the 7th International Conference on. 2003. Zagreb, Croatia: IEEE.
[19] Macedonia, M., *A Network Software Architecture For Large Scale Virtual Environments*. 1995, Naval Postgraduate School: Monterey, California, United States. p. 200.
[20] Macedonia, M., et al. *NPSNET: A Multi-player 3D Virtual Environment Over The Internet*. in Symposium on Interactive 3D Graphics. 1995. Monterey, California, United States: ACM.
[21] Macedonia, M., et al., *Eploiting Reality with Multicast Groups*. IEEE Computer Graphics and Applications, 1995. **15**(5): p. 38-45.
[22] Greenhalgh, C. and S. Benford. *MASSIVE: a Distributed Virtual Reality System Incorporating Spatial Trading*. in Distributed Computing Systems. 1995. Vancouver, British Columbia, Canada: IEEE.
[23] Barrus, J.W.W., R.C.; Anderson, D.B., *Locales: supporting large multiuser virtual environments*. Computer Graphics and Applications, IEEE, 1996. **16**(6): p. 50-57.
[24] Greenhalgh, C., *MASSIVE-2*. 1997, Communications Research Group.
[25] Greenhalgh, C., S. Benford, and G. Reynard. *A QoS Architecture for Collaborative Virtual Environments*. in Multimedia. 1999. Orlando, Florida, United States: ACM.
[26] Benford, S., C. Greenhalgh, and D. Lloyd. *Crowded Collaborative Virtual Environments*. in Human Factors and Computing Systems. 1997. Atlanta, Georgia, United States: ACM.
[27] Das, T., et al. *NetEffect: A Network Architecture for Large-scale Multi-user Virtual Worlds*. in Virtual Reality Software and Technology. 1997. Lausanne, Switzerland: ACM.
[28] Powers, S., M. Hinds, and J. Morphett, *DEE: an architecture for distributed virtual environment gaming*. Distributed Systems Engineering, 1998. **5**(3): p. 107-117.
[29] Greenhalgh, C., *MASSIVE-3 / HIVEK Introduction*. 1999, The University of Nottingham. p. 2.
[30] Greenhalgh, C., J. Purbrick, and D. Snowdon. *Inside MASSIVE-3: Flexible Support for Data Consistency and World Structuring*. in Collaborative Virtual Environments. 2000. San Francisco, California, United States: ACM.
[31] Lim, M.-G., *Scalable Inter-Region Interaction Management for Large Distributed Virtual Environments*. 2000, Information and Communications University: Taejon, Korea. p. 82.
[32] Lee, D., M. Lim, and S. Han. *ATLAS - A Scalable Network Framework For Distributed Virtual Environments*. 2002. Bonn, Germany: ACM.
[33] Verna, D., Y. Fabre, and G. Pitel. *Urbi et Orbi: Unusual Design and Implementation Choices for Distributed Virtual Environments*. in Virtual Systems and Multimedia. 2000. Gifu, Japan: IOS.
[34] Pettifer, S., et al. *DEVA3: Architecture for a Large Scale Distributed Virtual Reality System*. in Virtual Reality Software and Technology. 2000. Seoul, Korea: ACM.
[35] Hubbold, R., et al. *GNU/MAVERIK: a micro-kernel for large-scale virtual environments*. in Virtual Reality and Software Technology. 1999. London, United Kingdom: ACM.
[36] Aarhus, L., K. Holmgvist, and M. Kirkengen. *Generalized two-tier relevance filtering of computer game update events*. in Proceedings of the first workshop on Network and system support for games. 2002. Braunschweig, Germany: ACM.
[37] Oliveira, J. and N. Georganas. *VELVET: An Adaptive Hybrid Architecture for VEry Large Virtual EnvironmenTs*. in Communications. 2002. New York, New York, United States: IEEE.
[38] Fuhrer, P., G. Mostefaoui, and J. Pasquier-Rocha, *MaDViWorld: a software framework for massively distributed virtual worlds*. Software: Practice and Experience, 2002. **32**(7): p. 645-668.
[39] Bharambe, A.R., S. Rao, and S. Seshan. *Mercury: a scalable publish-subscribe system for internet games*. in Proceedings of the 1st workshop on Network and system support for games. 2002. Braunschweig, Germany: ACM Press.
[40] Pang, J. and J. Weisz, *Object Placement in Distributed Multiplayer Games*. 2003, Carnegie Mellon University. p. 11.
[41] McGregor, D., et al. *Requirements for large-scale networked virtual environments*. in Telecommunications, 2003. ConTEL 2003. Proceedings of the 7th International Conference on. 2003. Zagreb, Croatia: IEEE.
[42] Lety, E., T. Turletti, and F. Baccelli, *SCORE: a scalable communication protocol for large-scale virtual environments*. Networking, IEEE/ACM Transactions on, 2004. **12**(2): p. 247-260.

Using Abstraction in the Verification of Simulation Coercion

Xinyu Liu, Paul F. Reynolds, David C. Brogan

Department of Computing Science, University of Virginia, Charlottesville, VA 22903
{xl3t, reynolds, dbrogan}@cs.virginia.edu

Abstract

Simulation coercion concerns the adaptation of an existing simulation to meet new requirements. Interactions among course-of-action options available during coercion can become sufficiently complex that full verification of the simulation as it is adapted becomes cost-prohibitive. To address this issue we introduce two forms of abstraction, as employed in the model-checking community, to support verification of critical features of the simulation. We extend existing abstraction methods to facilitate our goals, and propose a useful abstraction method based on partial traces. As a case study, we apply our abstraction methods to the verification of a coercion of an existing simulation.

1 Introduction

Simulation reuse and composition as well as multi-resolution modeling all share a common need: the ability to adapt existing simulations to meet new requirements. The traditional method for carrying out required adaptations is manual code modification, which can be extremely time-consuming. With a rise in interest in dynamic data-driven application systems (DDDAS) [2] users are now exploring dynamic adaptation of simulations in response to real-time requirements. Clearly, methods - both static and dynamic - for efficiently adapting simulations to meet new requirements have become necessary.

Simulation coercion [1], [3] is the semi-automated adaptation of a simulation with the goal of reducing the time required to meet new requirements. Coercion is characterized by a sequence of semi-automated code transforming optimizations and manual code modifications occurring in an order determined by a subject matter expert (SME) guiding the coercion process. By manipulating flexible points [4], the optimization portion of coercion transforms a simulation to satisfy specified objectives and properties. However, optimization-based coercion alone is not sufficient to guarantee that validity-determining properties, physical laws and user conceived constraints, are preserved. Thus, coercion-oriented verification methods become indispensable to the production of correct adapted simulations.

Complete verification of a simulation is often intractable. Simulation coercion compounds the problem. Similar issues have arisen in the software engineering and hardware design communities owing to the complexity of the systems to be verified. To address the complexity issues, we borrow from the software and hardware verification communities and introduce the use of abstraction. Abstraction has been used successfully in model checking and theorem proving to reduce the complexity of verification. Our primary contribution here is to extend its use to the verification of simulation adaptation.

In simulation coercion verification, a good abstraction will:
- reduce search space by eliminating invalid combinations of flexible point values
- reduce the number of verification test runs required to demonstrate correctness of a coerced simulation

In the following sections we present two uses of abstraction in the coercion verification process, we discuss the extension of several abstraction methods, and we propose an abstraction based on partial trace which dramatically decreases the complexity of coercion verification. Finally, we present a case study.

2 Related Work

Abstraction is a recognized method for simplifying verification. It has been used in combination with both model checking and formal theorem proving to represent properties of programs that are of greater importance to the user. We review the literature germane to our goals.

Cousot et al [5] present a framework for using

abstraction in software verification. They argue that most formal methods for reasoning about programs do not reason directly about the operational program semantics but rather about an abstract model of the semantics. They propose Abstract Interpretation, a formalization of their abstraction methods.

Two forms of abstraction have been advocated in the literature: data abstraction and control abstraction. Data abstraction has been employed to reduce an infinite or intractably large program state space into a finite abstract version. A survey of data abstraction methods used in model checking can be found in Holzmann [6].

Control abstraction creates essential models of system behavior. Hudak et al [8] present control abstraction techniques in the context of model-based verification (MBV). In hybrid I/O automaton (HIOA) systems [7], modular system decomposition and abstraction are used to reason about the system's behavior at a high level of abstraction.

Sargent [9], reviews the literature of simulation validation and verification. None of the verification techniques reviewed addresses the complexity of verifying simulation adaptation. Motivated by this issue, we build upon ideas from previously published work to extend abstraction to coercion verification.

3 Abstraction in Coercion Verification

In cases where full verification is complex, possibly intractable, abstraction can enable partial verification. Benefits of an 80/20 variety often arise: 80% of what is important to the user is verified using 20% of the effort required for full verification. Building on application of abstraction methods, verification techniques such as testing, model checking and theorem proving can then be applied. In this section we propose two novel uses of abstraction, as it has been used in the formal verification and model checking communities, for verification of simulation coercion.

3.1 Use Abstraction to Guide Optimization

Coercion involves a user-guided exploration of opportunities occurring in variations of bindings made to simulation flexible points. The exploration of possibilities for even one flexible point can be computationally prohibitive. Consider a simulation with two flexible points, where each flexible point has 100 potential bindings. A search process will need 100*100 runs of the simulation. If a simulation run consumes two minutes, the coercion will cost 20000 minutes, almost 14 days. Complexity grows exponentially as more flexible points are added.

In practice we have found that many combinations of flexible point bindings are invalid: they violate the simulation's correctness properties. So a reasonable goal is to reduce as many combinations of flexible point bindings as possible before entering the optimization stage. Abstract models can be used to screen incorrect combinations of flexible point values. The verification time of a well-designed abstract model can be considerably less than the time to verify all possible combinations of bindings to flexible points. Furthermore, the incremental use of abstraction during coercion adds user insight to the optimization process by revealing various boundary conditions relating to correctness.

3.2 Use Abstraction to Check Coercion

The primary goal of simulation coercion is to adapt an existing simulation to meet a new set of requirements. The degree to which this goal is satisfied is usually characterized by an objective function. For example, the objective function for a physical combustion simulation might be to optimize fuel delivery velocity. However, a satisfactory solution may give a good value for burning velocity, but the simulated flame structure (e.g. temperature and chemical species spatial profiles of the fuel) may be unacceptable, e.g. the flame is too broad or various species are not properly consumed. In achieving an objective the simulation violates critical abstract constraints. Satisfaction of an objective function does not guarantee satisfaction of important properties. By capturing critical properties, we can address the need to satisfy an objective within given constraints.

As another consideration, one should be able to extrapolate the results of a coercion, to apply to cases not specifically covered in the coercion process. Coercion is typically performed based on selected cases, so the resulting coerced model may not maintain critical properties under more general circumstances. By employing an abstract verification model one can ensure the correctness of coerced models when they are used under conditions that did not arise directly during coercion.

4 Abstraction Methods

We have just argued that guiding optimization and verifying a coerced simulation are two uses for abstraction methods in support of coercion. Next we present the existing abstraction methods that can be used to implement them. For coercion, method choice should not only address critical properties but should also take flexible points into consideration. An important part of the abstraction process will be to reduce the potential combinations of flexible point bindings likely by orders of magnitude.

4.1 Data Abstraction

Data abstraction refines the state diagram of a program by reducing possible total states. We discuss the extension of data abstraction to simulation coercion verification.

Selective Data Hiding
As traditionally used, selective data hiding removes those data objects that are not relevant to critical properties. As long as the irrelevance of removed objects can be proven, selective data hiding retains both logical soundness and completeness. For coercion verification, selective data hiding can be implemented by identifying irrelevant objects using data flow and data dependency analyses. Irrelevancy would be determined by user-guided designation of which flexible point bindings have no impact on user-specified critical properties. By removing unrelated flexible point bindings, the dimensionality of the verification space can be effectively reduced. Thus the complexity of filtering through combinations of flexible point bindings is also reduced. The process for carrying out selective data hiding can be assisted by existing program slicers [6] [7].

Data Approximation
Often, data approximation is used to map uncountable sets of data values to countable sets of values. Generally this reduces the set of values that must be considered in a verification. Data type abstraction is an example. It reduces the type of a variable to one of its subtypes. For example, floating point values are often mapped to a subset of the integers.
When verifying simulations, one is often concerned with properties associated with observable behaviors of the simulation rather than single data variables. In fact it may not be evident how to represent a given property in terms of mapping the range of values variables may take on to smaller sets. In such a case data interpolation can be used to approximate a set of data. Interpolation has been used in numerical analysis to approximate a complex function. Used as an abstraction method for verification, interpolation can be employed in cases where observable behaviors are viewed as functions over aggregations of sets of variables.

4.2 Control Abstraction

Control abstraction refines the possible control flow of a simulation by removing unused control transitions. In this section, we discuss the use of control abstraction in coercion verification.

Behavior Reduction
Behavior reduction removes uninteresting components of a simulation while preserving characteristics relevant to verification of those properties deemed important. For example, in a simulation of combustion, if only the rate of combustion is of concern, then factors such as motion of the combustion chamber can be elided.
Behavior reduction applied to coercion verification facilitates separation of concerns. Behaviors related to a property deemed important are isolated, as are relevant flexible points. Others can be ignored. Employing only isolated flexible points in analysis and verification of the abstract model, a clearer view of their impact on a particular property arises, thus reducing verification complexity. This method applies only to the optimization portion of coercion, where flexible point selection is involved. Manual code modification requires its own verification methods.

Decomposition
Decomposition is a technique for systematically partitioning a system into structural or functional components. By leveraging the simplicity and independence of components, when possible, decomposing a system and verifying each component separately can greatly simplify verification of the whole system. Decomposition can work well with federations. By decomposing a federation, each component can be verified separately, and results from individual verifications can be combined at a higher level of abstraction. Of course, one must exercise caution in such cases because a federation can take on properties not present in individual components. However, one should always be aware of the opportunity to exploit decomposition.

4.3 Partial Trace Abstraction

The methods presented in sections 4.1 and 4.2 are used often in formal verification and model checking. However, they have some shortcomings when applied to simulation coercion, including: 1) they only employ static information and are not applicable to studying behaviors resulting from simulation execution or real system states; 2) they require execution of most of the simulation, consuming significant time and resources; 3) the abstract model they generate is subject to change during the modification and optimization process of coercion.

To address these issues, we propose an abstraction method based on partial trace, which has been employed in other verification methods. Our contribution is the consideration of partial trace for simulation coercion verification.

Partial Trace

A finite partial execution trace $s_0 s_1 ... s_n$ begins in a state $s_0 \in \Sigma$ and transitions from one state $s_i, i < n$, to another s_{i+1} such that $<s_i, s_{i+1}> \in T$. [10]

Σ is the set of possible states a simulation can enter. T is the set of possible traces. We define our partial trace-based abstraction method as follows:

1. Analyze a particular invalid coerced simulation, and extract profiles of the run which lead to violations of user required properties;
2. Compare trace results with expected results;
3. Construct a starting state s_0 from valid profiles in 2), and select trace length n long enough to let the coerced simulation manifest or violate the property;
4. Develop an abstract model represented as a Partial Trace ($s_0 s_1 ... s_n$).

Since the starting state of the abstract model resulting from step 4 is obtained from an analysis of expected results, it will not vary during the coercion process. The length of a partial trace is often very short compared to a trace for the entire simulation. This makes it an efficient abstraction method to filter invalid flexible point combinations.

5 Case Study

To demonstrate the application of abstraction techniques to simulation coercion and verification, we utilize a pair of physical simulations that have been published in previous studies of simulation coercion [11]. The two physical simulations, differing in their simulation fidelity, reproduce the movements of a human bicyclist following a target path. The coercion goal of this study seeks to make the low-resolution hockey puck, which is a one-degree-of-freedom particle-based simulation, generate the same trajectories as those generated by the high-resolution bicyclist, which uses a rigid body simulation composed of 15 controlled degrees of freedom to model the bicyclist's limbs and bicycle components. The coercion process will manipulate two flexible points of the hockey puck simulation:

- *maximum rotation acceleration* (*MRA*), the maximum degrees per second the hockey puck is allowed to change turning speeds. This variable influences the overshoot observed when bicyclists are unable to accomplish tight corners.
- *lookahead*, an internal parameter of the hockey puck's steering control algorithm. To simulate how bicyclists smooth, or "cut," corners, the hockey steering controller steers towards a position on the target path that is ahead of it by an amount proportional to the *lookahead*.

All models in this case study are based on a looping target path, shown in Figure 1. The path robustly tests the simulation behavior by presenting smooth and sharp corners that turn left and right. In the following sections, we use abstraction to expedite coercion and to validate its results.

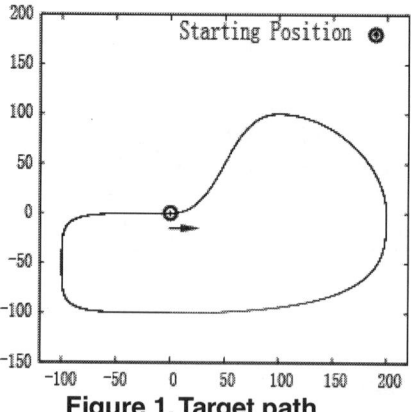

Figure 1. Target path

5.1 Abstraction for Guiding Optimization

The optimization stage of coercion requires finding the best values for the flexible points, *MRA* and *lookahead*. In this study, candidate flexible point values for *MRA* and *lookahead* are identified by the SME. According to the SME's insight, sampling of *MRA* and *lookahead* values should not be constant. There is a sweet spot that must be explored carefully. For example, for values of the *MRA* between 18 and 180, steps of size one are used, while steps of size ten are used for values between 180 and 1,800. A total of 18,821 combinations of the two flexible points are sampled. If brute-force search were to be used, days of simulation would be required to perform a hockey puck simulation trial around the entire target path for each possible pair of flexible point values.

We reduce the time required to evaluate all the flexible point values by deriving two properties that the coerced simulation must satisfy. These properties support the overriding objective of the hockey puck simulation coercion, to duplicate the behavior of the high-resolution simulation.

Property 1

The distance between a point on the hockey puck path and the closest point on the given target path must be less than ε.

Property 2

The angle between the hockey puck's orientation and the path's tangent (measured at the closest point to the hockey puck) must be smaller than 90 degrees.

To a degree dictated by the high-resolution simulation, Property 1 ensures that the hockey puck is close to the target path while Property 2 ensures it does not move erratically.

Data abstract model for Property 1

The parameter sweeping required by the flexible point optimization will evaluate Property 1 at each simulation step. However, it is expensive to compute the closest point on the path for the calculation of tangent because there is no closed-form solution and an iterative procedure is used. Compounding the cost of this iterative process, the process's inner loop requires the evaluation of a third-order spline (because the target path is a cubic spline formed from eleven control points). A detailed analysis shows that calculating the closest points on the target path consumes 50% of the total simulation time. We use data abstraction to reduce the computational burden of calculating the closest point on the target path while preserving an adequate degree of accuracy. Continuity of the path is important for Property 1, but the derivatives can be discontinuous. By converting the path to a piecewise-linear curve and using linear interpolation, the computational complexity becomes little greater than the lower-resolution versions. Figures 2 and 3 show multiple discretizations of the target path and the corresponding effects on the hockey puck simulation. In both figures, the path constructed from 500 segments is so similar to the continuous spline that it is not indicated in the left pane. Figure 2 demonstrates how significant discretizations can have little effect on simulation behavior. Figure 3, however, demonstrates that although these four versions of the target paths are quite similar, they can produce dramatically different behavior.

The hockey puck simulation results reveal that behavior degrades as the target path is simplified. Because there is little cost to computing the 500 segment path, we chose to use it for the parameter sweep optimization. Additionally, we set ε to 20 for the parameter sweeping. It takes about 3 hours to run all combinations of different flexible point values and to verify Property 1 in each combination. Of 18,821 pairs of flexible point values tested, 2,336 tests could be preempted because Property 1 was violated. A filtering percentage of 12.4% reveals a significant reduction in the number of tests required to conclude the optimization stage of coercion.

The graphs in figure 4 demonstrate exactly where in the flexible point search space Property 1 was able to cull inadequate flexible point settings. Grey dots are valid combinations and the black ones near the origin are invalid ones. Note that the grey dots are not evenly distributed because of the heterogeneous sampling recommended by the SME. The right pane gives an enlarged picture of the corner area. It can be

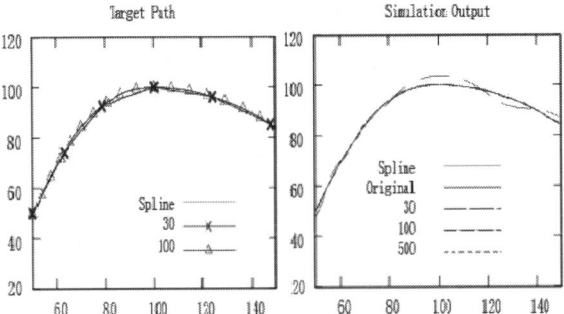

Figure 2. Path discretization (left) and the resulting hockey puck behavior (right) in a smooth curve

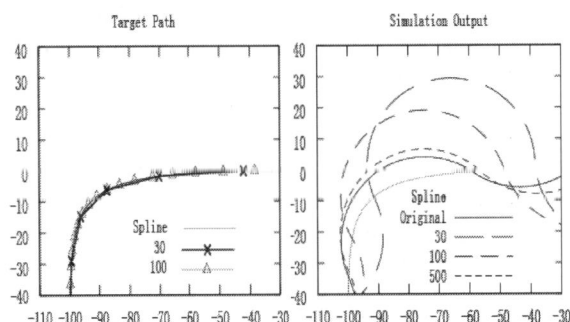

Figure 3. Path discretization (left) and the resulting hockey puck behavior (right) in a sharp curve

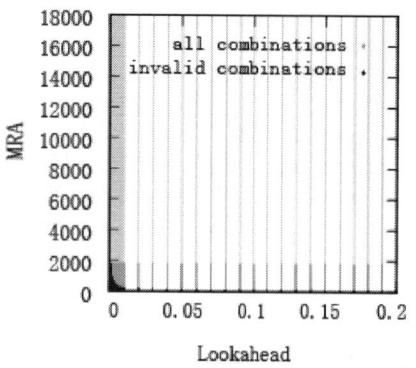
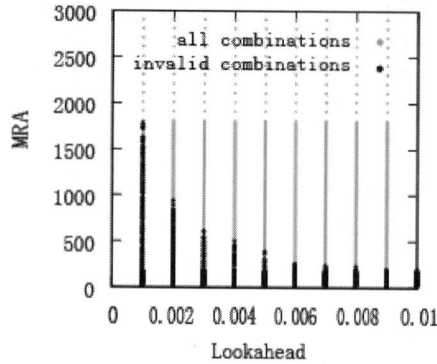

Figure 4. Results from the verification of the data abstract model

concluded that when lookahead and MRA are small, the hockey puck easily falls out of the target path. The conclusion is expected since the hockey puck, with the limitation in lookahead and MRA, cannot respond quickly to high frequency variations in the prescribed path.

Partial trace abstract model for Property 2

When searching for optimal flexible point values, the Property 2 must be satisfied throughout each simulation trial. Violation of Property 2 at any time step during the trial eliminates the candidate flexible point values from consideration. It is therefore only necessary to detect any single violation of Property 2 in simulation trials even though multiple violations may exist. This motivates the use of partial trace abstraction.

Following the steps in section 4.3, we first look for a typical invalid simulation state. Figure 5 shows the hockey puck path under the combination (lookahead=0.01, MRA=10). Taking a close look at the figure we can find that in several positions the hockey puck violates Property 2. By using the partial trace abstraction, we define a partial trace that begins before the invariant violation occurred. For example, in figure 5 the black circle at position (128.515, 59.576) serves as a valid state that precedes an invalid one. In this valid state, the hockey puck satisfies Property 2 but its direction is going to be contradictory to the target path direction in the next few steps. By initializing the simulation to perform a parameter sweep at this partial trace, we aim to eliminate flexible point values that are inappropriate for the path following requirements. The flexible point values that permit the hockey puck to successfully navigate this partial trace should be retained as candidates that will produce optimal hockey puck behavior across the entire path.

The combinations are shown in Figure 6, where grey dots are valid combinations and black dots on the bottom are invalid ones. The right pane of figure 6 gives an enlarged picture of the lower-left corner area. We observed that when *MRA* is less than 600, the hockey puck will violate Property 2. Above this threshold, the hockey puck has sufficient rotational acceleration to allow it to adjust its direction quickly enough to be consistent with the target path direction.

5.2 Abstraction for Checking Coerced Simulation

In previous coercion studies of the hockey puck, a brute-force parameter search process was used to optimize the flexible points for a single target path [14]. A limitation of this optimization process is that only a specific target path was considered. Because the final goal is to let the hockey puck mimic the high-resolution simulation of the bicyclist as closely as possible, we are concerned with how well the resulting coerced hockey puck behaves on other target paths. We extend Property 2 to Property 3 in order to investigate how well the coerced hockey puck behaves on target paths *similar* to the one on which it was coerced.

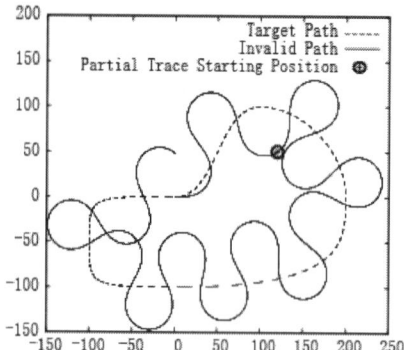

Figure 5. Invalid run of the hockey puck

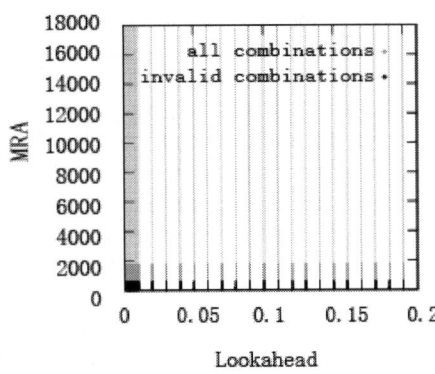 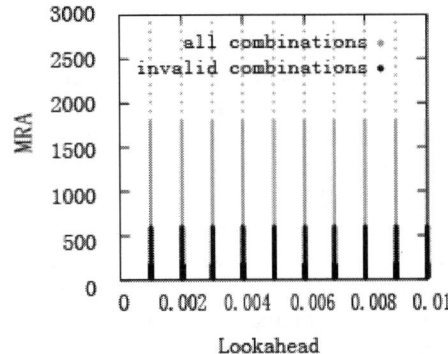

Figure 6. Results from the verification of the partial trace abstract model

Property 3

The angle between the hockey puck's orientation and the path's tangent (measured at the closest point to the hockey puck) must be smaller than 90 degrees in target paths "similar" to the one in figure 4.

Control abstract model for property 3

A steering control algorithm determines the orientation of the hockey puck at each simulation time step. We utilize control abstraction methods to investigate this algorithm. First we exploit decomposition by extracting the entire steering control procedure from the simulation, and then use behavior reduction to identify all behaviors related to the hockey puck's trajectory. Based on Property 3 and the steering control algorithm, we identify two key parameters to construct the abstract model:

- θ_1: local curvature of the target path. We measure θ_1 by measuring the change in the target path's tangent (its second derivative) along the entire loop. For the target path shown in figure 5, the change in tangent direction, θ_1, is always within the range of +/- 0.24 degrees per timestep.
- θ_2: tangent direction of the target path. We measure θ_2 in the target path between the point on the path closest to the hockey puck and at the location determined by the *lookahead*. Inspection of the target path in figure 5 reveals the difference is within the range of +/- 0.85 degrees.

Given this analysis of the relevant properties of the target path as they relate to Property 3, we define *similar* target paths to be those that have curvature properties within the identified ranges:

1) $-0.24 \leq \theta_1 \leq 0.24$ and
2) $\theta_1 - 0.85 \leq \theta_2 \leq \theta_1 + 0.85$.

In the verification we create test cases that vary path curvatures and hockey puck initial conditions. We vary θ_1 by 0.001 degrees in the range of $-0.24 \leq \theta_1 \leq 0.24$.

The distance between the hockey puck and the path is varied from 0.0 to 20 meters by increments of 0.5 meters. Our careful analysis of the hockey puck's steering control algorithm reveals the hockey puck's new orientation is a linear function of θ_2 and its orientation relative to the path. Therefore, we can test for violations of Property 3 at the boundary values of θ_2 and the hockey puck's orientation. The value of θ_2 is tested at $\theta_1 - 0.85$ and $\theta_1 + 0.85$. The value of the hockey puck's orientation is tested at +/- 90.0 degrees. Using the boundary conditions and discretizations listed above, we created 76,800 test conditions to verify Property 3, and the simulation was executed for one timestep in each of these test conditions.

To evaluate the effectiveness of Property 3, we analyzed previously published coercion results to generalize to similar paths. Carnahan et al reported *MRA* and *lookahead* flexible point values of 1,580 and 0.008 respectively for a target path identical to that in figure 5 [14]. Upon testing those flexible point values for our similar paths, Property 3 was found to be violated. Figure 7 shows values for θ_1 and θ_2 that violate Property 3 when the distance between the hockey puck and the curve is *0.0 meters* and the hockey puck's orientation is *90 degrees*.

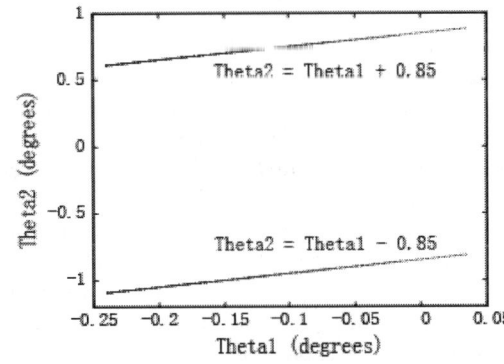

Figure 7. Invalid combinations of θ_1 and θ_2

6 Discussion

Our experiences reveal some particular strengths and limitations of each abstraction method in coercion verification. *Data abstraction* is useful in the optimization of a simulation's flexible points when they involve continuous data or data sets. However, it can produce misleading results when the selected samples fail to characterize their sets. In our case study, the discretized target path may cause hockey puck trajectories that are dramatically different from what would be produced by the continuous path.

Partial traces takes both normal and boundary cases into account like test cases. However, it integrates dynamic runtime information and only executes a few simulation steps. This fundamental difference makes rapid culling of flexible point values possible. But poor selection of partial traces can produce useless culling of flexible point values.

Control abstraction simplifies the control flow of a program and in our case study it permits us to reverse engineer the critical simulation states that must be tested to validate the behavior of the coerced simulation. Another advantage of control abstraction is its capability of dealing with large, complex simulations. Because most modern simulations follow a modular structure, the complexity of coercion verification can be significantly reduced by decomposition.

Additional abstraction can be achieved by using more than one abstraction method in sequence. In our case study, we can combine two filtering abstraction methods, e.g., a partial trace abstraction can be followed by a data approximation. Combination of abstraction methods should be used with caution because sampling errors inherent to each method can compound.

7 Conclusions And Future Work

In this paper we presented two uses of abstraction in the verification of simulation coercion: guiding optimization and checking coercion. We discussed extension of existing abstraction methods for coercion verification, and proposed an abstraction based on partial trace, which is particularly useful in coercion verification. Our case study of the coercion of an abstract bicyclist (hockey puck) simulation demonstrated the use of abstraction methods in coercion verification. Using a data approximation method, it took three hours to filter out 12.4% invalid combinations of flexible point values. Using partial trace abstraction it took five minutes to filter 31.6% invalid combinations. Then we used a control abstraction method to check the coerced simulation. Our results show, as an unexpected but correct outcome of our analysis, that previously determined optimal bindings for flexible points in the hockey puck coercion do not extrapolate to similar but different paths for the bicyclist to follow. We interpret this finding as an excellent demonstration of the benefit of the abstraction methods we advocate in this paper.

There are additional abstraction methods that can be employed to simplify validation. For example, interval arithmetic [12] supports abstraction of real valued variables to a manageable number of potential states. We will be investigating additional abstraction methods, such as interval arithmetic, as we continue our study of ensuring the efficient demonstration of correctness during the coercion process.

References

[1] P. F. Reynolds, "Using Space-Time Constraints to guide model interoperability," *Proc. 2002 Spring Simulation Interoperability Workshop*, Sep. 2002.

[2] F. Darema, "Dynamic data driven application systems: A new paradigm for application simulations and measurements," *Proc. 2004 International Conf. on Computational Science*, June, 2004.

[3] S. Waziruddin, D. C. Brogan and P. F. Reynolds, "Coercion through Optimization: A Classification of Optimization Techniques," *Proc. 2004 Fall Simulation Interoperability Workshop*, Sep. 2004.

[4] J. C. Carnahan, P. F. Reynolds and D. C. Brogan, "Simulation-specific Characteristics and Software Reuse," *Proc. 2005 Winter Simulation Conf.*, Nov. 2005.

[5] P. Cousot, "On Abstraction in Software Verification," *International Conf. on Computer-Aided Verification (CAV 2002)*, Copenhagen, Denmark, Jul. 2002.

[6] G. J. Holzmann, *The SPIN Model Checker*, Addison-Wesley, 2004.

[7] N. Lynch, R. Segala, and F. Vaandrager. Hybrid, "I/O Automata," *Technical Report: MIT-LCS-TR-827d*, MIT Lab. for Computer Science, Jan. 2003.

[8] J. Hudak, S. Comella-Dorda, D. Gluch, G. Lewis, C. Weinstock, "Model-Based Verification: Abstraction Guidelines," *Technical Note: CMU/SEI-2002-TN-011*, Carnegie Mellon University, 2002.

[9] R. G. Sargent, "Validation and Verification of Simulation Models," *Proc. 2004 Winter Simulation Conf.*, Nov. 2004.

[10] P. Cousot, R. Cousot, "Basic concepts of abstract interpretation," *IFIP World Computer Congress*, 2004.

[11] J. C. Carnahan, P. F. Reynolds, Jr., and D. C. Brogan, "An Experiment in Simulation Coercion," *Proc. 2003 Interservice/Industry Training, Simulation, and Education Conference*, Dec. 2003.

[12] C. Muñoz and D. Lester, "Real Number Calculations and Theorem Proving," *Proc. 18th International Conference on Theorem Proving in Higher Order Logics*, 2005.

Principles of Advanced and Distributed Simulation

Session 6: Abstracts

Model-Based Services for Computing Grid Performance Analyses & Tuning

Rob Simmonds and Brian Unger
Grid Research Centre
University of Calgary, Canada
E-mail: simmonds@cpsc.ucalgary.ca

Abstract

Grid computing environments typically federate heterogeneous resource "clusters" belonging to several organizations. To fully realize the promise of a grid environment, it is necessary to support analysis tools that help obtain insights into the behavior of individual clusters. The Grid Research Centre at the University of Calgary (http://grid.ucalgary.ca/) is developing a cluster service called "replay" that simplifies the development and maintenance of such tools. The service provides a single, consistent, model-based interface for obtaining current and historical information about a cluster.

Replay will manage multiple views of a cluster which enables tools to obtain data from an existing cluster as well as information that shows how a cluster might have behaved under alternate "simulated" configurations and workloads. Using information collected at a series of time instants, tools can "replay" the activity observed over a given time period. This replay can reproduce actual historical data or observe simulated alternatives. The system will support "rollback" to recover the state of a cluster at a particular time.

The model-based nature of the service also permits tools to obtain information transparently regardless of the underlying cluster. Another unique feature of replay is its use of different mechanisms to manage information that typically changes infrequently and information that can change in a more dynamic, continuous manner.

This work is primarily motivated by the analysis tools developed for WestGrid, a grid-enabled high performance computing facility in Western Canada.

The Reconfiguration Problem in Sensor Networks: An Optimization Approach

El Moustapha Ould-Ahmed-Vall, George F. Riley, and Bonnie S. Heck
School of Electrical and Computer Engineering
Georgia Institute of Technology
Atlanta, GA 30332-0250, USA
E-mail: {eouldahm,riley,bonnie.heck}@ece.gatech.edu

Abstract

The objective of reconfiguration in sensor networks is to maximize the overall network lifetime while maintaining a minimum quality of service. This is performed by turning some of the nodes off whenever they are not needed to maintain the required quality of service. This requires a way of detecting node failures to reconfigure accordingly.

The reconfiguration problem can be formulated as an integer linear programming optimization problem. A solution to this problem consists of a binary vector, where a "0" in position k means that the corresponding node can turn itself off in the next reconfiguration period, while a "1" means that the node is required to remain active. A centralized solution to this problem is designed and implemented. However, this solution suffers high energy costs and long delays. In addition, it does not scale well with the network size. A cluster-based solution is derived, and we are currently working on a localized solution where nodes interact only with neighbors to decide whether to turn off or remain active.

To solve the reconfiguration problem in a simulation setting, it was decided to interface the Georgia Tech Sensor Network Simulator (GTSNetS) with the GNU Linear Programming Kit (GLPK). GTSNetS is a highly scalable sensor network simulator that allows users to evaluate the effects of different architectural choices and strategies on the lifetime and performance of a sensor network. GLPK is a software package intended to solve large-scale optimization problems, such as linear programming and mixed integer programming.

A Generic Symbiotic Simulation Framework

Shell Ying Huang, Wentong Cai, Stephen JohnTurner, Wen Jing Hsu, and Suiping Zhou
Nanyang Technological University, Singapore
E-mail: assyhuang@ntu.edu.sg

Malcolm Yoke Hean Low
Singapore Institute of Manufacturing Technology, Singapore

Richard Fujimoto
Georgia Institute of Technology, USA

Rassul Ayani
Royal Institute of Technology, Sweden

Abstract

A symbiotic or online simulation is defined as one that interacts with the physical system in a mutually beneficial way. The simulation is driven by real time data collected from a physical system under control and needs to meet the real-time requirements of the physical system. In turn, the results from the "what-if" experiments performed by the simulator can be used to control the dynamic behaviour of the physical system. Such a simulation tool is for real-time planning and is to foresee and advise on real time problems. It aims to improve performance, to adapt to sudden and unexpected events and to improve aspects of safety and security of the physical system.

There are some research efforts, for example, the Dynamic Data-Driven Application Systems (DDDAS) which are currently advocated by the National Science Foundation (NSF) of the United States. However, work in this area is far from complete and many of the research issues are not fully addressed.

We see the need for a general framework for symbiotic simulation. In this project, simulators based on the same general framework will be developed using symbiotic simulation techniques and will be used to provide adaptive decision support to manage the resources in several application environments. The objectives of this project are:

- *To develop a generic, agent-based, symbiotic simulation system architecture.*
- *To develop mechanisms to support dynamic coupling between the symbiotic simulation system and the physical system.*
- *To conduct pilot case studies of the simulation framework.*
- *To explore and evaluate the service oriented architecture approach for parallel simulation in the multi-agent symbiotic simulation framework.*

Intelligent Management of Data Driven Simulations to support Model Building

Catriona Kennedy and Georgios Theodoropoulos
School of Computer Science
University of Birmingham, UK
E-mail: {cmk,gkt}@cs.bham.ac.uk

Abstract

Artificial intelligence (AI) can contribute to the management of a data driven simulation system, in particular with regard to adaptive selection of data and refinement of the model on which the simulation is based. We consider two different classes of intelligent agent that can control a data driven simulation: (a) an autonomous agent using internal simulation to test and refine a model of its environment and (b) an assistant agent managing a data-driven simulation to help humans understand a complex system (assisted model-building).

In the first case, the agent is situated in its environment and can use its own sensors to explore the data sources. In the second case, the agent has much less independent access to data and may have limited capability to refine the model on which the simulation is based. This is particularly true if the data contains subjective statements about the human view of the world, such as in the social sciences. For complex systems involving human actors, we propose an architecture in which assistant agents cooperate with autonomous agents to build a more complete and reliable picture of the observed system.

This research is undertaken in the context of the project "AIMSS: Adaptive Intelligent Model-Building for the Social Sciences using Symbiotic Simulation", http://www.cs.bham.ac.uk/research/projects/aimss/, ESRC Project RES-149-25-1053.

Towards an Efficient Branching Mechanism for Simultaneous Events in Distributed Simulation

Patrick Peschlow and Peter Martini
Institut für Informatik IV
Universität Bonn, Germany
E-mail: peschlow@cs.uni-bonn.de

Abstract

In distributed discrete-event simulation, simultaneous events can considerably influence simulation results as well as hinder reproducibility. As tie-breaking rules do not solve these problems satisfactorily [4], it makes sense to examine different event execution orders by using a branching mechanism. Branching guarantees reproducibility and increases confidence in simulation results, and we have already shown techniques for an efficient implementation with sequential simulation in [1]. However, branching poses additional challenges in distributed simulation.

There are already different possibilities of designing branching mechanisms. For example, branches may be executed one by one, requiring global state saving. Alternatively, branches may be executed concurrently with on-demand state-replication (as already applied in related research on simulation cloning, see e.g. [2, 3]). Additionally, the efficiency of branching depends on the type of synchronization mechanism. Some combinations of synchronization and branching mechanisms perform poorly, while others work together efficiently. To illustrate this: in optimistic simulation, rolling back branched events might prove costly. On the other hand, both optimistic synchronization and branching use state saving which can potentially be combined. We address these challenges by evaluating different combinations of branching and synchronization algorithms. The goal is to identify those with stable and good performance, resulting in an efficient implementation of branching.

Our research will also yield a better understanding concerning the question of which synchronization mechanism to use in distributed simulation. This will remain open in the general case, but we expect interesting results in the context of branching mechanisms.

References

[1] Christoph Barz, Rolf Göpffarth, Peter Martini and Andre Wenzel, "A New Framework for the Analysis of Simultaneous Events", in Proceedings of the Summer Computer Simulation Conference (SCSC 2003), July 20-24, 2003, Montreal, Canada.

[2] Dan Chen, Boon-Ping Gan, Nirupam Julka, Stephen J. Turner, Wentong Cai and Junhu Wei, "Evaluating Alternative Solutions for Cloning in Distributed Simulation", in Proceedings of the 36th Annual Simulation Symposium (ANSS 2003), March 30 - April 2, 2003, Orlando, Florida, USA, pages 201-208.

[3] Maria Hybinette, "Just-In-Time Cloning", in Proceedings of the 18th Workshop on Parallel and Distributed Simulation (PADS 2004), May 16-19, 2004, Kufstein, Austria, pages 45-51.

[4] Vikas Jha and Rajive Bagrodia, "Simultaneous Events and Lookahead in Simulation Protocols", in ACM Transactions on Modeling and Computer Simulation, Vol. 10, No. 3, July 2000, pages 241-267.

Parallel Execution of Region-Scale Evacuation Traffic Models

Kalyan S. Perumalla
Oak Ridge National Laboratory, USA
E-mail: perumallaks@ornl.gov

Abstract

Simulation-based planning by emergency management agencies for region-scale evacuation scenarios requires fast execution of large vehicular traffic models. The planning problem is characterized by the need to capture micro behaviors of population as well as the far-reaching dependencies inherent in heavily stressed network conditions spanning wide spatial scales. Parallel execution is, thus, required to sustain the required detail, size and speed. However, few parallel simulators exist for such applications, partly due to the challenges underlying their development. While most existing simulators are limited in size to a few hundred thousand road segment intersections, region-scale scenarios can involve millions of intersections. Moreover, many simulators are based on time-stepped models, which can be computationally inefficient for the purposes of modeling evacuation traffic. We are addressing the speed and scalability problems using a two-fold approach. First, we are developing discrete event models of vehicular traffic that accommodate complex driver behavior, operation of intersection controllers and complex individual trip patterns. Secondly, we are developing new model partitioning methods and applying parallel discrete event simulation techniques to enable efficient parallel execution on high-performance computing platforms. These are being incorporated into a new parallel simulator of discrete event models of transportation networks, called SCATTER, which we are developing in support of large-scale emergency evacuation scenarios. The end goal of this effort is to greatly exceed the current vehicular simulation capabilities, and enable the simulation at unprecedented scales with millions of intersections and vehicles.

NBS Supply Chain Simulation using Simul8 and HLA

Navonil Mustafee and Simon Taylor
Centre for Applied Simulation Modelling
School of Information Systems, Computing and Mathematics
Brunel University, Uxbridge, Middlesex, UB8 3PH, UK
E-mail: {navonil.mustafee,simon.taylor}@brunel.ac.uk

Korina Katsaliaki and Sally Brailsford
School of Management,
University of Southampton
Southampton SO17 1BJ, UK
E-mail: {korina,s.c.brailsford}@soton.ac.uk

Abstract

Commercial Off-The-Shelf Simulation Packages (CSPs) are widely used in industry to perform standalone simulations. A lack of widespread demand for distributed simulation within the industry has meant that there are few commercially available options for end user simulation modellers. However, from time to time, the simulation modeller is faced with a problem to which distributed simulation can provide a viable alternative solution. One such problem is the basis of our current work involving creation of a distributed simulation federation using the CSP Simul8 and the High Level Architecture (HLA). It is collaboration between the modellers and the members of the CSP Interoperability Product Development Group (CSPI-PDG).

The UK National Blood Service (NBS) supply chain simulation models the Southampton Process, Testing and Issuing (PTI) centre that serves around 20 hospitals. It is modelled in the CSP Simul8. Due to the complexity of the NBS supply chain only a limited number of hospitals can be effectively executed as a standalone simulation. To overcome this limitation we have distributed the Southampton PTI model and 4 hospital models over multiple computers and have created a 5 federate Simul8-HLA distributed simulation federation. Further work will involve distributing all the 20 hospitals and thereby modelling the entire blood supply simulation in the Southampton area. This work should be of interest to the PADS community as it concerns the development of interoperability standards and solutions driven by end user needs.

Principles of Advanced and Distributed Simulation

Session 7: Keynote Presentation

Distributed Simulation in Manufacturing and Logistics

Peter Lendermann
Production & Operations Management Group
Singapore Institute of Manufacturing Technology
71 Nanyang Drive, Singapore 638075
E-mail: peterl@SIMTech.a-star.edu.sg

Abstract

Distributed simulation technology was originally developed for application in the military domain. Subsequently, the availability of synchronisation middleware such as the Runtime Infrastructure of the High Level Architecture has also inspired research looking at application of distributed simulation for modelling and analysis of other large-scale, heterogeneous systems such as supply networks. In this keynote talk, research accomplishments that have been made in Singapore in the area of distributed simulation in the context of manufacturing and logistics will be reviewed. With a dozen wafer fabrication plants and more than 20 assembly & test facilities currently being operated in Singapore, potential application scenarios have naturally been looking at the semiconductor manufacturing domain. Challenges in view of implementation of distributed simulation in an industrial environment and application for the resolution of real-world problems will be discussed as well.

Biodata

Peter Lendermann is a Senior Scientist in the Production and Operations Management Group at Singapore Institute of Manufacturing Technology (SIMTech) where he is leading the research efforts looking at simulation-based decision support technologies for asset-intensive businesses. He is also a Principal Investigator in the Integrated Manufacturing and Service Systems (IMSS) Thematic Strategic Research Programme of the Science and Engineering Research Council (SERC) at A*STAR in Singapore. He holds a concurrent appointment as Adjunct Associate Professor at the Department of Industrial and Systems Engineering at the National University of Singapore.

Before joining SIMTech, he was a Managing Consultant with agiplan in Germany where his focus was on the areas of supply chain management and production planning. He also worked as a Research Associate at the European Laboratory for Particle Physics CERN in Geneva (Switzerland) and Nagoya University (Japan). He obtained a Diploma in Physics from the University of Munich (Germany), a Doctorate in Applied Physics from Humboldt-University in Berlin (Germany) and a Master in International Economics and Management from Bocconi-University in Milan (Italy).

Principles of Advanced and Distributed Simulation

Session 8: Network Simulation

Modeling Autonomous–System Relationships

Xenofontas Dimitropoulos
Georgia Tech
fontas@ece.gatech.edu

George Riley
Georgia Tech
riley@ece.gatech.edu

Abstract

The development of realistic topology generators that produce faithful replicas of Internet topologies is critical for conducting realistic simulation studies of Internet protocols. Despite the volume of research in this area the last several years, current topology generators fail to capture an inherent aspect of the autonomous–system (AS) topology of the Internet, namely the fact that AS links reflect business agreements between competing entities, which impose restrictions on how traffic is routed between ASs. These restrictions result in inflated AS paths and generally in suboptimal routing in the Internet. In this work, we first evaluate the importance of modeling AS relationships when conducting accurate and realistic simulation studies. We demonstrate that ignoring AS relationships produces different simulation results than modeling AS relationships based on known relationships between Internet Internet Service Providers (ISPs). Then, we introduce a framework for generating synthetic AS topologies annotated with realistic relationships. In addition to modeling the degree distribution of a network, which is the property that most existing topology generators model, our framework also models new properties that capture the characteristics of AS relationships. Finally, we propose a novel algorithm for generating synthetic graphs, annotated with AS relationships, that reproduce these AS relationships-aware properties.

1 Introduction

In recent years several efforts have focused on developing topology models and topology generators that produce synthetic topologies with characteristics that accurately reflect properties of real Internet networks. Accurate topologies are essential for performing realistic simulations of new protocols, routing, and architectures. They are especially important in areas such as multicasting, routing and overlay networks, where protocol performance is strongly coupled with the structure of the underlying topology. For example, in the case of multicasting, the study in [18] demonstrated that the performance of a well-studied protocol changed drastically after deploying more accurate topology models. For this reason, accurate and realistic topology generators are of paramount importance in conducting reliable performance evaluation experiments.

Here, we take at a completely new approach to topology generation, which is based on the idea of modeling different node relationships. Node relationships are an inherent aspect of many real networks. Links of *AS* topologies represent different types of business relationships, like customer-to-provider (c2p) peer-to-peer (p2p) and sibling-to-sibling (s2s) relationships [10]. Links in social networks represent different types of social relationships while links in protein networks represent different types of protein interactions. However, current network topology generators overlook the diversity of node relationships by modeling networks as abstract undirected graphs. Such graphs identify all the links of a network as equivalent, missing the different types of node relationships. Yet, knowing the types of relationships between network nodes and having realistic models of these relationships is very important for several applications.

The main application that motivates this work is determining routing *AS* paths in synthetic *AS* topologies. Routing paths between *AS*s are determined by *AS* relationships. These relationships result in the valley-free routing model which states that every *AS* path has a hierarchical structure [10]. Given an *AS* topology annotated with inferred *AS* relationships, we can compute the policy-compliant *AS* path between any two *AS*s using a modified version of Dijkstra's algorithm [14]. On the other hand, without knowing *AS* relationships we are forced to assume shortest path routing which leads to unrealistic results. It is well known that actual *AS* paths in the Internet are substantially longer [22, 21, 11, 20] than the shortest path. Unfortunately, the shortest path routing assumption is made by default in most simulation studies without further investigation. The reason is that all existing topology generators do not model *AS* relationships, which makes it impossible to simulate path inflation effects.

The second reason for which modeling of node relationships is important is that it enables us to produce more accurate synthetic topologies. Different types of links are likely to exhibit different topological properties. For example, borrowing the terminology of [13], c2p links are more *radial*, in that they connect small degree to large degree *ASs*. However, p2p links are more *tangential* in that they connect *ASs* of similar degree. To capture this diversity of properties, it is necessary to build a topology generator that takes into account the existence of different types of links that may have different topological characteristics. Then, we can effectively model a wider range of topological properties than can currently available generators.

In this work, we first focus on the importance of modeling *AS* relationships in conducting accurate and realistic network simulations. We identify and discuss the following three shortcoming of ignoring *AS* relationships: 1) *AS* paths are substantially shorter than in reality, 2) the traffic load on *AS* links and on individual *ASs* is substantially lower than in reality, and 3) the number of alternative *AS* paths available to an *AS* is substantially larger than in reality. We use simulation experiments to demonstrate these shortcoming and to show how they can effect commonly used performance evaluation metrics.

Next, we introduce a framework for modeling *AS* relationships and for generating realistic *AS* topologies annotated with realistic *AS* relationships. We start by identifying topological properties that capture important *AS* relationships characteristics. Then, we use statistical tools to model these properties in real *AS* topologies annotated with inferred *AS* relationships. Finally, we introduce an algorithm for reproducing these properties in synthetic *AS* topologies.

In the next section we briefly review related work in the area of topology modeling and topology generation. Then, in section 3 we discuss and demonstrate shortcomings of ignoring *AS* relationships in conducting realistic network simulations. In section 4 we introduce the topological properties that enable us to model *AS* relationships. In section 5 we outline our framework for modeling these properties and for generating synthetic *AS* graphs. Finally, in section 6 we conclude our paper and discuss future research directions.

2 Related Work

A large number of published works have focused on modeling Internet topologies and on developing realistic topology generators. The first topology generator that became widely known was introduced by Waxman [23]. Waxman generator is a variation of the classical Erdos-Renyi random graphs. Later, after it became evident that networks do not have a random structure, new generators like GT-ITM [25] and Tiers [9] emphasized the hierarchical structure of networks. Consequently, these topology generators were characterized as *structural*. In 1999, Faloutsos et al. discovered that the degree distributions of router- and AS-level topologies of the Internet follow a power-law. Structural generators failed to reproduce this power-law, which triggered a number of new topology generators that tried to achieve this goal. These newer topology generators can be classified into causality-aware and causality-oblivious. The first class includes the Barabasi-Albert (BA) [2] preferential attachment model and the model by Chang *et al.* [4] based on the idea of *highly optimized tolerance* [3]. These models grow a network by incrementally adding nodes and links into a graph based on some evolution process so that the resulting graph follows a power-law degree distribution. In the same family belongs the BRITE [15] topology generator, which employs the BA model to generate synthetic Internet topologies. On the other hand, causality-oblivious generators like PLRG [1], Inet [24] and the model by Gkantsidis *et al.* [12] try to match the power-law degree distribution of the Internet without accounting for different rules that might drive the evolution of the topology.

3 AS relationships on simulations

AS relationships reflect business agreements between *ASs* and can be classified in three categories. In the c2p category, a customer *AS* pays a provider *AS* for transiting traffic from the customer and also for delivering traffic to the customer. In the p2p category, two *ASs* exchange traffic between their customers but do not exchange traffic from or to their providers or peers. Two sibling *ASs* exchange traffic between their providers, customers, peers or other siblings. Sibling *ASs* usually belong to the same organization or to strongly affiliated organizations. For example, the relationship between the European and North American divisions of a global ISP would be s2s. To honor these agreements network administrators configure export policies on BGP routers according to the following rules:

- Exporting to a provider: When exporting routes to a provider, an *AS* advertises routes received from customer *ASs* and local routes. It does not advertise routes received from peer and provider *ASs*.

- Exporting to a customer: When exporting routes to a customer, an *AS* advertises all its routes, i.e., local routes and routes received from customer, provider, peer and sibling *ASs*.

- Exporting to a peer: When exporting routes to a peer, an *AS* advertises routes received from customer *ASs* and local routes. It does not advertise routes received from peer and provider *ASs*.

- Exporting to a sibling: When exporting routes to a sibling, an *AS* advertises all its routes, i.e., local routes and routes received from customer, provider, peer and sibling *ASs*.

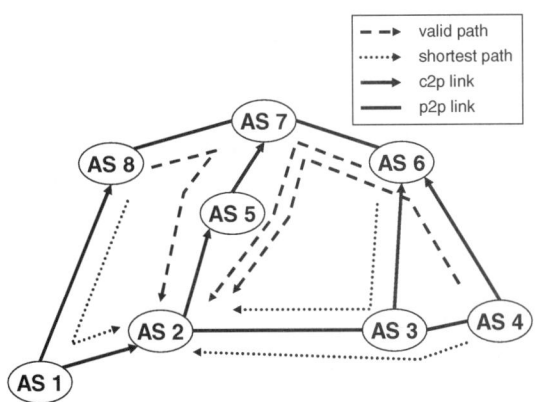

Figure 1. Example AS topology annotated with AS relationships. The topology is extracted from a real AS topology and the AS relationships are inferred using the heuristics in [7]. The dotted lines represent shortest paths between ASs 4, 6 and 8 to AS 2. The dashed lines represent policy compliant paths from the same sources to the same destination.

If all *ASs* strictly adhere to these export policies, then every *AS* path must comply with the following hierarchical pattern: an uphill segment of zero or more c2p or s2s links, followed by zero or one p2p link, followed by a downhill segment of zero or more provider-to-customer (p2c) or s2s links. The paths that follow this hierarchical structure are called *valley-free* [10] or *valid*.

In addition to export policies, network administrators also configure route selection policies. The most widely used route selection policy is that *ASs* prefer customer routes over routes through peers or providers. This is because *ASs* do not have to pay for sending traffic to a customer and also because they tend to avoid congestion at peering exchange points. This route selection policy is referred as *prefer-customer* routing [10].

Routing policies reflect business agreements and economic incentives, and for this reason they are deemed more important than quality of service criteria and thus they take precedence in the route selection process. Consequently, suboptimal routing and inflated *AS* paths often occur. The study by Gao and Wang [11] used BGP data to measure the extent of *AS* path inflation due to valley-free and prefer-customer routing in the Internet. They found that at least 45% of the *AS* paths observed in BGP data are inflated by at least one *AS* hop and that *AS* paths can be inflated by as long as 9 *AS* hops.

Taking into account such inflation effects is important for conducting meaningful and realistic simulation studies.

Consider, for example the *AS* topology in Figure 1 that we extracted from a real topology[1]. Directed links represent c2p relationships that point towards the provider and undirected links represent p2p relationships. If we ignore *AS* relationships then the shortest paths from *ASs* 4, 6 and 8 to *AS* 2 are shown with dotted lines. On the other hand, if we account for *AS* relationships these paths are no longer valid. In particular, the path 4→3→2 transverses two p2p links; the path 6→3→2 transverses a p2c link followed by a p2p link; and the path 8→1→2 transverses a c2p link after having gone through a p2c link. All these paths violate the hierarchical structure of the valley-free model and thus are not used in practice. The paths actually used are the policy compliant paths marked with dashed lines.

The first effect of taking *AS* relationships into account is that paths become longer than the corresponding shortest paths. From a performance perspective, longer paths can affect metrics such as end-to-end (e2e) delay, server response time, jitter, convergence time and others. To demonstrate this we simulated the topology in Figure 1 using BGP++ [8, 5]. BGP++ is a BGP simulation module based on Zebra routing software. We use a single router for each *AS* and configured appropriate export rules between *ASs* according the guidelines discussed above. We set the delay of each link to 10 milliseconds and the bandwidth to 400kbps. Then, we configured exponential on/off sources at *ASs* 4, 6 and 8 that send traffic to *AS* 2 at a rate of 500kbps. We run the simulation for 120 seconds; for the first 100 seconds we wait for routers to converge[2] and at the 100th second we start the traffic sources. We first measure the e2e delay between the sources and the destination under the following two configuration scenarios: 1) *AS* relationships disabled, and 2) AS relationships enabled.

In Figure 2 we depict the cumulative distribution function (CDF) of the e2e delays for the two scenarios. First, notice that the CDF corresponding to simulating *AS* relationships is skewed to the right, which means that there is a significant increase in the e2e delay. In particular, the average e2e delay with *AS* relationships enabled is 0.853 seconds whereas without *AS* relationships it drops to 0.389 seconds. Besides this decrease in the e2e delay, note that in Figure 2 the CDF corresponding to simulating *AS* relationships is much smoother than the second CDF, which exhibits a step-wise increase. This difference shows that the e2e delay with *AS* relationships enabled exhibits a much higher variability compared to ignoring *AS* relationships. This variability is likely to affect other performance metrics like jitter and buffer occupancy.

---

[1]*AS* numbers have been anonymized since *AS* relationships are considered sensitive information by the ISPs.

[2]Typically routers take much less than 100 seconds to converge, but to be conservative we used a longer period.

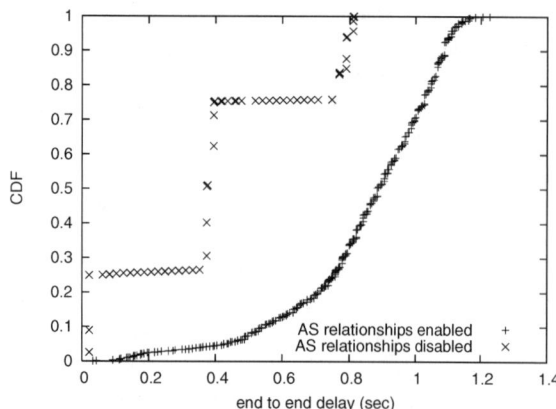

Figure 2. CDF of e2e delay between traffic sources and destination.

Table 1. Total number of paths for each AS with AS relationships enabled and AS relationships disabled.

AS number	1	2	3	4	5	6	7	8
AS relationships enabled	12	9	10	8	8	7	9	6
AS relationships disabled	12	13	16	15	13	15	15	13

A second implication of policy routing is that *ASs* have fewer alternative *AS* paths. For example, in Figure 1 when ignoring *AS* relationships *AS* 7 has three (one through each neighbor) disjoint paths to reach destination 2. One the other hand, with *AS* relationships enabled, *AS* 7 has only one possible path through *AS* 5, since the other two paths are not valley-free. In Table 1, we show the total number of paths we find in the BGP tables of the 8 simulated *ASs*. The consistent decrease in the number of paths when *AS* relationships are enabled highlights that *ignoring AS relationships increases the path diversity* of the *ASs* in a simulation. Path diversity is a property that can play an important role in simulations measuring such properties as network resilience, vulnerability to attacks, links and router failures, load balancing, multi-path routing, convergence of routing protocols and others.

An additional implication of policy routing is that due to the smaller number of available *AS* paths as compared to shortest path routing, some *ASs* or *AS* links are likely to receive greater load than when assuming shortest path routing. For example, in Figure 1 the dashed paths share the links from *AS* 7 to *AS* 5. On the other hand, when assuming shortest path routing the three paths are mostly disjoint, with only the link between *AS* 3 and *AS* 2 being shared by two flows. Thus, *AS* links and *ASs* will receive greater load than when ignoring *AS* relationships, which is likely to pro-

Table 2. Average bandwidth per flow with AS relationships enabled or disabled.

Flow	$4 \to 2$	$6 \to 2$	$8 \to 2$
AS relationships enabled Bandwidth (Kbps)	113	164	121
AS relationships disabled Bandwidth (Kbps)	202	196	397

duce more packet drops, increased delay, congestion, router failures and other important events. In our simulations, we find that because of the increased load on the links between *AS* 7 and *AS* 5 the average bandwidth of the three flows decreases substantially. In Table 2, we list the average bandwidth for each of the three flows with and without *AS* relationships enabled.

In summary, we highlight that ignoring *AS* relationships produces the following important artifacts:

- *AS* paths are substantially shorter than in reality.

- The number of alternative *AS* paths available to an *AS* is substantially larger than in reality.

- The traffic load on *AS* links and on individual *ASs* is substantially lower than in reality.

4 AS Relationships-aware topological properties

To represent *AS* topologies annotated with *AS* relationships, we use a graph G with edges annotated as c2p or p2p. c2p edges are *directed* from the customer *AS* to the provider *AS*, while p2p edges are *undirected*. We call such graphs G *annotated graphs*. Annotated graphs can also be used to represent other link characteristics, like link bandwidths, link latencies, or node characteristics, like router vendor models or router locations. In this study, we focus on using annotated graphs to model *AS* topologies annotated with *AS* relationships.

The topological property that most state-of-the-art topology generators reproduce is the degree distribution of a network. For our topology generator we choose to reproduce the following three properties.

AS-degree distribution. Along the lines of existing topology generators, we reproduce the degree distribution of the *AS* topology of the Internet. The degree distribution tells us how many nodes of each degree are in the network.

Annotation-degree distributions. The degree distribution of an *AS* topology does not convey any information about the different types of *AS* relationships in a topology.

To take into account *AS* relationships we look at the number of customers, providers and peers each *AS* has. We define the *customer-degree* d_{p2c} of an *AS* as the number of its customers, the *provider-degree* d_{c2p} as the number of its providers and the *peer-degree* d_{p2p} as the number of its peers. We collectively refer to d_{p2c}, d_{c2p} and d_{p2p} as *annotation degrees*. The second property we select to reproduce is the annotation-degree distributions of an *AS* topology. These distributions are a natural generalization of the degree distribution of a network that take into account the presence of different types of *AS* relationships. The customer-degree distribution tells us how many nodes with a specific number of customers are in the network. Similarly, the provider- and peer-degree distributions tell us how many nodes with a specific number of providers and peers, respectively, are in the network.

Annotation-degree correlations. The annotation-degree distributions do not tell us anything about the correlations between these degrees, i.e., how many customers, providers and peers a specific *AS* has. Correlations between different annotation degrees appear often in the Internet. For example, large tier-1 *AS*s typically have a large number of customers, i.e., large d_{p2c}, no providers, i.e., zero d_{c2p}, and a small number of peers, i.e., small d_{p2p}. On the other hand, medium size ISPs have a small set of customers, several peers, and few providers. Note, that simply ignoring these correlations can lead to graphs that follow the previous two properties, but have artifacts, like high degree nodes with many providers.

The exact correlations between the annotation degrees of an *AS* are captured in the joint distribution $P(d_{p2c}, d_{c2p}, d_{p2p})$, which is defined as the number $n(d_{p2c}, d_{c2p}, d_{p2p})$ of nodes in the network with d_{p2c} customers, d_{c2p} providers and d_{p2p} peers over the total number of nodes n:

$$P(d_{p2c}, d_{c2p}, d_{p2p}) = n(d_{p2c}, d_{c2p}, d_{p2p})/n.$$

We call this distribution the *joint annotation-degree distribution* (JADD). JADD is a multivariate distribution and its marginals[3] are the annotation-degree distributions, i.e., our second property. From JADD we can also derive the *AS*-degree distribution simply by summing the annotation degrees of a node. Consequently, JADD is a union of the three properties we have discussed thus far.

5 *AS* Topology Generator

In this section we outline our framework for modeling and reproducing the JADD of real *AS* topologies. Our topology generation scheme proceeds in two phases. In the first phase, given the number of nodes N in the target graph we produce N degree triplets d^i_{p2c}, d^i_{c2p} and d^i_{p2p}, $1 \leq i \leq N$, such that the JADD of these triplets follows the JADD of real *AS* topologies. In the second phase given the N degree triplets we contract the annotated graph.

5.1 Modeling JADD

We model JADD using *copulas* [17], an powerful statistical tool that fully quantifies the dependence among multiple random variables. In contrast to other well-known correlation metrics, like Pearson's coefficient, Kendall's tau or Spearman's rho, copulas do not provide a single scalar value but a function that can capture complex correlations and fine-grained details of the dependence structure.

According to Sklar's theorem [19], any continuous[4] 3-dimensional multivariate cumulative distribution function (CDF) F can be written in the form:

$$F(x_1, x_2, x_3) = C(F_1(x_1), F_2(x_2), F_2(x_3)), \quad (1)$$

where F_1, F_2 and F_3 denote the marginal CDFs. The function C is called a copula and has uniform distributed marginals in $[0, 1]^3$. Given the copula function and the marginal CDFs F_1, F_2 and F_3, we can determine the joint distribution F using equation 1. Thus, copulas have two important properties: 1) given the marginals they *fully* describe the joint distribution F, and most importantly, 2) they enable the practitioner to model the dependence structure *independently* of the marginal distributions.

Modeling marginal distributions is a fairly easy task, since there exist a wealth of statistical methods and distributions for matching univariate samples. To find the appropriate marginal distributions we constructed an *AS* topology from RouteViews [16] data. We downloaded a BGP table from the collector `route-views2.oregon-ix.net` on 07/18/2005 and extracted *AS* links, ignoring private *AS* numbers and *AS* sets. We inferred c2p and p2p relationships using the heuristics in [7, 6]. This way, we derived a real *AS* topology annotated with c2p and p2p relationships. From this topology, we extracted the customer-, provider- and peer-degree distributions and evaluated alternative fitting models. We find that the customer-degree distribution can be well approximated using a generalized Pareto distribution (GPD). Moreover, the peer-degree distribution can be accurately modeled with a pair of GDPs, one for the body and one for the tail of the distribution. For the provider-degree distribution, we were not able to fit a parametric model. For this reason, we model the distribution by

---

[3]Given three jointly distributed random variables X, Y and Z, the marginal distribution of X is the probability distribution of X ignoring information about Y and Z, typically calculated by summing or integrating the joint probability distribution over Y and Z.

[4]Degree distributions are inherently discrete distributions. Nevertheless, they can be turned into continuous by adding a random uniform noise $U(-0.5, 0.5)$ to each degree sample.

treating its six highest quantiles as invariant. This approximation results in underestimating the degree of the nodes in the tail of the distribution. However, the tail accounts for only 2% of the nodes and the maximum provider-degree (17) is relatively small. Thus our approximation is not expected to induce significant bias. The first step to reproduce JADD is to generate N customer, N provider and N peer degrees from the corresponding fitted models.

Next, we model the copula by resampling historical correlation data. We first construct a set with all the degree triplets of the collected *AS* topology. Then, we sample N degree triplets from this set. These N triplets include information on both the actual annotation degrees and the correlations between them. We extract the correlation information by mapping each triplet into the $[0,1]^3$ space. To do so, we replace each annotation degree with its rank normalized by $1/N$. The resulting triplets $(u_{p2c}^i, u_{c2p}^i, u_{p2p}^i)$ reflect the correlations between the annotation degrees in the original *AS* topology and are independent of the actual annotation degrees. Each of the u_{p2c}^i, u_{c2p}^i and u_{p2p}^i is uniformly distributed in $[0,1]$.

Finally, we combine the $(u_{p2c}^i, u_{c2p}^i, u_{p2p}^i)$ triplets with the generated annotation degrees to derive the final degree triplets that follow the JADD of the original topology. Each $(u_{p2c}^i, u_{c2p}^i, u_{p2p}^i)$ triplet is resolved into a degree triplet $(d_{p2c}^i, d_{c2p}^i, d_{p2p}^i)$ by mapping each u_{p2c}^i, u_{c2p}^i, u_{p2c}^i into the inverse CDF of the corresponding annotation degrees. For example, we map u_{p2c}^i into d_{p2c}^i, where d_{p2c}^i is the value of the inverse CDF of the generated customer degrees at the point u_{p2c}^i. Thus, we derive the N annotation-degree triplets $(d_{p2c}^i, d_{c2p}^i, d_{p2p}^i)$, $1 \leq i \leq N$, that follow the JADD of the original topology.

5.2 Generating annotated AS topologies

Given the N annotation-degree triplets, we construct a random annotated graph using the following algorithm:

1. For each of the generated triplets, we introduce a node with d_{p2c}^i customer stubs, d_{c2p}^i provider stubs and d_{p2p}^i peer stubs[5].

2. We connect stubs by performing one random matching between p2p stubs and a second random matching between c2p and p2c stubs. If the number of p2p stubs is odd or if the number of c2p stubs is not equal to the number of p2c stubs, then some stubs will remain unmatched. We ignore such stubs.

3. Random matchings can lead to self-loops and multi-edges. We extract the final graph by removing self-loops and multi-edges.

---
[5]A stub is a half edge that is adjacent to a single node. By connecting two stubs we get a regular edge.

This algorithm for constructing random graphs is a generalization of the algorithm used by the PLRG topology generator [1]. The PLRG algorithm uses random matching to create an undirected graph ignoring *AS* relationships. We extend this algorithm by using different types of stubs to account for customer, provider, and peer edges. Then, we perform two random matchings[6] between stubs of the same type and of compatible direction. A limitation of the PLRG topology generator is that it produces graphs that contain self-loops and multi-edges. Self-loops and multi-edges usually appear on or between large degree *ASs*. This is because large degree *ASs* have many stubs and thus it is quite likely that the random matching will match two stubs that belong to the same *AS* or more then two stubs between two *ASs*. In our generalization this two problems are diminished. This is because edges of high degree *ASs* are mainly customer edges that can only connect to customer *ASs*, which usually are of small degree, and not to other high degree *ASs*.

To make a first evaluation of the accuracy of the resulting synthetic graphs, we generate a topology with 20,305 *ASs*, which is the number of *ASs* we found in the *AS* topology we constructed from RouteViews. Then, we compare the customer-, provider-, and peer-degree distributions of the synthetic topology with the corresponding distributions of the real topology. In Figure 3 we plot the CDF of the customer, provider, and peer degrees. The empty points show the distributions observed in the real *AS* topology, whereas the solid points depict the same distributions in the synthetic topology. We first observe that the customer distribution exhibits the longest tail, followed by the peer distribution, followed by the provider distribution, which has a rather short tail. The maximum number of customers is 2,384, the maximum number of peers is 434 and the maximum number of providers is 17. These distributions confirm that different types of relationships can have radically different properties as we argued in the introduction. Next, we see that the generated degree distributions follow closely the real degree distributions, which highlights the effectiveness of our marginal models.

6 Conclusions

We highlighted the problems that the Internet community is facing due to the lack of *AS* relationship models and discussed its implications on conducting realistic and reliable simulation studies. We used simulation experiments to demonstrate that ignoring *AS* relationships can change a wide range of performance metrics, which are typically used by researchers in performance evaluation studies. We

---
[6]More generally, we need to perform as many random matchings as the number of different link annotations. Thus, if we also want to model s2s links, then we can add s2s stubs and perform a random matching between them.

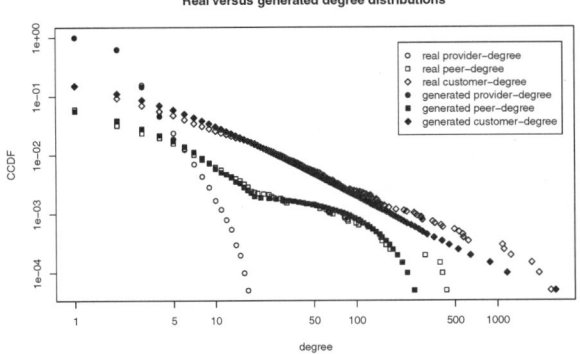

Figure 3. Customer, peer, and provider degree distributions of real graph and of synthetic graph of the same size.

draw motivation from our findings first to note that shortest path routing is a questionable assumption that should be used with great care in simulation studies and secondly to introduce a novel topology generation framework. Our framework improves the state-of-the-art by producing AS graphs that follow the degree distribution of the Internet as well as two new properties: 1) the annotation-degree distributions, and 2) the joint annotation-degree distribution (JADD). These two properties extract information about the number of customers, providers and peers of ASs in the Internet and enable us to create synthetic AS graphs with realistic customer, provider and peer assignments. We use powerful statistical tools to model these properties on real AS topologies and, finally, we introduce an algorithm to reproduce these properties in synthetic AS topologies.

Soon, we intend to supplement our framework with a comprehensive evaluation of the properties of the resulting graphs. An additional promising venue is to use our annotated graphs to model router level topologies and other interesting network characteristics, like link bandwidths, link latencies, router vendor models or router locations. Finally, we will make publicly available a new topology generator capable of modeling and generating annotated graphs.

References

[1] W. Aiello, F. Chung, and L. Lu. A random graph model for massive graphs. In *Proceedings of the 32nd Annual ACM Symposium on Theory of Computing (STOC)*, pages 171–180. ACM Press, 2000.

[2] R. Albert and A.-L. Barabási. Topology of evolving networks: Local events and universality. *Physical Review Letters*, 85(24):5234–5237, 2000.

[3] J. M. Carlson and J. Doyle. Highly optimized tolerance: A mechanism for power-laws in designed systems. *Physical Review E*, 1999.

[4] H. Chang, S. Jamin, and W. Willinger. Internet connectivity at the AS level: An optimization driven modeling approach. In *Proceedings of MoMeTools*, 2003.

[5] X. Dimitropoulos, S. Beeram, and G. Riley. BGP++ Home Page. http://www.ece.gatech.edu/research/labs/MANIACS/BGP++/.

[6] X. Dimitropoulos, D. Krioukov, M. Fomenkova, B. Huffaker, kc claffy, and G. Riley. AS relationships: Inference and Validation, 2006. Under Submission.

[7] X. Dimitropoulos, D. Krioukov, B. Huffaker, kc claffy, and G. Riley. Inferring AS relationships: Dead end or lively beginning? In *Proceedings of 4th Workshop on Efficient and Experimental Algorithms (WEA' 05)*, May 2005.

[8] X. Dimitropoulos and G. Riley. Creating realistic BGP models. In *Symposium on Modeling, Analysis and Simulation of Computer and Telecommunication Systems (MASCOTS'03)*, October 2003.

[9] M. Doar. A better model for generating test networks. In *IEEE GLOBECOM*, 1996.

[10] L. Gao. On inferring Autonomous System Relationships in the Internet. In *IEEE/ACM Transactions on Networking*, December 2001.

[11] L. Gao and F. Wang. The extent of AS path inflation by routing policies. In *IEEE Global Internet Symposium*, 2002.

[12] C. Gkantsidis, M. Mihail, and E. Zegura. The markov chain simulation method for generating connected power law random graphs. In *SIAM Workshop on Algorithm Engineering and Experiments (ALENEX)*, 2003.

[13] P. Mahadevan, D. Krioukov, M. Fomenkov, B. Huffaker, X. Dimitropoulos, kc claffy, and A. Vahdat. Lesson from three views of the Internet topology. Technical Report TR-2005-02, CAIDA, 2005. http://www.caida.org/outreach/papers/2005/tr-2005-02/.

[14] Z. M. Mao, L. Qiu, J. Wang, and Y. Zhang. On AS-level path inference. In *SIGMETRICS*, 2005.

[15] A. Medina, A. Lakhina, I. Matta, and J. Byers. BRITE: An approach to universal topology generation. In *MASCOTS*, 2001.

[16] D. Meyer. University of Oregon Route Views Project, 2004.

[17] R. B. Nelson. An introduction to copulas. *Springer-Verlag Lecture Notes in Statistics*, 139:216, 1999.

[18] C. Palmer and G. Steffan. Generating network topologies that obey power laws. In *GLOBECOM*, November 2000.

[19] A. Sklar. Fonctions de repartition a n dimensions et leurs marges, 1959.

[20] N. Spring, R. Mahajan, and T. Anderson. Quantifying the causes of path inflation. In *ACM SIGCOMM*, 2003.

[21] H. Tangmunarunkit, R. Govindan, and S. Shenker. Internet path inflation due to policy routing. In *SPIE ITCom*, 2001.

[22] H. Tangmunarunkit, R. Govindan, S. Shenker, and D. Estrin. The impact of routing policy on Internet paths. In *IEEE INFOCOM*, 2001.

[23] B. M. Waxman. Routing of multipoint connections. *IEEE JSAC*, 1988.

[24] J. Winick and S. Jamin. Inet-3.0: Internet topology generator. Technical Report UM-CSE-TR-456-02, University of Michigan, 2002.

[25] E. W. Zegura, K. Calvert, and S. Bhattacharjee. How to model an internetwork. In *IEEE INFOCOM*, 1996.

An Efficient Routing Mechanism in Network Simulation

Zhiyu Hao, Xiaochun Yun, Hongli Zhang
School of Computer Science and Technology, Harbin Institute of Technology
Harbin 150001, China
{hzy, yxc, zhl}@pact518.hit.edu.cn

Abstract

Simulation is widely recognized as an essential tool to analyze large-scale networks. Routing is a key factor which impacts the scale and efficiency of simulation. This paper presents a new approach to routing calculation, storage and lookup, named MTree_Nix. It maintains variable number of spanning trees as the base routing table and uses well-known Nix-Vector routing to compute on demand the routing states that cannot be covered by any of the spanning trees. Theoretically, we obtain the constraint condition on the optimized trade-off between space and time in MTree_Nix routing. Integrated with the advantages of the current routing mechanisms, MTree_Nix comes to a better trade-off between the storage space for the routing tables and the CPU time for routing lookup. Experimental results show that, with an increasing storage space of only about 1% more than Nix-Vector, MTree_Nix can reduce the simulation time for about 85% compared with Nix-Vector.

1. Introduction

The last decade has seen the rapid growth of Internet. Due to the complexity of networks, simulation plays a vital role in attempting to characterize both the behavior of the current Internet and the possible effects of proposed changes to its operation. The use of simulation is becoming increasingly prevalent in the networking research community.

Scale and efficiency are two key performance factors of the simulations. Researchers aim at increasing the scale and improving the efficiency of the simulation with the limitation of available resources on computers. Routing is the most important among many factors that affect simulation scale and efficiency. Firstly, memory requirement for routing states is one major bottleneck in large-scale network simulation, while limited memory resources severely constrains the size of the networks being simulated. Secondly, looking up routing states costs a lot of CPU time during the simulation, and greatly impacts simulation efficiency. Thus, an efficient routing computation, storage and lookup mechanism can improve simulation scale and efficiency remarkably.

Memory requirement for routing table and CPU time requirement for routing states lookup are two vital parameters that can be used to evaluate a routing mechanism. It will be more efficient for a routing mechanism to achieve a better trade-off between them.

After analyzing some of the current routing mechanisms, we present an efficient routing computation, storage and lookup approach, named *MTree_Nix*. *MTree_Nix* integrates the advantages of some well-known routing mechanisms, maintains variable number of spanning trees as the base routing table for most of the shortest-path routing states, and for those that can not be covered by any of the spanning trees, *MTree_Nix* uses *Nix-Vector* routing to compute them on demand. By analyzing the storage space requirement and CPU time for routing states lookup, we get the best trade-off between them, and the constraint condition to achieve this.

The remainder of this paper is organized as follows. Section 2 gives an overview of some existing routing mechanisms. Section 3 describes the design and implementation details of *MTree_Nix* routing mechanism. Section 4 gives the theoretical and experimental results. Finally, section 5 describes conclusions and future directions of our research.

2. Related work

The main difference between routing mechanisms in simulation and real networks is that the simulator knows all the characteristics of the network topology to be simulated. Simulators can then compute and store routing states in a centralized fashion[1] when details of message exchange are not crucial and memory or computation resource is scarce. In this section we will introduce some existing routing mechanisms.

Flat routing performs shortest route computation and generates a routing table that each node has the next hop information to every other node. Obviously *Flat* routing needs the largest space to maintain the routing table, its space complexity is $O(N^2)$ where N is the number of nodes. However, looking up a neighbor node is $O(1)$ for a given pair of a current node and a destination node, the time complexity is the smallest.

Huang et al. [2] have proposed algorithmic routing approach that greatly reduces the size of routing tables in a special case where any route between two nodes is covered in a unique spanning tree. In this case, instead of a general routing table, a simulator may keep a spanning tree as a routing table whose size is only $O(N)$ while a lookup operation needs $O(lgN)$. Algorithmic routing gets a better trade-off between the storage space and the CPU time for routing lookup, but it only provides partial shortest-path routing since not all the shortest paths are covered by the spanning tree.

Hiromori et al. [3] extended the algorithmic routing method to allow generic routings. It represents the general routing table as the combination of a spanning-tree based routing table and a partial general routing table, by translating a part of the given general routing table into the spanning-tree based one (we call it *STree_Flat* routing hereafter). When looking up a routing state, if an entry in the general routing table can be represented by the spanning tree using the algorithmic routing method (we say that the entry is covered by the spanning tree hereafter), then the entry is represented by the spanning-tree based routing table. Otherwise, it is represented in the general routing table as it is. The space and time complexity depends on how many entries in the given general routing table can be covered by the spanning-tree based routing table (we call it the *coverage percentage* of the spanning tree hereafter). Given that the coverage percentage is p, the space needed by *STree_Flat* routing is $O(N+(1-p)\times N^2)$, and the worst time of each lookup is $O(\lg N+(1-p)\times N^2)$. *STree_Flat* routing greatly reduces the space requirement, but highly increases the runtime, and gets even worse trade-off than *Flat* routing.

Chen et al. [4] further extended the *STree_Flat* routing method by maintaining multiple spanning trees combined with a partial general routing table to represent the general routing table in *Flat* routing (we call it *MTree_Flat* routing hereafter). *MTree_Flat* routing is almost the same as *STree_Flat*, except that when looking up a routing state, if it is covered by one of the spanning trees, *MTree_Flat* routing has to search all of them and choose one with the shortest path length. The space and time complexity of *MTree_Flat* routing also depend on the coverage percentage. Given that the coverage percentage is p and the number of spanning trees is k, the space requirement is $O(k\times N+(1-p)\times N^2)$, and the worst computation time of each lookup is $O(k\times \lg N+(1-p)\times N^2)$. Since it obviously has higher coverage percentage than *STree_Flat* routing, *MTree_Flat* routing has better space and time complexity than *STree_Flat* routing, and also better trade-off. However, as the size and complexity of the topology increase, the number of routing states which cannot be covered by the spanning trees will still be extremely large, and so will the space and time requirement.

Besides the routing mechanisms mentioned above, there is another kind of methods that doesn't maintain any routing state, but computes them only when the packet is generated. *Nix-Vector* routing mechanism, which is proposed by Riley et al. [5, 6], represented this kind of routing methods. *Nix-Vector* routing deletes completely the need for routing tables. Instead, it computes routing states on demand whenever a new packet is generated, and then includes the routing information into the simulated packet. When the packet arrives at a simulated node, the routing decision can be made by examining the packet, rather than looking up routing tables. *Nix-Vector* routing needs no space at all for routing states, and has the smallest space complexity. But it has to traverse the topology to compute the routing information that the packet needs whenever a new packet is generated, so the time complexity is pretty large. Using breadth first search algorithm, the time complexity is $O(N+E)$, where E is the number of links.

3. MTree_Nix routing

3.1. MTree_Nix routing approach

For any routing mechanism in network simulation, storage space requirement for routing tables and CPU time requirement for routing lookup operations are two key factors. However, there is a contradiction between them. To achieve faster lookup, larger space has to be used to store more routing information. *Flat* routing is implemented in case of unlimited memory resource, to achieve the best time complexity of $O(1)$ with the largest space complexity of $O(N^2)$. However, scarce memory resource is the main factor to limit the size of network simulation. Almost all the routing mechanisms after that regarded the reduction of storage space requirement as the only goal to design the routing mechanisms, such as *STree_Flat* and *MTree_Flat* routing. *Nix-Vector* routing mechanism even requires none of the storage space without any computation for routing information during the initialization of the simulator. However, as it needs to use *BFS* algorithm to compute shortest-path routing information whenever a new packet is generated, *Nix-Vector* routing mechanism has a large time complexity for routing lookup. So, it is not appropriate in some kinds of simulations of large-scale networks and complex applications, such as worm propagation.

As a result, it is unreasonable that we only take into consideration the space or time requirement when designing a routing mechanism. Instead, we should achieve a better trade-off between them according to the simulation.

Although *Nix-Vector* routing mechanism has the lowest space requirement for routing tables, it is not appropriate in certain kinds of simulations. If we can introduce a mechanism to compute and store routing tables, which needs storage space as small as possible to maintain most of the routing information and has faster lookup time, we can incredibly reduce the requirement to compute the *Nix-Vector* and use the more efficient routing lookup method instead, and enhance the efficiency of the routing mechanism.

In order to implement the idea mentioned above, we need to find a data structure to store routing information, which should have the characteristics of low space complexity and efficient lookup time for routing states between any pair of nodes. Spanning tree is an appropriate data structure. Since the Internet-like networks are typically not dense, if we generate a spanning tree for such graph, a relatively large percentage of shortest paths between vertices will be contained within the tree. As the space complexity of the spanning tree is $O(N)$, this will greatly reduce the space requirement for routing tables. When we create more spanning trees for the graph, each one will contain a different subset of the shortest paths between vertices. Thus, as the number of spanning trees increases, so does fraction of shortest paths that are in the set. One extreme is if we pick N spanning trees, they could potentially cover all the shortest paths, but the size of the trees would be $O(N^2)$, just like the general routing table in *Flat* routing. So it's a key parameter how many spanning trees we should use in the routing mechanism.

We also need a cache to record the routing information of the shortest paths that are not included in any of the spanning trees, so that we can use *Nix-Vector* routing to compute them. In the cache the information of the source and destination addresses should be stored. Data structure for the cache should also have low space complexity and efficient lookup time. We choose adjacency lists of the topology graph. According to the characteristics of adjacency lists, the source node index can be found in $O(1)$ time. To find the destination node faster, the adjacency lists of each node are ordered by the indices of the nodes, and binary search is used to get the destination node index in $O(lgm)$ time, where m is the number of neighbors of the source node. As the topology graphs are undirected, the information of a pair of nodes appears in the cache only once, which also reduces the space requirement.

Based on the description above, we present *MTree_Nix* routing mechanism. The concept of *MTree_Nix* routing mechanism is shown in Figure 1.

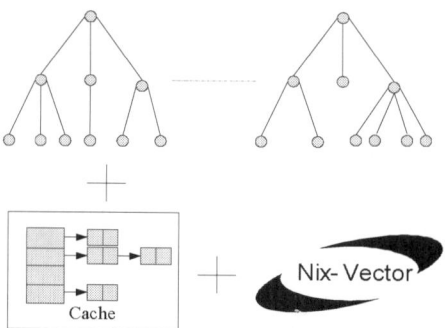

Figure 1. Concept of *MTree_Nix* routing

According to Figure 1, lookup time for *MTree_Nix* routing should be the time for looking up the cache plus the lookup time for either the multiple trees or the *Nix-Vector*. The average time of routing lookup for *MTree_Nix* routing is

$$T_{Lookup} = T_{Cache} + P_{Coverage} \times T_{MTree} + (1 - P_{Coverage}) \times T_{Nix-Vector} \quad (1)$$

where T_{Lookup} is the average lookup time, T_{Cache}, T_{MTree} and $T_{Nix-Vector}$ are the lookup time for the cache, spanning trees and *Nix-Vector*, $P_{Coverage}$ is the coverage percentage of the spanning trees. Since $T_{Nix-Vector}$ is much larger than T_{MTree}, according to equation (1), the larger the $P_{Coverage}$, the smaller the T_{Lookup}. While since $P_{Coverage}$ increases as the number of spanning trees increases, it can be concluded that T_{Lookup} will increase as the number of spanning trees increases.

As is shown in Figure 1, memory requirement of *MTree_Nix* routing includes storage space for the cache and spanning trees. The total space needed by *MTree_Nix* routing is

$$M_{MTree\_Nix} = M_{MTree} + M_{Cache} \quad (2)$$

where M_{MTree_Nix} is the total memory for *MTree_Nix* routing, M_{MTree} and M_{Cache} are the memory for the multiple spanning trees and the cache. As is described above, the relationship between M_{MTree} and M_{Cache} is that when we create one more spanning tree, M_{MTree} increases with a certain number of memory units, while M_{Cache} decreases with a variable number of units.

As the number of spanning trees increases, the increment of coverage percentage will become smaller when creating a new tree. Thus equation (2) has a minimum, and the condition to achieve the minimum is that when a new spanning tree is created, the increment of M_{MTree} is more than the decrement of M_{Cache}, or

$$\Delta M_{MTree} > \Delta M_{Cache} \qquad (3)$$

According to the implementation of *MTree_Nix* routing mechanism in this paper, the increment of memory space caused by a new tree is N storage units, while if the coverage percentage increases $\Delta P_{Coverage}$, the storage decrement of the cache is $\Delta P_{Coverage} \times N^2 / 2$ units, so equation (3) becomes

$$N > \Delta P_{Coverage} \times N^2 / 2 \qquad (4)$$

or $\qquad \Delta P_{Coverage} < 2/N \qquad (5)$

and the number of spanning trees k under this condition will lead to the lowest space requirement. For a certain network topology to be simulated, the relationship between k and $\Delta P_{Coverage}$ is determinate, and can be calculated by a recursive algorithm.

In order to get a better trade-off between storage usage and CPU time, we choose k which makes $\Delta P_{Coverage}$ satisfy equation (5) as the constraint condition of the optimization.

3.2. Implementation and algorithms

Some special techniques to achieve the routing lookup and improve the performance of *MTree_Nix* routing are described bellow.

Generation of spanning trees. When considering the generation of spanning trees, there are two key issues which greatly impact the shortest-path coverage percentage of the trees: where should the trees be rooted and what algorithm should be used. Experiments in [4] proved that short, fat spanning trees would incorporate a larger percentage of shortest paths within them. In *MTree_Nix* routing mechanism, we order the nodes by their degrees, and choose the next node with the highest degree as the root of the new spanning tree. In order to minimize their height, the spanning trees are generated using a simple breadth-first search algorithm.

Modification of *Nix-Vector*. in *MTree_Nix* routing, the method of looking up a routing state is based on either spanning trees or *Nix-Vector*, so we cannot compute the neighbor-index vector when a new packet is generated, instead, the computation should be put off until the simulator determines that *Nix-Vector* routing should be used by checking the cache when the packet needs to be routed at the first hop.

Carrying routing information within the packet header. when looking up routing states in the spanning trees, if the index of the spanning tree to be used has been determined, the simulator saves the index in the packet header, just as the neighbor-index vector in *Nix-Vector* routing. Then every time the packet is routed after that, the simulator does not need the computation of checking the cache and choosing the spanning tree with the shortest path length, so that much computation time is saved.

Algorithms of *MTree_Nix* routing computation and lookup are given in Figure 2 and 3.

Suppose N is the size of the network topology, and the next node index of maximum degree is saved in *node_max_degree*.

procedure ComupteMTree_Nix
    sort nodes ordered by degree;
    compute shortest-path lengths in flat routing;
    while TRUE do
        BFS(*node_max_degree*);
        $\Delta P_{Coverage}$=Compare_pathlength(*tree, flat*);
        if $\Delta P_{Coverage} < 2/N$ **then**
            break;
        end if
    end while
end procedure

Figure 2. Algorithm for routing table computation of *MTree_Nix*

Suppose that the header of the packet is saved in *pkthdr*, in which the information of source and destination nodes is stored. The index of current node is represented by *this*, *k* represents the number of spanning trees, and all the trees are stored in *Tree_Route[k]*.

procedure LookupRouting
    if *nix vector is saved in pkthdr* **then**
        nexthop = Extract(*nix-vector*);
        return *nexthop*;
    end if
    if *tree id is saved in pkthdr* **then**
        nexthop=LookupTree(*pkthdr->TreeID, this, pkthdr->dst*);
        return *nexthop*;
    end if
    IsFound = LookupCache(*pkthdr->src, pkthdr->dst*);
    if *IsFound* **then**
        ComputeNixVector();
        nexthop = Extract(*nix-vector*);
        save nix vector into packet header;
        return *nexthop*;
    else
        for *i* from *0* **to** *k* **do**
            nexthop=LookupTree(*i, pkthdr->src, pkthdr->dst*);
            get tree id with the shortest path length;
        end for
        save tree id into pkthdr->TreeID;
        return *nexthop*;
    end if
end procedure

procedure LookupTree(*TreeID, SrcID, DstID*)
    src = *SrcID*;
    dst = *DstID*;
    Tree = *Tree_Route[TreeID]*;
    while *dst* <> *root* **do**
        if *Tree[dst]->parent* = *src* **then**
            return *dst*;
        end if
        dst = *Tree[dst]->parent*;
    end while
    return *Tree[src]->parent*;
end procedure

Figure 3. Algorithm for routing states lookup of *MTree_Nix*

4. Performance

4.1. Complexity analysis

According to the description of *MTree_Nix* routing mechanism in section 3 and equation (1) and (2), the storage space requirement of *MTree_Nix* routing is

$$O(k \times N + (1-p) \times N^2 / 4)$$

and the lookup time is

$$O(\lg N + p \times k \times \lg N + (1-p) \times (N+E)).$$

Table 1 lists the space and time complexity of *MTree_Nix* routing and other mechanisms mentioned in section 2.

Table 1. Space and time requirement of different routing mechanisms

Methods	Storage space	Lookup time
Flat	$O(N^2)$	$O(1)$
STree_Flat	$O(N + (1-p) \times N^2)$	$O(\lg N + (1-p) \times N^2)$
MTree_Flat	$O(k \times N + (1-p) \times N^2)$	$O(k \times \lg N + (1-p) \times N^2)$
Nix-Vector	0	$O(N \cdot E)$
MTree_Nix	$O(k \times N + (1-p) \times N^2 / 4)$	$O(\lg N + p \times k \times \lg N + (1-p) \times (N \cdot E))$

Through table 1 we can conclude that *MTree_Nix* has better time and space complexity than *STree_Flat* and *MTree_Flat*, and much better space complexity than *Flat* routing. It also has much better time complexity than *Nix-Vector*, with the space complexity increasing not so much.

4.2. Experimental results

To investigate how our approach performs in a real simulator, we integrated *MTree_Nix* routing mechanism into well-known NS-2[7, 8], performed benchmarks, and compared the results with *Flat*, *STree_Flat*, *MTree_Flat* and *Nix-Vector*. In this section, we describe details of the experiments and analyze the experimental results.

We ran our experiments on a PC with a Pentium IV 1.0GHz CPU, 2 GB RAM, and running RedHat Linux operating system.

The simulation topologies were built using a synthetic topology generator *NEM*[9], which can generate topologies with different parameters such as topology size and average node degree. In each simulation topology, we created 10,000 TCP connections between random pairs of nodes, and send 1,040 bytes in each TCP connection. We repeated each experiment 5 times, and use the average as the experimental results.

4.2.1. Coverage percentage. The performance of *MTree_Nix* routing mechanism highly depends on the percentage of routing states covered by the spanning trees. We computed the coverage percentage and the number of spanning trees under the condition of equation (5) on topologies with different size and average node degree.

The characteristics of simulation topologies greatly impact the coverage percentage. Intuitively, topologies with larger size and higher average node degree will get lower coverage percentage, and need more spanning trees. The results of two sets of experiments below prove this.

Figure 4 shows the coverage percentage of different topology size, and Figure 5 shows the number of spanning trees to achieve the coverage percentage. In the experiments we generate different size of topologies from 200 to 3,000 nodes, with an average node degree of 2.6. We can see that as the topology

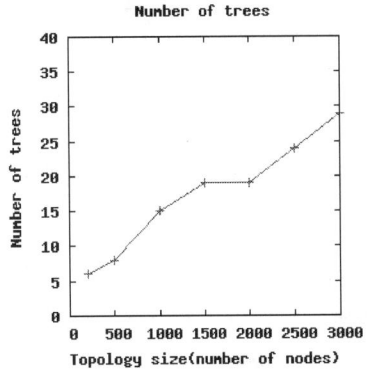

Figure 5. Number of trees to achieve the coverage percentage in Figure 4

size increases, the coverage percentage decreases, with the number of spanning trees increasing.

Figure 6 shows the coverage percentage changing with different average node degree of a fix topology size of 1,000. Figure 7 shows the number of spanning trees to achieve the coverage percentage reported in Figure 6. The average node degree varies from 4 to 14.

From Figure 6 and 7 we can see that the coverage percentage decreases as the average node degree increases, and the number of spanning trees to achieve the coverage percentage increases. This is expected, as the average node degree rises, there is an increasing number of shortest paths that share fewer edges, thus the set of spanning trees is less likely to cover as many routing states in the general routing table as the number of edges in any spanning tree.

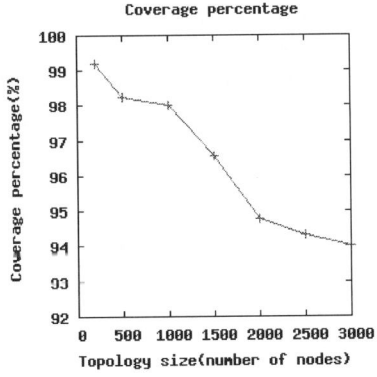

Figure 4. Coverage percentage as a function of topology size

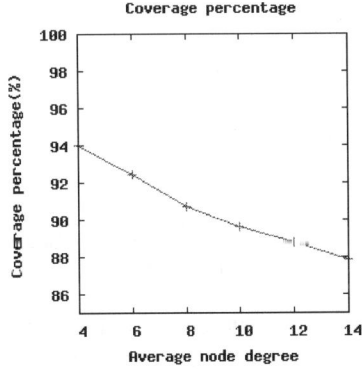

Figure 6. Coverage percentage with different average node degree

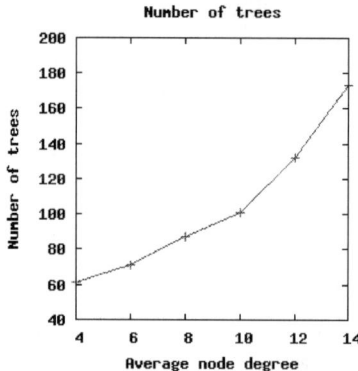

Figure 7. Number of trees to achieve the coverage percentage shown in Figure 6

4.2.2. Simulation performance. The performance of a routing mechanism in simulation can be indicated mainly by three parameters: pre-computation time, memory usage and simulation time. In this section we describe the experimental results of these parameters with different topology size and average node degree.

Figure 8 shows the pre-computation time with different topology size, with the coverage percentage and the relevant number of spanning trees reported in Figure 4 and 5. As is expected, with the topology size increasing, pre-computation time increases, too. However, it is rather faster compared with the regular simulation time.

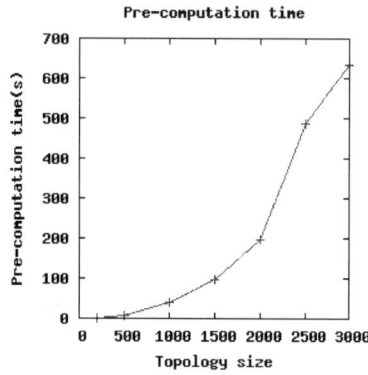

Figure 8. Pre-computation time with different topology size

The result of the memory usage measurement of different routing mechanisms is shown in Figure 9. As the size and connectivity of simulation topologies are all the same, the difference of memory usage between different routing mechanisms comes mainly from the routing table storage. According to the graph, *Nix-Vector* routing needs the smallest memory since there is no routing table necessary at all. *MTree_Nix* routing requires only 1% more memory than *Nix-Vector*, and *MTree_Flat* routing mechanism needs a little more than *MTree_Nix*. The memory usages of *STree_Flat* routing and *Flat* routing are much more than the other three because the routing tables of them are much more larger.

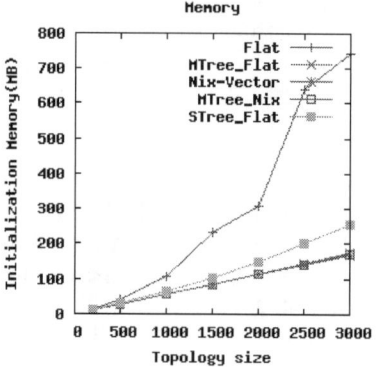

Figure 9. Memory usage with different topology size

Figure 10 shows the simulation time with different topology size. Like the memory usage, the difference of simulation time between different routing mechanisms comes mainly from the routing lookup. According to the graph, *STtree_Flat* routing requires more than ten times of simulation time than the other mechanisms, because as the topology size rises, the number of routing states that a spanning tree can cover becomes much smaller, and in each lookup, the simulator needs to search the partial general routing table with the space complexity of almost $O(N^2)$. *Flat* routing mechanism has the shortest simulation time, and *MTree_Nix* routing needs about 20% more time than *Flat* routing, and 85% less than *Nix-Vector* routing, just as is expected.

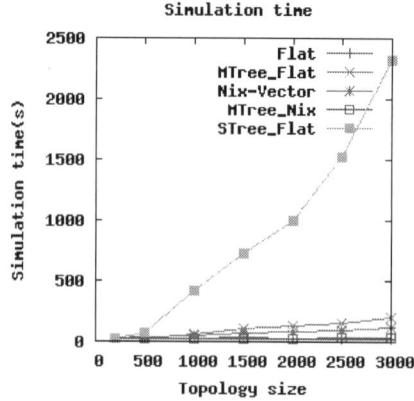

Figure 10. Simulation time with different topology size

Figure 11 shows the simulation time of different routing mechanisms with different average node degree of the same topology size. Since the time of *STree_Flat* routing is of too much difference compared with the others, here we didn't show the results of it. The graph shows that the time of *MTree_Nix* routing is the closest to the *Flat* routing mechanism, and much less than *Nix-Vector* and *MTree_Flat* routing.

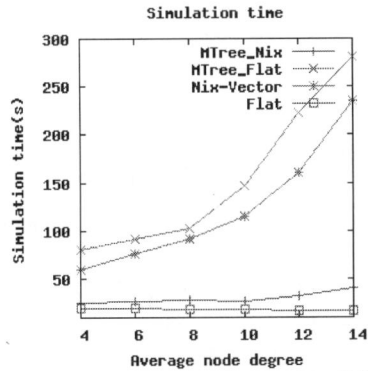

Figure 11. Simulation time with different average node degree

According to the experimental results and analysis above, the memory usage and simulation time of *MTree_Nix* routing mechanism are both close to the optimization, and *MTree_Nix* routing mechanism comes to a better trade-off than the current routing mechanisms.

5. Conclusions and future work

Routing mechanism is one of the most important factors which impact the performance of simulation. This paper presents *MTree_Nix* routing mechanism, which maintains certain number of spanning trees as the base routing table, and uses *Nix-Vector* routing to compute on demand the routing states that can't be covered by any spanning tree. By analyzing the space and time requirement, we obtain the constraint condition to achieve the best trade-off between space and time in *MTree_Nix* routing. *MTree_Nix* routing mechanism integrates the advantages of both the static and on-demand routing, and comes to a better trade-off between memory usage and lookup time than the current routing mechanisms. Based on the experimental results, *MTree_Nix* routing mechanism adds only about 1% more memory usage than *Nix-Vector* routing, and achieves about 85% decrement of simulation time than *Nix-Vector*.

Our implementation of *MTree_Nix* routing mechanism in NS-2 is somewhat quick and dirty, and we care more about the method of integrating the static and on-demand routing mechanisms in this paper. In the future we will improve *MTree_Nix* routing by proposing more efficient algorithm of choosing tree roots and so on. Besides, parallel and distributed network simulation is an efficient way to enable simulation of large-scale networks. Later we expect to extend *MTree_Nix* routing to parallel and distributed network simulators such as PDNS.

References

[1] P. Huang, D. Estrin, and J. Heidemann, "Enabling Large-scale simulations: selective abstraction approach to the study of multicast protocols," in Proceedings of the International Symposium on Modeling, Analysis and Simulation of Computer and Telecommunication Systems, Montreal, Canada, July 1998, pp. 241–248.

[2] P. Huang and J. Heidemann, "Minimizing routing state for light-weight network simulation," in Proceedings of the IEEE International Symposium on Modeling, Analysis and Simulation of Computer and Telecommunication Systems, August 2001.

[3] A. Hiromori, H. Yamaguchi, K. Yasumoto, T. Higashino and K. Taniguchi, "Reducing the Size of Routing Tables for Large-scale Network Simulation," in Proceedings of the IEEE International Symposium on Modeling, Analysis and Simulation of Computer and Telecommunication Systems, October 2003.

[4] J. Chen, D. Gupta, K.V. Vishwanath, A. C. Snoeren and A. Vahdat, "Routing in an Internet-Scale Network Emulator," in Proceedings of the IEEE International Symposium on Modeling, Analysis and Simulation of Computer and Telecommunication Systems, October 2004.

[5] G. F. Riley, M. H. Ammar, and E.W. Zegura, "Efficient routing with Nix-Vectors," in Proceedings of IEEE Workshop on High Performance Switching and RoutingHPSR 2001, 2001.

[6] G. F. Riley, R. Fujimoto, and M. H. Ammar, "Stateless routing in network simulations," in Proceedings of the 8th International Symposium on Modeling, Analysis and Simulation of Computer and Telecommunication Systems, May 2000.

[7] The VINT Project, http://www.isi.edu/nsnam/vint/, network simulator.

[8] S. McCanne and S. Floyd, "The LBNL network simulator," Lawrence Berkeley Laboratory, 1997.

[9] D. Magoni and J. Pansiot, "Internet Topology Modeler Based on Map Sampling," in Proceedings of the 7th IEEE Symposium on Computers and Communications, July 2002, pp. 1021-1027.

A Case Study in Understanding OSPF and BGP Interactions Using Efficient Experiment Design

David Bauer[†], Murat Yuksel[‡], Christopher Carothers[†] and Shivkumar Kalyanaraman[‡]
[†]Department of Computer Science
[‡]Department of Electrical, Computer, and Systems Engineering
Rensselaer Polytechnic Institute
110 8th Street, Troy, NY 12180, USA.
{bauerd, chrisc}@cs.rpi.edu, {yuksem, shivkuma}@ecse.rpi.edu

Abstract

In this paper, we analyze the two dominant inter- and intra-domain routing protocols in the Internet: Open Shortest Path Forwarding (OSPFv2) and Border Gateway Protocol (BGP4). Specifically, we investigate interactions between these two routing protocols as well as overall (i.e. both OSPF and BGP) stability and dynamics. Our analysis is based on large-scale simulations of OSPF and BGP, and careful design of experiments (DoE) to perform an efficient search for the best parameter settings of these two routing protocols.

1 Introduction

Understanding routing protocol dynamics and interactions on a large-scale is an important problem due to its immediate affect on current practice of inter- and intra-domain routing [1]. Network simulation allows us to consider multiple Autonomous Systems (AS), and to quantify the possible effects both from within and from outside a particular domain. However, because of the computational complexity within such models, the simulation community has primarily focused on tools which allow for large-scale parallel and/or distributed experimentation [2, 3, 4]. But beyond just model complexity, this problem equally has a Design of Experiment (DoE) complexity problem [4]. To address that problem in a real-world case study, we apply ROSS.Net in an attempt to begin to understand complex protocol interactions between the BGP4 and OSPFv2 routing protocols.

We illustrate how control plane update messages in OSPF and BGP could be reduced by 7-27% for competing network management perspectives. We quantify the impacts of using cold and hot potato routing and determined that the real issue in increased update messages may lie elsewhere within the BGP decision making algorithm. Finally, we study the effect of network robustness on the number of update messages generated. We found that by taking steps to minimize the interactions between protocols, messages could be reduced from 8 to 36%, or generally by around 20%.

In this paper, we focus on characterizing Internet routing protocol performance response by the number of update messages generated by each routing protocol model (i.e., OSPF and BGP) as a function of protocol timers, variables, and algorithm decisions. Measuring protocol response as a function of update messages generated is important because this is where the interactions between protocols are defined. For example, in a network where route flapping is occurring, routers may converge quickly between the two routes as they change. Measuring convergence as the response would lead us to believe there are no negative effects on OSPF from BGP. Similarly, measuring link congestion does not lead to the negative effect because we may observe only a fractional difference in bandwidth consumption over time. Each route removal/installation can be directly measured within the OSPF domain. By measuring the number of updates generated by the OSPF domain, a clearer picture of the negative effects emerges. Of course these negative effects lead to slower convergence times and greater link utilization, but these are secondary measures. By measuring the interactions directly (i.e., updates messages) we are able to quantify the direct impact on the network without having to separate out other effects. This allows us to begin answering the questions, *does my intra-AS management policy adversely affect my inter-AS policies, and vice-versa?* and *which is the best approach to minimizing negative effects between protocols?*

1.1 Why are Protocol Interactions Harmful?

Network protocol weaknesses are not fully understood until they have been deployed in large-scale production environments. There is probably no better example of this than the BGP protocol. Clear limitations of this protocol have been illustrated since its introduction (e.g. BGP storms [6, 7], the stability problem [8, 9]), and several solutions (e.g. route reflection) have been proposed and implemented to overcome them.

These investigations have typically focused on the individual effects of the parameter settings, and neglected the external effects on protocol performance. The problem that we see is that there are two conflicting views of the network: intra-domain and inter-domain routing. Our concern is that decisions made to efficiently route data *within* a domain are directly affecting the ability of the network to route data *across* the domain.

One immediate cause for concern is **Hot Potato Routing** [10], though some researchers have similarly voiced concerns over Cold Potato routing [11]. Hot Potato routing is interesting because it allows a router which does not necessarily contain an up-to-date view of the internal network to make decisions about how to route traffic through that network. As a practical example, the BGP protocol makes a decision about which routes to install based on the distance of each competing intra-domain route. The problem arises when this information is not stable. BGP routers typically are responsible for generating large flows of traffic data into and out of the network. The major concern is that a *small* degree of unstable routing information may inversely impact a *large* amount of network traffic.

Traffic shifts because of OSPF-BGP interactions happen

typically at ASes with multiple paths to another ISP. More than half of the non-ISP ASes have such multiple paths to a tier-1 ISP [12]. Previous work indicates that Hot Potato changes can cause major shifts in routing and network traffic. In addition, hot-potato routing may add to the degradation of forwarding plane convergence and generate temporary forwarding plane loops. Finally, Hot Potato routing leads to measurement inaccuracies in probes of the forwarding plane, and the external visibility of BGP routes.

1.2 Our Contributions

Our main goal is to minimize the number of negative interactions between the OSPF and BGP protocols in a multi-AS environment. In particular, the number of OSPF updates caused by BGP protocol dynamics, and the number of BGP updates caused by OSPF protocol characteristics should be *minimized*. Past investigations relying on measurement data have been constrained to one-way analysis of either BGP dynamics on the OSPF protocol, or OSPF dynamics on the BGP protocol, and then only for a single AS.

Our major contributions can be itemized as follows:

A framework to optimize OSPF and BGP protocol response: Based on a controlled large-scale simulation of OSPF and BGP, we present a framework to optimize a particular protocol performance metric over possible parameter search space through a heuristic search algorithm. We particularly use the number of updates with various original causes (i.e., OSPF-caused, BGP-caused) as metrics to optimize several OSPF and BGP parameters used in practice. Instead of measurement-based estimation and matching methods, we leverage a controlled simulation environment to trace exact causes of each routing update in the system.

Experiment design approach to understand OSPF and BGP interactions: We devise a systematic design of experiments methodology to investigate particular effects of three classes of protocol parameters in the total number of negative interactions between OSPF and BGP. We measure the negative interactions as the total number of OSPF-caused BGP updates and BGP-caused OSPF updates. We investigate three classes of parameters as factors into the negative interactions: (i) OSPF timers, (ii) BGP timers, and (iii) BGP decision making attributes.

Large-scale OSPF and BGP simulation: We present large-scale simulation of OSPF and BGP in a single model. Our simulation model uses realistic inter- and intra-domain topology generated from Rocketfuel [5] measurement data and nearly complete RFC implementations of the OSPF and BGP protocols.

2 Related Work

Analysis of interactions between inter- and intra-domain routing protocols has been an attractive research topic. In [13], through analysis of data from AT&T's BGP and OSPF traffic measurements, authors showed that majority of BGP updates are because of Hot Potato decision-making practices of ISPs. The main difference in our work is that we do not need any matching or estimation technique to determine OSPF-caused BGP updates or vice versa. Since our large-scale simulation environment is fully controlled, we can easily trace the causes of updates.

In [10], as a follow-up to their previous work [13], authors modeled sensitivity of BGP (and the network in general) to IGP-caused Hot Potato changes. The bottom line result is one needs to enumerate all possible Hot Potato IGP changes to perform BGP analysis.

Another major work on analysis of OSPF and BGP interactions was presented in [12]. In contrast to the research direction on analyzing effects of intra-domain changes on inter-domain routing as in [13, 10], the main goal of the work in [12] was to determine if BGP dynamics effect intra-domain routing behavior and in turn effect the traffic engineering of it.

There has been significant research on convergence time and stability of both BGP and OSPF [14, 15, 16, 17]; BGP security and misconfiguration [18, 19, 20] and BGP quality of service extensions [21, 22]. Our work can potentially enhance the key results already generated by these efforts.

In placing this work in the context of the larger modeling and simulation community, we are driven by the need to "obtain good results, fast". This performance driven need has been attacked on many fronts. Clearly one of the most popular approaches is the application of many processors to speedup the execution of a simulation, such as done with such systems as [23, 24, 25, 26, 27]. In this case, we employ a technique that greatly reduces the numbers the experiments that must be run and aides in the search process for the set of parameters that provides "good" protocol performance.

3 ROSS.Net

The goal of our black-box simulation was to simulate a portion of the Internet by simulating multiple ASes, with multiple OSPF areas per AS, and multiple sub-networks per area. The investigation centers around link weight changes at the OSPFv2 routers, and link status changes which occur globally throughout the topology. This section details how the model was built and what assumptions were made during model construction.

We use the ROSS.Net framework to perform systematic analysis of OSPF and BGP dynamics and interactions. Our framework includes (i) a simulation component for simulating large-scale network protocol scenarios, and (ii) a Unified Search Framework which currently employs the heuristic search algorithm, Recursive Random Search (RRS) [28], to seek the best parameter settings of the system under consideration. In our experiments, we use the count of routing updates as the metric to optimize, and several OSPF and BGP protocol parameters as the parameters of the optimization.

3.1 Network Protocol Simulation Models

The network protocols simulated include: BGP4, OSPFv2, and IPv4. For scalability, the TCP layer was not simulated for the BGP routers. The assumptions made for scalability and time available for development are addressed in this section.

OSPFv2 is a link-state routing protocol designed to run internal to a single AS. Each OSPFv2 router maintains an identical database describing the AS network's topology. From this database, a routing table is calculated by constructing a shortest-path tree. OSPFv2 recalculates routes quickly in the face of topological changes, utilizing a minimum of routing protocol traffic.

We developed our OSPFv2 simulation model as a nearly complete RFC implementation citeRFC2328. The only exception is that Network LSAs were not modeled, and so the topology was not configured with stub networks. Our **BGP4 model** simulates both eBGP and iBGP according to [29]. External peers were defined by connections to BGP routers outside the current AS. Internal peers were fully connected to all eBGP routers in a given AS. With the exception of the error notification details, we have nearly fully modeled the BGP4 protocol per the RFC specification. In BGP, the decision making process occurs in three phases. The first phase is related to

Table 1: Stages of the BGP decision algorithm for route selection.

BGP Decision Algorithm
1. Highest Local Preference
2. Lowest AS Path Length
3. Lowest Origin Type (0 iBGP, 1 eBGP, 2 Incomplete)
4. Smaller MED (iff next hops equal)
5. Lowest IGP Cost
6. Lowest Next Hop
7. Lowest BGP Identifier
8. Vendor-dependent Tie Break

calculating route preferences according to owner-defined policies. The second phase selects the best route to each destination based upon the route attributes, and installs those routes into the local RIB (Loc-RIB). Phase 3 involves route aggregation and dissemination, which we did *not* model since route aggregation and information reduction are not described in the RFC and are optional and commercially dependent. Routes are disseminated as appropriate for eBGP and iBGP, and external control traffic minimized by using the MinRouteAdvertisementInterval (MRAI). The specification simply calls for MRAI seconds to elapse between successive route updates between any two eBGP speakers.

We have modeled all other parts of the decision making algorithm, illustrated in Table 1, and the default decision if a tie exists at all levels is to keep the existing route. Conversely, if no route exists, the route in question is always added to the RIB. In our model the vendor dependent tie breaking decision is to keep the existing route.

In order to reduce the complexity of the design of experiments, input parameters are configurable at the AS level. Some of the variables in the BGP decision stage are simply on/off, such as MED and Hot Potato routing, which signify that these features are either enabled or disabled in the AS throughout the simulation. Other variables can take a value in a range, such MED, path padding and Local-Pref, which indicate the values of each feature, if enabled. So if MED is enabled in an AS, we can also select a value for it's policy. Conversely, if MED is disabled, then the AS will have no MED attribute set. Additional parameters involve the timers in BGP model, such as the MRAI which significantly affects the total number of update events in the system. KeepAlive messages are affected by the interval at which KeepAlives are sent; the HoldInterval, or just Hold, determines how many KeepAlive messages can be missed before a connection is disabled.

The IP simulation model we developed is very simple and only responsible for keeping statistical data such as packets forwarded, dropped or completed. The main function of the IP model is to determine the destination port for each packet in the system. The IP model determines which port should be used by first determining if a link to the destination exists for the packet. If not, then a routing table lookup is done. If this also fails, then the packet is dropped by the network.

4 Large-Scale Network Configuration

We used the topological data measured by the University of Washington's Rocketfuel project [5]. In totality, the Rocketfuel data identifies internal AS topologies for 10 major ISPs which cover a large area of the world. Our simulation included 5 of these ISP topologies. We chose the ISPs based upon reachability, ISP size and number of external routers detected. For example, for scalability purposes, the AT&T and Sprint topologies were excluded from this study, both having greater than 10,000 routers. The Verio map was not used because the high number of external routers would have required greater than 3.5 million iBGP connections. Finally, the Telstra and VSNL maps covering India and Australia were not used because they could not be connected to the remaining ISPs from the available data.

Rocketfuel data lists routers as having both internal and external ISP connections. We established an OSPFv2 router at each router in the topology. Also, we determined that routers which contained one or more external connections to be BGP4 routers in addition to an OSPFv2 router. This means that some routers were running only OSPF, while others modeled both BGP and OSPF protocols. Each ISP was configured as a single AS, and within routers were broken down into two additional levels: areas and subnets. To determine the areas and the subnets, we used the IP addresses of the individual machines. For example, if two machines shared the same class A, B and C address, then we placed them into the same subnet. Areas were determined in the same way using the class A and B prefixes.

Because the Rocketfuel data relies on traceroute to determine the ISP topologies, certain limitations had to be addressed. Rocketfuel data does not define the bandwidth, speed or delay of the links. Link bandwidth and delay classes were defined for the different Rocketfuel-determined router levels. The bandwidth and delay for the topology is as follows:

- **Level 0 routers:** 9.92 Gb/sec and 1 ms delay
- **Level 1 routers:** 2.48 Gb/sec and 2 ms delay
- **Level 2 routers:** 620 Mb/sec and 3 ms delay
- **Level 3 routers:** 155 Mb/sec and 50 ms delay
- **Level 4 routers:** 45 Mb/sec and 50 ms delay
- **Level 5 routers and below:** 1.55 Mb/sec and 50 ms delay

Table 2 outlines the details of the multiple AS topology. BGP routers within an AS are fully connected to form the iBGP domain. The degrees are listed for each AS to every other AS, and the total number of BGP connections is listed along the diagonal.

Table 2: Rocketfuel ISP Topology Parameters

ISP	#iBGP	AS0	AS 1	AS2	AS3	AS4
AS0: AboveNet	2,500	199	8	12	18	161
AS1: EBONE	16,384	8	38	6	12	12
AS2: Exodus	50,176	12	6	53	9	26
AS3: Tiscali	441	18	12	9	50	11
AS4: Level 3	7921	161	12	26	11	210

5 OSPF and BGP Interactions

We have generated 4 designs of experiments. The first design optimizes across 3 classes of parameters: BGP timers, OSPF timers, and BGP decision parameters. Taking these classes in different combinations will allow us to quantify the specific parameter effects first, then the feature interactions. The second design investigates the effects of cold versus Hot Potato routing in the BGP protocol model. This is significant because Hot Potato routing in BGP relies on information from the OSPF protocol. Because there is a direct correlation between the models, we expect there to be a direct feature interaction as well. The third design investigates the effects of various network management policies on the response. Broadly, there are two approaches to network management at the AS level: greedy and cooperative. We define a greedy strategy as one in which the management policy promotes efficiency within the AS without consideration of the effects on the surrounding ASes. By contrast, a cooperative strategy is one in which the efficiency goal is considered across all of the ASes first. The final design considers the effects of the parameters on the response with varying degrees of network robustness. Here we perform a full-factorial on the topology parameters: link stability and link weight changes. The goal is to determine the range of the parameters and their interactions under varying network conditions.

5.1 Response Surface

Our response surface is defined by the number of network topology update messages exchanged by the BGP and OSPF protocols in the control plane. There are four types of update messages possible:

- OSPF caused OSPF updates (OO)
- BGP caused BGP updates (BB)
- OSPF caused BGP updates (OB)
- BGP caused OSPF updates (BO)

There are two types of changes which may occur in the topology: link status changes and link weight changes. The OSPF protocol detects link status changes via the HELLO protocol, and the BGP protocol via the KeepAlive Timer. Link weight changes are only detected by the OSPF protocol and are detected directly. When the OSPF protocol detects a change in the topology, it creates new LSAs appropriate for the cause and floods them throughout the OSPF domain. As the new LSAs are flooded they are accounted for in the "OSPF caused OSPF updates" statistic. The same is true for BGP caused BGP updates, and we do not distinguish between eBGP and iBGP route updates.

OSPF caused BGP updates are measured when the connection between two iBGP peers changes. This signals a change in the underlying OSPF network between the peers, and so the cause of the subsequent updates are attributed to the OSPF protocol. For example, a link which was previously down in the intra AS domain becomes available again, and the OSPF network rebuilds the corresponding routing tables. The new routing tables allow BGP KeepAlive messages to suddenly start getting through again, and reachability information is exchanged via update messages.

BGP caused OSPF updates are measured when an eBGP router creates or installs a new route to a destination IP prefix. The AS External LSA created by the IGP domain is tagged as being caused by BGP and at every hop throughout the flood is measured as such. Not all AS External LSAs are caused by BGP. OSPF routers must exchange their entire LSA database when a link becomes available, and these LSAs must be flooded throughout a domain according to the OSPF RFC.

Because we are specifically interested in feature interactions between the OSPF and BGP protocols, our main response surface is defined as $BGP\ caused\ OSPF\ +\ OSPF\ caused\ BGP\ Updates$. Also, because the interactions are implicit in the models, specific code had to be added to the models to detect and mark updates as to their cause, and tracked throughout the system for quantification purposes.

5.2 Network Topology Stability

Recall that our network protocol models start in the converged state for each experiment generated by the optimization. In steady state, no control plane update messages are exchanged, other than periodic OSPF LSA refreshing. BGP does not require refreshing of the RIB. In order to generate update messages in the system, two types of network events were modeled: link status changes and link weight changes.

Link statuses are either *up or down* and occur with a uniform random probability over the simulation endtime. These events can model either link congestion in the data plane or actual link availability on a given timeline. The probability that a link status may change in the given simulation endtime is varied to model different levels of network topology stability. The stability levels are: 1%, 10% and %15 over runtime. While it was shown in [31] that some links fail far more frequently than others over a given interval, generalizing link failures uniformly allows us to investigate varying degrees of network topology stability. While the system has the capability of modeling individual links, creating a more "realistic" link failure model is beyond the scope of this investigation.

Link weight changes follow the same uniform random probability over the simulation endtime, but rather than act as up/down events, they affect the network by varying the metric on the links. Also, link weight change events are delivered directly to the affected OSPF routers and are modeled as network administration events which occur through either human contact or programmatically. Each router originating an LSA containing the affected link refreshes the LSAs containing the link in question. Each new link metric is chosen randomly over the ranges: ± 10, 25, and 50 units.

6 Design of Experiments

We present here three investigations with the goal of generally characterizing the system under test in variety of conditions. The first experiment design considers varying network management perspectives. These perspectives each attempt to minimize the response as related to either a global or local perspective. One example of a local perspective is optimizing the OSPF domain without considering the impact on the BGP domain. The global perspective implies all ISPs working together to reduce control plane traffic.

The second design investigates cold- versus hot-potato routing policies within an AS. This investigation focuses on the BGP attribute, MultiExitDiscriminator (MED) for cold-potato routing and the IGP hop count for hot-potato routing.

Design 3 analyzes the performance of protocol models under varying degrees of network stability and link weight management. Network stability is determined by the frequency and duration of link outages in the network.

For each experiment conducted, an efficient RRS search was performed for the given response value, and each RRS search generated 200 simulation samples. We then performed a multiple linear regression on the results of the RRS search. Please note that only $Adjusted R^2$ results are shown because experiments may have different input parameters. The $Adjusted R^2$ value indicates the degree to which the input parameters are related to the response. In each experiment the P value was always < 0.0001, indicating in each case that the regression model predicted the response in a statistically significant manner. In other words, in each experiment the predictions of the model are better than chance alone. In addition, the Degrees of Freedom are not reported per experiment. In each experiment the degrees of freedom was high, > 100. Finally, multi-collinearity was not observed to be a problem in any of the experiments (i.e., all R^2 with other X values were < 0.75.

6.1 Input Parameter Classes

Table 3: Detail of parameter space for the large-scale OSPF and BGP experiment designs.

Input Parameter Classes	Min, Max, Step	Defaults
OSPFv2 Timer Class:		
OSPF Hello Interval	[1,4,1] secs	2
OSPF Inactivity Interval	[2,5,1] multiplier	4
OSPF Flood Interval	[1,4,1] secs	1
BGP4 Timer Class:		
BGP KeepAlive Interval	[25,35,2] secs	30
BGP Hold Interval	[36,56,4] secs	45
BGP Min Update Interval	[20,40,4] secs	30
BGP Policy Routing Class:		
MED	ON/OFF	ON
Hot Potato	ON/OFF	ON
BGP Decision Algorithm Class:		
Local-Pref	{low, med, high}	low
MED	{low, med, high}	low
AS-PATH Padding	{0 thru 8}	4

The system under test can be characterized as different classes of input parameters. The four classes shown in Table 3 represent timers for OSPF and BGP, the BGP route selection policies and the BGP decision algorithm. Each class is defined at the AS level and the values generated are determined by the efficient search algorithm, RRS.

The BGP and OSPF timer classes represent router timers and the values they may have during each simulation run. The specified ranges and steps for each timer value determines the search sample space. The defaults shown are the values used per AS when a given class is not searchable within a given design.

The BGP Policy Routing Class allows hot- and cold-potato routing to be enabled/disabled within an AS. The ROSS.Net framework allows any of the stages in the BGP decision algorithm to be disabled, however these are the two of interest in this paper.

The BGP Decision Algorithm Class provides specific values for the AS routes. For example, if cold-potato routing is enabled within an AS, then the MED value is defined for routes created by that AS. In this paper we investigate cold-potato routing so must define MED values for those ASes where cold-potato routing in enabled. Values are *low, medium and high* and correspond to varying levels of aggressiveness within each AS. Recall that during the BGP decision algorithm, stage 1, we install the route with the higher Local-Pref value, so each AS must define this attribute for each route created. When these stages are enabled, but not searched by the experiment design, the default values are used.

When all of the input parameter classes are searched the sample space is greater than 14 million. Heuristic search algorithms such as RRS allow us to search this sample space efficiently, i.e., using a proportionally small number of experiments, while still achieving highly correlated results (high $AdjustedR^2$ values).

6.2 Experiment Design 1: Management Perspective

Our first investigation focuses on the role of network management perspectives in the response plane. We identify two disparate approaches to network management: local and global. The local approach involves performance tuning an AS domain without knowledge or concern for the impact on neighboring ASes, or even other protocols within the AS. The global approach attempts to optimize all of the ASes simultaneously and is semantic to optimal performance with respect to the internetwork as a whole. Here information about each neighboring AS is openly available and the optimization goal is across all ASes. BB, OO, OB, BO and BO+OB are considered local policies and the global policy is the addition of all update messages (BB+OO+OB+BO).

This design focuses on multiple response surfaces, as shown in Table 4 and optimizes across all input parameter classes. Each Experiment conducted generates a unique response plane corresponding to a network management perspective. For example, Experiment 1 generates a response plane where OSPF caused OSPF updates were minimized. The optimal response column indicates that of the 200 simulation runs, the minimum number of OO updates obtained was 27,424. The BO+OB column indicates the number of interactions that occurred between the OSPF and BGP protocols. A value of 59,429 indicates that minimizing OO updates does not greatly increase the number of updates between OSPF and BGP when compared to the other perspectives. The $AdjustedR^2$ value of 88% indicates that the search parameters highly correlated to the response, and the optimal values were 3 seconds for the OSPF HELLO timer, 4 seconds for the OSPF Flood timer, and 56 seconds for the BGP HOLD interval.

Table 5: Variation in the optimization of different perspectives. This table illustrates the tradeoffs made for each particular optimization. Bold values are the optimal response (i.e., not averages).

Exp	ΣBB	ΣOO	ΣBO	ΣOB	$\Sigma BO + OB$	$\Sigma Global$
0	**1,938**	27,624	20	77,004	77,024	106,586
1	2,574	**27,424**	20	59,409	59,429	89,427
2	9,565	27,864	245	**52,700**	52,945	90,374
3	2,507	27,672	**18**	75,481	75,499	105,678
4	8,619	27,888	211	52,748	**52,959**	89,466
5	2,687	27,847	24	52,703	52,727	**83,261**

How efficient is each management perspective? Table 5 lists the results from each of the experiments. We see that the lowest number of interactions occurred in Experiment 1 where OSPF caused BGP updates were optimized. Because we were optimizing OB updates, and OB updates account for greater than 99% of BO+OB updates, this result make sense. Experiment 5 generated the least number of updates overall and was 7-27% better than the local perspectives. Not only does optimizing globally lower the number of overall updates, it also lowers the number of interactions between the protocols, within $< 1\%$ of the best case. So it is clear that maintaining privacy between ISPs leads to an increase in the amount of update messages in the network.

Each row of the table represents the optimal value generated by the Experiment. Each column indicates the average number of each type of update message generated for those parameters. Experiments 1, 2 and 4 indicate that minimizing the interaction from OSPF in BGP has the most impact on reducing the total number of updates in the system.

Of the different types of update messages, BB and BO were insignificant in respect to the global number of updates. Con-

Table 4: Design 1: Search varying network management perspectives. The optimal response column relates to the specific management goal searched. The BO+OB column represents the interactions between protocols that occurred.

Design 1: Management Perspectives									
	Response Surfaces							Effects: optimal values	
Experiment	BB	OO	OB	BO	Optimal Response	BO+OB	$Adj\ R^2$		
0	+	-	-	-	1,938	77,024	0.30	Inactivity: 3	Keep: 26
1	-	+	-	-	27,424	59,429	0.88	Hello: 3	Flood: 4
2	-	-	+	-	52,700	52,945	0.88	Flood: 1	Keep: 34
3	-	-	-	+	18	75,499	0.18	MRAI: 34	
4	-	-	+	+	52,959	52,959	0.91	Keep: 34	Hold: 45
5	+	+	+	+	83,261	52,727	0.52	Flood: 1	Keep: 34
Sample Space Size: $4.82x10^{13}$								+ = searched	

versely, OO and BO were a significant fraction of all update messages, but the OO updates varied little. This leaves OSPF caused BGP (OB) update messages as the significant response to optimize when attempting to minimize both feature interactions and the overall number of update messages in the network.

Which protocol parameters effect the response? If we choose to minimize the number of updates and/or interactions in the network by minimizing OB updates, then Table 4 suggests settings for the OSPF Hello interval and Flood interval be set high. In our search, settings of 3 seconds for the Hello interval and 4 seconds for the Flood interval suggest that OSPF convergence times be lengthened in order to minimize overall updates. Generally, slow convergence is not a desirable feature in OSPF networks as it can lead to losses in the data plane. However, slower detection in OSPF may reduce the effects of highly unstable links.

An alternative is to optimize for one of the other local perspectives which prescribe aggressive OSPF convergence settings. In Experiments 2, 4 and 5 the important parameter appears to be the BGP KeepAlive timer. In each case, this timer is set to a high value. Since iBGP connections far outweigh eBGP connections, it makes sense then that by setting the KeepAlive timer to a high value would minimize the effects of highly unstable links in the path between iBGP neighbors.

6.3 Experiment Design 2: Cold vs Hot Potato Routing

Table 6: Design 2: Analyze protocol performance under competing goals of Hot and Cold Potato routing.

Design 2: Cold vs Hot Potato Routing				
	BGP Decision Classes			
Exp.	Hot Potato	MED	BO+OB	$Adj\ R^2$
0	-	-	52,722	0.91
1	+	-	52,494	0.91
2	-	+	52,675	0.91
3	+	+	52,908	0.91
Sample Space Size: 14,348,907			+ = searched	

When two otherwise equal routes are being considered for addition to the BGP RIB, and those routes are both from iBGP peers, the route selected should be from the nearest peer. To determine which peer is the shortest distance away, the IGP hop count path is considered. This is the definition of Hot Potato routing, and was highlighted as a potential cause of many OSPF caused BGP updates in [13]. In that study it was noted that it was not possible to quantify the causes of the updates through measurement data. Also, protocol timer settings in routers throughout the network were not known. Simulation allows us to have a global view of the network, and complete topological information. Searching the sample space allows us to quantify the causes of the updates as well as determine the effects of any potentially influential protocol parameters.

Now that we have a validation that the OSPF domain adversely impacts the BGP domain, we can begin to focus our experiments on the hypothesized cause of the interruptions. In Table 6 we investigate the effects of cold versus hot potato routing. In this design we perform a simple full-factorial of RRS optimizations, turning Hot Potato routing on/off, and the MED on/off within the BGP decision algorithm.

If the goal of Hot Potato routing is to transit data through the network by the shortest paths possible, the goal of cold potato routing is the opposite. Cold potato routing is employed when end-to-end quality of service is of importance to an ISP. By carrying data longer in the network, an ISP can exert more control over the data before handing it off to another ISP. The MED accomplishes this goal by advertising to an AS the *preferred* routes data should take. *Preferred* is a term which is open to interpretation, but in this sense it implies "highest quality" ingress points to a neighboring AS [32]. An ISP implements cold potato routing by setting the MED parameter.

Table 7: This table illustrates the steps used in the BGP decision algorithm for route updates. Each entry illustrates how many times a particular step resulted in a tie-breaking event.

BGP Decision Algo	Hot Potato	MED	Neither	Both
Local-Pref	6383	1,714	767	885
AS Path	15,251	5,503	2,240	5,874
Origin	1	8	50	204
MED	OFF	4	OFF	0
Hot Potato	199	OFF	OFF	1,229
Next Hop	123	369	175	113
Default	476	778	272	635
Total	22,433	8,376	3504	12,444
% Hot Potato	0.8	-	-	9
% MED	-	$\ll 1$	-	0

Which steps in the BGP decision algorithm are most important? Table 7 quantifies the tie-breaking steps in the BGP decision making algorithm. We expected MED and Hot Potato to play a larger role in the algorithm, based on previous work [13, 12]. In our model it appears that Local-Pref and AS Path Padding play a much larger role in the decision process. In practice, these parameters may not be implemented in some or all ISP networks. Clearly, these parameters do play an important role in dampening the effects of both Hot and Cold Potato routing.

While our statistical models show a high correlation between the input parameters and the response ($Adjusted R^2 =$

91%), we believe that this design is only an initial step towards systematic questioning of the BGP decision algorithm. For example, when hot-potato routing only is enabled, the number of times the AS Path length was the tie-breaker increased from about 2,000 to over 15,000. Clearly, hot-potato routing is generating longer AS Path lengths in the routes. But it is unclear why there would be a corresponding 10-fold increase in the number of times the Local Pref tie-breaker was used. When just cold-potato routing was employed, these tie-breakers only doubled, which indicates that cold-potato routing has the same problem, but to much less a degree. More importantly, Table 7 indicates that when both policies are enabled, cold-potato routing can dampen the negative effects of hot-potato routing.

We did not expect these policies to have such a large effect on the other stages in the BGP decision algorithm. More insight into these results may be gained by future designs which takes this into account.

6.4 Experiment Design 3: Network Robustness

Table 8 illustrates our third design. The purpose of this experiment design is to ascertain the effects of network robustness on our characterization of the system under test. Network robustness is varied in two dimensions: link stability and link weight changes. Link stability was varied randomly over the intervals 1, 10 or 15% and link weights randomly over the intervals 10, 25 or 50 units. The design computes a full factorial over the two parameters of network robustness.

Which parameters were most important in reducing interactions? We report that the liveness timers are the important parameter settings and are related to minimizing OSPF caused BGP updates (OB). KeepAlive is maximized in BGP, and the InactivityInterval is maximized in OSPF. In OSPF, the flood timer, when important is optimized to a value of 2 leading to slower convergence. As the network becomes less stable however, we begin to see that other parameters are having more of an impact on the response. In OSPF we begin to see the Hello frequency becoming more important, and maximized. This is interesting because delaying detection allows OSPF to aggregate (implicitly) more changes into a single LSA update, which would act to minimize the overall number of updates generated. This implicit aggregation is occurring in the BGP domain as well by setting the KeepAlive interval to 34 seconds and the Hold Interval to 45-55 seconds. By detecting fewer link status changes the models are generating fewer control plane update messages.

Table 9: Improvements over average BO+OB, Global and Defaults in design 3.

LW/LS	Optimal	Avg BO+OB	Avg Global	Defaults
±10,1%	50,450	17%	19%	18%
±10/10%	73,196	17%	8%	
±10/15%	99,564	36%	34%	
±25/1%	54,254	10%	13%	18%
±25/10%	75,819	17%	17%	
±25/15%	100,493	22%	21%	
±50/1%	52,959	19%	14%	20%
±50/10%	76,346	17%	19%	
±50/15%	110,009	18%	17%	

Table 9 shows that we continue to receive consistent improvements in the response over the average regardless of the robustness in the network. We see that the optimal simulation experiments are simply setting the link failure detection parameters in either protocol to their slowest convergence settings. By not detecting link status changes quickly, the number of updates generated can most effectively be minimized. The table compares the amount of improvement over the average cases of BO+OB and the global response, as well as over the default settings. Generally, this approach to minimizing updates yielded a 20% improvement over the average. This figure is primarily related to the intervals chosen for the protocol parameters. In the future we could relate the improvements to the rate of convergence, which would be a more meaningful representation of the trade-off.

From the table we also see that the response is independent of the link weight changes. Each link weight interval varies by $< 5\%$ for each fixed link stability interval. This is surprising since aggressive link weight policies are known to produce routing loops among other problems. While aggressive changes impact the OSPF domain internally, those updates do not appear to be propagating into the BGP domain via OSPF. We theorize that the link status changes have a much greater impact on the OB response because they have a direct impact on the iBGP connections which dominate the model.

7 Conclusions

In this paper, we have used the design of experiments tool in ROSS.Net [4, 33] to characterize OSPF and BGP behavior in combination as well as their interactions. Based on the Rocketfuel data repository, we have developed a "more realistic" large-scale simulation of these two dominant inter- and intra-domain routing protocols. We then employed an efficient heuristic search algorithm, RRS, to search for best protocol optimizations and parameter settings. The protocol parameters we investigated included OSPF timers, BGP timers and BGP decision algorithm attributes. We defined the number of routing updates as the metric to minimize in our heuristic search for the best parameter settings. We also classified the routing updates into four categories to help design our experiments more flexibly.

We found that in order to minimize the interactions between BGP and OSPF the OSPF caused BGP updates should be optimized, as they account for the largest percentage of overall updates in the system and are the best candidate for minimization. In our second design we were able to verify past results which showed that hot-potato routing does in fact have an impact on the control plane, however we have quantifiably shown the AS PATH padding and Local Preference route attributes to have a greater impact. In our final design we found that link status changes propagated heavily from the OSPF domain into the iBGP domain, and that the effects of link weight changes were relatively insignificant in comparison.

References

[1] A. Papachristodoulou, L. Li, and J. C. Doyle, "Methodological frameworks for large-scale network analysis and design," *ACM SIGCOMM Computer Communication Review*, vol. 34, no. 3, pp. 7–20, October 2004.

[2] M. Liljenstam, et. al., "Rinse: the real-time interactive network simulation environment for network security exercises," in *Proceedings of the 19th Workshop on Parallel and Distributed Simulation*, June 2005, pp. 119–128.

[3] A. Park, R. Fujimoto, and K. Perumalla, "Conservative synchronization of large-scale network simulations," in *Proceedings of the Workshop on Parallel and Distributed Simulation*, May 2004, pp. 153–161.

[4] D. Bauer, et. al., "A case study of meta-simulation and performance analysis of large-scale networks," in *Proceedings of Winter Simulation Conference*, 2004.

Table 8: Design 3: Analyze performance of protocol models under varying degrees of network stability and link weight management.

	Design 3: Network Robustness						
	Topology Parameters				**Effects: optimal values**		
Experiment	Link Stability (LS)	Link Weight (LW)	**Optimal Response**	$Adj\ R^2$			
0	1%	± 10	50,450	0.89	Keep: 34		
1	1%	± 25	54,254	0.91	Keep: 32	Hold: 46	MRAI: 33
2	1%	± 50	52,959	0.91	Keep: 34	Hold: 45	
3	10%	± 10	73,196	0.87	Keep: 34	Hold: 39	Inactivity: 4
4	10%	± 25	75,819	0.88	Keep: 34	Hello: 4	Inactivity: 5
5	10%	± 50	76,346	0.87	Keep: 34	Hold: 55	
6	15%	± 10	99,564	0.78	Keep: 35	Flood: 2	MRAI: 28
7	15%	± 25	100,493	0.78	Keep: 34		
8	15%	± 50	110,009	0.900	Keep: 34	Hello: 4	
	Sample Space Size: $4.82x10^{13}$				+ = searched		

[5] U. of Washington, "Rocketfuel internet topology database," 2002.

[6] J. Cowie, A. Ogielski, B. J. Premore, and Y. Yuan, "Global routing instabilities triggered by code red ii and nimda worm attacks," Renesys Corporation, Tech. Rep., 2001.

[7] L. Wang, et. al., "Observation and analysis of bgp behavior under stress," in *Proceedings of ACM SIGCOMM Workshop on Internet Measurement*, 2002.

[8] T. G. Griffin, F. B. Shepherd, and G. Wilfong, "The stable paths problem and interdomain routing," *IEEE/ACM Transactions on Networking*, vol. 10, no. 2, pp. 232–243, April 2002.

[9] T. G. Griffin and G. Wilfong, "A safe path vector protocol," in *Proceedings of INFOCOM*, 2000.

[10] R. Teixeira, A. Shaikh, T. Griffin, and G. M. Voelker, "Network sensitivity to hot-potato disruptions," in *Proceedings of SIGCOMM*, 2004.

[11] T. G. Griffin and G. Wilfong, "Analysis of the med oscillation problem in bgp," in *Proceedings of ICNP*, 2002.

[12] R. Agarwal, C. N. Chuah, S. Bhattacharyya, and C. Diot, "The impact of bgp dynamics on intra-domain traffic," in *Proceedings of SIGMETRICS*, 2004.

[13] R. Teixeira, A. Shaikh, T. Griffin, and J. Rexford, "Dynamics of hot-potato routing in ip networks," in *Proceedings of SIGMETRICS*, 2004.

[14] A. Basu and J. G. Riecke, "Stability issues in ospf routing," in *Proceedings of SIGCOMM*, 2001.

[15] D. Obradovic, "Real-time model and convergence time of bgp," in *Proceedings of INFOCOMM*, 2002.

[16] A. Shaikh and A. Greenberg, "Experience in black-box ospf measurement," in *Proceedings of the SIGCOMM Internet Measurement Workshop*, 2001.

[17] A. Shaikh, R. Dube, and A. Varma, "Avoiding instability during graceful shutdown of ospf," in *Proceedings of INFOCOMM*, 2002.

[18] T. W. Chim and K. L. Yeung, "Time-efficient algorithms for bgp route configuration," in *Proceedings of the IEEE International Conference on Communications*, 2004, pp. 1197–1201.

[19] R. Mahajan, D. Wetherall, and T. Anderson, "Understanding bgp misconfiguration," in *Proceedings of SIGCOMM*, 2002.

[20] O. Nordstrom and C. Dovrolis, "Beware of bgp attacks," in *ACM Computer Communications Review*, 2004.

[21] J. Feigenbaum, C. Papadimitrious, R. Sami, and S. Shenker, "A bgp-based mechanism for lowest-cost routing," in *Proceedings of the ACM Sysposium on Principles of Distributed Computing*, 2002.

[22] L. Xiao, K.-S. Liu, J. Wang, and K. Nahrstedt, "Qos extension to bgp," in *Proceedings of the Internation Conference Network Protocols*, 2002.

[23] D. Nicol and J. Liu, "Composite synchronization in parallel discrete-event simulation," *IEEE Transactions on Parallel and Distributed Systems*, vol. 13, no. 5, pp. 433–446, May 2001.

[24] R. Fujimoto and M. Hybinette, "Computing global virtual time in shared-memory multiprocessors," *ACM Transactions on Modeling and Computer Simulation*, vol. 7, no. 4, pp. 425–446, 1997.

[25] J. Cowie, et. al., "Towards realistic million-node internet simulations," in *Proceedings of the 1999 International Conference on Parallel and Distributed Processing Techniques and Applications*, 1999.

[26] R. Fujimoto, et. al., "Large-scale network simulation – how big? how fast?" in *IEEE/ACM International Symposium on Modeling, Analysis and Simulation of Computer Telecommunication Systems*, 2003.

[27] D. M. Nicol and G. Yan, "Simulation of network traffic at course timescales," in *Proceedings of the 2005 Workshop on Principles of Advanced and Distributed Simulation*, 2005.

[28] T. Ye and S. Kalyanaraman, "A recursive random search algorithm for large-scale network parameter configuration," in *Proceedings of SIGMETRICS*, 2003, pp. 196–205.

[29] Y. Rekhter and T. Li, "A border gateway protocol 4 (bgp-4)," IETF, Tech. Rep. RFC 1771, March 1995.

[30] R. Teixeira, K. Marzullo, S. Savage, and G. M. Voelker, "In search of path diversity in ISP networks," in *Proceedings of IMC*, 2003.

[31] A. Markopoulou, et. al., "Characterization of failures in an ip backbone network," in *Proceedings of IEEE INFOCOM 2004*, March 2004.

[32] Cisco Systems Inc., "How the bgp deterministic-med command differs from the bgp always-compare-med command," March 2005, document ID: 16046.

[33] G. Yaun, et. al., "Large scale network simulation techniques: Examples of tcp and ospf models," in *ACM SIGCOMM Computer Communication Review*, 2003.

Empirical Models of TCP and UDP End–User Network Traffic from NETI@home Data Analysis

Charles R. Simpson, Jr., Dheeraj Reddy, George F. Riley
School of Electrical and Computer Engineering
Georgia Institute of Technology
Atlanta, Georgia 30332–0250
{rsimpson,dheeraj,riley}@ece.gatech.edu

Abstract

The simulation of computer networks requires accurate models of user behavior. To this end, we present empirical models of end–user network traffic derived from the analysis of NETI@home data. There are two forms of models presented. The first models traffic for a specific TCP or UDP port. The second models all TCP or UDP traffic for an end–user. These models are meant to be network–independent and contain aspects such as bytes sent, bytes received, and user think time. The empirical models derived in this study can then be used to enable more realistic simulations of computer networks.

1. Introduction

The simulation of computer networks has become a popular method to evaluate characteristics of these networks across a wide range of topics, including protocol analysis, routing stability, and topological dependencies, to name a few. However, for these simulations to yield meaningful results, they must incorporate accurate models of their simulated components.

One such component is end–user traffic generation. This component should be network–independent so that it can be used in a wide variety of simulation configurations without dependency on the simulated environment. These traffic models should be updated frequently, using recent measurements, to accurately reflect the changing nature and uses of the Internet. Further, such measurements should represent the heterogeneous connection methods and diverse locations of Internet users. To this aim, we have developed network–independent traffic models for network users based on data gathered by the NETI@home infrastructure.

The remainder of this paper is organized as follows. Section 2 presents work related to this study. Next, Section 3 describes the dataset used for this study and the methodology used to create our models. Section 4 discusses the experimental results of our study and Section 5 describes the simulation used to demonstrate and validate our models. Finally, Section 6 discusses several areas of future work and we conclude in Section 7.

2. Background and related work

Portions of this work are based on work presented in [13] and [17] and we have chosen to adopt much of their nomenclature. However, we have attempted to expand upon their work in several ways. First, the work in [13] is based on packet traces collected from a campus network. In an attempt to represent more typical end–users, we use data collected by the NETI@home project. Also, the studies conducted in [13, 17] were specific to TCP connections on port 80. In this study, we model any given TCP or UDP port, as well as all TCP or UDP traffic aggregated.

NETI@home[16] (Network Intelligence at home) is an open–source software package named after the popular SETI@home[1] software. The NETI@home client is available on the NETI@home website[15] and is designed to be run by any client machine connected to the Internet. When run on a client machine, the NETI@home software reports end–to–end flow summary statistics to a server at the Georgia Institute of Technology. The statistics collected and the functionality of the software are discussed in [16]. Since NETI@home is designed to run on end–user systems, it provides a unique perspective into the behavior of both end–users and their systems.

Previously, NETI@home data analysis has focused on aspects relating to security[9]. In this paper, we utilize the measurements made by NETI@home to generate traffic models based on end–user behavior. NETI@home users represent a heterogeneous mixture of network users from various networks and geographical locations.

The need for accurate simulation models was discussed in [8]. Several other studies have discussed modeling of either application–specific [3, 4, 5, 6, 17] or general [2, 10, 11, 18] end–user network traffic. Also, several studies have used network traffic models in simulation environments including [7, 12, 19, 20].

3. Methodology

The models developed for this work are intended to be network–independent. To this aim, we define several characteristics of TCP and UDP flows that reflect this design choice and attempt to wholly represent network client behavior.

There are two categories of models created in this study. The first is specific to a TCP or UDP port, that is we create a model of client behavior for a given TCP or UDP port. Throughout most of this paper, we use the model created for TCP port 80, the most common port used by World Wide Web servers, as an example. The second category of model created is an aggregate of all port–specific models. This model can be likened to a TCP or UDP client model. Such a model may prove useful for studies that are more generic and are not attempting to study a particular type of network traffic. All of these models incorporate empirical distributions directly interpreted from the NETI@home dataset.

The dataset used in this study consists of NETI@home data collected over a one year period from October 1, 2004 to September 30, 2005. This dataset includes over 36 million TCP flows and 93 million UDP flows, which form the basis of this work, as well as various other flow types and information about their corresponding hosts. Although an exact calculation is not possible due to privacy settings and dynamically assigned IP addresses, we estimate that this data was collected by approximately 1700 users. These users represent a heterogeneous sampling of Internet users running some 8 different operating systems and reporting from approximately 28 nations and 43 US ZIP Codes.

The first two aspects we model are empirical distributions of *bytes sent* and *bytes received*. These values are based only on the payload of the packets and thus do not represent the sizes of the TCP or UDP headers and their underlying headers or TCP's flow control and congestion control algorithms, merely transferred application information. This allows our models to be used in simulations where variations of TCP or UDP are employed.

The next aspect modeled is *user think time*. User think time is the term we use for the amount of time a client waits before initiating another flow. For this aspect, we developed two empirical distributions. One distribution describes the user think time when consecutively accessing a specific destination and the other describes the user think time when contacting a new destination.

Another aspect modeled is *consecutive contacts*. Consecutive contacts is the term we use for the probability that a client will choose to initiate another flow with the last destination contacted, or the client will choose to initiate a flow with a new destination. For this aspect, we developed a single empirical distribution.

Finally, the last aspect modeled is *contact selection*. Contact selection is the term we use for the frequency distribution of contacting specific destinations. This distribution can be thought of as modeling the popularity of a destination. For this aspect, we developed a single empirical distribution.

One other aspect that we believe to be worth modeling is related to *idle time*. For applications such as World Wide Web transfers, this aspect has little meaning, as web pages are simply requested and served. However, for interactive applications such as SSH or telnet, there are periods of time, *during* the flow, when there is no data transferred. However, using the NETI@home data, it is difficult to differentiate between network–dependent flow time and network–independent flow time. We are aware of work [10, 11] that attempts to capture this behavior and are considering implementing a similar technique into the NETI@home client software so that future models can incorporate this aspect of user behavior.

4. Experimental results

From the analysis of the NETI@home dataset described previously, we were able to generate a set of empirical distributions for each component of our models. To download the complete set of distributions and for any updates to these distributions please visit http://neti.gatech.edu/research/user.html.

4.1. Bytes sent

The amount of bytes sent varies dependent on the port modeled. However, upon investigation of each modeled port, our findings seem intuitive.

Figure 1 depicts the cumulative distribution function of bytes sent for TCP port 80. Compared with previous studies [13], these results contain many more flows with zero bytes sent. However, upon investigation it does not appear that these results are due to a single NETI@home user or are anomalous. This difference in results is most likely due to the fact that [13] was based on data collected from a campus network, whereas NETI@home data contains users with less reliable network connections. The zero bytes sent flows typically represent flows in which the connection failed during the TCP three–way handshake. Although these flows do not generate much network traffic (usually no more than

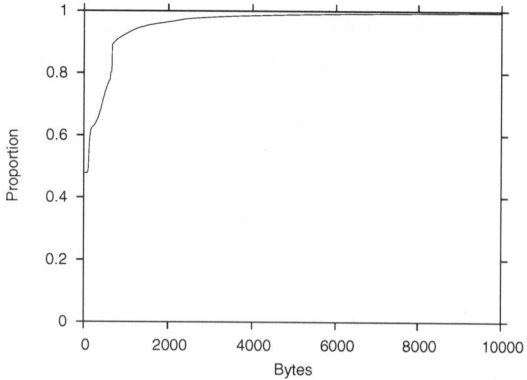

Figure 1. CDF of bytes sent for TCP port 80

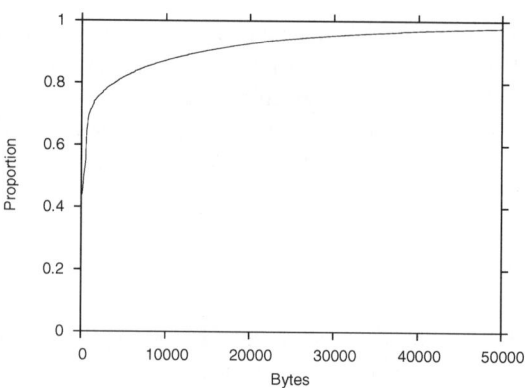

Figure 2. CDF of bytes received for TCP port 80

three packets), they are significant in terms of numbers of flows and most likely influence a user's behavior.

As can be seen in the figure, approximately 40 percent of flows to TCP port 80 send little or no data. There are several possible causes for the large number of flows sending little or no data. First, many of these flows are failed connection attempts. Many NETI@home users are utilizing less reliable network connections such as dial–up or wireless. Also, some of these flows may be to blocked sites. Many browsers and third–party software block advertisements and some organizations restrict the viewing of certain websites. Finally, a handful of NETI@home users periodically scan hosts on the Internet[9]. Considering that these users know that their network connections are monitored, it is unlikely that this scanning is intentional and may be the result of a virus or worm. While these results could be considered anomalous, we believe that this does indeed represent typical end–user behavior as seen on the Internet. Almost all remaining flows send no more than 10 KB of data to the server.

4.2. Bytes received

The amount of bytes received by the client is also dependent on the port modeled. Figure 2 depicts the cumulative distribution function of bytes received for TCP port 80. Compared with [13], we also find that there are many more flows with zero bytes received. As with our findings for bytes sent, this is most likely due to failed connection attempts.

The distribution for bytes received has a much longer tail than that for the bytes sent. Approximately 40 percent of flows with a remote TCP port of 80 receive little or no data. However, more than 10 percent of these flows receive greater than 10KB of data.

4.3. User think time

The cumulative distribution function for user think time to the same destination is given in Figure 3 and to differing destinations is given in Figure 4 for TCP ports 23 and 80. These findings show a tendency towards shorter user think times than was found in [13] for TCP Port 80. We can think of several reasons for this shortened user think time. First, the World Wide Web has become much more popular since the time of [13]'s publication. Also, it is likely that NETI@home captures data from users who are active more often than it does for inactive users as many users would simply turn off their machines while not using them, thus disabling NETI@home's monitoring. This would artificially inflate our numbers to show users that appear to be more active and is a source of bias.

We chose to model the user think time to the same destination separately from the user think time to a different destination. Figures 3(a) and 4(a) appear to be similar however. We believe that it is still appropriate to model these think times separately as these distributions can differ greatly for other TCP or UDP ports as is shown in Figures 3(b) and 4(b). These figures show the distributions for think times for TCP Port 23, the port commonly used for telnet.

For connections to TCP port 80, the majority of user think times tends to be less than 1 second. However, for connections to TCP port 23 (telnet), the user think times have a much heavier tail, with only approximately 40 percent of flows having think times less than 100 seconds.

4.4. Consecutive contacts

In Figure 5, we present the cumulative distribution function for consecutive contacts for TCP port 80. These results also show a tendency towards a lower number of consecutive contacts than was found in [13]. However, this is

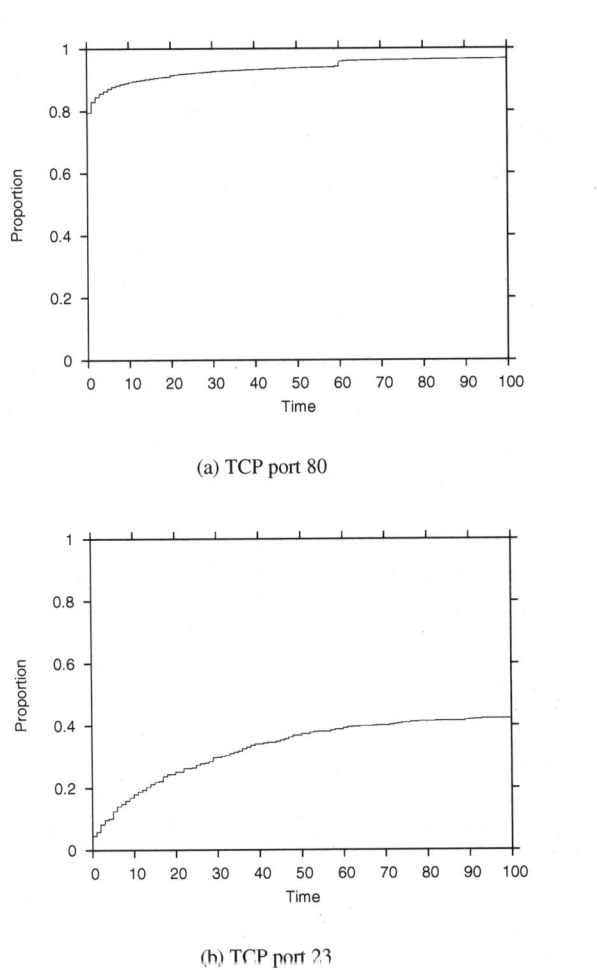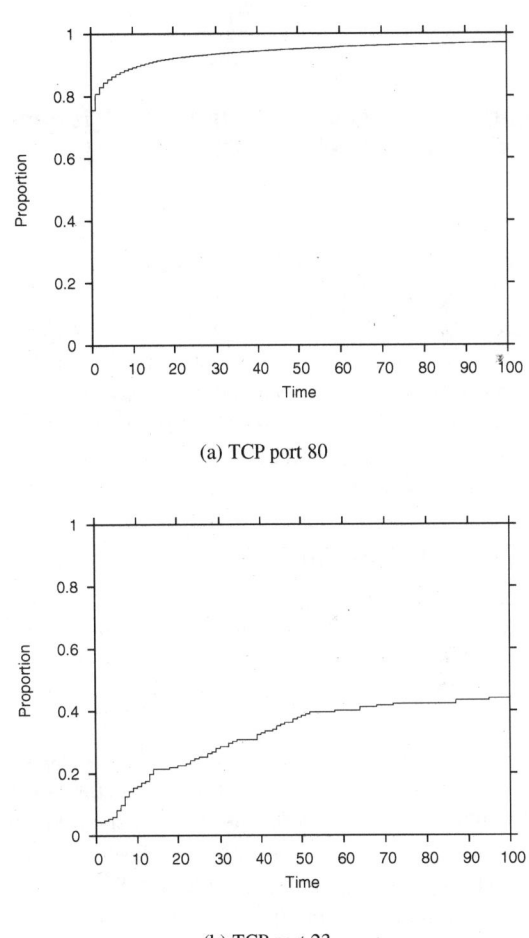

Figure 3. CDF of user think time to same IPs

Figure 4. CDF of user think time to differing IPs

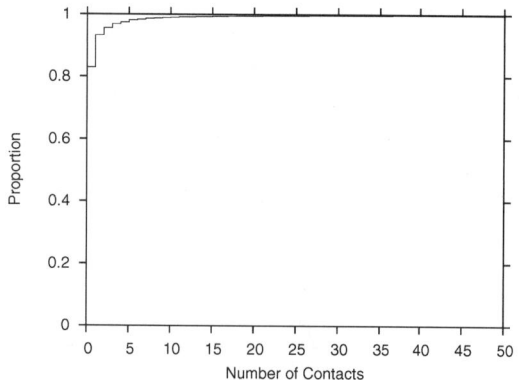

Figure 5. CDF of number of times an IP is contacted consecutively for TCP port 80

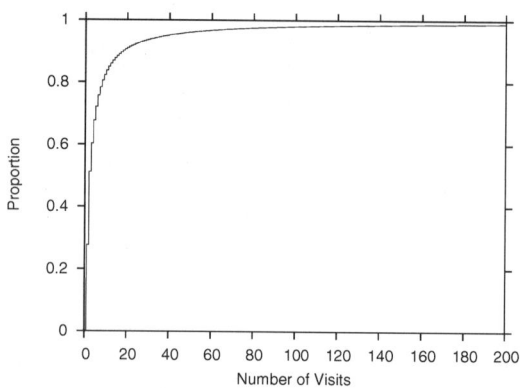

Figure 6. CDF of relative frequency of server visits for TCP port 80 over a one year period

intuitive considering the number of "failed" connection attempts observed previously.

Approximately 80 percent of the flows to TCP port 80 are not consecutive, that is the destination is contacted only once in a row. Further, over 99 percent of visits to a specific destination on TCP port 80 lasted for 10 or less flows in a row. Therefore, it appears that users tend to switch web destinations fairly often as was noted in [13].

4.5. Contact selection

Unlike [13], which used a Zipf distribution, we were able to construct a cumulative distribution function for contact selection due to the wide sampling offered by the NETI@home dataset. Figure 6 presents this CDF for TCP port 80. One possible source of inaccuracy for this aspect is the fact that we are unable to determine if a specific destination uses multiple IP addresses, thus reducing the frequency of selection a given contact may appear to have.

As can be seen in the figure, for TCP port 80 servers the distribution of the overall number of visits by NETI@home users is quite varied and has a heavy tail. Many servers are only visited a handful of times, however many other servers tend to be contacted quite often, with some servers receiving millions of visits over the year studied.

5. Simulation results

To judge the usefulness of our models, we have incorporated the above derived TCP traffic models into the GTNetS environment[14]. The GTNetS environment already has some HTTP traffic models as described in [13]. We incorporated the models derived from the analysis of the NETI@home datasets into GTNetS. We consider this approach to be a better one for traffic generation in network simulations, because NETI@home datasets are more current and continue to be so [16]. An analysis program generates these models automatically from the NETI@home datasets. The traffic distribution models can then be easily used by the application layer models which drive a network simulation. In our simulation experiments, we have concentrated on the World Wide Web traffic and the HTTP models. Our implementation samples the empirical distributions to determine the particular values used at a given time. This seems a logical choice since any single distribution doesn't seem to fit the complete dataset verifiably. We model the behavior of a web browser in GTNetS which sends a HTTP request to a designated webserver asking it to send a certain length of data that constitutes the response. When the simulation starts, the browser application chooses a server randomly from a list of target servers. It then chooses a *response size* that it wants to obtain from the webserver from the CDF that describes the *received bytes*. The size of the HTTP request packet is chosen from the *sent bytes* CDF plot. It may request one or more objects within the same TCP connection. Once the web browser application has received the appropriate response, it proceeds to select a different server or the same server for its next request and waits for an amount of time. This amount of time, which is obtained from the CDF that describes the *user think time*, depends on whether the same server is chosen or a different server is chosen.

The network topology for simulations is obtained from [7]. It consists of a large set of web browsers connected via a series of three routers to a webserver as shown in Figure 7. We have chosen this to be our baseline topology because we have earlier simulation experiments conducted using the models and datasets proposed in [7].

The simulation experiment is run using two HTTP traffic models. One of the traffic models is obtained from the datasets suggested in [13] and [7]. The other traffic model

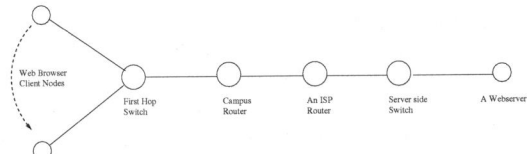

Figure 7. Network topology used for testing traffic models in simulation

Table 1. Variation in average and maximum response times when using HTTP traffic model presented in this paper

Number of browsers	Average response time	Maximum response time
10	0.316738	0.738639
25	0.301151	0.740423
50	0.318433	0.738642
75	0.321075	0.743916
100	0.304644	0.745433
125	0.305372	0.751632
150	0.312204	0.839426

Table 2. Variation in average and maximum response times when using HTTP traffic model presented in [13]

Number of browsers	Average response time	Maximum response time
10	0.461172	0.716738
25	0.339998	1.01388
50	0.344094	1.20155
75	0.375188	3.98217
100	0.380281	3.80786
125	0.332889	4.16023
150	0.405156	6.6588

is one that is obtained from the NETI@home datasets. Intuitively, empirical traffic models should be more representative of a realistic dataset than statistical traffic generators, although the former cannot be subjected to extrapolations. All the measurements are the averages of three runs of a simulation at a given data point.

Table 1 shows the average and maximum response times for a given number of web clients when they request data from a webserver using the traffic models presented in this paper. Table 2 shows the average and maximum response times for the same number of web browsers when they request data from a webserver using the traffic models presented in [13].

It can be seen from the results in Table 1 and Table 2 that the maximum response time for the HTTP traffic model presented in [13] is substantially larger than the model that is derived from NETI@home dataset. A careful observation of the cumulative distribution functions of the two datasets shows that the NETI@home data has a larger proportion of flow sizes that are very small, most likely due to the inclusion of a large number of failed connections. This results in lower load on the webserver and consequently lower latencies. This is evident in the lower average and maximum response times as the traffic increases. On the other hand, the traffic model presented in [13] has a lesser number of flow sizes that are very small. This results in a larger load on the server and on the network as the number of web browsers increases. When the number of web browsers is fairly small, the difference is not appreciable because the flow size does not influence the network.

The code used for these simulations, as well as the empirical models, are available in the latest official distribution of the GTNetS environment.

6. Future work

Several enhancements to our modeling technique can be made and are areas of future work. First, it would be useful to model idle times within a flow. As previously mentioned, certain applications have periods of time where the connection is idle as in interactive applications. Another enhancement to our model would be to determine if there is any correlation between the different aspects of our model. For example, in certain applications the number of bytes sent and the number of bytes received may be highly correlated. If so, these aspects should most likely be treated as bivariate data. Several enhancements could also be made to our consecutive contacts and contact selection components. It is intuitive that once a destination is visited and then left, that the original destination has a higher likelihood of being visited again. Thus, a model with memory, such as a Markov model, would be useful. Such a model may also incorporate zero byte flows. That is, if a connection fails, the likelihood of that connection's destination of being visited again may change. Further, our model could be extended to other protocols beyond TCP and UDP. Currently, NETI@home collects flow summary statistics for TCP, UDP, ICMP, and IGMP, so ICMP and IGMP models could easily be derived.

The models presented in this paper solely focus on network–independent characteristics. It would be useful however to model network–dependent aspects of the global Internet. Such a model could focus on parameters such as the proliferation of network address translation, the topology of the Internet, the number of servers visited overall, latency, loss, bandwidth, and the locality of network traffic.

The nature of the Internet and its usage is constantly changing. With an infrastructure such as NETI@home in place, changes to Internet usage, and thus updates to our models, should be studied. This will not only allow for studies comparing changing trends, but will ensure the availability of accurate and updated simulation models.

Finally, we have chosen to represent our models in empirical form. Such a form has its advantages, however analytical models could be developed from this data. These analytical models may have advantages for scaling, both temporally and spatially.

7. Conclusions

In conclusion, we have presented empirical models of end–user network traffic. There are two general forms of these models, one form is port–specific for a given TCP or UDP port. The second form is a generic model for TCP or UDP traffic. These models consist of network–independent distributions for the number of bytes sent, the number of bytes received, the user think time to the same destination, the user think time to a different destination, the number of times a destination will be contacted consecutively, and the popularity of specific destinations.

The distributions derived are based on the NETI@home dataset and are meant to represent a heterogeneous sampling of network users. Such a heterogeneous sampling of users from differing network and geographical locations provides more accurate models for simulations. As the NETI@home project is ongoing for the foreseeable future, we plan to continuously update the models. For these updates and to download the complete distributions please visit http://neti.gatech.edu/research/user.html.

Further, we have implemented these models in a simulation environment. In this simulation environment we tested the affect of network traffic on a webserver. These results were then compared to the results from previous models. The models and code used are available in the latest distribution of the GTNetS environment.

References

[1] D. P. Anderson and et al. SETI@home: Search for extraterrestrial intelligence at home. Software on-line: http://setiathome.ssl.berkeley.edu, 2003.

[2] C. Barakat, P. Thiran, G. Iannaccone, C. Diot, and P. Owezarski. Modeling internet backbone traffic at the flow level. *IEEE Transactions on Signal Processing – Special Issue on Networking*, 51(8), August 2003.

[3] P. Barford and M. Crovella. Generating representative web workloads for network and server performance evaluation. In *ACM SIGMETRICS*, 1998.

[4] J. Cao, W. S. Cleveland, Y. Gao, K. Jeffay, F. D. Smith, and M. C. Weigle. Stochastic models for generating synthetic HTTP source traffic. In *IEEE INFOCOMM*, March 2004.

[5] Y.-C. Cheng, U. Holzle, N. Cardwell, S. Savage, and G. M. Voelker. Monkey see, monkey do: A tool for TCP tracing and replaying. In *Proceedings of USENIX Technical Conference*, June 2004.

[6] H.-K. Choi and J. O. Limb. A behavioral model of web traffic. In *ICNP*, 1999.

[7] M. Christiansen, K. Jeffay, D. Ott, and F. D. Smith. Tuning RED for web traffic. *IEEE/ACM Transactions on Networking*, 9(3):249–264, June 2001.

[8] S. Floyd and V. Paxson. Difficulties in simulating the internet. *IEEE/ACM Transactions on Networking*, 9(4):392–403, August 2001.

[9] J. B. Grizzard, C. R. Simpson, Jr., S. Krasser, H. L. Owen, and G. F. Riley. Flow based observations from NETI@home and honeynet data. In *Proceedings from the sixth IEEE Systems, Man and Cybernetics Information Assurance Workshop*, pages 244–251, June 2005.

[10] F. Hernandez-Campos, A. B. Nobel, F. D. Smith, and K. Jeffay. Understanding patterns of TCP connection usage with statistical clustering. In *IEEE MASCOTS*, 2005.

[11] F. Hernandez-Campos, F. D. Smith, and K. Jeffay. Generating realistic TCP workloads. In *Computer Measurement Group International Conference*, December 2004.

[12] L. Le, J. Aikat, K. Jeffay, and F. D. Smith. The effects of active queue management on web performance. In *ACM SIGCOMM*, pages 265–276, August 2003.

[13] B. A. Mah. An empirical model of HTTP network traffic. In *IEEE INFOCOMM*, April 1997.

[14] G. F. Riley. The Georgia Tech Network Simulator. In *Proceedings of the ACM SIGCOMM workshop on Models, methods and tools for reproducible network research*, pages 5–12, 2003.

[15] C. R. Simpson, Jr. NETI@home. Software on-line: http://neti.gatech.edu, 2003. Georgia Institute of Technology.

[16] C. R. Simpson, Jr. and G. F. Riley. NETI@home: A distributed approach to collecting end-to-end network performance measurements. In *PAM2004 - A workshop on Passive and Active Measurements*, April 2004.

[17] F. D. Smith, F. Hernandez-Campos, K. Jeffay, and D. Ott. What TCP/IP protocol headers can tell us about the web. In *ACM SIGMETRICS*, pages 245–256, 2001.

[18] J. Sommers, H. Kim, and P. Barford. Harpoon: A flow-level traffic generator for router and network tests. In *ACM SIGMETRICS*, June 2004.

[19] M. Weigle, K. Jeffay, and F. D. Smith. Delay–based early congestion detection and adaptation in TCP: Impact on web performance. *ACM Computer Communications Review*, 28(8):837–850, May 2005.

[20] J. Xu and W. Lee. Sustaining availability of web services under distributed denial of service attacks. *IEEE Transactions on Computers*, 52(2):195–208, February 2003.

Principles of Advanced and Distributed Simulation

Session 9: High Level Architecture

Evaluation of a Fault-Tolerance Mechanism for HLA-Based Distributed Simulations

Martin Eklöf
Swedish Defence Research Agency (FOI)

Rassul Ayani
Royal Institute of Technology (KTH)

Farshad Moradi
Swedish Defence Research Agency (FOI)

Abstract

Successful integration of Modeling and Simulation (M&S) in the future Network-Based Defence (NBD) depends, among other things, on providing fault-tolerant (FT) distributed simulations. This paper describes a framework, named Distributed Resource Management System (DRMS), for robust execution of simulations based on the High Level Architecture. More specifically, a mechanism for FT in simulations synchronized according to the time-warp protocol is presented and evaluated. The results show that utilization of the FT mechanism, in a worst-case scenario, increases the total number of generated messages by 68% if one fault occurs. When the FT mechanism is not utilized, the same scenario shows an increase in total number of generated messages by 90%. Considering the worst-case scenario a plausible requirement on an M&S infrastructure of the NBD, the overhead caused by the FT mechanism is considered acceptable.

1. Introduction

Modeling and Simulation (M&S) have an important role in realizing the concept of a Network-Based Defence (NBD). In this context, simulations provide support for efficient training, and can also function as a decision support tool for the commander. When simulation tools are used in the decision process, these must meet certain requirements. Above all, simulations must be reliable and respond in a timely fashion. The latter is of particular importance in short decision cycles. An important aspect of these requirements is support for Fault-Tolerance (FT). Mechanisms for detection of failures in a simulation, as well as measures for failure recovery are needed. If these functions are properly designed and implemented the reliability of simulation results will be increased.

Also, the effectiveness of simulation executions may be increased, i.e. reruns of erroneous simulations are avoided.

Today, distributed simulation is often employed in the military domain since it efficiently decomposes a simulation system into logical units, better enabling reuse and availability of simulation models. Also, a distributed simulation system exhibits better tolerance against failures. Given that components of a simulation are distributed over several nodes, a failure will most often not affect the entire system.

The most well-known and used standard for distributed simulations within the military domain is the High Level Architecture (HLA). The HLA standard is implemented by a Run-Time Infrastructure (RTI), which can be seen as an operating system for distributed simulations. In HLA a simulation is referred to as a federation, whereas individual components of the federation are referred to as federates. Until now, FT has not been treated as a core component of the HLA standard, thus federations are typically developed disregarding this important aspect. Given that HLA is the main architecture for distributed simulations within the Swedish Defence, and simulations are crucial in the NBD, it is important to evaluate the possibilities for inclusion of FT mechanisms in HLA.

In [6] and [5] an architecture and partial implementation of an execution environment for distributed simulations, referred to as the Distributed Resource Management System (DRMS), are described. Also, in [5] an FT mechanism within the framework of DRMS is presented. This mechanism specifically addresses FT in federations synchronized according to the time-warp protocol [9]. In this paper we investigate the feasibility of the proposed FT mechanism and present some performance results. The performance is evaluated in terms of the overhead, in number of messages, caused by the FT mechanism. The FT mechanism in DRMS does not consider software errors, in terms of federates producing erroneous result, but handles situations where the host environment of a federate crashes, the federate itself crashes for some reason, or a federate's link to the RTI is lost. Moreover, we assume that federates executed within the scope of DRMS are portable, meaning that they are not bound to a specific piece of hardware and can easily be migrated between different host environments. In the present implementation of the FT mechanism, it is not possible to recover from multiple concurrent failures. However, the DRMS supports recovery from non-transient errors, i.e. permanent failures.

2. Handling fault-tolerance in distributed simulations

DRMS is a component of a network-based M&S environment, referred to as NetSim, currently under development at the Swedish Defence Research Agency (FOI). NetSim provides services for distributed storage and look-up of resources, e.g. federates, federations and computing resources. Further, the NetSim environment aims at providing services for Computer Supported Collaborative Work (CSCW), which means that users of the environment can cooperate in developing a federation, regardless of their physical location. The purpose of the DRMS in this setting is to provide transparent access to computing resources, which are utilized for execution of federations composed by a user, or a group of users. DRMS comprises services for automatic deployment of distributed simulations and fault-tolerant execution of federations. The NetSim environment is described in greater detail in [7].

DRMS is based on a service-oriented architecture, which is realized using Web Services, more specifically the Axis Web Services platform [14]. DRMS comprises two basic service types, namely a *worker service* and a *coordinator service*. A worker is responsible for execution of one or more jobs, e.g. federates, whereas a coordinator is responsible for the coordination of one or more workers when managing a batch of jobs. In addition to these basic services, the DRMS relies on a *repository service*. A repository is used by a worker to advertise its presence on the network and thereby its availability for execution of jobs. Furthermore, the repository is used by a coordinator for localization of available workers. A repository also contains advertisements of other resources available on the network, federates for instance, and is therefore used as entry point when worker services fetch resource files and executable code. The implementation of DRMS is described in greater detail in [5].

2.1. Fault-tolerance in HLA

A distributed simulation, or distributed system for that matter, has a higher failure rate than a simulation or system executed on a single machine. However, a failure in a distributed system is often partial, that is, one of the components of the system fails. The failure may, or may not, affect other components of the system. In the past, several techniques for fault-tolerance in distributed systems have been developed. These techniques can be classified into two main categories; replication-based and check-pointing-based approaches [4]. In replication based approaches one or more copies of a Logical Process (LP) is maintained in addition to the main LP. In case of failure, one of these replicas will take the failed LP's place. In check-pointing based approaches, states of the individual LPs are saved on stable storage. In case of failure, an LP is restarted using the last stable state saved on stable storage.

According to [10] research in fault-tolerant distributed simulation has been quite sparse. Application of fault-tolerance techniques in the context of HLA is even scarcer. However, there is some work that aims in this direction. In [12] a structured view of fault-tolerance in parallel and distributed simulations is given and possible solutions are proposed. In [11] a Resource Sharing System (RSS) is presented that in a future extension could serve as the basis for fault-detection, check-pointing and replication of federates. In [1] a concept, named R-FED (Replica Federate), in support of fault-tolerant HLA federations is presented. As the name implies, the approach is based on replication of individual federates in a federation. Several papers address the issue of federate migration, which is an important cornerstone in designing an infrastructure for fault-tolerant distributed simulation; see for example [6], [15], [2], [3] and [11]. However, these papers usually address federate migration in the context of load-balancing and do not explicitly address fault-tolerance.

The present version of HLA is IEEE 1516-2000. Currently, work is carried out to define the next version of HLA, through the *HLA Evolved* [13]. An interesting aspect of *HLA Evolved* is that fault-tolerance has been given more focus than before. *HLA Evolved* is aimed at providing a common semantics for failure and mechanisms for fault-detection. At the core, two additions have been made to the Management Object Model (MOM), namely *federate lost* and *disconnected*. These interactions provide the basic mechanisms for signaling a fault from the context of a federation, through *federate lost*, and from the perspective of a federate, through *disconnected*. Upon failure, the RTI has the responsibility to do resign on behalf of the lost federate using an *Automatic Resign Directive*. This line of development is important for future realization of fault-tolerant distributed simulations, based on the HLA.

2.2. Fault-tolerance in DRMS

At present, a mechanism for FT in federations synchronized according to the time-warp protocol is implemented in DRMS. The recovery phase of this mechanism is based on a rollback-recovery scheme, which is commonly used for FT in message-passing systems; see for example the survey made by Elnozahy et al [8]. In this approach, states of individual federates are periodically saved on stable storage throughout the federation execution. In case of failure, recovery of the federation is accomplished by rolling back individual federates to a consistent system state. In DRMS, federate states are check-pointed using a remote stable storage component. This means that states are distributed outside of the local scope (host environment) of an executing federate. The communication required for distribution of checkpoints, to and from the stable storage, is implemented by means of the RTI communication infrastructure, utilizing an extension to the Federation Object Model (FOM). Thus, the stable storage component is also a member of the federation. Interactions imposed by the FT mechanism are outlined in table 1.

Table 1. Interactions added to the FOM to support the fault-tolerance mechanism (P = Publish, S = Subscribe).

Interaction	Description	Federate	Stable Storage
reportCP	Reports state to Stable Storage	P	S
requestCP	Requests latest state from stable storage	P	S
latestCP	Delivers latest state to recovered federate	S	P
requestResend	Requests resend of messages with time stamp greater than GVT[1]	P, S	-

---

[1] GVT – Global Virtual Time

The check-pointing protocol must assure that states, reported to stable storage, are safe i.e. a state represents a federate at a point in time that can not be invalided due to rollback. This means that federates report checkpoints for a point in time that is less than the smallest timestamp of a message that could ever be delivered to the federate. The time-stamp of states reported to the stable storage are used by the stable storage component to control the advancement of GVT. This control is required to stop advancement of GVT in case of federate failure. The check-pointing is not synchronized through-out the federation, but federates report states individually.

2.3. Federate restoration in DRMS

Next, the fault-recovery scheme of the FT mechanism is explained in greater detail based on a simple example. In case of federate failure, the DRMS automatically restores the concerned federate in a new host environment. This is accomplished by using a previously saved state from the stable storage. The state used for restoration represents the federate at the current GVT.

Consider the simple exchange of event-messages as illustrated in figure 1. Fed2 processes event-message A at time T_a, which induces scheduling of event-message B at time T_b in Fed1. Fed1 processes event-message B at time T_b, which leads to scheduling of event-message C in Fed2 at time T_c. Next, Fed2 processes event-message C at time T_c, leading to scheduling of event-message D in Fed3 at time T_d, and so on.

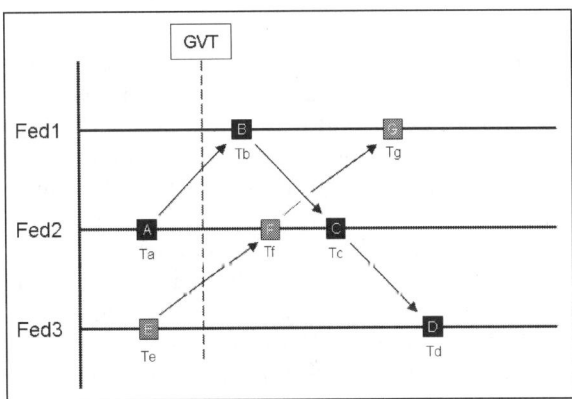

Figure 1. Exchange of event-messages in a federation.

Three types of time-stamps are associated with each event-message in figure 1, these are; T_{send}, $T_{process}$ and $T_{schedule}$. Looking at an event-message from the perspective of Fed2, for example event-message C, T_{send} represents the processing time of event-message

B by Fed1, i.e. T_b. $T_{process}$ represents the processing time of event-message C by Fed2, i.e. T_c and $T_{schedule}$ represents the scheduled time of event-message D in Fed3, i.e. T_d. $T_{process}$ and $T_{schedule}$ of each event-message are inherently known to each federate. T_{send} is added to all interactions, or objects, as an additional parameter.

Upon failure of a federate its execution is resumed in a new host environment. After rejoining the federation execution, the resumed federate requests its state from stable storage using the *requestCP* interaction. Next, the resumed federate issues the *RequestResend* interaction that instructs other federates to execute the recovery procedure. The recovery procedure, carried out by all federates besides the resumed federate, can be described in terms of the following pseudo-code:

```
ID = name of failed federate

For each event-message, E, sent from ID do
    If T_send of E is greater than GVT then
        If E is not processed then
            Delete E
        Else If E is processed then
            Retract E

For each retracted E do
    Rollback to T_process of E

For each E destined for ID do
    If T_schedule of E is greater than GVT
        Resend E to ID
```

Given the procedure outlined above, if Fed1 fails the following sequence of events will be executed to restore the federation; Fed2 retracts event-message C, since in this case T_{send} of C is greater than GVT. The retracted event-message induces rollback of Fed2 to $T_{process}$ of event-message C, i.e. Fed2 will rollback to a state that does not record the processing of event-message C, but reflects the processing of event-message F. The rollback will in turn induce retraction of event-message D from Fed3. This causes rollback of Fed3 to $T_{process}$ of event-message D. The state used for the rollback does not record the processing of event-message D, but reflects the processing of event-message E. After completion of the rollback phase, event-messages destined for Fed1 are resent. This means that Fed2 resends event-message B, since $T_{schedule}$ of event-message A is greater than GVT. Also, Fed2 resends event-message G, since $T_{schedule}$ of event-message F is greater than GVT. After this the federation is restored and can resume normal execution.

3. Test federation

To evaluate the FT mechanism, as described above, a simple test federation was developed. This federation employs time-warp as synchronization protocol and comprises four federates. The federates form a fully connected network, i.e. each federate is capable of sending an event-message to an arbitrary neighbor federate.

The processing of an event-message in the test federation simply means updating a statistics object, describing the message exchange during a simulation run, and scheduling of the event-message in a neighbor federate. The scheduled time is randomly calculated within each federate.

The federates of the test federation process and produce events optimistically, thus when an event-message is received in a federate's past, a rollback is triggered. Similarly, when an anti-message is received that will annihilate an already processed event-message a rollback is also triggered. The rollback relies on a record of locally saved checkpoints. The advancement of GVT triggers garbage collection of this record. The test federation utilizes the following interactions:

- *Event-message*: this is the standard event of the federation. It is simply a message that when processed by a federate means scheduling its arrival in another federate.
- *Anti-message*: this message is used for annihilating sent event-messages in case of rollback. In this case the standard way of retracting messages in HLA is employed, i.e. using *requestRetraction* of the *FederateAmbassador* and *retract* of the *RTIAmbassador*.
- *ReportCP*: this message represents the state of a federate at a specific point in time. It is sent to the stable storage to enable restoration of a failed federate.
- *RequestCP*: this message requests a state of a particular federate at the current GVT from stable storage.
- *LatestCP*: this message is used to deliver a requested state from stable storage to the concerned federate.
- *RequestResend*: this message triggers resend of messages to a federate that has been migrated due to failure.

Of the message types defined above, the *ReportCP*, *RequestCP*, *LatestCP* and *RequestResend* are specifically employed to enable use of the FT mechanism. Thus, when the federation is executed without the FT mechanism, these message types are not used.

4. Experiments and results

The following section describes the experiments used to evaluate the proposed FT mechanism and the results generated through these experiments. The purpose of the experiments was to get an estimate of the communication overhead generated when utilizing the FT mechanism. Thus, the difference in number of generated messages between the case when FT is employed and the case when FT is not used was measured. Also, the difference in total number of messages generated between the FT and non FT cases, when faults are introduced during the simulation run, was measured. When faults are introduced during the simulation execution, in the non FT case, the entire simulation has to be restarted completely. During the experiments the test federation was executed using a logical time interval from 0 to 500. Table 2 outlines the characteristics of the simulation runs carried out to evaluate the proposed FT mechanism.

Table 2. Characteristics of experimental simulation runs. The simulation was executed using a logical time interval from 0 to 500.

Simulation Run	Failures	Time of failures	Using FT
1	0	-	Yes
2	0	-	No
3	1	50	Yes
4	1	150	Yes
5	1	250	Yes
6	1	350	Yes
7	1	450	Yes
8	1	50	No
9	1	150	No
10	1	250	No
11	1	350	No
12	1	450	No
13	3	125, 250, 375	Yes
14	3	125, 250, 375	No

Figure 2 shows the total number of event-messages and anti-messages for three simulation runs that does not utilize FT. In the first case, no failures were triggered during the simulation run. In the second case, a failure was triggered at local time 250 in one of the federates. In the last case, three failures were introduced during the simulation execution. These occurred at local time 125, 250 and 375 of three different federates. When a failure occurs the federation must be restarted, since it is assumed that no checkpoints are available to allow for federate recovery. Thus, a failure at the early stages of the simulation execution will induce minimal extra communication, whereas in the extreme case, the total communication cost will increase by 100 %.

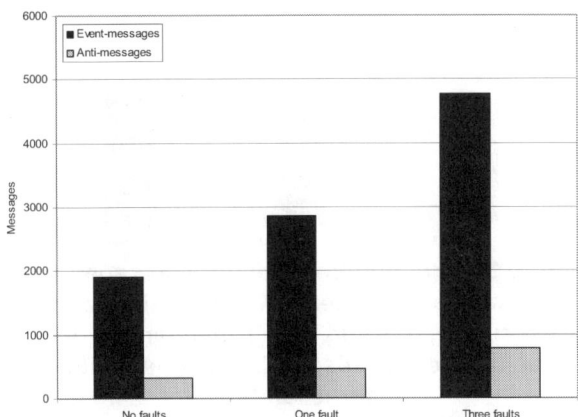

Figure 2. Total number of event-messages and anti-messages generated during simulation execution, not utilizing the FT mechanism, for three different cases; no faults, one fault and three faults.

Figure 3 shows the total number of event-messages and anti-messages for three simulation runs when the FT mechanism is used. In the first case, no failures were triggered during the simulation run. In the second case, a failure was triggered at local time 250 in one of the federates. In the last case, three failures were introduced during the simulation execution. These occurred at local time 125, 250 and 375 of three different federates. The difference between the zero faults, one fault and three faults cases is small. The total number of messages generated for each message type increases slightly as the number of faults triggered increases.

Figure 4 shows a comparison between the FT and non FT cases. The bars in this chart represent the total number of messages generated within the federation. In the one fault case the failure was triggered at local time 250 in one of the federates, whereas in the three faults case, the failures were triggered at local time 125, 250 and 375 in three different federates. As the chart illustrates, using the FT mechanism when no faults are present in the system will impose an extra cost. In this case the *reportCP* interactions to stable storage induce the cost. However, in the one fault case the applied approaches (FT and non FT) almost perform equally. As expected, the three faults case reflects a high number of messages for the non FT simulation execution.

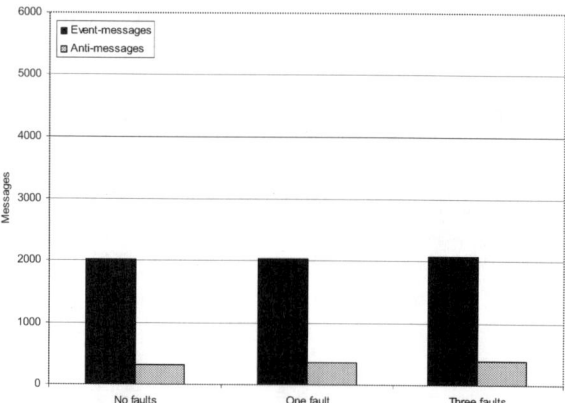

Figure 3. Total number of event-messages and anti-messages generated during simulation execution, utilizing the FT mechanism, for three different cases; no faults, one fault and three faults.

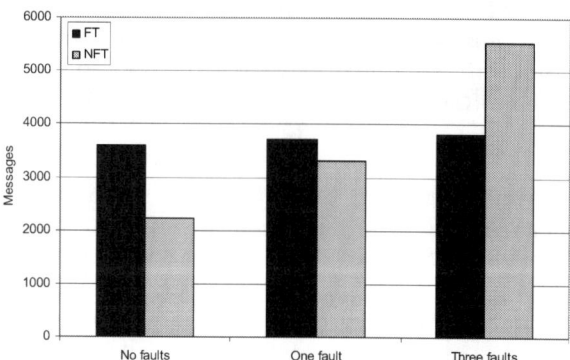

Figure 4. Total number of messages generated for the no faults, one fault and three faults cases, with and without utilization of the FT mechanism.

The failure of individual components of a simulation is probably best described in terms of a stochastic process. Making general conclusions based on mean estimates of failure times will not reflect the behavior of a real-world system. Thus, it is not entirely justified to make conclusions based on a mean value that expresses when a federate will fail during the simulation run. To provide an alternative view of the cost of having fault-tolerance, three different cases were tested. The purpose of these cases was to represent the mean failure time within five consecutive intervals of the federation execution. Thus, these cases represent a mean failure time within the first fifth, second fifth and so forth of the logical time interval used for the simulation execution. Table 3 summarizes the total number of messages generated, with and without FT, for these intervals.

Table 3. Total number of messages for the FT and non FT cases.

Failure time	FT	NFT
50	3841	2474
150	3774	2856
250	3714	3321
350	3754	3747
450	3740	4258

Figure 5 depicts the difference between the FT and non FT cases, in terms of total number of generated messages, for the intervals described above. As indicated in the chart, the overhead for the FT cases is greater than the extra communication caused by the faults in the non FT cases for the first three intervals. In the fourth interval the total communication cost is almost equal, whereas in the fifth interval the FT case shows better performance over the non FT case.

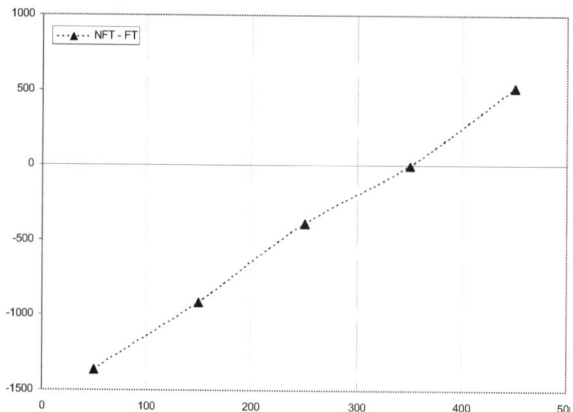

Figure 5. Difference in total number of messages, assuming one fault, between the FT and non FT cases for mean failure time of five intervals of the federation's logical time interval.

5. Discussion

When simulations are integrated in the decision process, to serve the commander in an NBD context, the requirements on the supporting infrastructure are high. An essential aspect of these requirements is enabling fault-tolerant distributed simulations, since this is the fundament for a robust execution environment that can respond to user needs in a timely fashion. The most widely adopted standard for distributed simulations within the military community, the HLA, does not in its present form treat fault-tolerance extensively. Thus, it is desirable to develop efficient and scalable methods for fault-tolerance in HLA in order to successfully deploy HLA simulations within the framework of the NBD.

We have shown that it is feasible to develop FT mechanisms within the framework of HLA. However, in our case a supporting infrastructure is needed to enable automatic re-deployment of a federate upon failure. As the HLA develops, through the *HLA Evolved* track, there will be stronger support for fault-tolerance within the standard, which will ease development of robust federations.

Regardless of the approach taken for implementation of fault-tolerant federations, there will always be an extra cost associated to it. The fault-tolerance support will inherently lead to increased network traffic and/or heavier consumption of hardware resources. However, this extra cost must be evaluated in terms of the consequences that may result from not having a fault-tolerant federation. In the federation developed to evaluate the proposed FT mechanism, the cost, in terms of number of extra messages generated to handle failures, is relatively low, as indicated in figure 3. The total number of messages rises from 2013 to 2075, comparing the no faults case with the three faults case, not taking into account the *reportCP* interactions. The reason for this increase is the resending of event-messages and potential rollbacks caused by recovery of a failed federate. However, depending on the mutual relations existing between federates of a federation, the recovery phase may result in disparate numbers of resent event-messages and/or rollbacks. Different relations among a set of federates have not been treated in the present evaluation. Currently, the federates form a fully connected network and thus the message exchange is fairly homogeneous.

As seen in figure 4, the total number of generated messages, for the non FT cases, rises sharply as the number of faults increases, whereas in the FT cases, the increase is almost negligible. Of course, the timing of the faults has a large impact on the end result in these cases. If a simulation is considered being a critical component of an NBD framework, the worst-case must be considered a plausible scenario, i.e. failure near the end of the simulation execution. Looking at the mean failure time of the last 20% of the simulation execution in figure 5 the non FT case results in 4258 messages (given by table 3). In comparison with the total number of generated messages for the zero failures case without FT of 2221 messages, presented in figure 4, a failure in the last 20% of the simulation execution would increase the total number of messages by approximately 90% on average. Note that this estimate is for the one fault case. If additional faults are introduced in this interval the cost will grow immensely. In the one fault case, utilization of the FT approach will result in 3740 messages (given by table 3). This equals an increase in number of generated messages by approximately 68%. However, note that this figure is tightly coupled with the total number of event-messages of the federation. If a federation generates more event-messages than the test federation, the FT mechanism will perform even better (since the number of *reportCP* interactions will remain the same). Thus, the overhead, in number of generated messages, for having fault-tolerance is certainly justifiable, considering the worst-case scenario a likely requirement on an M&S infrastructure of the NBD.

6. Conclusions

We showed how to implement fault-tolerance in time-warp federations using a check-pointing-based scheme within the HLA communication infrastructure. The overhead cost when utilizing the FT mechanism is justifiable, especially when considering worst-case scenarios for federate failure times i.e. failures near the end of the federation execution. In our example, when the FT mechanism is employed, a failure in the last 20% of the simulation execution would result in a total of 3740 generated messages, which should be compared with the 4258 messages generated when the FT mechanism is not employed. If no failures occur, the simulation execution will generate 2221 messages on average, given that the fault-tolerance mechanism is not used. This means that for one failure in the last 20% of the simulation execution, utilization of the fault-tolerance mechanism will increase the total number of messages by 68%. This should be compared to the case when fault-tolerance is not present where the total number of generated messages is increased by 90%. Thus, the FT mechanism will in this case decrease the total number of messages by approximately 12%. If additional faults occur the reduction will be greater.

7. Future work

As a starting point we have evaluated the overhead in number of additional messages generated by the FT mechanism. As a next step it would be valuable to estimate the degradation in the effectiveness of a simulation execution when using the FT mechanism. In this context it would be of interest to look at various sizes of the checkpoints to see how different federate types may have an impact on the effectiveness, i.e. some federates will require more memory than others for representation of their states. Also, we will consider tests of the FT mechanism where the timing of the faults are not pre-defined, but randomly generated throughout the simulation execution by a probability function at each node.

Moreover, the test federation used in this work comprises no complex issues of ownership of objects in the federation. In more complex federation types, the issue of transferring ownership of objects between federates, in case of failure, must be resolved as well. This issue is of great concern to enable use of the FT mechanism on a more general level and in more complex federation types.

8. References

[1] C. Berchtold, and M. Hezel. 2001. An architecture for fault-tolerant HLA-based simulation *Proceedings of 15th European Simulation Multiconference*.

[2] L. Bononi, G. D'Angelo, and L. Donatiello. 2003. HLA-based adaptive distributed simulation of wireless mobile systems *Proceedings of 17th Workshop on Parallel and Distributed Simulation*.

[3] W. Cai, S. Turner and H. Zhao. 2002. A load management system for running HLA-based distributed simulations over the grid *Proceedings of the IEEE International Symposium on Distributed Simulation and Real Time Applications*.

[4] P. Damani, and K. Garg. 1998. Fault-tolerant distributed simulation *Proceedings of the 12th Workshop on Parallel and Distributed Simulation*.

[5] M. Eklöf, R. Ayani, and F. Moradi. 2005. A Framework for fault-tolerance in HLA-based distributed simulations *Proceedings of the 2005 Winter Simulation Conference*.

[6] M. Eklöf, M. Sparf, F. Moradi, and R. Ayani. 2004. Peer-to-peer-based resource management in support of HLA-based simulations *SIMULATION*. Volume 80, Issue 4-5.

[7] M. Eklöf, J. Ulriksson, and F. Moradi. 2003. NetSim: an environment for network based modeling and simulation *Symposium on C3I and M&S Interoperability (MSG-22)*. NATO Modeling and Simulation Group.

[8] E. Elnozahy, L. Alvisi, Y-M, Wang, and D. Johnson. 2002. A Survey of Rollback-Recovery Protocols in Message-Passing Systems *ACM Computing Surveys*. Volume 34, Number 3.

[9] D. Jefferson. 1985. Virtual time *ACM Transactions on Programming Languages and Systems*. Volume 7, Number 3.

[10] T. Kiesling. 2003. Fault-tolerant distributed simulation: a position paper. Available via http://fakinf.informatik.unibwmuenchen.de/~tkiesling/documents/ftds-position-paper.pdf [accessed March 21, 2005].

[11] J. Lüthi, and S. Großmann. 2001. The resource sharing system: dynamic federate mapping for HLA-based distributed simulation *Proceedings of the 15th Workshop on Parallel and Distributed Simulation*.

[12] J. Lüthi, and C. Berchtold. 2000. Concepts for dependable distributed discrete event simulation *Proceedings of the International European Simulation Multi-Conference*.

[13] B. Möller, M. Karlsson, and B. Löfstrand. 2005. Developing fault tolerant federations using HLA evolved *Proceedings of the Spring Simulation Interoperability Workshop*.

[14] U. Saleem. 2004. Developing java web services with AXIS. Available via http://www.developer.com/java/web/article.php/3443951 [accessed March 21, 2005].

[15] G. Tan, A. Persson, and R. Ayani. 2004. HLA federate migration *38th Annual Simulation Symposium*.

A Framework for Robust HLA-based Distributed Simulations

Dan Chen
School of Computer Science
University of Birmingham
United Kingdom, B15 2TT
E-mail: chendan@pmail.ntu.edu.sg

Stephen John Turner, Wentong Cai
School of Computer Engineering
Nanyang Technological University
Singapore 639798
E-mai: {assjturner, aswtcai}@ntu.edu.sg

Abstract

The High Level Architecture (HLA) is a standard for the interoperability and reuse of simulation components, referred to as federates. Large scale HLA-compliant simulations are built to study complex problems, and they often involve a large number of federates and vast computing resources. Simulation federates running at different locations are liable to failure. The failure of one federate can lead to the crash of the overall simulation execution. Such risk increases with the scale of a distributed simulation. Hence, fault-tolerance is required to support runtime robustness.

This paper introduces a framework for robust HLA-based distributed simulations using a "Decoupled Federate Architecture". Our framework exploits the architecture to provide a generic fault-tolerant model, that exploits a "dynamic substitution" approach to deal with failure. A sender-based method is designed to ensure reliable in-transit message delivery, which is coupled with a novel algorithm to perform effective fossil collection. The fault-tolerant model also avoids any unnecessary repeated computation when handling failure. The framework supports reusability of legacy federate code, and it is platform-neutral and independent of federate modeling approaches. Experiments have been carried out to validate and benchmark the fault-tolerant federates using an example of a simple supply-chain simulation. The experimental results show that the framework provides correct failure recovery and indicate that the overhead for facilitating fault-tolerance is minimal.

1. Introduction

Distributed simulation technology facilitates the construction of a large-scale simulation with component models that can be developed independently on heterogeneous platforms and distributed geographically. The High Level Architecture (HLA) defines the rules, interface specification and object model template to support reusability and interoperability amongst the simulation components, known as federates. The Runtime Infrastructure (RTI) software supports and synchronizes the interactions amongst different federates conforming to the HLA standard [5] to give an overall simulation application, known as a federation.

In the case where the problem domain is particularly complex or involves multiple collaborative parties, the analysts often need to construct a large scale federation with individual simulation federates interacting over the Internet. Some typical examples are: military commission rehearsal, Internet gaming and supply chain simulation, etc. Those applications usually are time consuming and computation intensive and require vast distributed computing resources. Simulation federates running at different locations are liable to failure: as the current IEEE 1516 HLA does not support a formal fault tolerant model [7], crash of a federate or a part of a federation will lead to the failure of the whole federation. When failure occurs, even it is feasible to restart the simulation from a previous checkpoint [8], repeating the execution could either be costly or lose the functions of the failed simulation (for example, a rare event may not be regenerated in the new "recovered" simulation execution). The risk of such failure increases with the number of federates inside one single federation. Although fault tolerance support has been informally proposed in the latest HLA Evolved specification and some design patterns for fault tolerant federations were suggested in [10], there are only few preliminary and non-standard implementations for this purpose. Hence, there exists a pressing need for a mechanism to support runtime robustness in HLA-based distributed simulations.

A normal federate usually exists as a single process at runtime, and the simulation model shares the same memory space with the Local RTI Component (LRC) [9, 11]. In the case where the RTI crashes or meets congestion, the failure of any LRC prevents the simulation execution from proceeding correctly even though the simulation model contains no error at all. Thus, providing fault-tolerance to federates requires an approach to "isolate" the error of the LRC from the simulation model in addition to the challenge to develop a generic state saving and recovery mechanism. In [4], a "Decoupled Federate Architecture" approach has been proposed to enable state saving and recovery for federate cloning. In this paper, we investigate the fault-tolerance issue, and whether the Decoupled Federate Architecture can be used for this purpose.

This paper proposes a framework that takes advantage of the decoupled architecture to handle an RTI failure. The basic idea is to prevent a local failure from affecting the overall distributed computation (simulation). A generic fault-tolerant model has been developed as middleware transparent to the user. The model dynamically substitutes the crashed RTI components with backups while the simulation federates still continue to operate as normal without being disrupted. The fault-tolerant model avoids repeating the execution of federates when handling failure. Furthermore, the framework uses a sender-based method to ensure reliable in-transit message delivery in case of failure. We have also designed a novel algorithm to dispose of buffered events after they have been successfully delivered to the subscribers. A series of experiments has been performed to validate and benchmark the fault-tolerant model.

The rest of this paper is organized as follows: Section 2 addresses related work and analyses the problems to be solved. Section 3 gives an overview of the Decoupled Federate Architecture. Section 4 details the functionalities and design of the framework as well as the algorithms for dealing with in-transit messages. Section 5 presents the experiments based on a distributed supply-chain simulation example, which examine the correctness of the fault-tolerant model and compare the robust federates with normal federates in terms of performance. In Section 6, we conclude with a summary and proposals on future work.

2. Background and scope

People have developed many technologies for facilitating fault-tolerance in distributed applications. Cristian pointed out some principles about fault-tolerance in distributed system architectures [3], and these are: understanding failure semantics, masking failure and balancing design cost.

The checkpoint and message-logging approach is commonly used. For example, as proposed in [8], a process records each message received in a message log while the state of each process is occasionally saved as a checkpoint. A failed process can be restored using some previous checkpoint of the process and the log of messages. The federation save and restore services [11] could be used to save the RTI states at some checkpoints. In the case of failure, a new federation could be created to "restore" the federation with the saved states. In the checkpoint approach, the simulation model should have the functionality to manipulate the states at the model level, and it repeats the computation from one of the checkpoints onwards. Moreover, the overhead for executing federation save and restore can be significant [12, 15].

Fault-tolerant techniques often employ redundant/backup components to achieve system robustness. Birman used backup to ensure fault-tolerance in building reliable network applications [2]. In [6], fault-tolerance was enabled in a distributed system using rollback-recovery and process replication. Principally these methods take advantage of replication to ensure reliability of distributed applications. Another typical example is the Replica Federate approach proposed in [1]. This approach produces multiple identical instances of one single federate, and failures can be detected and recovered upon the outputs of those identical instances. However, replication consumes extra resources and requires synchronization of the replicas to maintain consistency, and redundancy is liable to result in lowered system performance. Furthermore, extra federate replicas in a single federation increase the probability of overall system fault due to an RTI failure, and this may also limit the scalability of the approach.

Considering the drawbacks of the above approaches, our framework has been designed with the following objectives and scope:
- Tackling unpredictable failure of RTI services regardless of what causes the failure.
- Minimizing overhead for providing runtime robustness to ensure execution efficiency.
- Resuming normal execution exactly from where a failure occurs without repeating or disrupting the global simulation execution.
- Avoiding the need for developers to include extra "fault-tolerant codes" in modeling federates, to minimize development cost and support reuse of legacy federates.

- Allowing developers to model their federates freely independent of the software package or platform.
- Providing user transparency, which (1) masks failure from the users at runtime and (2) allows users to deploy/execute fault-tolerant federations in the same way as normal federations.

However, it is a challenge to develop a generic fault-tolerant model. One of the difficulties is due to the assumption that developers can model their federates in a totally free manner. It is unlikely that a generic state saving and replication mechanism can be provided that will be suitable for any federate. Even given such a mechanism, it is unlikely that all developers will use the same standard package to model their simulations. Without the ability to customize the user's simulation code, it is almost impossible to make snapshots of all system states of any federate. The principle of reusing existing federate code increases the difficulty of this task. On the other hand, the HLA standard makes it relatively easy to intercept the system states at the RTI level using a middleware approach. Furthermore, we can see that the simulation model and the Local RTI Component have very different characteristics. Therefore, it suggests a distinction should be made between these two modules when dealing with failure.

3. Decoupled federate architecture

As shown in Figure 1(A), in an HLA-based distributed simulation, a normal simulation federate can be viewed as an integrated program consisting of a simulation model and Local RTI Component (LRC) [11]. The simulation model executes the representation of the system being analyzed, whereas the LRC services it by interacting and synchronizing with other federates. In a sense, the simulation model performs local computing while the LRC carries out distributed computing for the model.

The Decoupled Federate Architecture [4] was initially designed to tackle the problems involved in replicating running federates for distributed simulation cloning. The Decoupled Federate Architecture separates a federate's simulation model from the Local RTI Component. A virtual federate is built with the same code as the original federate. Figure 1(C) gives the abstract model of the virtual federate. Compared with the original federate, the only difference is in the module below the RTI interface, which remains transparent to the users. A physical federate (PhyFed) is designed as shown in Figure 1(B), and it associates itself with a real LRC. Physical federates interact with each other via a common RTI and form a "physical federation" serving the overall simulation. Both virtual federate and physical federate operate as independent processes. Reliable external communication channels link the two modules into a single federate executive.

A well-designed Decoupled Federate Architecture can provide federated simulations with almost equivalent execution efficiency to that obtained using normal federates in terms of both latency and time advancement performance [4]. As the Decoupled Federate Architecture keeps the standard HLA interface, developers are allowed to customize their own RTI++ library (middleware) to expand the functionalities of the original RTI software without altering the semantics of RTI services. With these merits, the architecture seems to be an infrastructure suitable for developing the fault-tolerant model (see Section 4.1).

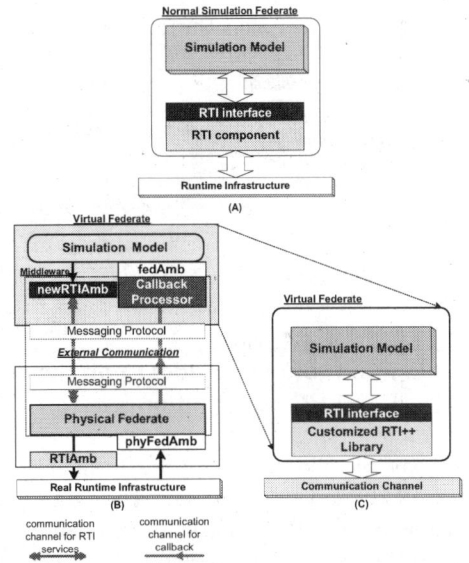

Figure 1. Normal federate versus decoupled federate architecture

4. A framework for supporting robust HLA-based simulations

This section introduces the internal design of the fault-tolerant model and related issues. No implementation can ensure that any program is immune from all faults, and the focus of this study is to develop a robust infrastructure for facilitating distributed simulations rather than to free developers from validating their simulation models. Therefore, the fault-tolerant model does not consider federate crashes due to the incorrect implementation of its simulation model or address deadlock in federation synchronization. It assumes also that the messages sent and received in the network are not corrupted. An RTI failure in the current implementation can be: (1) time-out of an RTI invocation, (2) a critical RTI exception[1], (3) any other unknown error from the RTI or (4) crash of the physical federate or RTIEXEC. In the rest of this paper, a federate means one that contains a virtual federate and a physical federate, and we will explicitly refer to a traditional federate that directly interacts with the real RTI as a "normal federate".

4.1. Fault-tolerant model

In the framework, the fault-tolerant model is embedded in the customized RTI++ library (middleware of the Decoupled Federate Architecture). As shown in Figure 2, the model contains a Management Module and a Failure Detector in the middleware. The Management Module comprises an RTI States Manipulator and a Buffer Manager.

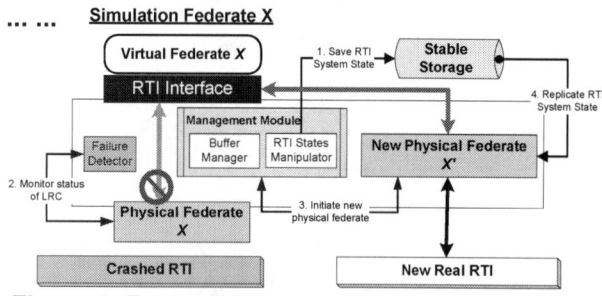

Figure 2. Fault-tolerant model upon dynamic LRC substitution

At runtime the middleware intercepts the invocation of each RTI service method. The RTI States Manipulator saves RTI states immediately before passing the RTI call to the physical federate to execute it. For example, when the virtual federate invokes *publishObjectClass*, the RTI States Manipulator intercepts this call and saves the information, after which it will call the physical federate via the External Communication channel. In this way, the RTI States Manipulator logs all the RTI system states into stable storage. Some RTI states are relatively static, such as the federate identity, federation information, the published/subscribed classes and time constrained/regulating status. Other states include the registered or deleted object instances, and granted federate time. Some event data may also need to be saved, such as sent and received interactions, updated

---

[1] e.g. *RTI::RTIinternalError* or any other exception specified as critical by the user.

and reflected attribute values of object instances, etc. The RTI States Manipulator logs those states through the standard RTI interface, and its design is transparent and independent to the underlying RTI implementation. The Buffer Manager makes use of saved attribute updates and interactions for dealing with in-transit events (see Section 4.2 for details). The Failure Detector monitors the status of the LRC or even the RTIEXEC if necessary. In the four cases of RTI failure (see above), the first three cases can be detected passively via the physical federate while the fourth requires the failure detector actively checking the status of the physical federate or RTIEXEC. Subsequent to confirming an occurrence of an RTI failure, the Management Module will start a failure recovery procedure. Management Modules of other federates will eventually detect the "remote" failure. In this section, we describe a straightforward recovery scheme (as shown in Figure 3) from the perspective of the first failed federate(s) using the following steps:

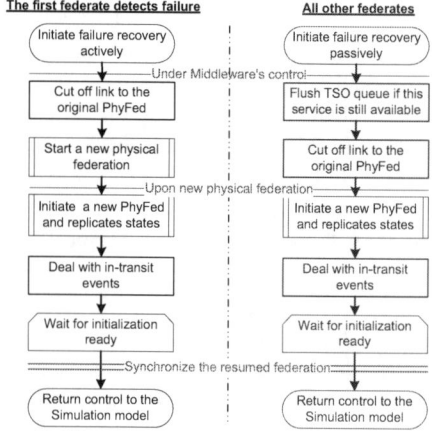

Figure 3. Illustration of straightforward failure recovery procedure

- Preparation for recovery. The Management Module cuts off the connection from its PhyFed and terminates it, while other federates' middleware attempt to extract received events before doing this.
- Initiation of new physical federation. The Management Module creates a new physical federation and initiates a new PhyFed instance. Other federates' middleware also perform exactly the same operation. All virtual federates switch to the new PhyFeds and form a new workable federation together.
- State recovery. All RTI States Manipulators recover RTI states from stable storage to the PhyFeds.

- Handling in-transit events. All Buffer Managers ensure in-transit events are delivered properly to the subscribers.
- Coordination among Management Modules. The Management Module synchronizes the recovered federation to guarantee that all federates are fully reinitialized and ready to proceed.

Finally, the virtual federates obtain control again and continue execution with the support of a new physical federation. Therefore, physical federates work as plug-and-play components, and they can be replaced at runtime. The fault-tolerant model functions as a firewall to prevent failure of local or remote LRCs from stopping the execution of the simulation model.

4.2. Dealing with in-transit events

The current design of the fault-tolerant model supports the conservative time synchronization scheme [7]. The RTI treats updates of attributes and some other events as transient ones. Thus, the recovered federates may miss some events previously generated with a timestamp greater than the federation time on failure, which should be delivered to them. Examples of this problem are shown in Figure 4. Although the example is discussed based on the timestamp ordered (TSO) events, it is similar for receive order (RO) events.

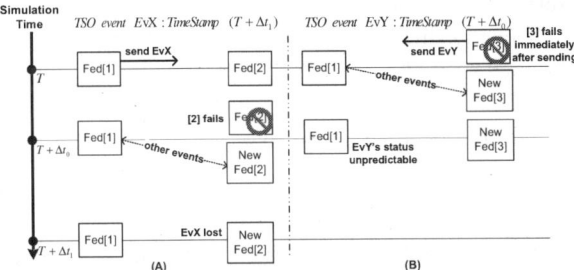

Figure 4. Illustration of the problems in dealing with in-transit events

As illustrated in Figure 4(A), at simulation time T, $Fed[1]$ sends a TSO event EvX with timestamp $T + \Delta t_1$ ($\Delta t_1 > \Delta t_0 > Lookahead$) to subscribers (e.g. $Fed[2]$). In the case that $Fed[2]$ fails at time $T + \Delta t_0$, $Fed[2]$ resumes with a new PhyFed. But the recovered federate will never receive the event EvX as it has already been lost due to the failure. In another case (Figure 4(B)), $Fed[3]$ fails at time T immediately after sending a TSO event EvY with timestamp $T + \Delta t_0$, it is totally unpredictable whether or not subscribers (e.g. $Fed[1]$) have received this event or buffered it in their PhyFeds' TSO queues [11].

In order to ensure that in-transit events are delivered to the receivers when the simulation resumes from failure, a solution is proposed to resend "image" events with an identical content/timestamp to the corresponding in-transit events generated previously. The Buffer Manager (Figure 2) at the sender side records each outgoing TSO event and indexes the event according to the sequence in which it is created. The buffer can be flushed to stable storage from time to time. This approach has similarity to the commonly-used message logging approach in the sense of recording events, but it does not require rollback of the model's execution [14]. The approach needs to make a tradeoff between redundancy in message passing and complexity of the control mechanism under the condition that the new PhyFed must not miss any event that ought to be received. A general principle in designing the resending approach is to ensure that all federates operate in the same way as normal federates that have not encountered a fault.

To minimize extra networking overhead, the proposed approach requires the sender only to resend those events that (1) have been subscribed and (2) have not been received or buffered in the subscriber's TSO queue. The middleware can be designed to help the subscribers notify the particular sender(s) about the reception status of the events originating from the sender. According to the feedback, the sender can selectively generate the image events. The approach is as follows, including preparation before a crash and the action on failure recovery:

- Collecting Subscription/Publication/Registration Data. Each federate builds a Federate Subscription/Publication/Registration (FSPR) Table, which records the classes subscribed/published and the objects registered by other federates. Each federate broadcasts its subscription/publication information that enables other federates to update corresponding entries in their own FSPR Tables. When an object instance is registered (with federate ID encoded using middleware), each subscriber updates the table according to the object class and federate to which it belongs. Thus, when attribute updates of an object instance (events) are received, the receiver can trace the source of this event.
- Buffering Events. Each sender records its local updates in time stamp order according to their associated object classes. Thus each sender records what events it has generated. Referring to the FSPR Table, each sender also knows which federates should receive these events.

- Regenerating Events. On recovering from failure, the PhyFed being recovered requests the senders to deliver those events with timestamp greater than its current granted time[2]. Thus the recovered federate can receive those events and pass them to the simulation model with the advance of time.

The same approach is applicable for processing interactions. For processing RO events, the Buffer Manager indexes the outgoing RO events according to the sequence in which they are created, thus the index can be used to order the RO events. Consequently we can also apply this approach in processing RO events.

4.3. Fossil collection

Using the scheme described in the previous section, sent events are buffered at the senders' side against any potential unpredictable failure. As the simulation execution proceeds, the buffered data will accumulate indefinitely; at some stage this will become a bottleneck as system resources are wasted in maintaining a huge amount of redundant data. Therefore, it is necessary to perform fossil collection on the logged events. The fossil collection should (1) ensure that events that any subscriber might miss in case of failure are always available, as well as (2) dispose of events that have been received by all subscribers as soon as possible.

The RTI ensures that a federate receives all events with timestamp less than its granted time. Therefore, senders do not need to keep events with timestamp less than the granted time of a receiver. Based on this fundamental assumption, the main task of fossil collection is to determine which logged TSO events are safe for a sender to dispose according to its current granted time.

A time constrained federate has an associated Lower Bound Time Stamp (LBTS), which is the timestamp of the earliest possible TSO event that may be generated by any other regulating federate [9, 11]. In the scenario depicted in Figure 5, we write the lookahead of the ith federate ($Fed[i]$) as La_i, its current granted time as T_i and the time of the next request this federate may make to the RTI to advance time as $T_i^{'}$. We define a

---

[2] It is possible that the timestamps of some events to be resent are less than the sender's granted time plus lookahead. In this case, the RTI++ middleware can be designed to encode the content and timestamps of these events in a special RO message, which can then be decoded in the form of TSO events at the receiver's end.

"timestep" by which $Fed[i]$ advances its time in each loop as $\delta_i = T_i^{'} - T_i$.

Considering the simplest scenario consisting of only two federates, from $Fed[1]$'s perspective, failure may occur in $Fed[2]$ either (1) after $Fed[2]$ has been granted time T_2 but before $Fed[2]$ makes another request to advance time, or (2) after $Fed[2]$ has made a request to advance time to $T_2 + \delta_2$ but before the request is granted.

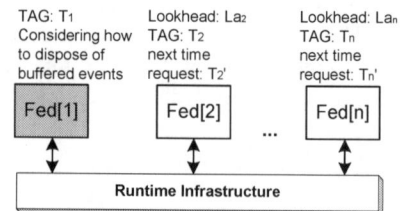

Figure 5: Example for calculating timestamp of events to be disposed

$Fed[1]$'s LBTS is $T_2 + La_2$ in the first case (hence $T_1 \leq T_2 + La_2$), and its LBTS is $T_2 + La_2 + \delta_2$ in the second case (hence $T_1 \leq T_2 + La_2 + \delta_2$). It is safe for $Fed[1]$ to dispose of buffered events earlier than $Fed[2]$'s current granted time T_2, which means any event with timestamp less than $T_1 - (La_2 + \delta_2)$ can be removed immediately.

Generalizing to n federates, suppose that $Fed[k] (k \neq 1)$ has the smallest federate time T_k of the other federates, so that it is safe for $Fed[1]$ to dispose of events with time earlier than T_k. It is obvious that: $La_k + \delta_k \leq \max\{(La_i + \delta_i) | i \neq 1\}$. Thus, in the worst case, it is safe for $Fed[1]$ to dispose of all logged TSO events with timestamp less than $T_1 - \max\{(La_i + \delta_i) | i \neq 1\}$, and we define this value as $Fed[1]$'s *safe lower bound*. The fossil collection algorithm can determine this safe lower bound easily given that the lookahead and timestep of other federates are available, and this can be achieved easily using a middleware approach.

Furthermore, for any federate, its "timestep" may change from time to time. To minimize global propagations, a simulation time window can be defined with an upper and lower bound specified. The window of a federate (say $Fed[i]$) is an interval around $T_i + \delta_i$, i.e. $[(T_i + \delta_i) - \xi_1, (T_i + \delta_i) + \xi_2]$, for some $\xi_1 < \delta_i$ and $\xi_1, \xi_2 > 0$.

When $Fed[i]$ requests to advance its time to $T_i^{'}$, there are four cases:

(1) If $T_i^{'} \leq (T_i + \delta_i) - \xi_1$, set new $\delta_i = (\delta_i - \xi_1)$;

(2) If $(T_i + \delta_i) - \xi_1 < T_i^{'} \leq (T_i + \delta_i)$, δ_i is unchanged;

(3) If $(T_i + \delta_i) < T_i^{'} \leq (T_i + \delta_i) + \xi_2$, set new $\delta_i = (\delta_i + \xi_2)$;

(4) If $T_i^{'} > (T_i + \delta_i) + \xi_2$, set new $\delta_i = (T_i^{'} - T_i)$.

When δ_i decreases, it is safe for the other federates to calculate safe lower bounds using a larger δ value for *Fed[i]*. In case (1), we still need to send other federates the new δ_i, as it is out of the window. For cases (3) and (4), using middleware can ensure other federates have received the new δ_i before *Fed[i]* requests the RTI to advance time. After *Fed[i]* is granted a new time, the time window will be moved forward to adapt to the change.

4.4. Optimizing the failure recovery procedure

The failure recovery procedure starts from the point where a failure is detected by the first federate to the point where all federates are completely re-initialized and ready for resuming normal execution. The straightforward recovery scheme (see Figure 3) requires two time-consuming RTI related operations to be performed, which are (1) to create the physical federation and (2) for each federate, to join the existing federation. The *joinFederationExecution* call incurs costly federation-wide operations. For example in DMSO RTI-NG, this operation usually requires opening TCP sockets to all other federates in the federation, which is expensive [12]. To minimize the overhead (which can be greater than 20 seconds, see Section 5), a possible solution is to avoid these calls during the procedure itself. We attempt to solve this problem using a *Physical Federate Pool* approach as shown in Figure 6.

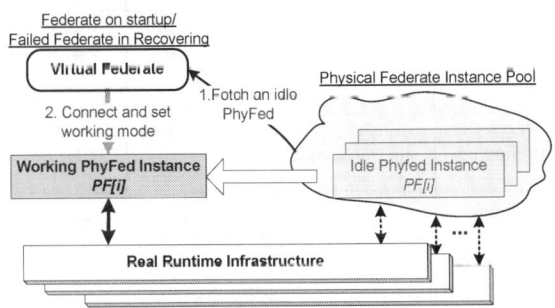

Figure 6. Physical federate pool approach

This approach creates one or multiple "backup" physical federations concurrently with the normal simulation execution. An appropriate number of PhyFed instances are created, which join their respective backup federations and form PhyFed instance pools (one pool for each federation). In the context of the pool approach, a PhyFed instance may operate in two modes: (1) *working mode*, servicing a virtual federate as normal, and (2) *idle mode*, calling *tick* regularly to maintain connection session with the RTI while checking for invocation from a virtual federate. On startup, a virtual federate connects to a PhyFed from the pool and the PhyFed operates in working mode from then onwards. The backup physical federations are purely constituted of idle PhyFeds instances, which are neither time regulating nor time constrained, and only have minimum interaction with each other. The backup physical federations potentially serve for recovery in the future. On failure recovery, an idle PhyFed instance can be fetched from the pool by the virtual federate to provide the required RTI services immediately. Thus, this approach avoids consuming time for creating and joining federation execution prior to state replication. Maintaining spare PhyFed instances consumes extra system resources, and we need to investigate the overhead this may cause. Correspondingly, the straightforward fault recovery scheme (Section 4.1) can be optimized using the pool approach as in Figure 7.

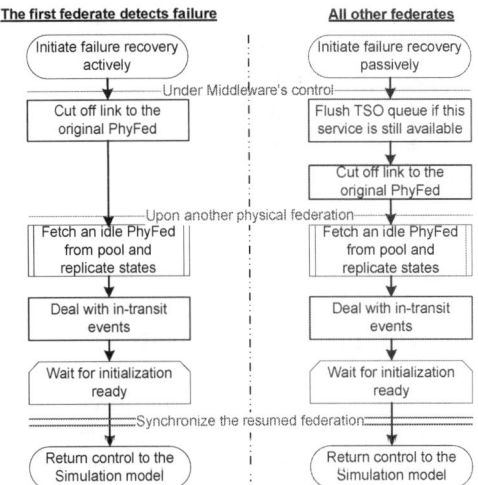

Figure 7. Illustration of the optimized failure recovery procedure using PhyFed pool

Another uncertain factor is the time needed for the remaining federates to detect the failure propagated from the origin. It depends on the form in which the failure appears and how the fault-tolerant model handles it. If the failure is detected as one of the last three cases defined in Section 4, other federates' middleware need only immediately initiate a passive failure recovery. For the first case, the time required to confirm the occurrence of a failure must be longer than the specified "time-out" period.

The situation becomes even more complicated if the "symptoms" of failure cannot be explicitly identified at all. For example, suppose a federate does not receive a *timeAdvanceGranted* (TAG) for a significantly long period after it requests advancing its time from the RTI [11]. Basically this may due to the fact that (1) some LRCs have failed, or (2) the condition for granting its request has not been met yet or (3) some other reason not related to failure, e.g. an unexpected communication delay for the RTI to convey callbacks. There needs to be a method to distinguish the first case from the others. The PhyFed pool approach can be used to solve this issue: a pre-selected backup physical federation can also serve as an out-of-band channel for a failed federate to notify the remaining federates of the occurrence of failure. We define a special "system" object class ("RTI_FAIL") and have all idle PhyFed instances subscribe to and publish it. The Management Module of the first failed federate registers an RTI_FAIL object instance in the selected backup physical federation. The remaining federates' Management Modules periodically check the existence of such an object from the selected backup physical federation to decide whether to start a passive fault recovery procedure. Hence, it is possible for the whole federation to quickly respond to a local failure.

5. Experiments and results

In order to verify the correctness and investigate the overhead incurred in the proposed fault-tolerant model, we perform a series of experiments to compare the robust federates with normal federates using a simple distributed supply chain simulation.

5.1. Configuration of experiments

The simulated supply chain comprises an agent company, a factory and a transportation company. The agent keeps issuing orders to the factory, and the latter processes these orders and plans production accordingly. The transportation company is responsible for delivering products of the factory and reporting the delivery status. The three nodes in the supply chain can be modeled as three federates as shown in Figure 8, namely *simAgent*, *simFactory* and *simTransportation*. These federates form a simple distributed simulation to simulate the supply chain's operation in almost a year (from simulation time 0 to 361). Two object classes "*Order*", "*Products*" and one interaction class "*deliveryReport*" are defined in the Federation Object Model (FOM) [7] to represent the types of events exchanged amongst the federates. The *simFactory* reports the cost incurred for each order at the end of the simulation. The simulation starts with an initialization procedure then enters the "real" simulation procedure after a global synchronization. The initialization procedure denotes the interval from the point a federate is started to the exact point where it has completed the following operations: create/join the federation, enable time regulating/constrained, publish/subscribe object/interaction classes and register object instances. During the simulation procedure, federates interact and coordinate time advancement with each other using the conservative synchronization scheme. In this paper, the elapsed times of the initialization procedure and the simulation procedure of each run are called its *initialization time* and *simulation execution time* respectively.

Using the same codes for the simulation models, the federates are built into two versions by linking to: (1) the DMSO RTI library directly (normal) and (2) the RTI++ middleware library supporting fault-tolerance (robust). The RTI++ in these experiments adopts the PhyFed pool approach and uses the IPC *Message Queue* [13] as the external communication to bridge the virtual federate and its PhyFed. The PhyFed pool maintains one backup physical federation consisting of three idle PhyFeds.

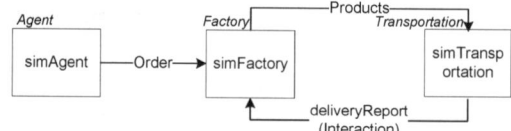

Figure 8. A simple distributed supply chain simulation

Table 1. Configuration of experiment test bed

Specification	Computers		
	Workstation1~2	Workstation3	Server1
CPU	Sparcv9 CPU, at 900 MHz	Sparcv9 CPU * 2, at 360 MHz	Sparcv9 CPU * 6, at 248 MHz
RAM	1024M	512M	2048M
Processes running on	SimAgent or simTransportation	simFactory	RTIEXEC&FEDEXEC
Compiler	GCC 2.95.3		
OS	Sun Solaris OS 5.8		
Underlying RTI	DMSO NG 1.3 V6		

The experiment architecture and platform specification are listed in Table 1. The experiments use four computers in total (three workstations and one server), which are interlinked via a 100Mbps-based backbone. Each federate occupies one individual workstation, with the RTIEXEC and FEDEXEC processes running on the server.

5.2. Correctness of fault-tolerant model

To verify the correctness of the fault-tolerant model, we specify federate *simAgent* to generate the same set of orders in different runs. There are three sets of experiments in this session. We first execute the normal federates, in which the outputs are used as a reference in subsequent experiments. Secondly, we repeat the simulation using the robust federates without introducing failure (FAULT_FREE). The last experiment still uses robust federates but with failure abruptly triggered once by manually terminating a working PhyFed during the simulation procedure (FAULT_INCURRED). The outputs obtained using normal federates are summarized as follows:

- *simAgent* issues 240 orders, in which the first and the last order carries timestamp 2.5 and 362.5 respectively.
- *simFactory* receives 239 orders (note the last order is not received as it is after the simulation end time) and makes products accordingly.
- *simTransportation* receives all product updates issued earlier than the end time and sends *deliveryReport* interactions with respect to these updates.

From the FAULT_FREE and FAULT_INCURRED experiments, we check the orders issued and received, products produced and delivered as well as the calculation of costs. Outputs (including the timestamps and values of all events) in these experiments match exactly those using normal federates. This indicates that the fault-tolerant model does not introduce any variation to the simulation results, and our framework provides a correct robustness mechanism for HLA-based distributed simulations.

5.3. Efficiency of fault-tolerant model

To investigate the performance of the fault-tolerance mechanism, another set of experiments are performed to collect the overall execution time using normal and robust federates. We specify federate *simAgent* to generate orders randomly in each run. For normal federates, we have a number of runs, and the average execution time of these runs is referred to as the NORMAL time of executing one simulation session. As for the robust federates, we first repeat the FAULT_FREE experiments then carry out a number of the FAULT_INCURRED experiments. From FAULT_INCURRED experiments, we select three runs in which the failure of federate *simFactory* occurs at simulation time 43, 182 and 320. These points represent failure at the start (FI_S), middle (FI_M) and end (FI_E) stages respectively.

The average CPU utilization of a single normal federate or a virtual federate (in workstation 1 or 2) is reported as above 80%. A PhyFed has an average CPU utilization as low as <0.5% in working mode and <0.02% in idle mode.

The initialization time of normal federates varies between 19 to 27 seconds in different runs, and it varies between 21 to 27 seconds using robust federates. The latency for initiating the PhyFed pool is well hidden. The simulation execution times of different experiments are reported in Figure 9. The normal simulation execution time is ~584 seconds using normal federates, which is almost the same as the average simulation execution time in FAULT_FREE experiments. This means the overhead for federate decoupling and maintaining the PhyFed pool has little influence on execution efficiency. In the FAILURE_INCURRED experiments, the simulation execution time is only 11~13 seconds longer than the normal case. In the experiments, if an RTI call issued from the virtual federate has not been returned by the PhyFed after more than 6 seconds a time-out will occur. Because of this, a large part of this slight overhead is due mainly to the failure detection procedure.

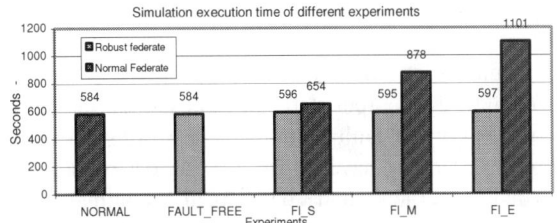

Figure 9. Simulation execution time

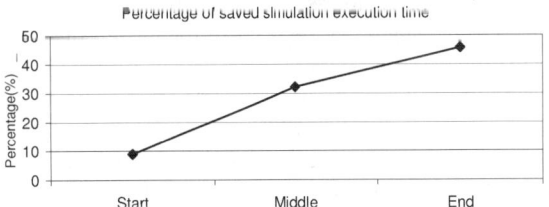

Figure 10. Percentage of saved execution time with failure occurring at different stages

When failure occurs, we assume that the normal federates have to start from the beginning, and the sum of the elapsed times of both the failed and repeated simulation executions is used for comparison with the simulation execution times using robust federates. The percentage of saved execution time is shown in Figure 10. Obviously, the later the failure occurs, the more execution time can be saved (up to 50%).

6. Conclusions and future work

In this paper, we introduce a framework for supporting runtime robustness to HLA-based distributed simulations. We have investigated the issues and design of a generic fault-tolerant federate model. Based upon the Decoupled Federate Architecture, the model is developed to prevent an RTI error from disrupting the execution of simulation federates and ensures correct recovery of a distributed simulation session. Algorithms have been presented to ensure reliable delivery of in-transit messages as well as perform safe fossil collection.

All the objectives set at the beginning of this paper have been fulfilled. The fault-tolerant model supports the reuse of legacy federates while enabling robustness, and it minimizes developers' effort for modeling robust federates. The model is platform-neutral and model independent. User transparency has been provided with failure properly masked. Robust federates do not require rollback of simulation execution in the case of failure.

A series of experiments has been performed to investigate the correctness and performance of the fault-tolerant model using an example of a distributed supply chain simulation. The experimental results are compared for normal and robust federates in terms of uniformity of output statistics and computing efficiency. The output statistics indicate that the model provides correct fault recovery. The results show that robust federates have a very close performance to normal federates and only incur minimal extra overhead. Our work indicates that the fault-tolerant model is a feasible and efficient solution to the support of runtime robustness in HLA-based distributed simulations, which can be used in the design of robust RTI software in the future.

For future work, it is necessary to investigate the framework's scalability which is absent in this study due to limited computing resources. Other work involves the benchmarking of alternative ExtComm backbones such as Sockets, MPI or Web/Grid services and on various platforms. Another issue is to test the implementation and performance of the framework with federates developed using Commercial-off-the-shelf (COTS) simulation packages.

References

[1] C. Berchtold and M. Hezel. "An Architecture for Fault-tolerant HLA-based Simulation", *Proceedings of the 15th International European Simulation Multi-Conference (ESM) 2001*, Prague, Czech Republic, June 2001, pp. 616-620.

[2] Birman, K. P. "Building Secure and Reliable Network Applications", *Prentice Hall and Manning Publishing Company*, 1997.

[3] F. Cristian, "Understanding Fault-Tolerant Distributed Systems", *Communications of the ACM*, 34:2, February 1991, pp. 57-78.

[4] D. Chen, S. J. Turner, B. P. Gan, W. Cai, M. Y. H. Low and J. Wei, "A Decoupled Federate Architecture for Distributed Simulation Cloning", *15th European Simulation Symposium*, Delft, the Netherlands, October 2003, pp. 131-140.

[5] J. S. Dahmann, F. Kuhl and R. Weatherly, "Standards for Simulation: As Simple As Possible But Not Simpler, The High Level Architecture for Simulation", *Simulation*, 71:6, December 1998, pp. 378-387.

[6] Elnozahy, E. N. "Fault-tolerance in Distributed systems Using Rollback-Recovery and Process Replication", *Ph.D. Thesis*, Rice University, Texas, USA, 1993.

[7] IEEE 1516, IEEE Standard for High Level Architecture, 2001.

[8] Johnson, D. B. "Distributed System Fault-tolerance Using Message Logging and Checkpointing", *Ph.D. Thesis*, Rice University, Texas, USA, 1989.

[9] Kuhl, F. R., Weatherly and J. Dahmann, *Creating Computer Simulation Systems: An Introduction to HLA*, ISBN 1-3-022511-8, Prentice Hall, 1999.

[10] B. Möller, B. Löfstrand and Mikael Karlsson, "Developing Fault Tolerant Federations Using HLA Evolved", *Proceeding of 2005 Spring Simulation Interoperability Workshop*, San Diego, California, USA, April 2005, paper no. 05S-SIW-048.

[11] RTI 1.3-Next Generation Programmer's Guide Version 5, *DoD, DMSO*, February 2002.

[12] K. Rycerz, M. Bubak, M. Malawski and P. Sloot, "A Framework for HLA-Based Interactive Simulations on the Grid", *Simulation*, 81:1, January 2005, pp. 67-76.

[13] Stevens, W. R., *UNIX Network Programming, Inter-Process Communications*, Vol. 2, 2nd Edition, Prentice Hall, 1999.

[14] Tanenbaum, A. S. and M. van Steen. "Distributed Systems: Principles and Paradigms", Prentice Hall, 2002.

[15] K. Zając, M. Bubak, M. Malawski and P. Sloot, "Towards a Grid Management System for HLA-based Interactive Simulations", *Proceedings of the 7th IEEE International Symposium on Distributed Simulation and Real Time Applications*, Delft, Netherlands, October 2003, pp. 4-11.

Transparent Optimistic Synchronization in HLA via a Time-Management Converter

Andrea Santoro and Francesco Quaglia
Dipartimento di Informatica e Sistemistica
Università di Roma "La Sapienza"

Abstract

In this paper we present the design and implementation of a Time Management Converter (TiMaC) for HLA based simulation systems. TiMaC is a layer interposed in between the federate and the underlying RTI in order to map the conservative Time Management interface onto the optimistic one. In this way, TiMaC transparently supports optimistic execution for federates originally designed for the conservative approach, which is achieved without the need for developing any ad-hoc RTI system. TiMaC relies on a recently proposed software architecture for transparent treatment of checkpointing/recovery of the federate state, namely Magic State Manager (MASM), and implements a set of additional facilities required to support all the tasks associated with the mapping of conservative onto optimistic Time Management interfaces. The implementation has been tailored to the Georgia Tech B-RTI package, although the underlying design principles would allow it to be integrated with any RTI system. We also report an experimental study demonstrating the viability and effectiveness of our proposal in allowing conservative federates to be supported with highly increased run-time effectiveness in general contexts for what concerns the features of the underlying computing systems (e.g. LAN vs WAN based systems).

1 Introduction

The High Level Architecture (HLA) is a standard for the integration and the interoperability of autonomous simulators [9]. Its target is the building of complex simulation systems (*federations* in the HLA terminology) through the use of a Run-Time Infrastructure (RTI) acting as a middleware component, which offers a general set of services to each involved simulator (i.e. to each *federate*).

The HLA interface specification [10] defines a suite of services, called Time Management, to be offered by the RTI in support of synchronized execution among federates. However, while it is relatively easy to implement the conservative synchronization approach using the HLA, the optimistic approach introduces a set of additional complications. One complication is related to the fact that this kind of synchronization requires checkpointing and state recovery mechanisms to be built in the federate code. Another complication is the burden of handling the whole set of tasks, and their schedule, related to rollback management (e.g. event retractions) at the application level. Unfortunately, the effort to implement all these mechanisms inside the federate code discourages the adoption of the optimistic synchronization approach, possibly at the cost of reduced performance.

To provide a building block to address such an issue, the work in [14] has presented a software architecture, called MAgic State Manager (MASM), allowing transparent checkpointing/recovery of the federate state. Specifically, it offers the possibility to identify the portion of the memory image of the federate (i.e. the federate state), within the memory image of the whole application, namely federate plus middleware layer (i.e. RTI), and also the possibility to incrementally determine the portions of the federate state modified by the execution of simulation events, so to checkpoint/recover them selectively.

In this paper we present the design and implementation of a Time-Management-Converter (TiMaC) that, exploiting the capabilities of MASM, allows not only transparent state management, but completely transparent optimistic synchronization. TiMaC is a software layer interposed in between the federate and both a conventional RTI (the Georgia Tech B-RTI package [7] in our implementation) and MASM. It integrates the functionalities of MASM and of the conventional RTI so to expose to the overlying federate the Time Management interface proper of conservative synchronization, while actually supporting optimistic synchronization (hence interacting with the underlying conventional RTI through the interface for optimistic synchronization). In other words, it performs a conversion between the (conservative) synchronization mode seen by the overlying federate, and the real (optimistic) synchronization mode selected for the execution among the ones supported by the underlying RTI. Therefore, our proposal enlarges the spectrum of synchronization possibilities within HLA federations independently of the specific nature (conservative or optimistic) of the involved federates. This has the strong advantage of allowing to cope with performance problems related to (i) poor or zero lookahead within the specific federation and (ii) large costs for the preventive computation of event safety in case the simulation system is hosted by an infrastructure with, e.g., non-minimal delivery delay among the different instances of the RTI. Additionally, supporting optimistic synchronization transparently is relevant also in the context of federates based on commercial-off-the-shelf (COTS) simulation packages, typically programmed for interfacing only to the conservative portion of Time Management services. For those packages, there would be no way to achieve an optimistic execution without the synchronization facilities offered by a middleware architecture like the one proposed in this paper.

The remainder of this work is structured as follows. In Section 2 a brief overview of MASM is presented. In Section 3 we provide the description of TiMaC, including design choices and some implementation details. Finally, Section 4 is devoted to an experimental evaluation of TiMaC.

2 MASM Overview

As hinted, the objective of MASM is transparency in the treatment of state related operations for optimistic synchronization in the context of HLA. This is clearly not sufficient for achieving completely transparent optimistic synchronization, but is a significant building block, which we briefly overview in order to facilitate the comprehension of the whole TiMaC design.

Contrary to the appearances, the problem addressed by MASM is not merely a problem of transparent checkpointing/recovery of a process state. Specifically, although being defined as separate objects by the HLA standard, the federate and the underlying simulation middleware, i.e. the RTI, are typically parts of a same application program, thus they are executed within the same process and share the same data area. Additionally, classical RTI process models, supported by many commercial and non-commercial implementations (see, e.g., [6, 8, 16]), are based on interactions between the federate and the RTI through methods exposed by RTI and invoked by the federate. Hence, the federate and (at least a portion of) the RTI are executed within the same thread, thus they share the same stack. These peculiarities make techniques traditionally employed to checkpoint/recover a whole process state transparently (see, e.g., [13]) not directly applicable to the HLA context, where we have a single process/thread and we want to transparently checkpoint/recover only a portion of its whole state selectively. To solve this problem, MASM adopts a set of compile-time and run-time techniques allowing the split of the whole process memory areas into two separate sections. One section contains the RTI state, and the other one contains the federate state. A checkpoint operation performed by MASM will save the content of the federate section into buffers within the RTI section. Conversely, a recovery of the federate state will consist in copying the saved data back into the federate section. The compile-time techniques deal with such a separation for what concerns statically allocated memory, whereas, the run-time techniques deal with such a separation for what concerns both the heap (and hence the memory area treated by the `malloc` library) and the stack areas.

MASM performs checkpointing by incrementally logging only dirty pages within the memory image portion related to the federate. This is achieved by exploiting Operating System memory protection mechanisms. Analogously, it restores only the pages which have been dirtied after the causality violation to be recovered. MASM API entails:

- `SaveState(Timetype VirtualTime)`. When this service is invoked, MASM performs an incremental checkpoint of the federate state. The parameter passed to this service is the current simulation time for the federate, which is associated by MASM with the currently taken checkpoint.

- `RecoverState(Timetype VirtualTime)`. When this service is invoked, MASM restores a previously checkpointed state. The parameter passed to this service is the simulation time to be recovered for the federate, which determines the checkpointed state to be selected for the recovery procedure.

- `PruneStateLog(Timetype GVT)`. When this service is invoked, MASM frees the memory that keeps the oldest checkpoints. All checkpoints whose simulation time is lower than `GVT` will be removed from the log.

As a final note MASM has been originally developed in one version based on LINUX kernel patches [14], which performs low level memory management operations with extremely reduced overhead directly within the kernel, and, more recently, in another version exploiting UNIX APIs and entirely working at the application level [15]. The TiMaC layer we present in this paper is actually independent of the specific MASM version since it does not interact with MASM internals. Hence, one could decide to employ TiMaC with one or the other MASM version, e.g., depending on whether performance in state management operations provided by one version might be slightly sacrificed at the expense of installation simplicity provided by the other version.

3 Design of the Time Management Converter

To provide a clear context for understanding the structure of the TiMaC layer, we initially recall basic concepts related to both conservative and optimistic Time Management services to be offered by the RTI. Then we proceed with the presentation of TiMaC in terms of mapping the two different Time Management interfaces on each other. Actually, Time Management services are specified in a manner allowing the treatment of two different categories of messages associated with coordination along the HLA time-axis, namely TimeStamp Ordered (TSO) and Receive Ordered (RO) messages [10]. However, since synchronization primarily deals with the advancement in simulation time, subject to (possible) delivery of TSO messages, TiMaC has been structured to primarily address the problem of mapping conservative simulation time advancement onto optimistic one just in the presence of TSO messages. Then, the design has extended the capabilities of TiMaC to treat RO messages. For this reason we present TiMaC incrementally by first discussing the treatment of TSO messages and then going to the treatment of RO messages. Finally, the last part of this section is devoted to a discussion on the effects of (and also on current limitations from) the Time Management conversion performed by TiMaC for what concerns the relation between Time Management services and other kind of HLA services to be supported by the underlying RTI.

3.1 Recall on Time Management Services

The typical RTI service used for conservative synchronization of event-driven federates is *Next Message Request* (NMR). This service allows the federate to ask for an advancement of its local simulation clock to a given value t specified as an input parameter to the service invocation (typically this is the time of the next event in the federate local event queue). The effect of an NMR invocation is twofold: (i) The delivery of all the TSO messages with the minimum timestamp destined to the federate and having time up to t, if any. (ii) The delivery of all the incoming RO messages already buffered by the RTI and destined to the federate, if any. In case the RTI knows that no TSO message will be ever delivered to the federate with simulation time less than or equal to t, the RTI grants to the federate the advancement to time t. On the other hand, in case there is a chance that a future TSO message will arrive to the federate with time less than or equal to t, the RTI delivers to the federate the RO messages and will eventually deliver the incoming TSO message with the minimum simulation time. Then, the RTI will eventually grant the federate with the simulation time of that message. The grant is delivered to the federate through the *Time Advance Grant* (TAG) callback invoked by the RTI. Note that the granted time is greater than or equal to the current simulation clock of the federate.

For optimistic synchronization, the Time Management service is called *Flush Queue Requests* (FQR), which allows the federate to ask the RTI to deliver all the already buffered RO messages and the already buffered TSO messages with time up to t so that the federate itself can proceed processing those messages without the need for assurance of their safety. Also in this case the RTI replies to a FQR call with a TAG callback. However, the difference with the NMR request is that a TAG in response to FQR may grant to the federate a time less than the current simulation clock of the federate. Hence this grant is not used to determine whether it is safe to process messages, but to determine whether "fossil collection" of recovery information maintained by the federate to support rollback procedures can be discarded.

For both conservative and optimistic synchronization, the delivery of TSO and RO messages to the federate, after an NMR or FQR request is issued, occurs through a set of callbacks that RTI can invoke. The typical callbacks are *Reflect Attribute Values* (RAV), *Receive Interaction* (RI) and *Remove Object Instance* (ROI). These callbacks are issued by the RTI after the NMR or FQR request from the federate and before the TAG callback. The typical trigger for all these callbacks (including TAG) is an additional call to the RTI-tick service (also defined as Evoke Callback in the HLA specifications) issued by the federate after NMR or FQR.

Independently of the optimistic or conservative nature of synchronization, the RTI offers also services to send information to remote federates. This always takes place through both TSO and RO messages. Common services for sending the information are *Update Attribute Values* (UAV), *Send Interaction* (SI) and *Delete Object Instance* (DOI), which will result in the previously described RAV, RI and ROI callbacks executed by the RTI supporting the remote federates so to deliver the information.

There are also services for retracting a previously sent message, like for example the *Retract* (R) service. This might result in the *Request Retraction* (RR) callback on remote federates in case the delivery has been already executed by the destination federates (if the delivery has not yet been executed, then R will simply result in an annihilation of the information to be delivered, which is performed internally by the RTI). These are typically used in the context of optimistic synchronization, where there is the possibility to undo previously issued message exchanges when a rollback occurs. However, it is important to note that retraction can be invoked only in case the corresponding sent message to retract is a TSO message. Instead, no retraction action can be invoked in case of a sent RO message. To support the retraction correctly, when calling whichever service causing the send of a TSO message, the service returns a federation-unique message retraction designator. The different treatment of TSO and RO messages for what concerns retraction actions is one main point for having two different message treatment policies within the TiMaC layer, as we shall de-

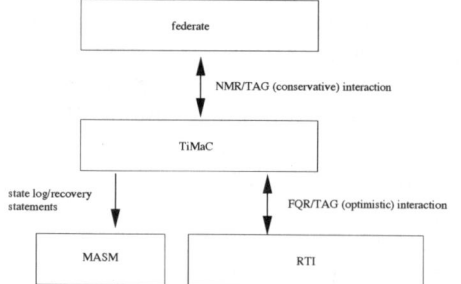

Figure 1. System Architecture with TiMaC.

tailedly discuss later.

3.2 Mapping of Conservative to Optimistic Time Management Services

The problem of how to map the Time Management interface for conservative synchronization onto the one for optimistic synchronization entails removing the need for the federate code to: (1) Log message retraction designators for sent messages (e.g. via UAV), which might be retracted in case of rollback. (2) Explicitly handle the retraction of messages upon a rollback (i.e. via R). (3) Explicitly handle retraction callbacks for previously received information (i.e. RR callbacks). (4) Explicitly log/recover state information.

As shown in Figure 1, we address this problem through the TiMaC layer by interposing it in between the federate and the RTI in order to mask to the federate all the previously listed tasks. TiMaC interacts with the conventional RTI with classical Time Management services and callbacks in support of optimistic synchronization. It also interacts with MASM so to perform checkpointing and recovery of the federate state transparently. On the other hand it exposes to the federate a conventional conservative interface based on NMR and TAG.

3.2.1 Treatment of TSO Messages

In our design, the treatment of TSO messages while mapping conservative onto optimistic Time Management services takes place by logically partitioning the simulation time into epochs. Each epoch is defined as the simulation time interval between two subsequent NMR requests issued by the federate according to the conservative Time Management interface. The following steps are executed by TiMaC during each epoch:

Step 1. Upon the NMR request with time t, TiMaC logs the federate state through the SaveState() MASM facility. Given that the local simulation clock of the federate upon the NMR request is equal to the last time granted by TiMaC to the federate, say $t' \leq t$, then the logged state is associated with such a simulation time value by TiMaC when calling SaveState(). We

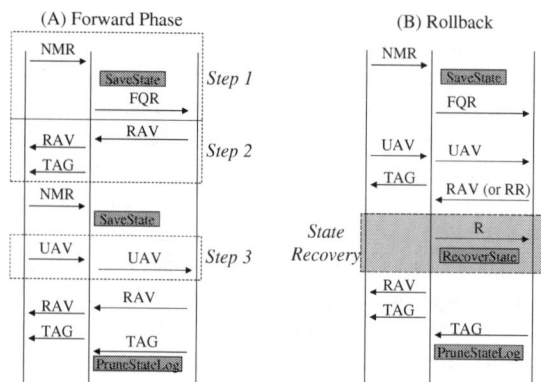

Figure 2. TiMaC Behavior During both Forward Computation and Rollback.

denote this logged state value as $log(t')$. Afterwards, TiMaC issues the FQR request to the underlying RTI ([1]), unless TiMaC itself is not in time granted state. This might occur due to the fact that the underlying RTI might have not yet delivered the TAG callback to TiMaC for an FQR call issued in a previous epoch.

Step 2. When receiving the RTI-tick call, TiMaC behaves as follows. It invokes the RTI-tick call to the underlying RTI, and buffers all the TSO messages delivered by the RTI via the appropriate callbacks. At this point it checks whether there are TSO messages with time up to t to be delivered to the federate. If there is no such a message, TiMaC grants to the federate permission to advance to time t via TAG. Otherwise it delivers to the federate all the TSO messages with the minimum time, say t'', in the interval between t' and t, and then grants the federate to advance to time t''.

Step 3. It logs the message retraction designators for all the TSO messages sent by the federate in the current epoch (through UAV, SI and DOI calls issued towards TiMaC). Each message is also really sent by TiMaC to the destination federate by issuing the corresponding UAV, SI and DOI calls to the underlying RTI.

An example of the steps performed by TiMaC is shown in Figure 2.A (RTI-tick invocations are omitted for simplicity). One important point deriving from such a structuring of TiMaC is that we have decoupled time advancement grants (i.e. TAG callbacks) coming from the underlying RTI, from time advancement grants delivered by TiMaC

---

[1]The simulation time associated with FQR is selected as the minimum among the time associated with NMR and the time of both incoming and outgoing messages not yet committed. This is done in order not to violate Time Management constraints related to HLA specifications for optimistic synchronization.

to the federate. Hence, TAG callbacks are delivered to the federate with speed independent of the speed of TAG callbacks issued by the underlying RTI. This also allows the TAG rate seen by the federate to be independent of the latency of the algorithm implemented within the underlying RTI for supporting the TAG service.

By the previous organization, it is clear that TiMaC issues the TAG callback to the federate in **Step 2** even if it is not safe to advance to the granted time. In fact, it is possible that new messages which must be delivered to the federate will arrive in the future with time in the interval $[t', t]$. If this really occurs, then a causality violation has occurred while managing TSO messages on that federate. Also, it is possible that the underlying RTI issues a RR callback to TiMaC for annihilating a message that has been delivered to TiMaC in reply to a FQR call. If TiMaC has already delivered that message to the federate during the execution of **Step 2** of whichever epoch, then there is again a causality violation on TSO messages that needs to be recovered.

On the basis of the previous observations, TiMaC recovers causality violations according to the following scheme. When the violation is detected, the simulation time for the violation is determined, say $t_{violation}$. Then the following two recovery actions are executed by TiMaC:

Recovery-Action A. All the TSO messages sent by the federate during the epoch associated with the interval containing $t_{violation}$ and during any subsequent epoch are undone. This is done by TiMaC through R calls issued to the underlying RTI, one for each retraction designator of a message logged by TiMaC (see **Step 3**) during the epochs to be undone.

Recovery-Action B. The federate state is recovered to the last logged value with simulation time $t_{recovery} \leq t_{violation}$, namely $log(t_{recovery})$. This is done through the RecoverState() MASM facility.

One example of such a behavior is shown in Figure 2.B (also in this case RTI-tick calls are omitted for simplicity), where, in case of arrival of a RAV (or RR) causing a rollback, TiMaC undoes incorrect outgoing TSO messages via R, recovers the federate state and then delivers a pending TSO message, if any, in correct order by RAV. By the previous rollback scheme, the federate state is always recovered at the point of an NMR call to the TiMaC layer. This means that, upon state recovery, the federate automatically re-starts from the epoch with initial time $t_{recovery}$. As a consequence, after having performed the state recovery phase through the **Recovery-Action B**, TiMaC skips execution of **Step 1** and immediately goes on executing **Step 2** and **Step 3** for that epoch. In other words, **Step 1** is not executed since the state log for the current epoch, i.e. $log(t_{recovery})$, is already available and has been just used for recovery purposes.

3.2.2 Treatment of RO Messages

The main problem when dealing with the treatment of RO messages in the context of transparent optimistic synchronization via TiMaC is that RO messages have no retraction designator associated with them. Hence, once sent, an RO message has no way to be undone. Concerning this point the treatment of RO messages performed by TiMaC is based on the following distinction of application level software into two different types for what concerns the awareness about interactions associated with RO messages:

RO-Awareness. We say that a federate is RO-aware in case its data structures keep track of issued interactions associated with RO messages. As an example, a federate which just maintains a counter of issued interactions associated with RO sent messages is a simple instance of RO-aware federate.

RO-Unawareness. We say that a federate is RO-unaware in case it keeps no data structure recording information about issued interactions associated with RO messages. (Trivially, a federate which issues only TSO messages is within the RO-unaware class.)

For an RO-unaware conservative federate, state recovery actions transparently performed by TiMaC through MASM facilities do not alter the consistency of state information with respect to issued interactions associated with RO messages. Instead, in case of an RO-aware conservative federate, a transparent state recovery operation might yield to the situation in which the federate state loses knowledge about already issued interactions associated with RO messages. Given that, in general, we cannot assume those same interactions are replied by the federate when the computation resumes after the rollback, then the situation might arise in which some RO messages have been sent, but are not anymore (and will not eventually be) registered as sent by the federate. This problem does not appear in the context of optimistic federates since they perform state recovery operations acting on the so called "state vector" (i.e. the data structure explicitly representing the federate state at a given simulation time), instead, TiMaC performs state recovery through MASM acting on the whole memory image portion associated with the federate (hence not only the state vector is rolled back, but all the application level data structures). To address this problem, TiMaC supports the following two different policies for the treatment of RO messages, dealing with the case of RO-unawareness and RO-awareness, respectively:

Immediate-Forward Policy. Upon the receipt of an interaction (RAV, SI and DOI) from an overlying RO-unaware federate during whichever epoch, TiMaC simply issues (forwards) that same interaction to the underlying RTI.

Delay-Until-Commit Policy. Interactions issued by an overlying RO-aware federate during whichever epoch are kept pending by TiMaC until that epoch gets committed. This happens when the TAG provided by the underlying RTI grants simulation time advancement beyond the upper limit of that epoch. When this happens, the pending interactions are issued to the underlying RTI. On the other hand, if an epoch is rolled back (i.e. it does not eventually get committed) the pending interactions associated with RO messages issued during that epoch are simply cancelled by TiMaC.

By using the Delay-Until-Commit policy, there will never be an interaction associated with RO-messages which, due to rollback, will eventually not be recorded as issued by an RO-aware federate. On the other hand, this policy has the effect of delaying the real send operation of RO messages. However, this does not contrast with the HLA specification [10] since no explicit indication on the timeliness according to which RO messages need to be handled by the RTI is provided. In the current TiMaC implementation, the selection of one or the other policy takes place by appropriately selecting a parameter value which indicates to TiMaC whether the overlying federate is RO-aware or RO-unaware. Note that the Delay-Until-Commit policy is safe with both RO-aware and RO-unaware federates, thus care has been taken to select this policy as the default one. Finally, the effects of transparent state recovery supported by TiMaC need to be considered also for what concerns received interactions associated with RO messages. Specifically, given that a state recovery procedure for the federate executed by TiMaC via **Recovery-Action B** through `RecoverState()` also undoes the delivery of interactions (i.e. RAV, RI and ROI) associated with RO messages (starting from those delivered to the federate during the epoch associated with the interval containing $t_{violation}$ and then going through any subsequent epoch), the TiMaC layer also keeps incoming RO messages buffered for re-delivery after a rollback. These messages are then discarded, together with other logged information, once the epochs within which they have been delivered get committed.

3.2.3 Effects of TiMaC on the Interaction between Time Management and other RTI Services

By taking a wider view, we observe that the same problem associated with the treatment of RO messages appears also when considering other RTI services, such as Federation Management or Declaration Management services. Specifically, RTI specifications do not offer any way to undo an already issued request to these services. Hence, TiMaC cannot undo such requests while supporting transparent rollback of a conservative federate.

This issue does not represent a concern for federates that invoke these types of RTI services only during the federation setup phase (as it often happens). In such a case, invocations to these services occur only before any synchronization action associated with Time Management takes place. However to cope with federates which use these types of services during simulation progress, a Delay-Until-Commit like policy needs to be supported. Specifically, calls to these RTI services need to be intercepted and the corresponding invocations to the underlying RTI should be forwarded only when the corresponding epoch gets committed. We are currently working on an extension of TiMaC implementation in order to support such an intercept operation.

Anyway, a peculiar case of a Federation Management service that is currently intercepted by TiMaC is the *Resign Federation Execution* service, which the federate must invoke when terminating its interaction with the rest of the federation. A federate synchronized using TiMaC may believe that its computation is complete (having received the final TAG) and invoke the Resign Federation Execution. Yet its computation might not be over, since the underlying TiMaC may not have yet received the final TAG from the RTI. Therefore the Resign Federation Execution service is intercepted by TiMaC which keeps control until the underlying RTI delivers to it the final TAG. Only after TiMaC has received that TAG, the Resign Federation Execution service can be forwarded to the underlying RTI and control can be returned to the federate.

3.3 Some Implementation Details

Although the previously outlined TiMaC design is independent of the specific underlying RTI, based on such a design we have developed an implementation tailored to the Georgia Tech B-RTI package [7].

Using the types defined within the B-RTI package, our implementation of TiMaC relies on a data structure consisting of a double linked list of records, each one structured as in Figure 3 and keeping track of information associated with a given epoch. The two fields of type `struct RO_msgs*` keep track of additional lists of incoming, respectively outgoing, RO messages delivered to, respectively sent by, the application during that epoch. The `outgoing_RO_message` list is used for temporarily buffering outgoing RO messages in case the Delay-Until-Commit policy is employed. These messages are flushed towards the underlying RTI when the corresponding epoch is committed. On the other hand, the `incoming_RO_message` list is used for re-delivery of RO messages in case the epoch in which they were originally delivered is rolled back. Care is taken to maintain the receive order for RO messages while re-delivering them. Finally, the `struct TSO_EventRetractionHandle *TSO_EventRetractionList` field keeps track of the list of all the retraction designators associated with TSO

```
struct epoch_entry{
TM_Time epoch_start_time;
TM_Time epoch_end_time;
struct TSO_EventRetractionHandle *TSO_EventRetractionList;
struct RO_msgs *incoming_RO_message;
struct RO_msgs *outgoing_RO_message;
}
```

Figure 3. Data Structure for the Double Linked List of Epoch Information Records.

messages sent during the epoch. These are used by TiMaC in a rollback phase while invoking the R service to the underlying RTI. Each retraction designator is obtained and recorded by TiMaC into that list when a call to the B-RTI function `RTI_UpdateAttributeValues()` is issued on behalf of the overlying federate. As a final observation, TiMaC handles additional lists of entries of type `struct MsgS` which are used to temporarily buffer both pending RO and TSO messages. Association between TSO messages and epochs is done on the basis of timestamps.

4 Experimental Evaluation

In this section we report the results of an experimental evaluation of TiMaC. The evaluation has been focused on the comparison of the run-time behaviors of a federation synchronized via the conservative approach, and of that same federation synchronized optimistically via the transparent approach supported by TiMaC.

Actually, the main factor affecting both previous configurations is the communication latency between distinct federates. For conservative synchronization, that latency affects the timeliness in the preventive detection of event safety. As also recently discussed in [12], this detection results in a distributed reduction to be performed by the RTI, whose completion time depends on the timely delivery of messages. On the other hand, for optimistic synchronization the communication latency between federates may affect the rollback pattern, which, in its turn, may affect the speed of simulation time commitment. For these reasons, we have decided to parameterize the performance study vs the Round-Trip-Time (RTT) among different federates within the federation, so to draw conclusions on the effects of TiMaC while emulating underlying computing systems ranging from, e.g., LAN based to WAN based ones. In order to parameterize the performance study vs the RTT, we have developed an application level TCP forwarder (TCP-F) towards which all the messages sent by an instance of B-RTI are redirected. Each time data are received by TCP-F, this module forwards the data to the correct destination after a delay which models the RTT in between the two communication end-points.

In the experimental study we have used the portable (application level based) version of MASM presented in [15]. We have also used the same application level simulation code used in that study for the evaluation of MASM overhead in forward computation when employed in a stand alone federate scenario. This code simulates a Personal Communication System (PCS) with fixed base stations offering communication services to mobile devices and performing power regulation based on the Signal-to-Interference Ratio (SIR) evaluated considering cross channel interference within a same cell [11].

The experiments have been conducted on a self-federation of this simulation code, realized by having three different instances of that same PCS simulator organized in a coverage area of three groups of cells. These have been supported by two machines with 2GHz Xeon CPU - 4 GB of RAM, and a machine with 2.4GHz Pentium 4 CPU - 2 GB of RAM, interconnected via a 100 Mb switched Ethernet LAN. To examine the effects of TiMaC on different model sizes, we have considered two configurations, namely a larger one in which each federate simulates a group of 1024 hexagonal micro-cells, and a smaller one in which each federate simulates a group of only 256 micro-cells. For both configurations, each cell manages 100 channels. The movement of mobile devices follows a classical random walk model [1] with cell switch time exponentially distributed with mean 5 minutes, and the average call holding time has been set to 2 minutes. Each federate includes the modules for pseudo-random generation of the call arrival within the corresponding group of cells so that the interaction between different federates takes place only in case of hand-off occurrence for a mobile involved in an ongoing call, which switches between cells in different groups. The threshold SIR to be achieved by power regulation at the start of a call has been set at about 10 DB, similarly to what happens in standard GSM transmission, and the inter-arrival time of calls per each cell follows an exponential distribution [2, 4, 5] with mean value selected to achieve channel utilization factor of about 60%.

Figure 4 reports the execution speed of the simulation, evaluated in terms of simulated time units per wall-clock time unit, for the two different investigated configurations (i.e. conservative synchronization and optimistic synchronization via TiMaC), while varying the RTT among the different federates up to 200 milliseconds. Each reported value is the average of a number of samples that ensures a confidence interval of 10% around the mean at the 95% confidence level. Actually, RTT set to 0 in the plots does not mean that communication is instantaneous, it only means that TCP-F (i.e. artificial network delay) is excluded. By the results, we observe that, for large model size, the execution with optimistic synchronization via TiMaC exhibits speed between 60% and 108% better than the speed observed with conservative synchronization, with gain that increases vs the RTT among the different federate instances. Similar re-

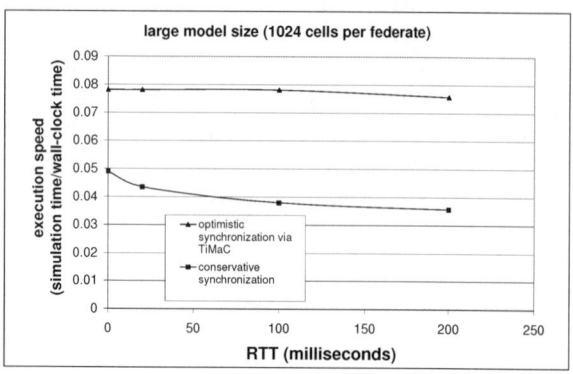
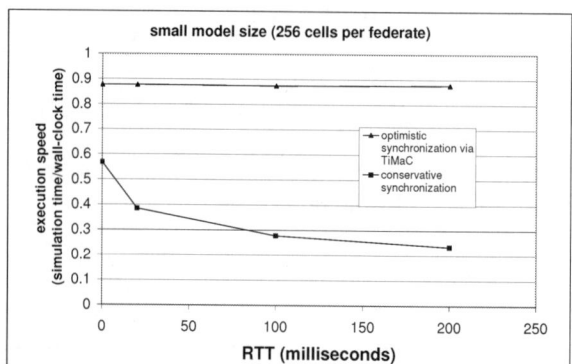

Figure 4. Execution Speed Results.

sults are obtained for the smaller model size configuration, where the execution with TiMaC provides speed between 53% and 270% better than conservative synchronization. Additionally, and perhaps even more important, optimistic synchronization via TiMaC allows flat execution speed vs the RTT for both model sizes, which is not achieved with conservative synchronization. This is a manifestation of a classical phenomenon associated with the relation between communication latency and the behavior of the two different synchronization approaches. Specifically, while the increase of RTT has a sure impact on the detection of event safety in case of conservative synchronization, it does not surely affect the rollback pattern in optimistic synchronization. More precisely, increase in the communication delay has the potential to affect the rollback pattern [3], but this does not always occur in practice, which is one reason for preferring optimistic synchronization in a large amount of contexts for what concerns the underlying computing platform. This preference can be supported by TiMaC to definitely accelerate the execution speed of the simulation in case we employ any kind of conservative federate in such contexts.

References

[1] I. F. Akyildiz, Y. B. Lin, W. R. Lai, and R. J. Chen. A new random walk model for PCS networks. *IEEE Journal on Selected Areas in Communications*, 18(7):1254–1260, 2000.

[2] A. Boukerche, S. K. Das, A. Fabbri, and O. Yildz. Exploiting model independence for parallel PCS network simulation. In *Proceedings of the 13th Workshop on Parallel and Distributed Simulation*, pages 166–173. IEEE Computer Society, May 1999.

[3] C. D. Carothers, R. M. Fujimoto, and P. England. Effects of communication overhead on Time Warp performance. In *Proceedings of the 8th Workshop on Parallel and Distributed Simulation*, pages 118–125. IEEE Computer Society, 1994.

[4] C. D. Carothers, R. M. Fujimoto, P. England, and Y. B. Lin. Distributed simulation of large-scale PCS networks. In *Proceedings of the 2nd IEEE International Workshop on Modeling, Analysis, and Simulation of Computer and Telecommunication Systems*, pages 2–6. IEEE Computer Society, 1994.

[5] C. D. Carothers, R. M. Fujimoto, and Y. B. Lin. A case study in simulating PCS networks using Time Warp. In *Proceedings of the 9th Workshop on Parallel and Distributed Simulation*, pages 87–94. IEEE Computer Society, June 1995.

[6] DMSO. Runtime Infrastructure (RTI). *https://www.dmso.mil/public/transition/hla/rti*, 2004.

[7] R. M. Fujimoto, T. McLean, K. S. Perumalla, and I. Tacic. Design of high performance RTI software. In *Proceedings of the 4th International Workshop on Distributed Simulation and Real-Time Applications*, pages 89–96. IEEE Computer Society, 2000.

[8] Georgia Tech Research Corporation. FDK - Federated Simulations Development Kit. *http://www.cc.gatech.edu/computing/pads/fdk/*, 2003.

[9] IEEE Std 1516-2000 (2000). IEEE Standard for Modeling and Simulation (M&S) High Level Architecture (HLA) – Framework and Rules. New York, NY, Institute of Electrical and Electronics Engineers, Inc.

[10] IEEE Std 1516.1-2000 (2000). IEEE Standard for Modeling and Simulation (M&S) High Level Architecture (HLA) – Federate Interface (FI) Specification. New York, NY, Institute of Electrical and Electronics Engineers, Inc.

[11] S. Kandukuri and S. Boyd. Optimal power control in interference-limited fading wireless channels with outage-probability specifications. *IEEE Transactions on Wireless Communications*, 1(1):46–55, 2002.

[12] T. McLean and R. M. Fujimoto. Predictable time management for real-time distributed simulation. In *Proceedings of the 17th Workshop on Parallel and Distributed Simulation*, pages 89–96. IEEE Computer Society, 2003.

[13] J. Plank, M. Beck, and G. Kingsley. Libckpt: Transparent checkpointing under UNIX. In *Proceedings of USENIX Winter Technical Conference*, pages 213–223. USENIX Association, 1995.

[14] A. Santoro and F. Quaglia. Transparent state management for optimistic synchronization in the High Level Architecture. In *Proceedings of the 19th Workshop on Principles of Advanced and Distributed Simulation*, pages 171–180. IEEE Computer Society, 2005.

[15] A. Santoro and F. Quaglia. A version of MASM portable across different UNIX systems and different hardware architectures. In *Proceedings of the 9th International Symposium on Distributed Simulation and Real Time Applications*. IEEE Computer Society, 2005.

[16] Virtual Technology Corporation. RTI NG Pro^{TM} version 2.0.2. *http://www.virtc.com/Products/prdFulltext.jsp?ID=1z_RTI*, 2004.

COTS Simulation Package (CSP) Interoperability – A Solution to Synchronous Entity Passing

Xiaoguang Wang   Stephen John Turner
School of Computer Engineering, Nanyang Technological University
Singapore 639798
xgwang@pmail.ntu.edu.sg   assjturne@ntu.edu.sg

Simon J E Taylor
School of Information Systems, Computing and Maths, Brunel University
Uxbridge, UB8 3PH UK
Simon.Taylor@brunel.ac.uk

Abstract

In this paper we examine Commercial-Off-The-Shelf (COTS) Simulation Package (CSP) interoperability for one type of distributed simulation problem, namely synchronous entity passing. Synchronous entity passing is also referred to as the bounded buffer interoperability reference model. It deals with the case where for entities passed between models the receiving queue is bounded or the receiving workstation has limited capacity. This means the sending model must check the status of the receiving model before it can send entities. Correspondingly, the receiving model should update the status information dynamically when it changes. Similar to the work done on asynchronous entity passing, the High Level Architecture is chosen as the underlying standard to support reuse and interoperability. To simplify the integration of the CSP and the HLA, a middleware layer called DSManager is provided. Some new problems generated for synchronous entity passing are discussed and solutions are proposed together with a description of their implementation. Two sets of experiments are conducted to evaluate the solutions using a CSP Emulator (CSPE) which supports both standalone and distributed simulation.

1. Introduction

Commercial-Off-The-Shelf (COTS) Simulation Package (CSP) interoperability aims to enable distributed simulation by linking multiple simulation components built using appropriate CSPs (possibly from different companies, even in geographically dispersed locations). A CSP supports the creation of a discrete event simulation model using some kind of visual interactive modeling interface. Examples of CSPs include: Simul8, Witness, Arena and ProModel. The advent of the High Level Architecture [1] makes it possible to link together these CSPs. The HLA standard was originally developed by the U.S. Department of Defense (DoD) and later adopted as an IEEE standard to facilitate interoperability and reusability. It provides a common technical framework for the interoperability of simulation models.

In 2005, the CSPI-PDG (COTS Simulation Package Interoperability - Product Development Group) [2] was approved by the Simulation Interoperability Standards Organization (SISO). Previously known as the HLA CSPI Forum, it is dedicated to creating a standardized approach to support the interoperation of discrete event models created in CSPs using the IEEE 1516 High Level Architecture. The Interoperability Reference Models (IRMs) are one set of products produced by the CSPI-PDG. The aim of the IRMs is to categorize the integration problem into different requirements, thereby providing an easy way to create solutions for each specific integration problem. There are six IRMs currently identified by the CSPI-PDG.

Based on previous work [3] to successfully link some of the CSPs with the HLA, a generic architecture [4] was proposed for CSP interoperability using middleware named DSManager that adopts an implicit approach from the modeler's point of view. While the explicit approach needs the modeler (those who develop the model using the CSP) to enhance the model with HLA functionality, the implicit approach means all HLA functionality is hidden from the modeler since the CSP and its underlying middleware handle all the HLA synchronization and communication. Obviously, the implicit approach makes it easier for the modeler to link simulation models together. In this way, the modeler only needs to focus on designing the model components without intervention due to the need of interoperability.

However, currently CSPs are heterogeneous in terms of their properties and extensibility, and different CSPs have different degrees of capabilities for their external interfaces. This makes it extremely difficult to find a general approach for the integration. To solve this problem, a CSP Emulator (CSPE) [5] was designed to emulate the functionality and interface to a CSP and this can be used to investigate and compare various interoperability approaches. Based on the CSPE, the requirements for the integration of CSPs and the HLA were investigated and interfaces were proposed for asynchronous entity passing, the Type I Interoperability Reference Model (IRM) [6].

While asynchronous entity passing focuses on the general problem of entity representation specification, synchronous entity passing (CSPI-PDG Type II IRM) represents another more complicated type of model. In the Type II IRM, the sending model may transfer entities into a bounded queue or a workstation with limited capacity in the receiving model. Thus, entities can be transferred only when the sending model is sure that the destination side is not full (queue) or blocked (workstation). This introduces a synchronous feature into the model, which can be solved by exchanging status information dynamically between the models.

In addition, another problem arises from the existence of inter-model simultaneous events. For example, entities of the same type from different models may need to be sent into the same bounded queue in the receiving model. If there is only space for one entity available, only one model can successfully transfer one such entity and all other such entities need to wait for new space to be available. Different orderings of these inter-model simultaneous events may generate dramatically different simulation results. Usually, the tie is broken by allowing the modelers to specify different priorities for each entry point through which the entity will be transferred into the local model. However, it is possible one entry point may have multiple priorities and the priority may be changed dynamically due to some simulation activities. This requires the priority information to be updated and exchanged at run time. In many simulation systems, the priority is represented by adding a hidden field to the simulation time. In this paper, we state the new problems introduced by synchronous entity passing and describe the solutions and their implementation using the DSManager and two hidden fields appended to the simulation time. To verify the solutions, several sets of experiments are conducted using some typical Type II IRMs.

The rest of this paper is organized as follows: Section 2 discusses related work in CSP interoperability as well as the simultaneous events problem. The special problems of synchronous entity passing are stated in Section 3 and solutions are provided in Section 4. Section 5 describes some issues in implementing the solutions. To evaluate the proposed solutions, several sets of experiments are conducted and discussed in section 6. Conclusions and future work are presented in Section 7.

2. Related work

2.1. CSPI Emulator (CSPE) and DSManager

As one part of the suite of CSPI-PDG standards, the CSP Emulator (CSPE) is intended to emulate the functionality and interface to a CSP. It supports the creation of a standalone model or a model component that is part of a distributed simulation. Based on the CSPE, various interoperability approaches can be investigated and compared. Another benefit of the CSPE is to provide a suggestion how current CSPs may add HLA capability to support distributed simulation.

The CSP or CSPE integrates with the HLA through a generic interface called DSManager. The interface consists of a set of functions to be invoked by the CSP or CSPE when necessary. The C++ / Java based HLA RunTime Infrastructure (RTI) is wrapped by "normal" C functions, that can easily be integrated with most of the current CSPs written in C, C++, Java or VB. Another important feature of the DSManager is to try to hide the HLA concept from both the CSP and the model. It is difficult to match model information represented in the CSPs to the object/interaction concept in the HLA standard. In addition, the terminology between different CSPs differs as there is no internationally recognized naming convention. The interface adopts a generic approach based on the concept of entity transfer, and will be proposed as a standard by the CSPI-PDG in the future.

Based on the CSPE, the requirements for integration of CSPs and the HLA were investigated and interfaces were proposed for the Type I IRM. In this paper, with new features added into the DSManager and the CSPE, the Type II IRM synchronous entity passing is investigated and the solutions are evaluated.

2.2. Simultaneous events problem

In a discrete event simulation, the events are timestamped and executed in increasing order to ensure causality. It is possible two or more events are scheduled at exactly the same simulation time, or at a slightly different simulation time but below the level of the machine precision. These events are considered as simultaneous events. Different orderings of the simultaneous events may generate different simulation results, which may conflict with the requirement of repeatable execution of the simulation programs. Repeatability means the execution of the simulation should produce exactly the same results on each execution when using the same initial state and external inputs.

Much work has been proposed to solve this problem [7]. Usually the solution is to execute these events in an arbitrary order unless the modeler explicitly specifies some tie-breaking technique, for example, FIFO (first-in, first-out), LIFO (last-in, first-out), or dependency order. Some tie-breaking mechanisms can be implemented by extending the timestamp to include additional, lower-precision bits that are hidden from the application program [8]. With different values to these bits, the simulation engine can ensure no two events in the simulation contain exactly the same timestamp. The values could be assigned based on the specified tie-breaking techniques to satisfy the simulation modeler's requirements.

3. Problems of synchronous entity passing

The Type II IRM synchronous entity passing deals with the case where a receiving queue is *bounded* or the receiving workstation has *limited* capacity. An example is shown in Figure 3.1, where the distributed simulation (federation) is composed of two factory models (federates), M_1 and M_2, interacting in the way denoted by the arrows. Each model consists of an entry point En_i, a queue Q_i, a workstation W_i, a resource R_i, and an exit point Ex_i (where i is the model identifier). After being processed in W_1, entities need to be sent periodically via Ex_1 and then entry point En_2 into a bounded queue Q_2 (or a workstation with limited capacity) in M_2. It indicates the requirement that M_1 containing the sending workstation W_1 must, when the processing of an entity is complete, check to determine that there is space in Q_2. If there is space available then the entity may be transferred. Otherwise M_1 must ensure that W_1 is blocked until space becomes available. In this paper, we call the entry point designed to receive entities from external models 'external entry point' and give it the abbreviation of 'EEP'. On the sending side, the EEP in the receiving model is referred to as the remote EEP, and on the receiving side the EEP is referred to as the local EEP.

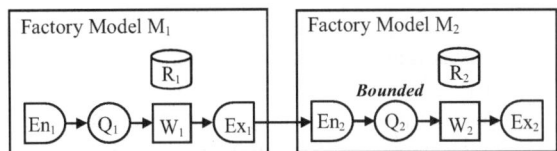

Figure 3.1: Synchronous entity passing

3.1. Status information

As discussed above, it is essential to update the status information of a bounded queue or a workstation with limited capacity in synchronous entity passing. Different from simply updating the status information in a standalone simulation, the status information should also be transferred between the models. In Figure 3.1, when Q_2 becomes full, a message with a small increment to the current simulation time is sent back to M_1, which causes M_1 to block. The small increment is added because the status event is dependent on the entity sending event from M_1. At some later simulation time, when the entity is processed in workstation W_2, M_2 clears a slot in Q_2 and sends another message with a small increment to the current simulation time to M_1, which allows new entities to be transferred.

Due to the complexity of distributed simulation scenarios, the status information may not be updated in time to external models. One case is for inter-model simultaneous events. For example, two models may want to send entities to the same remote EEP at the same simulation time. In the situation where there is only space available to receive one entity, the status of the remote EEP cannot be shown as idle for both sending models. Another case is for passing more than one entity with the same simulation time to the same remote EEP from the same sending model. Suppose two entities from M_1 are waiting to be transferred into M_2 via En_2. After receiving the first entity at time t, it is possible En_2 becomes blocked and the status information of 'blocked' will be transferred to the DSManager in M_1 a short time later at $t+\delta$ (δ is the small increment due to the dependency order). However, M_1 is trying to send the second entity at t since the new status information can only be received at $t+\delta$. Therefore, even though the receiving model has already updated the status of En_2 as 'blocked' or 'idle' based on local information, the status of the remote EEP may be uncertain for the DSManager in the sending model. The possible status of a remote EEP specified by the DSManager in the sending model can be summarized as follows.

0: idle and it is safe for the sending model to send an entity
1: blocked
-1: uncertain since there are possibly some other entities sent from other models to this remote EEP at the same simulation time
-2: uncertain since the entity just sent from the local model may cause the remote EEP to be blocked

To avoid the need for the CSP to handle the uncertain status information (the status of a remote EEP known by the CSP is only 'idle' or 'blocked'), the DSManager should update the status automatically and forward 'blocked' to the sending model when the status is uncertain ('-1' or '-2'). After the DSManager is sure it is safe to send an entity from the sending model, 'idle' will be returned instead.

3.2. Inter-model simultaneous events

In a standalone simulation, it is relatively easy to order the simultaneous events in the local event list based on some tie-breaking mechanisms. In distributed simulation, however, there may exist some simultaneous events transferred between different model components. In the example discussed in section 3.1, two models may want to send entities to the same remote EEP at exactly the same simulation time. These simultaneous events are generated in different models but interleave with each other, referred to as inter-model simultaneous events.

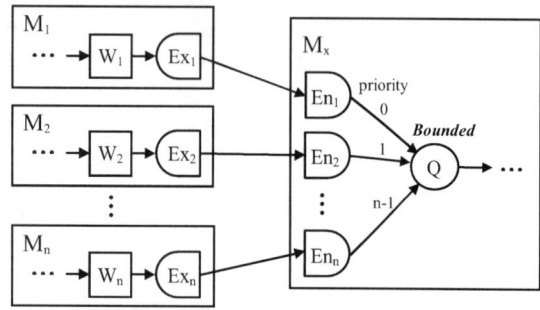

Figure 3.2: Inter-model simultaneous events to external entry point with single priority

Usually, the modeler will assign a priority to order the entities from different sending models. For those cases where no priority is explicitly specified, the DSManager will order them in an arbitrary order. Here our discussion is based on the assumption that the priority is already assigned for each local EEP.

In figure 3.2, Model M_i (i = 1, ... , n) generates entities in workstation W_i, and sends them periodically via Ex_i and En_i to a bounded queue Q in Model M_x. In M_x, each local EEP En_i is assigned a different priority for accessing Q. It is possible two or more inter-model simultaneous events exist to transfer entities to Q. In a standalone simulation these entities can be ordered in the event list waiting to be processed. In distributed simulation the entities from each sending model can be transferred to M_x only when the sending model makes sure there is space available in Q and no entities from other sending models with higher priority need to be transferred to the same queue.

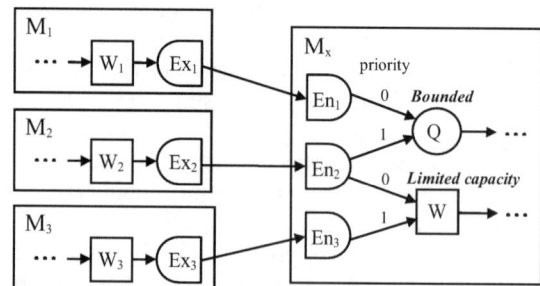

Figure 3.3: Inter-model simultaneous events to external entry point with multiple priorities

Another case is shown in Figure 3.3. The entities may be scheduled with different priorities into multiple queues or workstations via the same local EEP. That means each local EEP is associated with multiple priorities. Therefore, in addition to status information, the priority information should also be updated dynamically based on the simulation activities.

4. Solutions to synchronous entity passing

To address the new problems introduced by synchronous entity passing, solutions are proposed including extending the DSManager and introducing two hidden fields in the timestamp representation.

4.1. Extension to DSManager

Our solution to CSP interoperability is based on a generic interface and associated middleware named DSManager which wraps the HLA synchronization and communication, and provides a set of functions for entity transfer. It provides the necessary functionality used by the CSP simulation engine to support distributed simulation during the whole simulation life cycle.

As discussed in section 3.1, the status information in the Type II IRM is transferred with the timestamp of the current simulation time plus a small increment, considered as a NZL (near zero lookahead) message [9]. Lookahead represents a guarantee from a federate (model) that it will not generate any external message with a timestamp smaller than its current time plus the value of the lookahead. It is critical for conservative synchronization to achieve better performance. In the

Type II IRM, however, the lookahead value has to be set to near zero due to the status information. The DSManager will collect information from the model and automatically set the lookahead value. The CSP needs to tell the interface whether each local EEP is restricted or not. Here 'restricted' means the local EEP may be blocked as it is linked to a bounded queue or a workstation with limited capacity. If any one of the local EEPs is restricted, the DSManager has to set the lookahead as near zero. Otherwise, a larger lookahead may be adopted based on the scenario of the model itself.

Other new functions need be provided to allow the model to update and check status information. In the model which will receive entities from an external model, it must set the status of the local EEP each time it changes. When necessary, it also associates the priority information with the status since it is possible the local EEP has different priorities when it sends entities to different queues or workstations. The local DSManager will transfer such information to the DSManager for the sending model. Before the sending model transfers entities, it will invoke the necessary function to check the status of the appropriate remote EEP. As discussed in section 3.1, to hide the complicated implementation details from the CSP and the model, the status returned by the DSManager is only idle or blocked.

4.2. Hidden fields in timestamp representation

4.2.1. Purposes of hidden fields.
Hidden fields in the timestamp can be used to solve the problems of simultaneous events. In the DSManager designed for the Type II IRM, we utilize hidden fields for three purposes.

The first purpose of the hidden fields is to represent the small increment to the simulation time for status information. Different CSPs may have different time units and machine precisions in simulation execution. It is difficult to select a suitable value as the smallest time increment. By appending a hidden field of integer type to the simulation time, it can ensure the small increment will not conflict with the timestamp of any event scheduled by the model since the hidden field is transparent to the model layer.

Another purpose of the hidden fields is to contain priority information to order the inter-model simultaneous events. The lower the priority, the larger the value of the hidden field. In this way, the events with higher priority will be associated with a smaller timestamp and will be processed earlier.

The third purpose of the hidden fields is especially for the case when the sending model needs to send more than one entity to the same remote EEP simultaneously, as discussed in section 3.1. These simultaneous events should be ordered using a hidden field in logical time.

4.2.2. Two hidden fields for synchronous entity passing.
There are two hidden fields appended to the simulation time to support synchronous entity passing: one is priority for priority value to order inter-model simultaneous events (status of '-1'), the other is age used to order those simultaneous events sent from the same source model to the same remote EEP (status of '-2'). The small increment to the simulation time for status information is also contained in the second hidden field age. Thus, the logical time is defined as (t, priority, age) where t is the simulation time shown to the model. Importantly, the first hidden field priority has precedence (assigned to more significant bits) over the second hidden field age (more sensitive). Even for the entities with the same type sent to a remote EEP with a specific priority, it is also possible to schedule simultaneous events with different values of age (the first entity sent is with age 0, the second one is with age 1, and so on). It is easier to use two hidden fields to represent the precedence relationship instead of one hidden field.

To ensure the status information is updated as soon as possible, the small increment of simulation time is added to the second hidden field, which is more sensitive than the first one. The value sent for the small increment is less than the value increased each time the model needs to send another entity to the same remote EEP. Here, we represent each age a (a is a non-negative integer 0, 1, 2, ...) as $10*a$ (0, 10, 20, ...) and use 5 (any value between 1 to 9 is acceptable) as the small increment in age for status information. Consequently, the near zero lookahead discussed previously is also set as 5 in the second hidden field since it is the smallest increment for the logical time.

Let us illustrate the hidden fields using the case in Figure 3.2. Suppose the status of Q at time t is idle. Only M_1 can directly transfer an entity to Q because the corresponding remote EEP En_1 has the priority of 0. For each other sending model M_i (i = 2, 3, ..., n) that wants to transfer the a_j^{th} (a_j = 0, 1, ...) entity at time t, the DSManager sets priority as p_i (p_i = 1, 2, ... , n-1) and age as $10*a_j$, and tries to advance time to (t, p_i, $10*a_j$). Only when the granted time is equal to the requested time and no status information of 'blocked' is received during the time advancement, is the 'idle' status returned to the model by the DSManager for M_i. If the a_j^{th} entity sent from M_i causes Q to be blocked, the new status information will be sent to all sending models at time (t, p_i, $10*a_j+5$), which stops M_i sending other entities and meanwhile allows the models, including M_{i+1} to M_n, to receive the 'blocked' signal before their requested time is granted. In this way, the entities from the sending models can be sent in the correct order as specified by the priority of the corresponding remote EEP.

5. Implementation issues

The proposed solutions are implemented in the DSManager middleware as well as the logical simulation time defined by the IEEE HLA standard.

5.1. DSManager

The DSManager provides an interface consisting of a set of functions to be invoked by the CSP when a distributed simulation is created. Through the interface, the DSManager invokes necessary calls to the RTIAmbassador on behalf of the CSP and transfers the information received from the FederateAmbassador to the CSP. The basic communication protocol between the CSP, DSManager and RTI for CSPI-PDG Type I IRM is described in [6]. Here we only discuss the new features in the interface to the CSP for Type II IRM.

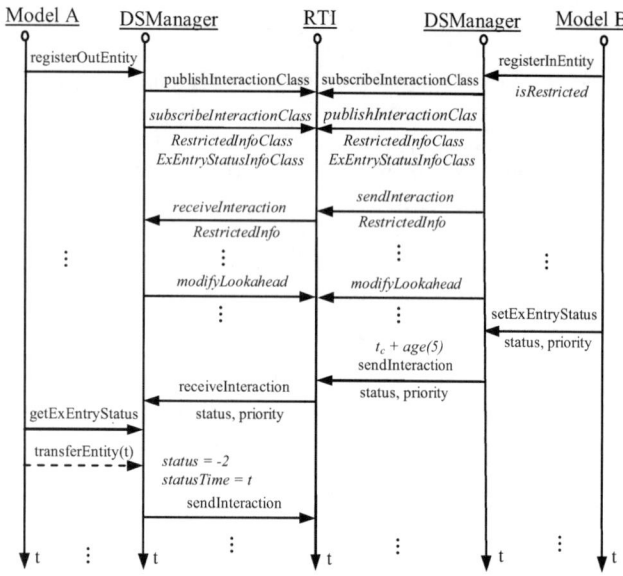

Figure 5.1 New features of interface for Type II IRM

In Figure 5.1, we use model A and model B to demonstrate the sending and receiving models respectively. Suppose model A transfers entities to a bounded queue or a workstation with limited capacity in model B. On each side, there is a DSManager used to communicate with the HLA RTI on behalf of the model.

In the initialization phase, model A and model B need to register the entity which is exchanged via *registerOutEntity* and *registerInEntity*. It should be noted that the 'isRestricted' information is also provided by each local EEP in model B. If any local EEP is restricted, the DSManager in Model B will call *modifyLookahead* to modify the lookahead value to near zero. Correspondingly, the lookahead in Model A should also be set to near zero by the DSManager in Model A. This information can be forwarded to the DSManager in model A by invoking *sendInteraction*. Before that, the DSManager on each side needs to declare the interest to send or receive such information by calling *publishInteractionClass* and *subscribeInteractionClass*. Additionally, the DSManager also automatically declares the interest to send or receive the status information as well as the priority for each EEP.

During the simulation execution, if the status of a local EEP is changed due to the simulation activities, model B will inform the DSManager by calling *setExEntryStatus* with the new status ('idle' or 'blocked') and current priority. Instead of increasing the time at the model level, the hidden field *age* is increased by the small increment which is transparent to the model. Then the DSManager will transfer the information to model A via *sendInteraction*.

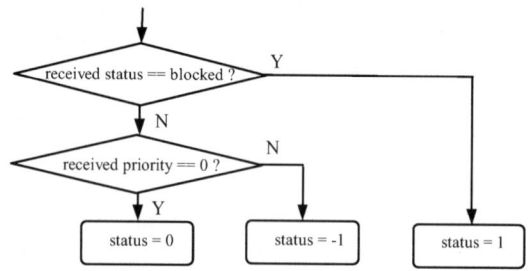

Figure 5.2: Receive ExEntryStatus procedure

In model A, the DSManager will set the status based on the received information (as shown in Figure 5.2). If the status is idle while the priority value is larger than 0, it is possible entities may be transferred to a remote EEP with a higher priority which also shares the queue or workstation with the remote EEP for this entity. In this case, the status is uncertain and has be set as '-1'. Before transferring an entity to model B, the CSP needs to check the status of the corresponding remote EEP in model B using *getExEntryStatus*. The DSManager will return 'idle' or 'blocked' after considering the simulation activities in the local model in addition to the status and priority information received from model B (as shown in Figure 5.3). After transferring an entity via *transferEntity* to model B, the DSManager in model A will locally change the status of the corresponding remote EEP to '-2' since the entity may cause the remote EEP in model B to be blocked.

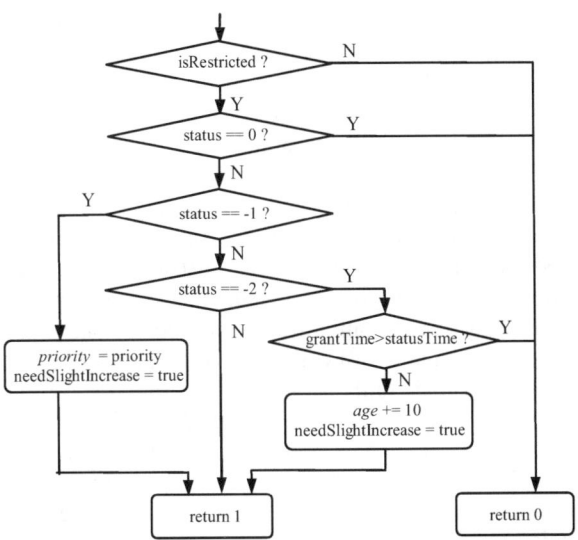

Figure 5.3: getExEntryStatus procedure

As we know, each model needs to advance time to progress the whole distributed simulation. Specifically, in the Type II IRM, the requested time forwarded to the RTI is possibly associated with a slight increase represented by the hidden fields. This may slow down the simulation if the hidden fields are added for each time request. The variable '*needSlightIncrease*' is used to identify whether it is necessary to set the hidden fields in the next request to advance time. Figure 5.3 shows that it is only set to 'true' when the hidden field needs to be appended. Another variable '*statusTime*' gives the time when the new status is updated. After sending the entity to the external model, the status is set as '-2' and the *statusTime* is updated to the current logical time. However, if the current granted time is larger than *statusTime* and the status is still '-2', this means there is no new status information of 'blocked' received from the external model. In this case, 'idle' is returned to the model. Otherwise, 'blocked' is returned since the status is still uncertain, and the hidden field age should be increased enough to see whether there is new status information received in the next request to advance time.

Figure 5.4 shows the general procedure for time advancement. Each model advances time by invoking *advanceTime* to the DSManager. In the procedure, the hidden fields may be added to the requested time (requestedTime) provided by the CSP and passed to the RTI (by calling *setHiddenField* method). After a safe time is granted from the RTI, the DSManager will clear the hidden fields and update the uncertain status information based on the granted time and received status information (if any) during the time advancement. If the granted time is equal to requested time and the status is still '-1' or '-2', the status is updated to '0' since that means no new status information of 'blocked' is received before the requested time during the time advancement. Finally, the simulation time without hidden fields (by calling *getTime* method) is returned to the model since the hidden fields are transparent to the model.

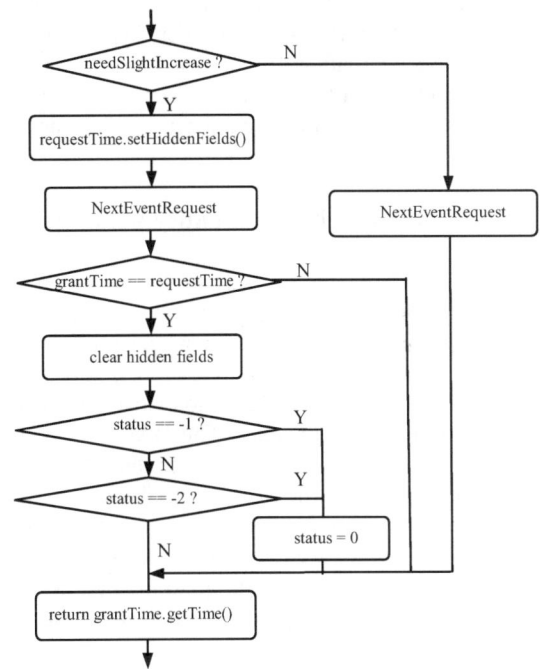

Figure 5.4: advanceTime procedure

5.2. FedTime in the RTI implementation

In the HLA standard, logical time is defined as an abstract class which allows the user to implement a version of this class for their own purposes. This provides the possibility to add the hidden fields to the *FedTime* in the RTI implementation. To extend *FedTime* with the new attributes of '*priority*' and '*age*', some supported functions are provided for operation and comparison between logical time values. For instance, for comparison using the '>' operator, suppose there are two timestamps: T_1 (t_1, $priority_1$, age_1) and T_2 (t_2, $priority_2$, age_2). If t_1 is larger than t_2, the result is 'true'; else if t_1 is equal to the t_2, the result is 'true' when $priority_1$ is also larger than $priority_2$; else if t_1 is equal to t_2 and $priority_1$ is equal to $priority_2$, the result is 'true' only when age_1 is also larger than age_2. Modifications also need to be made to the *encode* and *decode* functions in the *FedTime* class to include and exchange the hidden fields via the network.

In our implementation, the *FedTime* class provided by DMSO RTI1.3NG-V6 [10] was extended and the new generated library *libFedTime* was linked to the DSManager.

6. Experiments

Some experiments are designed to test the proposed solutions for Type II IRM synchronous entity passing. The experiments are conducted using the CSPE which is linked with the DSManager for Type II IRM. To ensure the simulation results are correct, we choose Simul8 [11], one of the popular discrete event CSPs, to run a standalone simulation for the same simulation model.

6.1. Normal synchronous entity passing model

Figure 6.1 shows a distributed and deterministic simulation for the bicycle manufacturing system [5]. It consists of three main parts: a wheel production line (WPL), a frame production line (FPL), and a bicycle assembly line (BAL) that assembles two wheels to one frame to produce a bicycle. The BAL checks wheels for faults and can return them to the WPL for re-machining (an example of valid feedback). To achieve a deterministic model for evaluation, the *Circulate* routing-out rule is used here at workstation W_{3a}. This means that the first entity will go to the first destination (exit point Ex_{3b}), the second work item to the second (queue Q_{3b}) and so on. A corresponding standalone and deterministic model is also created, where the simulation process is the same as the distributed one except that all the process is completed in one combined model named Bicycle Manufacturing System (BMS). To demonstrate the Type II IRM, the maximum length of all the queues in the model is set as 1, 10 and 100 separately for three sets of experiments.

Moreover, another set of experiments is carried out for stochastic models by introducing some probability distributions into the system. Instead of a fixed distribution, a normal distribution is used for the processing time in all workstations. For instance, the processing time of W1a is changed from *Fixed* (20) to *Normal* (20, 5) and the routing-out rule for W_{3a} is changed from *Circulate* to *Percent* (25%, 75%), which also introduces some stochastic property into the model. It is due to the fact that the destination is decided randomly based on the specified percentage going to each.

The experiments for the distributed simulation were run on four DELL 2.8GHz P4 1GB memory computers connected via a 1Gbps network. One computer was used to run the rtiexec (DMSO RTI1.3NG-V6), and the other three for three separate component models (WPL, FPL and BAL models respectively). The experiments for the standalone model were run on one of these computers.

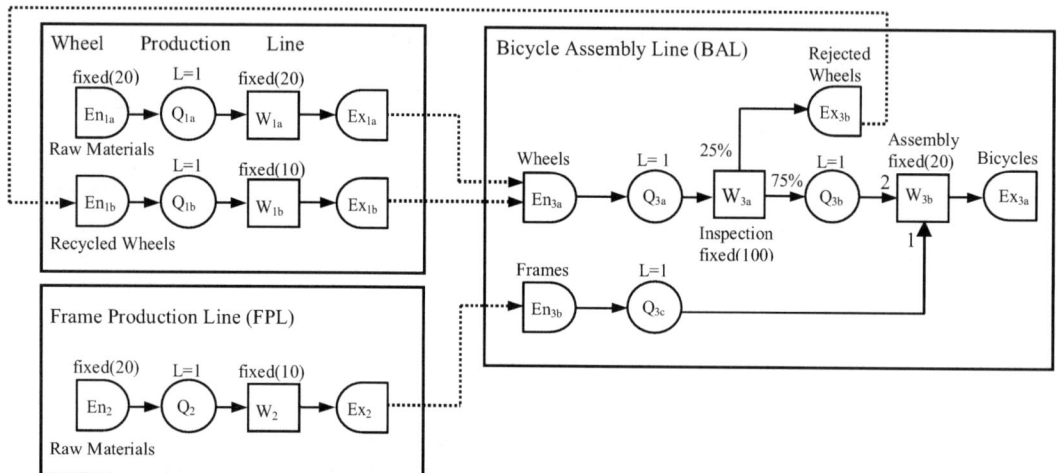

Figure 6.1: The Type II Bicycle Manufacturing System (distributed & deterministic)

Table 6.1: Experimental results for distributed and standalone simulation on CSPE and Simul8 (L=1)

		Deterministic			Stochastic		
		Simul8	CSPE(SA)	CSPE(DS)	Simul8	CSPE(SA)	CSPE(DS)
En_{1a}	Arrival Entities	5000	5000	5000	5000	5000	5000
En_2		5000	5000	5000	5000	5000	5000
En_{1a}	Refused Entities	4496	4496	4496	4843	4822	4822
En_2		4747	4747	4747	4921	4910	4910
Q_{1a}	Total Entered Entities	504	504	504	157	178	178
Q_{1b}		500	500	500	47	64	64
Q_2		253	253	253	79	90	90
Q_{3a}		1001	1001	1001	200	238	238
Q_{3b}		499	499	499	151	172	172
Q_{3c}		251	251	251	77	88	88
Q_{1a}	Queue Length at End Time	1	1	1	1	1	1
Q_{1b}		0	0	0	1	1	1
Q_2		1	1	1	1	1	1
Q_{3a}		1	1	1	1	1	1
Q_{3b}		0	0	0	0	0	0
Q_{3c}		1	1	1	1	1	1
W_{1a}	Completed Entities	503	503	503	156	177	177
W_{1b}		500	500	500	46	63	63
W_2		252	252	252	78	89	89
W_{3a}		999	999	999	199	237	237
W_{3b}		249	249	249	75	86	86
W_{1a}	Status at End Time	busy	busy	busy	busy	busy	busy
W_{1b}		busy	busy	busy	busy	busy	busy
W_2		busy	busy	busy	busy	busy	busy
W_{3a}		busy	busy	busy	busy	busy	busy
W_{3b}		busy	busy	busy	busy	busy	busy
Ex_1	Completed Entities	249	249	249	75	86	86

Table 6.1 shows the experimental results for simulating the system for 100,000 time units in Simul8, CSPE(SA) (standalone model) and CSPE(DS) (distributed simulation) with a maximum queue length of 1. The final throughput of the system as well as the statistics for each simulation object are identical for all three cases when the deterministic model is used, showing the correctness of the CSPE and successful interoperability of Type II IRMs. As for the stochastic model, CSPE(SA) and CSPE(DS) generate identical results. The results between Simul8 and CSPE are also almost identical, showing the correctness of the CSPE. The minor differences between the CSPE and Simul8 are mainly due to different ways of generating random numbers. With a queue length of 10 and 100, similar experimental results were generated (not shown here).

These results show that the CSPE integrated with the DSManager for Type II IRM can generate correct simulation statistics, indicating the status information is successfully transferred between the models. It is also interesting to investigate the overhead introduced by the new features in the DSManager in situations where the EEP is not restricted. We carried out another set of experiments using a Type I IRM, the same BMS except all the queues are unbounded. The experimental results were compared between the CSPE with DSManager for Type I IRM and the CSPE with DSManager for Type II IRM. We found the simulation results were identical and only around 2 more seconds were spent in execution time using the Type II DSManager, 36.56 seconds as compared to 34.38 seconds using the Type I DSManager. It is not a large overhead and optimization will be applied to the DSManager in the future.

6.2. External entry point with multiple priorities

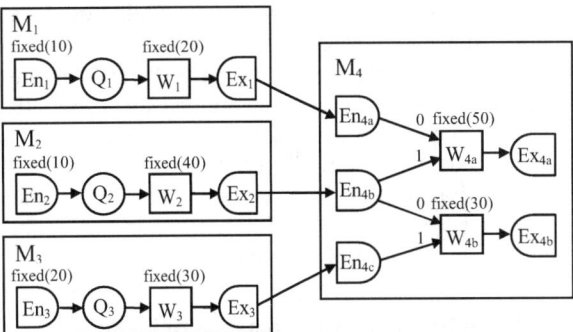

Figure 6.3: Type II IRM with external entry points having multiple priorities

Table 6.2: Experimental Results for Type II IRM with external entry points having multiple priorities

		Simul8	CSPE(SA)	CSPE(DS)
En_1	Arrival Entities	100	100	100
En_2		100	100	100
En_3		50	50	50
En_1	Refused Entities	0	0	0
En_2		0	0	0
En_3		0	0	0
Q_1	Total Entered Entities	100	100	100
Q_2		100	100	100
Q_3		50	50	50
Q_1	Queue Length at End Time	79	79	79
Q_2		83	83	83
Q_3		33	33	33
W_1	Completed Entities	21	21	21
W_2		17	17	17
W_3		16	16	16
W_{4a}		19	19	19
W_{4b}		31	31	31
W_1	Status at End Time	busy	busy	busy
W_2		busy	busy	busy
W_3		busy	busy	busy
W_{4a}		busy	busy	busy
W_{4b}		busy	busy	busy
Ex_{4a}	Completed Entities	19	19	19
Ex_{4b}		31	31	31

To test the Type II IRM with EEPs having multiple priorities, we create another distributed simulation consisting of 4 models M_1, M_2, M_3 and M_4. M_1, M_2 and M_3 transfer entities to two workstations with fixed capacity in M_4 via three EEPs. As is shown in Figure

6.3, En_{4b} has lower priority than En_{4a} for W_{4a}, but has higher priority than En_{4c} for W_{4b}. So it is possible the priority of En_{4b} may be changed dynamically when an entity is passed to a different workstation.

Table 6.2 shows the distributed simulation produces identical results to the standalone simulation. This proves that priority as well as status information is correctly transferred between different models. Also the inter-model simultaneous events are processed in the correct order when updating the priority dynamically.

From the above two sets of experiments, we found the CSPE integrated with the new DSManager can run both a normal Type II IRM with bounded queue and those special models with EEPs having multiple priorities. Furthermore, the new DSManager designed for Type II IRM can also be applied for Type I IRM without too much overhead. In this way, the model only needs to inform the DSManager whether each local EEP is restricted (linked with a bounded queue or a workstation with limited capacity) or not, without identifying the type of the model itself.

7. Conclusions and future work

This paper investigates the integration of CSPs for CSPI-PDG Type II IRM synchronous entity passing. We describe solutions to the new problems introduced by status information transfer and inter-model simultaneous events. The implementation was achieved by adding new features into the DSManager and extending the HLA RTI logical time with two hidden fields. Importantly, all the complicated details are transparent to the CSPs and the modelers. This allows the modelers to design their model components in a "plug & play" manner without worrying about interoperability. Several sets of experiments were conducted for Type II IRM. The simulation results were compared between standalone and distributed simulation using the CSPE, as well as standalone simulation using Simul8, showing the correctness of proposed solutions. It was also observed that the DSManager designed for Type II IRM using the modified DMSO RTI1.3NG-V6 logical time can also be applied for Type I IRM, without introducing too much additional overhead.

Future work is necessary in this area. Synchronous entity passing leads to the situation of near zero lookahead, which is the main constraint to performance in applying conservative synchronization in distributed simulation. It is worthwhile to see how optimistic synchronization could improve the performance. By integrating a rollback controller [12] into the DSManger, the modelers and CSPs can be released from the burden of the complex rollback procedure.

More work can also be done to investigate CSP interoperability for other types of IRMs. Each IRM type categorizes a particular problem and we hope the DSManager could provide a generic interface to the CSP for other types of IRMs.

References

[1] IEEE P 1516, "Standard for Modeling and Simulation (M&S) High Level Architecture (HLA)", April 2002.

[2] CSPI-PDG, www.cspi-pdg.org, viewed 28th Oct., 2005.

[3] S. Straßburger, "Distributed Simulation Based on the High Level Architecture in Civilian Application Domains", PhD Dissertation, University of Magdeburg, Germany, April, 2001.

[4] X.G. Wang, S.J. Turner, M.Y.H. Low and B.P. Gan, "A Generic Architecture for the Integration of COTS Packages with the HLA", *UK Operational Research Society Simulation Workshop*, Birmingham, UK, Mar. 23-24, 2004, pp. 224-233.

[5] X.G. Wang, S.J. Turner, S.J.E. Taylor, M.Y.H. Low and B.P. Gan, "A COTS Simulation Package Emulator (CSPE) for Investigating COTS Simulation Package Interoperability", *Proc. 2005 Winter Simulation Conference*, Florida, Dec. 4-7, 2005, pp. 402-411.

[6] S.J.E. Taylor, X.G. Wang, S.J. Turner and M.Y.H. Low, "Integrating Heterogeneous Distributed COTS Discrete-Event-Simulation Package: An Emerging Standards-Based Approach", *IEEE Transactions on Systems, Man and Cybernetics*, Jan. 2006, Vol. 36, No. 1, pp. 109-122.

[7] F. Wieland, "The Threshold of Event Simultaneity", *Transactions of the Society for Computer Simulation International*, 1999, Vol. 16, No. 1, pp. 23-31.

[8] R.M. Fujimoto, "Parallel and Distributed Simulation Systems", *Wiley Interscience*, January 2000.

[9] F. Wieland, "Parallel Simulation for Aviation Applications", *Proc. 1998 Winter Simulation Conference*, Washington DC, Dec. 13-16, 1998, pp. 1191-1198.

[10] Defense Modeling and Simulation Office (DMSO), "High Level Architecture RTI 1.3NG Programmer's Guide, Version 5", February 2002.

[11]. Simul8, www.simul8.com, viewed on 28th Oct., 2005.

[12] X.G. Wang, S.J. Turner, M.Y.H. Low and B.P. Gan, "Optimistic Synchronization in HLA Based Distributed Simulation", *Proc. 18th Workshop on Parallel and Distributed Simulation*, IEEE Computer Society, Kufstein, Austria, May 16-19, 2004, pp. 225-233.

Principles of Advanced and Distributed Simulation

Author Index

Ayani, Rassul 131, 175	Oguara, Tom 29
Back, Godmar 19	Oguara, Ton 37
Bartlett, Robert 111	Ould-Ahmed-Vall, El Moustapha 130
Bauer, David W. 158	Park, Alfred 3
Bergstrom, Craig 19	Perumalla, Kalyan S. 74, 134
Brailsford, Sally 135	Peschlow, Patrick 133
Brogan, David C. 119	Prandi, Davide 92
Cai, Wentong 65, 131, 183	Priami, Corado 92
Carothers, Christopher D. 158	Quaglia, Francesco 193
Chen, Dan 29, 183	Quaglia, Paola 92
Chen, Xinjun 65	Rao, Dhananjai M. 45
Chung, Moo-Kyoung 11	Reddy, Dheeraj 166
Dan, Chen 37	Reynolds, Paul F. 119
Dimitropoulos, Xenofontas 143	Riley, George F. 130
Eklöf, Martin 175	Riley, George 143, 166
Ewald, Roland 29	Santoro, Andrea 193
Fujimoto, Richard M. 3	Shen, Haifeng 103
Fujimoto, Richard 131	Simmonds, Rob 129
Hao, Zhiyu 150	Simpson, Charles R. 166
Heck, Bonnie S. 130	Ta, Duong Nguyen Binh 103
Himmelspach, Jan 92	Taylor, Simon J. E. 201
Hsu, Wen Jing 131	Taylor, Simon 135
Huang, Shell Ying 131	Theodoropoulos, Georgios K. 29
JohnTurner, Stephen 131	Theodoropoulos, Georgios 37, 132
Kalyanaram, Shickumar 158	Tolk, Andreas 55
Katsaliaki, Korina 135	Turner, Stephen John 65, 183, 201
Kennedy, Catriona 132	Uhrmacher, Adelinde M. 29
Kiesling, Tobias 82	Uhrmacher, Adelinde 92
Kyung, Chong-Min 11	Unger, Brian 129
Lecca, Paola 92	Varadarajan, Srinidhi 19
Lees, Michael 29, 37	Wang, Xiaoguang 201
Lendermann, Peter 139	Wang, Yong 65
Liu, Xinyu 119	Wilsey, Philip A. 45
Logan, Brian 29, 37	Yuksel, Murat 158
Low, Malcolm Yoke Hean 131	Yun, Xiaochun 150
Martini, Peter 133	Zhang, Hongli 150
Moradi, Farshad 175	Zhou, Suiping 103, 131
Mustafee, Navonil 135	

Press Operating Committee

Chair
Roger U. Fujii
*Vice President
Northrop Grumman Mission Systems*

Editor-in-Chief
Donald F. Shafer
*Chief Technology Officer
Athens Group, Inc.*

Board Members

Thomas Baldwin, *Manager, Conference Publishing Services (CPS)*
Hal Berghel, *Associate Dean, University of Nevada at Las Vegas*
Mark J. Christensen, *Independent Consultant*
James Conrad, *Associate Professor, UNC-Charlotte*
Herb Krasner, *Senior Lecturer, University of Texas at Austin*
Phillip Laplante, *Associate Professor, Penn State University*
Ted G. Lewis, *Professor, Computer Science, Naval Postgraduate School*
Deborah Plummer, *Manager, Authored Books*
Linda Shafer, *Professor Emeritus, University of Texas at Austin*
Richard Thayer, *Professor Emeritus, California State University, Sacramento*

IEEE Computer Society Executive Staff

David Hennage, *Executive Director*
Angela Burgess, *Publisher*

IEEE Computer Society Publications

The world-renowned IEEE Computer Society publishes, promotes, and distributes a wide variety of authoritative computer science and engineering texts. These books are available from most retail outlets. Visit the CS Store at *http://computer.org/cspress* for a list of products.

IEEE Computer Society *Conference Publishing Services* (CPS)

The IEEE Computer Society produces and actively promotes conference publications for more than 200 acclaimed international conferences each year in a variety of formats, including soft-cover books, hard-cover books, CD-ROMs, video, and on-line publications. For information about the IEEE Computer Society's *Conference Publishing Services* (CPS), please e-mail: tbaldwin@computer.org or write to: *Conference Publishing Services* (CPS), IEEE Computer Society, P.O. Box 3014, 10662 Los Vaqueros Circle, Los Alamitos, CA 90720-1314. Telephone +1-714-821-8380. Fax +1-714-761-1784. Additional information about the IEEE Computer Society's *Conference Publishing Services* (CPS) can be accessed from our web site at: *http://www.computer.org/cps*.

IEEE Computer Society / Wiley Partnership

The IEEE Computer Society and Wiley partnership allows the CS Press authored book program to produce a number of exciting new titles in areas of computer science and engineering with a special focus on software engineering. IEEE Computer Society members continue to receive a 15% discount on these titles when purchased through Wiley or at: *http://wiley.com/ieeecs*. To submit questions about the program or send proposals, please e-mail dplummer@computer.org or write to: Books, IEEE Computer Society, 10662 Los Vaqueros Circle, Los Alamitos, CA 90720-1314. Telephone +1-714-821-8380. Additional information regarding the Computer Society's authored book program can also be accessed from our web site at: *http://www.computer.org/portal/pages/ieeecs/publications/books/about.html*.

Revised: 03 January 2006